Actively Caring at Your School

How to Make it Happen

E. Scott Geller, Ph.D.

Published by
Make-A-Difference, LLC.
Newport, Virginia

Actively Caring at Your School: *How to Make it Happen*

Copyright © 2014 by E. Scott Geller, Ph.D.
Text processing: Jenna McCutchen
Editorial assistance: Dave Johnson
Illustrations: George V. Wills
Cover design: Nancy Poes

All rights reserved, including the right to reproduce this work in a form whatsoever without permission in writing from the publisher, except for brief passages in connection with a review. For more information write:

Make-A-Difference, LLC.
161 Make-A-DiffRanch
P. O. Box 73 • Newport, Virginia 24128-0073
www.ac4p.org • www.safetyperformance.com

ISBN 0-615893-87-2

Library of Congress Control Number is available upon request

Printed in the United States of America

Praise for
Actively Caring for People ™

THIS NEW BOOK by Dr. E. Scott Geller and colleagues provides an inspiring example of how theory and practice can come together to change lives. The Actively Caring for People Movement builds upon the spirit of service that defines Virginia Tech through its motto Ut Prosim (That I May Serve). As Provost, I have seen firsthand how our students have embraced and used actively caring in many different situations. Under the leadership of Scott Geller, this Movement has the potential to benefit the lives of millions of individuals and groups. This book provides the research-based principles and real-life stories that will help advance the Actively Caring for People Movement.

Mark McNamee
Senior Vice President and Provost
Virginia Tech
Blacksburg, Virginia

SCOTT GELLER'S CONCEPT of Actively Caring for People (AC4P) has been fundamental to keeping our employees safe for over ten years. Regardless of the type of work, reaching people is what makes the difference. Many might think Actively Caring is not a comfortable fit for rough necks in the oil-drilling business, but that's simply not true. With AC4P we have achieved "Best in Class" in our industry. The AC4P principles and applications have benefitted the lives of our employees at work and at home.

Dave Werner
Vice President and General Manager for California Operations
Nabors Completion and Production Services

ON THEIR RECENT speaking tour in Western Australia, Scott and Joanne Geller touched the hearts and minds of nearly 600 workers engaged in the "pointy end" of organizational safety and improvement efforts. One might think with our geographically dispersed workplaces, remote lifestyles and harsh outback working environments, the average West Aussie is a rough and tumble type who could care less about the welfare of fellow employees and the well-being of their community. But this stereotype was destroyed by the manner in which the Actively Caring for People concept was embraced by those fortunate enough to see Scott and Joanne in action. We now have researchers, school and community groups queuing up to explore how AC4P can make a difference in their lives. This is a long and no doubt challenging road we set upon, but Scott and Joanne inspired us to take the first step.

Martin Ralph
Managing Director
Industrial Foundation for Accident Prevention (IFAP)
Perth, Western Australia

This book is dedicated to the families and friends of the thirty-three Hokies who lost their lives on April 16th, 2007.

Ross A. Alameddine

Christopher James Bishop

Brian R. Bluhm

Ryan Christopher Clark

Austin Michelle Cloyd

Jocelyne Couture-Nowak

Kevin P. Granata

Matthew Gregory Gwaltney

Caitlin Millar Hammaren

Jeremy Michael Herbstritt

Rachael Elizabeth Hill

Emily Jane Hilscher

Jarrett Lee Lane

Matthew Joseph La Porte

Henry J. Lee

Liviu Librescu

G.V. Loganathan

Lauren Ashley McCain

Partahi Mamora Halomoan Lumbantoruan

Daniel Patrick O'Neil

Juan Ramon Ortiz-Ortiz

Minal Hiralal Panchal

Daniel Alejandro Perez Cueva

Erin Nicole Peterson

Michael Steven Pohle, Jr.

Julia Kathleen Pryde

Mary Karen Read

Reema Joseph Samaha

Waleed Mohamed Shaalan

Leslie Geraldine Sherman

Maxine Shelly Turner

Nicole Regina White

All book proceeds support the Actively Caring for People Foundation, Inc.

The Actively Caring for People Foundation, Inc. is dedicated to researching and teaching principles and procedures to cultivate a worldwide Actively Caring for People Culture of Compassion.

Preparation and printing of this book was supported by the
American Psychological Foundation
750 First Street NE, Washington, DC, USA

Contents

Foreword ix

Preface: Why Read This Book? xi

Part I: The Evidence-Based Principles 3
    1 The Foundation: Applied Behavior Analysis 5
    2 The Psychology of Actively Caring 33
    3 The Psychology of Self-Motivation 61
    4 The Courage to Actively Care 87
    5 Nudging AC4P with Social Influence 113

Part II: Applications of AC4P in Schools 147
    6 AC4P to Prevent Bullying 153
    7 AC4P in a Middle School 175
    8 Empowering People to Prevent Bullying 179
    9 Pedagogy for AC4P 187
   10 Sustaining Compassion after Tragic School Shootings ... 201
   11 AC4P after a Tragedy 213
   12 Feeling and Spreading Compassion 217
   13 The AC4P Movement at the University of Kansas 221
   14 Is it Realistic to Expect Quality AC4P Education? 231

Part III: Personal Stories of AC4P 239
   15 My 60/60 AC4P Challenge 241
   16 Memorable AC4P Experiences 245
   17 Living with Cancer 249
   18 My Starting Block and AC4P 257
   19 How I Get There Matters More 261
   20 Learning AC4P and Passing it On 263
   21 AC4P in My Military Career 267
   22 AC4P in Australia 269
   23 Making Time for People 273
   24 The Positive Addiction of AC4P 277
   25 Cultivating an AC4P Family 281
   26 Barriers to AC4P in Families 283

Part IV: Wristband Stories from ac4p.org 287

Contents

Epilogue: Where Do We Go From Here? 297

Acknowledgements 303

About the Authors 307

Subject & Name Index 311

Foreword

Dave Johnson

IT WAS THE ANNUAL MEETING of the National Safety Congress back in 1987 when I first came across Dr. E. Scott Geller. All that separated us was a standing-room-only crowd of six- or seven-hundred safety pros at a session where Dr. Geller paced up and down aisles and across the speaker's platform. Actually, I couldn't even get into the room at first; the audience spilled out into the hallway.

So I listened from outside and soon realized I'd never heard anyone talk about safety like this guy. His voice boomed like a football coach as he told jokes and stories and ripped through a stack of overhead transparencies. The man was seriously pumped and passionate, and his vitality was contagious. Laughs rolled through the large room and echoed out into the hall, where a group of us stood on our toes peeking through the door, trying to figure out this wiry professor with the energy of a rock-and-roll drummer.

But this was not another motivational speaker. What separated Scott was his message, his substance. He's always had this knack for making ivory-tower research somehow interesting. Scott's research is all about why we do the things we do, and how to help people do better, and how to help people actively care for one another. "I've got to get him to write articles for *Industrial Safety & Hygiene News (ISHN)*," I thought after listening for maybe five minutes.

As it turned out, Scott wrote a monthly *ISHN* article for a *Psychology of Safety* column for 19 years. Many of his articles focused on topics you'll read about in the following pages: systems thinking, culture, servant leadership, actively caring, self-motivation, observation and feedback, coaching, courage, interpersonal recognition, empowerment, self-esteem, student engagement, seeking success vs. avoiding failure, fixed vs. growth mindset, personality traits vs. states, bystander intervention, commitment, reciprocity, pro-social behavior, intrinsic vs. extrinsic reinforcement, and the do's and don'ts of incentive/reward programs.

They say a preacher has maybe ten good sermons in him – after that it's all recycling and repackaging. With a microphone in his hand, Scott works a room with a missionary's zeal, but his mission is to always give his audience and readers something new. New research, insights, and ideas are delivered to reach his vision of an Actively Caring for People (AC4P) culture.

The ultimate humane behavior, believes Scott, is to go above and beyond what is asked of us in our daily lives. Beyond the call of duty, he says, which infers that to actively care is an obligation to be met, certainly not ignored. We are obliged to actively care because we have it within us to do so. We can learn how to actively care through books such as this, and through related workshops and group discussions. Armed with this profound knowledge, how can we fail to act on our caring and our empathy?

Scott is a distinguished expert on the foibles of human nature, and he'll tell you right off that AC4P is a tall order. For any number of reasons. We fear our good intentions will be misinterpreted or rejected. We don't believe ourselves capable. "I'm just not feelin' it, dude." "I just don't want to take the time or expend the energy." "Someone else will do it." "Don't you see, I'm really an introvert, timid, and tend to veer to pessimistic thinking." "Actively caring is not in our DNA."

But this book challenges the excuses and provides evidence that thousands of people have upped their game to actively care. They have risen above their more hesitant, uncertain selves. Most of the time they have had help: friends, family, teachers, peers and strangers who have given them face-to face-encouragement, role modeling, and positive reinforcement.

Today, sufficient numbers of people are engaged in AC4P to call it a "Movement". This is really no surprise; AC4P behavior is viral, it's contagious, it's rewarding and fun. It's a cultural value around which communities of like-minded AC4P participants gravitate and reinforce one another.

Scott and his team at Virginia Tech have, through technology and creative thinking, constructed a global infrastructure to support AC4P. Their Movement is ambitious, idealistic, bold and grounded. It's based on psychological science and field research, not high hopes and do-gooder intentions. It aspires to increase the competence, commitment, and courage needed to sustain AC4P behavior in all the nooks and crannies of daily life: our schools, workplaces, the military, communities, families, heath care, and counseling. The book you are holding is Exhibit A.

Anything less aspiring would disappoint one of Dr. Geller's life-long inspirations, B.F. Skinner. Skinner, the Harvard psychologist and founder of behavior analysis, was preoccupied not with the manipulation of rats and mice in mazes, as his critics would have it, but to help people lead more satisfying and more productive lives. Skinner was convinced communities should actively shape human behavior to promote social justice and harmony. Scott and his team have done just that with the AC4P Movement.

Care to join them?

Preface: Why Read This Book?

E. Scott Geller

I coined the term "actively caring" in 1990 when working with a team of safety leaders at Exxon Chemical in Baytown, Texas.[1] Our vision was to cultivate a brother's/sister's keepers culture. Everyone would look out for each other's safety. People would routinely go above and beyond the call of duty for the benefit of the health, safety, and well-being of others.

We agreed "actively caring for people" (AC4P) was an ideal description for this company-wide paradigm shift.[2] Everyone naturally cares about the well-being of others. But certainly not everyone "acts" on their feelings of caring. Our challenge was to get everyone to *actively* care – to take effective action based on their caring.

This marked the beginning of systematic research in our Center for Applied Behavior Systems (CABS) at Virginia Tech (VT) to develop, evaluate, and continuously improve intervention techniques to increase the frequency and quality of person-to-person and group-to-group AC4P throughout a culture. For more than three decades we have continued this research, up to the present.

Applications have been tested in educational and work settings and throughout communities. A variety of behaviors affecting human and community welfare have been targeted. This book presents evidence-based interventions we developed to increase occurrences of AC4P behavior in educational settings, from elementary and middle schools to high schools and universities.

Following the VT campus shooting rampage on April 16, 2007 that took the lives of 33 people and injured 17 others, the mission of AC4P took on a new focus and prominence for my students and me. In a time of great uncertainty and reflection, those most affected by the tragedy did not think about themselves, but rather acted to help classmates, friends, and even strangers. This collective effort was manifested in an AC4P Movement for culture change (see www.ac4p.org).

My current and former students helped me compile this book to provide: a) the behavioral and psychological science behind the AC4P Movement, b) practical and successful applications of the evidence-based AC4P principles in educational settings, and c) inspirational evidence of the beneficial consequences from the AC4P approach.

We hope this book empowers and motivates you to join the Movement and spread AC4P among your friends, family, co-workers, peers, and even strangers in your schools, workplaces, organizations, and throughout communities. Apply these principles and applications in school, at home and throughout your community and you will contribute to reducing interpersonal conflict and aggression by cultivating AC4P cultures of compassion.

The AC4P Approach for Behavior Change

We are besieged by daunting societal problems. Thanks to the 24/7 news cycle and the Internet, smartphones and tablet devices, we know more than perhaps we'd like about the nation's obesity epidemic, millions of medical errors, Wall-Street greed, online scams, cyberbullying, violence and drugs in schools, bankrupt cities, terrorism, political gridlock, and global warming. This is a time of significant adversity. Since human behavior contributes to each of these societal problems; it must also be part of the solutions.

What if people were only more considerate and empathic to the circumstances, opinions, and behaviors of others? Imagine the beneficial impact of a world with more interpersonal compassion and AC4P – more empathy and kindness. The practical research-based AC4P interventions described in this book illustrate how such a culture can be achieved. The AC4P Movement combines humanism and behaviorism (i.e., *humanistic behaviorism*) to improve behaviors related to the health, safety, and well-being of people worldwide.

In 1971, B.F. Skinner told us, "Our culture has provided the science and technology to save itself".[3] The AC4P Movement reflects this assertion. It empowers individuals to be self-motivated to actively care and to increase the occurrence of AC4P behaviors from others as well. AC4P cultures empower people to improve their own school, work, and home environments, and as they do we will see AC4P cultures begin to flourish in schools, organizations and communities worldwide.

Chapters 1 to 5 define evidence-based strategies for increasing AC4P behavior in various settings, while reviewing the supportive theory and research for each intervention approach. We aren't talking about common-sense solutions here; we're sharing practical techniques verified through empirical research.

The lead authors of the remaining chapters in this book are change agents who have successfully applied the AC4P principles and procedures for diverse circumstances in educational settings. They have experienced firsthand the beneficial impact of applying the AC4P approach to prevent interpersonal conflict, bullying, and violence.

My students and I regularly hear many heartwarming personal stories of the profound positive effects of AC4P applications. A sample of those stories that teach practical AC4P lessons are included in Part III of this book. Each personal story illustrates how the benefits of AC4P behavior far outweigh the costs.

In every case, the mutual rewards from the AC4P exchange exceed any inconvenience of the AC4P behavior. Many stories show how one simple AC4P act can go viral, in effect be transmitted to other people and contribute to cultivating an AC4P culture of compassion. We call this "the AC4P ripple effect."

The Quality and Quantity of AC4P Behavior

Why isn't AC4P behavior more frequent? After all, the consequences of AC4P behavior are typically positive for both the giver and the receiver. And the beneficial impact of an AC4P interaction can serve as an activator and vicarious reinforcer for observers (see Chapter 5).

First, consider that AC4P behavior is more common than we realize. Daily occurrences of behavior opposite to AC4P make the news, but there are many untold stories of people worldwide reaching out daily to help others deal with unfortunate situational and/or dispositional factors.

Thousands of these people are professionals – fire fighters, police officers, doctors, nurses, home health aides, social workers, ministers, teachers, and personnel in the safety and human-relations departments of organizations. These AC4P professionals look out for the safety, health, and well-being of others morning, noon and night, every day and every shift.

Consider too the vast number of ordinary people who volunteer their time daily on behalf of the health and well-being of others, or who step out of themselves without forethought to instantaneously actively care for another person.

Quality of AC4P Behavior

I am actually more concerned about the quality of AC4P behavior than the quantity. Our behaviors at work, school, on the road, and at home with our families often come across as self-serving and non-caring.

Sure, most of our interpersonal behaviors might be well-intentioned, but too often they are not executed well. We might be well-intended, but for a variety of reasons, including "unconscious incompetence," the behavior performed to help another person (e.g., like offering feedback to improve someone's performance) is not viewed as AC4P behavior.

Our society, thanks to our legal system, is overly focused on using punitive consequences to stop people's undesirable behaviors, with limited attention to applying positive consequences to motivate desirable behavior.

Our popular culture can be a detriment. Hundreds of self-help books and many TV and radio talk shows make behavior and attitudinal change seem easier than it is.

Misinformed but popular authors proclaim that using incentives and rewards to increase the occurrence of desirable behavior does more harm than good.[4] The success of many positive AC4P interventions explicated in this book show the flaw in this silly assertion.

More importantly, the AC4P applications in Part II illustrate practical ways to improve any attempt to actively care by incorporating evidence-based principles of behavioral and psychological science. The quality of AC4P behavior can often be readily enhanced, and this book shows you how to do that.

Quantity of AC4P Behavior

The quantity of AC4P behavior can be increased by considering the variety of successful applications of the AC4P principles and procedures illustrated throughout this book. Most influential, for me, are the personal stories of individuals who experienced the rewards of performing and receiving a simple AC4P behavior (i.e., Parts III and IV).

Part III includes a sample of the numerous AC4P stories posted on our website at ac4p.org. Since January 2011, more than 2,000 individuals have posted brief AC4P stories, illustrating the positive consequences of actively caring for both those performing and those receiving AC4P behavior. These stories simply inspire me. Sharing their occurrence will contribute to making AC4P behavior a social norm.

Posting an AC4P story on our website connects immediately to your Facebook, and communicates to your friends the occasion of one more AC4P behavior, and its positive consequences. As more and more people post their AC4P tales, people will begin to accept AC4P behavior as the norm. Successive approximations of a worldwide culture of compassion will follow. So we hope you will, "Think globally and act locally".

Read this book and learn what you can do to increase the quantity and improve the quality of AC4P behavior in your life, starting at your school. Make your learning practical. Commit to being more intentional at actively caring for others and at rewarding people for their AC4P behaviors. When you share your AC4P stories on our website, others see your kind acts and consider modeling your AC4P behavior. Your stories may in fact find their way into the next edition of this book.

Our world brims with caring and compassion that goes untapped. A world filled with interpersonal compassion! This vision will become reality if more people reach out to help others more effectively and more often. This book shows you how to make that happen, and thereby live an AC4P lifestyle and lead the AC4P Movement.

Notes

1. Geller, E.S. (1991). If only more would actively care. *Journal of Applied Behavior Analysis, 24*, 763-764.
2. Geller, E.S., (1994). *Actively caring for safety.* Dallas, TX: Westcott Communications [Three 25-min. instructional videotapes with workbooks on the psychology of safety. One videotape teaches techniques to motivate safe work practices, another teaches a behavior-based process for addressing the human dimension of safety problems, and the third videotape teaches strategies for interpersonal coaching to improve industrial safety]; Geller, E.S. (1997). *Actively caring for safety: The psychology of injury prevention.* Blacksburg, VA: Safety Performance Solutions [Twelve 30-min. audiotapes with a workbook to teach principles and procedures for preventing unintentional injury at work, at home, and on the road.]
3. Skinner, B.F. (1971). *Beyond freedom and dignity.* New York, NY: Knopf.
4. Kohn, A. (1993). *Punished by rewards: The trouble with gold stars, incentive plans A's, praise, and other bribes.* Boston, MA: Houghton Mifflin; Pink, D.H. (2009). Drive: *The surprising truth about what motivates us.* New York, NY: Penguin Group.

Actively Caring at Your School

How to Make it Happen

E. Scott Geller, Ph.D.

Part I: Evidence-Based Principles of AC4P

E. Scott Geller

THE FIRST FIVE CHAPTERS of this book define principles you can use to cultivate an actively caring for people (AC4P) culture at your school. Then in Part II, successful applications of these AC4P principles are illustrated to prevent conflict and interpersonal bullying in educational settings and increase interpersonal caring and sharing. Subsequently, Part III includes a number of personal stories by individuals who applied one or more of the AC4P principles delineated and illustrated in Part I.

Throughout this book authors refer to particular AC4P principles they applied to activate and support AC4P behavior in a variety of situations. So what's a "principle" anyway?

The first definition in my *American Heritage Dictionary* is "a basic truth, law, or assumption".[1] How does this definition connect to the behavioral and psychological science referenced in the following five chapters?

Note we use the adjective "evidence-based" when referring to the AC4P principles. This means the principles are based on objective research that demonstrates the validity of the principle. Does this mean an AC4P principle is a basic truth or fact?

I think it's risky to consider these principles immutable or changeless, like the Law of Gravity. However, the AC4P principles are as close to valid as any other principle in psychological science.

In contrast to evidence-based principles, consider statements used to explain or influence human behavior which are not evidence-based, but are quite popular. In fact, some of these are themes of self-help books and pop-psychology seminars. I hope my comments make you skeptical of these so-called "principles" of human behavior.

1. **We learn more from our mistakes.** This popular myth, along with the popular slogan "trial-and error" learning, influences more emphasis on failure than success, and this can be detrimental to learning. Think about it. Animals, including humans, learn more when a consequence indicates their behavior was correct than incorrect.

2. **After 21 times, behavior becomes habit.** There's no empirical evidence of this popular but overly simplistic and silly statement. Many factors determine habit formation, especially the nature of the behavior. Plus, many behaviors require mindful attention to be effective, and should not become habitual.

3. **The "secret" to success is self-affirmation.** Telling yourself you can do something is the surest way to accomplishment. This popular myth may sound good, but it's wrong. Chapter 1 explains why the secret to achievement resides in behavioral consequences, not the self-talk preceding behavior.

4. **Live by the "Golden Rule," meaning treat others the way you want to be treated.** We've heard this rule all our lives, yet in Chapter 2 you'll learn why this principle is not optimal. For now, consider the value of treating others the way *they* want to be treated.

5. Incentive and rewards are detrimental to self-motivation. This pop-psychology statement is rarely supported by research; you'll learn evidence-based ways to increase self-motivation in Chapter 3. For example, behavior-based rewards and supportive feedback (e.g., recognition) are more likely to increase than decrease self-motivation.

6. Reprimand privately and recognize publically. Never recognize people publically without their permission. Some people are embarrassed in these situations, especially if others on their teams think they deserve recognition. Furthermore, public recognition of individuals on a team can promote win-lose independency over win-win interdependency. Chapter 3 details evidence-based ways to recognize teams, and Chapter 4 delineates strategies for rewarding individuals for their achievements.

7. Practice makes perfect. Practice without proper feedback can lead to permanence but certainly not perfection. Evidence-based principles for improving behavior through feedback are detailed in Chapter 4.

I could list many more assumptions people make about human dynamics which are not supported by research. And, some of these are incorrectly considered "principles" of human behavior. But, these seven make my point. What's my point? First, be skeptical about the pop-psychology "principles" you hear. My main point, however, is the AC4P principles illustrated in the next five chapters are founded on research.

One final point, the evidence-based principles explained in the following five chapters were selected from literally hundreds of verifiable principles related to understanding, predicting, and influencing the psychology of human experience. Those discussed in Chapters 1 to 5 were selected because at this point in our understanding of AC4P they are most relevant.

As we learn more about ways to enhance quality AC4P behavior in various situations, additional principles of psychological science will become relevant. Plus, additional research and continuous learning could influence refinements or extensions of the AC4P principles defined and illustrated in Part I of this book.

These chapters offer state-of-the-art AC4P principles from psychological science relevant to cultivating a culture of compassion at your school, and beyond.

Note

1. *The American Heritage Dictionary (1985).* (2nd College Edition). p. 985.

CHAPTER 1

The Foundation:
Applied Behavior Analysis

E. Scott Geller

COUNTLESS SOCIETAL PROBLEMS are brought to our attention every day by the news media. Violence and drug abuse, highway crashes, epidemics such as obesity and bullying, untold numbers of medical errors, conflicts both geopolitical and intensely personal, and environmental degradation – particularly climate change – carry significant economic burdens. They pose dehumanizing costs in terms of individual suffering and loss of life.

Human behavior contributes to each of these perplexing problems – but human behavior is also a critical part of the solution. For more than 50 years, applied behavior analysts have helped people by developing, implementing, and evaluating interventions to increase positive acts of caring and decrease damaging behaviors.

Effective applications of Applied Behavior Analysis (ABA) generally follow the seven key principles described below. Each principle is broad enough to include a wide range of practical operations, but narrow enough to define the ABA approach to managing behaviors relevant for promoting AC4P (e.g., for benefitting teaching/learning, safety, health, work productivity, parenting, and environmental conservation).[1]

1. Target Observable Behavior

B. F. Skinner conceptualized and researched the behavioral science upon which the ABA approach is founded.[2] Experimental behavior analysis, and later ABA, emerged from Skinner's research and teaching, and laid the groundwork for numerous therapies and interventions to improve the quality of life among individuals, groups, and entire communities.[3]

Whether working one-on-one in a clinical setting or with teachers and/or students throughout a school, the intervention procedures always target specific behaviors relevant to promoting constructive change. ABA focuses on what people do, analyzes *why* they do it, and then applies an evidence-based intervention to *improve* what people do.

Acting people into thinking differently is the focus. This contrasts with *thinking people to act differently*, which targets internal awareness, intentions, or attitudes. Many clinical psychologists successfully use this latter approach in professional therapy sessions. But in group, organizational, or community-wide settings it's not cost-effective. To be effective, thinking-focused intervention requires extensive one-on-one interaction between a client and a specially-trained intervention specialist.

Few intervention agents in the real world (e.g., teachers, parents, coaches, healthcare workers, and safety professionals) possess the educational background, training, and experience to implement an intervention focused on internal and unobservable person states. A basic tenet of ABA is that interventions should occur at the natural site of the behavioral issue (e.g., school, home, or athletic field) and be administered by an indigenous change agent (e.g., teacher, parent, or coach).

2. Focus on External Factors to Explain and Improve Behavior

Skinner did not deny the existence of internal determinants of behavior (such as personality characteristics, perceptions, attitudes, and values). These unobservable inferred constructs were rejected by Skinner for *scientific study* as causes or consequences of behavior. Factors in both our external and internal worlds obviously influence what we do – how we act. But it's difficult to objectively define internal traits or states. It's simply more cost-effective to identify environmental conditions that influence behavior, and then change these factors when behavior change is called for.

Bottom line: ABA focuses on the external environmental conditions and contingencies influencing a target behavior. A careful analysis is conducted of the situation before deciding on an intervention approach. The target behavior(s) and the individual(s) involved in any observed discrepancy between the behavior observed and the behavior desired (i.e., real vs. ideal behavior) are studied. A behavior-focused intervention is designed and implemented if the gap between the actual and the desired behavior warrants change. This is accomplished by adhering to the next three principles.

3. Direct with Activators and Motivate with Consequences

This principle enables us to understand why behavior occurs, and guides the design of interventions to improve behavior. It runs counter to common sense or "pop psychology." When people are asked why they did something, they make statements such as, "Because I wanted to do it," "Because I needed to do it," or "Because I was told to do it." Such explanations sound as if the cause of behavior precedes it. A multitude of "pop psychology" self-help books, audiotapes and DVDs support the belief we motivate our behavior with self-affirmations, positive thinking, optimistic expectations, or enthusiastic intentions.

The fact is, as Dale Carnegie put it, "Every act you have ever performed since the day you were born was performed because you wanted something."[4] We do what we do because of the consequences we expect for doing it. Carnegie cited Skinner's research and scholarship as the foundation for this basic principle of motivation.

Activators (or signals preceding behavior) are as powerful as the consequences supporting them. Activators tell us what to do in order to receive a positive, reinforcing consequence. Or they tell us what not to do to avoid an unpleasant consequence.

Take a ringing telephone. If we see from the "call waiting" phone number the call is from a friend we haven't spoken with in a long time, we pick up the receiver and begin a rewarding conversation. But if the "call waiting" number is unknown to us we might not pick up the receiver. We just let the call go to voicemail.

How about the ringing of a doorbell? Years ago, people always answered the door. Now, due to fears of unknown strangers and a plethora of visitors who want something from us ("Would you sign this petition?," "Can I count on your vote?," "Do you need your driveway blacktopped?"), we are more likely to peer through a window to see who it is, and note whether the consequence of opening the door will be pleasant or unpleasant.

We follow through with the particular behavior activated (from answering or ignoring a telephone to opening or refusing to open a door) based on whether we expect a pleasant consequence or can avoid an unpleasant consequence.

This principle is typically referred to as the ABC model or three-term contingency, with A for Activator (or antecedent), B for Behavior, and C for Consequence. Applied behavior analysts use this ABC principle to design interventions for improving behavior at individual, group, organizational, and community levels. More than 50 years of behavioral-science research has demonstrated the efficacy of this general approach to directing and motivating behavior change. The ABC (Activator – Behavior – Consequence) contingency is reflected in the illustration.

The dog will move if he expects to receive food after hearing the sound of the can opener. The direction provided by an activator is likely to be followed when it is backed by a soon, certain, and significant consequence. This operation is termed operant or instrumental conditioning. The consequence is a positive reinforcer when behavior is emitted to obtain it. When behavior occurs to avoid or escape a consequence, the consequence is a *negative* reinforcer.

If the sound of the can opener elicits a salivation reflex in the dog, we have an example of classical or respondent conditioning. The can-opener sound is a conditioned stimulus (CS) and the salivation is a conditioned response (CR). The food that follows the sound of the electric can opener is the unconditioned stimulus (UCS), which elicits the unconditioned response of salivating without any prior learning experience. This UCS – UCR reflex is natural or "wired in" the organism.

Perhaps you recall this terminology from a basic learning course in psychology. We review it here because ABA is founded on these learning principles, especially operant conditioning. People choose behavior to obtain a pleasant consequence or to escape or avoid an unpleasant consequence. But as shown in the illustration, operant (instrumental) and respondent (classical) conditioning often occur simultaneously.

Although we operate on the environment to achieve a desired consequence or avoid an unwanted consequence, emotional reactions are often classically conditioned to specific stimulus events in the situation. We learn to like or dislike an educational context and/or the teacher involved in administrating the ABC contingency. This is how the type of behavioral consequence influences attitude, and why ABA interventions focus on positive consequences.

4. Focus on Positive Consequences to Motivate Behavior

Skinner's concern for people's feelings and attitudes is reflected in his antipathy toward the use of punishment (or negative consequences) to motivate behavior. "The problem is to free men, not from control, but from certain kinds of control."[5] Skinner proceeds to explain that control by negative consequences must be reduced to increase perceptions of personal freedom.

The same situation can often be viewed both ways: control by punishment of unwanted behavior or control by positive reinforcement of desired behavior. Some students in my university classes, for example, are motivated to avoid failure (e.g., a poor grade). Other students are motivated to achieve success (e.g., a good grade or increased knowledge).

Which of these groups of students feel more empowered and in control of their class grade? Which have a better attitude toward my classes? Of course, you know the answer. Reflect on your own feelings or attitude in similar situations where you perceived your behavior as influenced by positive or negative consequences.

Achieving Success vs. Avoiding Failure

Years ago, John W. Atkinson and his associates[6] found dramatic differences when comparing the decision-making of individuals with a high need to avoid failure and those with a high need to achieve success. Those motivated to achieve positive consequences set challenging but attainable goals. Participants with a high need to avoid failure were apt to set goals either overly easy or overly difficult.

Setting easy goals assures avoidance of failure; setting unrealistic goals provides an excuse for failure – termed self-handicapping by more recent researchers.[7] Thus, a substantial amount of behavioral research and motivational theory justifies advocacy of positive reinforcement over punishment contingencies. This is the case whether an ABC contingency is contrived to improve someone else's behavior or imagined to motivate personal rule-following behavior.

Figure 1.1 depicts four distinct achievement typologies initially defined by Covington and Omelich.[8] These four classifications have been researched to explain differences in how people approach success and/or avoid failure.

It's most desirable to be a *success seeker*. These are the optimists, responding to setbacks (e.g., corrective feedback) in a positive and adaptive manner. They are self-confident and willing to take risks as opposed to avoiding challenges in order to avoid failure. They wake up each day to an *opportunity* clock rather than an *alarm* clock. It's a mindset or attitude toward life you can influence in yourselves and others. This book teaches you how to do that.

Overstrivers are diligent, successful, meticulous, and at times optimistic. But they have self-doubt about their abilities and experience substantial evaluation anxiety. This drives them to avoid failure by working hard to succeed.[9] Covington and Roberts[10] found overstrivers are preoccupied with perfection, often over-preparing for a challenge (e.g., a test of knowledge or ability).

Failure avoiders have a low expectancy for success and a high fear of failure. They do whatever it takes to protect themselves from appearing incompetent. They often use self-handicapping and defensive pessimism to shield themselves from potential failure.[11] These individuals are motivated but are not "happy campers." They are the students who say, "I've *got* to go to class; it's a requirement," rather than "I *get* to go to class; it's an opportunity."

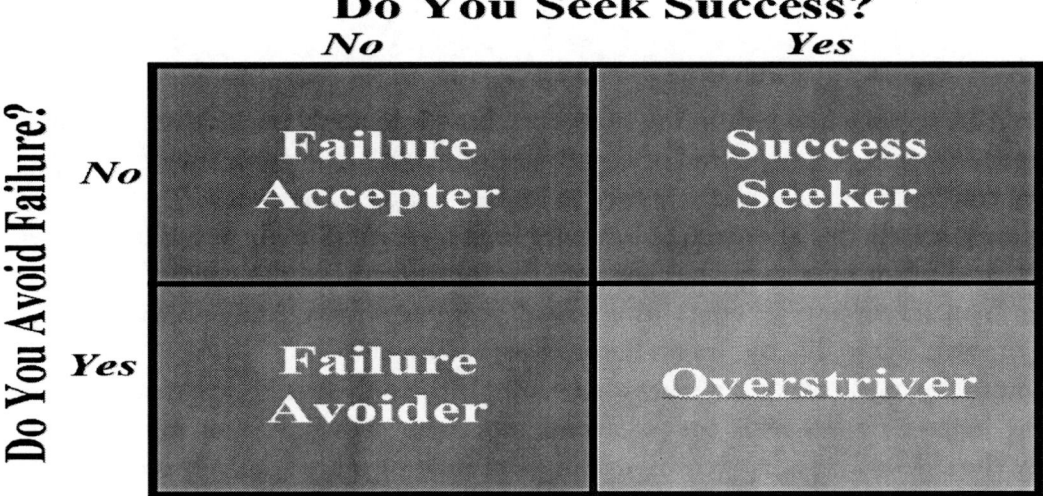

Figure 1.1. Achieving success vs. avoiding failure define four motivational typologies.

Finally, the *failure accepters* score low in terms of both expecting success and fearing failure. Failure is merely accepted as indicative of low ability. Unlike failure avoiders, though, these individuals don't worry about failure or their inability to succeed. They have given up. Their behavior is analogous to learned helplessness.[12]

Interestingly failure accepters are better adjusted psychologically than the failure avoiders and overstrivers, according to Covington and Roberts.[10] They score relatively high on well-being, tolerance, self-control, and social presence. They report being relatively self-assured and self-disciplined. Theirs is a passive lifestyle relatively free of worry. Why? Perhaps because they've abandoned achievement, and in so doing they experience relatively few stressors throughout their days.

Personality Traits vs. States

Much of the research literature addressing these four achievement typologies seem to imply they reflect relatively stable and persistent qualities of individuals. They represent personality traits rather than states.[13] However, other researchers and practitioners, especially proponents of ABA, view these characteristics as fluctuating states. They exist under the influence of the environment and the three-term (ABC) contingency. Environmental conditions and contingencies set the stage for success seeking, overstriving, failure avoiding, or failure accepting. The results or consequences of one's efforts can maintain or change one's perspective.

Success seeking is cultivated through positive reinforcement. Overstriving and failure avoiding result from negative reinforcement and punishment. A failure accepter might simply surrender after a history of consistent failure. Passive failure accepters who have "accepted their fate" are apparently "happier campers" than failure avoiders and overstrivers. But in their surrendering they are not motivated to even try a challenging task. Wouldn't you rather have a failure avoider or overstriver on your team, and attempt to move their state toward success seeking?

The Contingency for Success Seeking

The ABA approach to promoting success seeking is to apply positive reinforcement contingencies strategically instead of negative reinforcement or punishment. Still, punishment contingencies are relatively easy to implement on a large scale. That's why our government selects this approach to behavior management. Simply pass a law and enforce it. And when monetary fines are paid for transgressions, the controlling agency obtains financial support for continuing its enforcement efforts. And punishment often seems to work, as the illustration on the next page shows.

Control by negative consequences is seemingly the only feasible approach in many areas of large-scale behavior management, especially transportation safety. Consequently, the side-effects of aggressive driving and road rage are relatively common and observed by anyone who drives.

Most of us have experienced the anxious emotional reaction of seeing the flashing blue light of a police vehicle in our rear-view mirror—another example of classical conditioning. You've probably witnessed the temporary impact produced by this enforcement threat.

Classic research in experimental behavior analysis teaches us to expect only temporary suppression of a punished behavior,[14] and to predict that some drivers in their "Skinner box on wheels" will speed up to compensate for the time they lost when slowing down in an "enforcement zone".[17]

Regardless of situations, teachers, administrators, coaches, team leaders, and parents can often intervene to increase people's perceptions they are working to achieve

success rather than avoid failure. Even our verbal behavior directed toward another person, perhaps as a statement of genuine approval or appreciation for a task well done, can increase perceptions of personal freedom, empowerment, and self-motivation (see Chapter 3).

Words of approval, though, are not as common as words of disapproval. So while ABA change agents focus their interventions on observable behavior, they are concerned about attitude, as reflected in the next principle.

5. Design Interventions with Consideration of Internal Feelings and Attitudes

Skinner was certainly concerned about unobservable attitudes or feeling states. This is evidenced by his criticism of punishment's impact on people's feelings and perceptions. This perspective also reflects a realization: Intervention procedures influence feeling states, and these can be pleasant or unpleasant, desirable or undesirable. Internal feelings or attitudes are influenced indirectly by the type of behavior-focused intervention procedure implemented, and this relationship must be carefully considered by developers and managers of a behavior-change process.

The differential feeling states provoked by positive reinforcement versus punishment procedures is the rationale for using more positive than negative consequences to motivate behavior. Similarly, the way we implement an intervention process can increase or decrease feelings of empowerment, build or destroy trust, and cultivate or inhibit a sense of teamwork or belonging.[16]

Thus, it's important to assess feeling states or perceptions occurring concomitantly with an intervention process. This can be accomplished informally through one-on-one interviews and group discussions, or formally with a perception survey.[17] However, surveys with few response alternatives have obvious limitations when it comes to assessing feelings or attitudes, as the illustration shows.

Social Validity

Decisions regarding which ABA intervention to implement, and how to refine existing intervention procedures, should be based on both objective behavioral observations and subjective evaluations of feeling states. Often, it's possible to employ empathy to evaluate the indirect internal impact of an intervention. Imagine yourself going through a particular set of intervention procedures. Then, ask the question, "How would I feel?"

Almost two decades ago when my daughter wanted to drive my car to her high school I installed a sign on the back, as shown in the illustration. I bolted the sign to the vehicle after she achieved 100 percent safe on three consecutive coaching sessions with a Critical Behavior Checklist (CBC), as described later in this chapter. We had this "if-then" contingency: "Achieve a perfect score on three consecutive trips with the CBC, and you may drive my car to school."

I was sure she'd accept the addition of the sign on my vehicle. Note how this activator is more than an awareness prompt; it implies a consequence. We talked about the value of positive or supportive consequences, so I thought Krista would view this sign as a "fun" and positive approach to promote safe driving. "Let's be optimistic about this," I said to her, "and see how many positive phone calls I get about your safe and courteous driving behavior."

"Are you kidding me, Dad, there's no way I'd park that car and sign at my high-school," was Krista's reply. "I'd be the laughing stock of the whole school. I'll talk to mom about this." My lesson: Don't assume you know how a well-intentioned intervention will be received by the participant(s); ask first.

Assessment of social validity is a more comprehensive and systematic approach advocated by ABA researchers and practitioners.[18] Social validity assessment includes the use of rating scales, interviews, and focus-group discussions to assess: (a) the societal significance of the intervention goals, (b) the social appropriateness of the procedures, and (c) the societal importance or clinical significance of the intervention effects.[19]

The Four Components of ABA Intervention

The four basic components of an ABA intervention process – selection, implementation, evaluation, and dissemination – are addressed in a comprehensive social validity evaluation.

Selection refers to the importance or priority of the behavioral problem and the people targeted for change. Addressing the large-scale problems of inferior education, transportation safety, climate change, prison management, identity theft, child abuse, interpersonal bullying, and medical errors is clearly important, but given limited resources, which issue should receive priority? The answer to this question depends partly on the availability of a cost-effective intervention.

Assessing the social validity of the *implementation* stage of ABA intervention includes evaluating the behavior-change goals and procedures of the behavior-change process. How acceptable is the plan to potential participants and other parties, even those tangentially associated with the intervention?[20]

In the case of a bullying-prevention program, answering this question entails obtaining acceptability ratings not only from teachers, students, and school administrators, but also from the students' family members and the community members whose tax dollars support the intervention.

Are the intervention procedures consistent with the school's values and mission statement, and do they reach the most appropriate audience? And, it's recommended to consult with the recipients of an intervention regarding acceptability and methodology, as depicted in the illustration.

The social validity of the *evaluation* stage refers, of course, to the impact of the intervention process. This includes estimates of the costs and benefits of an intervention as well as measures of participant or consumer satisfaction. The numbers or scores obtained from various measurement devices (e.g., environmental audits, behavioral checklists, interview forms, output records, and attitude questionnaires) need to be reliable and valid. But they also need to be understood by the people who use them. If they are not, the evaluation scheme does not provide useful feedback and cannot lead to continuous improvement.

Meaningless or misunderstood evaluation numbers also limit the *dissemination* potential and large-scale applicability of an intervention. Now we're talking about the social validity of the *dissemination* stage of the ABA intervention process. This is the weakest aspect of ABA intervention, and perhaps applied psychology in general.

Intervention researchers and scholars justify their efforts and obtain financial support based on the scientific rigor of their methods and the statistical significance of their results. Rarely do these scholars address the real-world dissemination challenges of their findings.

Unfortunately, dissemination and marketability are left to corporations, consulting firms, and "pop psychologists." As a result, there are often disconnects between the science of ABA (and other psychological processes) and behavior-change intervention in the real world. One solution to this dilemma is to teach the real-world users of ABA how to conduct their own evaluations of intervention impact. This brings us to the next ABA principle.

6. Apply the Scientific Method to Improve Intervention

Some people believe dealing with the human dynamics of behavior change requires only "good common sense".[21] Surely you realize the absurdity of such a premise. Common sense is based on people's selective listening and interpretation, and is usually founded on what sounds good to the individual listener, not necessarily on what works.[22] In contrast, systematic and scientific observation enables the kind of objective feedback needed to know what works and what doesn't work to improve behavior.

The occurrence of specific behaviors can be objectively observed and measured before and after the implementation of an intervention process. This application of the scientific method provides feedback with which behavioral improvement can be shaped. I use the acronym "DO IT," as depicted in Figure 1.2, to teach this principle of ABA to change agents (e.g., teachers, coaches, parents, work supervisors, and students) empowered to improve the behavior of others and who want to continuously improve their intervention skills. This process represents the scientific method ABA practitioners have used for decades to demonstrate the impact of particular behavior-change techniques.

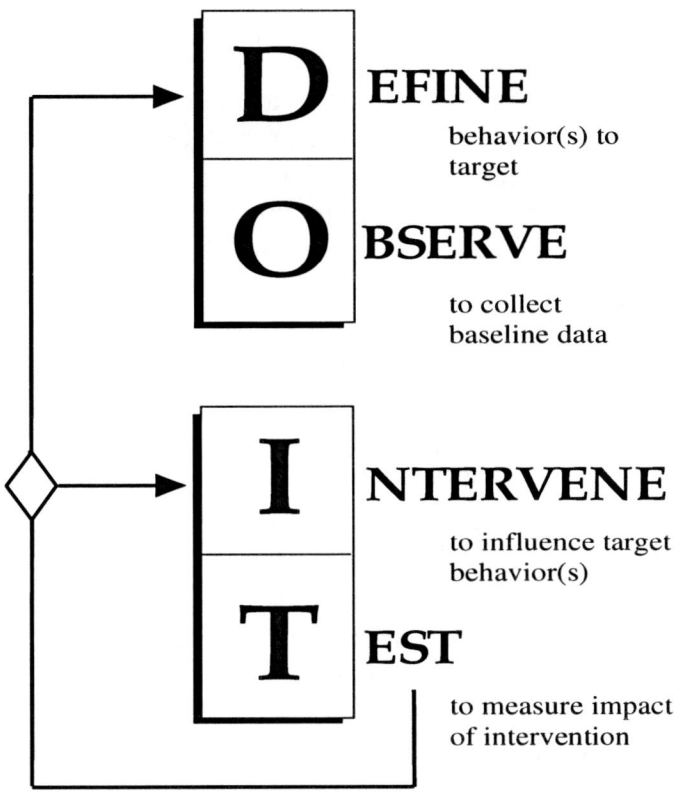

Figure 1.2 The scientific method of ABA is represented by DO IT.

"D" for Define

The process begins by defining specific behaviors to target, which are undesirable behaviors that need to decrease in frequency and/or desirable behaviors that need to occur more often. Avoiding certain unwanted behaviors often requires the occurrence of alternative behaviors, and so target behaviors might be behaviors to substitute for particular undesirable behaviors. On the other hand, a desirable target behavior can be defined independently of undesired behavior.

An AC4P approach to prevent interpersonal bullying applied reward techniques to increase interpersonal caring and sharing behaviors, and resulted in a decrease in bullying behavior without ever mentioning bullying as a target (see Chapters 6, 7, & 8). An undesirable behavior can be decreased in frequency by targeting desirable behavior(s) incompatible with the unwanted behavior.

Defining and evaluating ongoing behavior is often facilitated by the development of a behavioral checklist to use during observations. Development of behavioral definitions invoke an invaluable learning experience. When people get involved in deriving a behavioral checklist, they own a training process that can improve human dynamics on both the outside (behaviors) and the inside (feelings and attitudes) of people.

"O" for Observe

When people observe each other for certain desirable or undesirable behaviors, they realize everyone performs undesirable behavior, sometimes without even realizing it. The observation stage is not a fault-finding procedure. It's a fact-finding learning process to discover behaviors and conditions that need to be changed or continued in order to be competent at a task. No behavioral observation needs to be made without awareness and explicit permission from the person being observed. Observers should be open to learning as much (if not more) from the process as they expect to teach from completing the behavioral checklist.

The Critical Behavioral Checklist. There's not one generic observation procedure for every situation. Customization and refinement of a process for a particular setting never stops. You might begin the observation process with a limited number of behaviors and a relatively simple checklist. This reduces the possibility of people feeling overwhelmed at the beginning. Starting small also enables the broadest range of voluntary participation, and provides numerous opportunities to improve the process successively by expanding coverage of both behaviors and environmental settings.

I used the critical behavioral checklist (CBC) depicted in Figure 1.3 to teach my daughter safe-driving practices. She actually thought the "driver's ed program" she had in high school was sufficient. I knew better. We needed to develop and apply a CBC. Through one-on-one discussion, Krista and I derived a list of critical driving behaviors and then agreed on specific definitions for each item. My university students practiced using this CBC a few times with various drivers, resulting in a refined list of behavioral definitions.

After discussing the revised list of behaviors and their definitions with Krista, I was ready to implement the second stage of DO IT – observation. I asked my daughter to drive me to the university – about nine miles from home – to pick up some papers. I overtly recorded observations on the CBC during both legs of this roundtrip. When returning home, I totaled the safe and at-risk checkmarks and calculated the percentage of safe behaviors. Her percentage of safe driving was 85%. I considered this quite good for our first time. (Note my emphasis on achieving safe rather than avoiding at-risk.)

I told Krista her "percent safe" score and proceeded to show her the list of safe checkmarks, while covering the few checks in the at-risk column. To my surprise, she was not impressed with her percent safe score. Rather she pushed me to tell her what she did wrong. "Get to the bottom line Dad," she asserted, "Where did I screw up?"

This reaction was enlightening in two aspects. First, it illustrated the unfortunate reality that the "bottom line" for many people is "where did I go wrong?" My daughter, at age 15, had already absorbed that people evaluating her performance are more interested in mistakes than successes. This perspective activates failure-avoiding over success-seeking, an undesirable mindset I introduced earlier.

The realization people can be unaware of their at-risk behavior was a second important outcome from this CBC experience. Only through objective behavior-based feedback can we improve. Krista did not readily accept my corrective feedback regarding her four at-risk behaviors. She emphatically denied she did not always

Critical Behavior Checklist for Driving

Driver:	Date:		Day:
Observer 1:	Origin:		Start Time:
Observer 2:	Destination:		End Time:
Weather:			
Road Conditions:			

Behavior	Safe	At-Risk	Comments
Safety Belt Use:			
Turn Signal Use:			
Left turn			
Right turn			
Lane change			
Intersection Stop:			
Stop sign			
Red light			
Yellow light			
No activator			
Speed Limits:			
25 mph and under			
25 mph- 35 mph			
35 mph- 45 mph			
45 mph- 55 mph			
55 mph- 65 mph			
Passing:			
Lane Use:			
Following Distance (2 sec):			
Totals:			

% Safe = $\dfrac{\text{Total Safe Observations}}{\text{Total Safe + At-Risk Obs.}}$ = _____ %

Figure 1.3. A critical behavior checklist can improve driving.

come to a complete stop at intersections with stop signs. However, she became convinced of her error when I showed her my data sheet and my comments regarding the particular intersection where there was no traffic and she made only a rolling stop before turning right.

Obviously, we are now in the *intervention* phase of DO IT, with interpersonal feedback being the ABA intervention tactic. I reminded Krista she used her turn signal at every intersection, and she should be proud of that behavior. To make this behavior-based coaching process a positive, success-seeking experience, I emphasized the behaviors I observed her do correctly.

"I" for Intervene

During this stage, interventions are designed and implemented in an attempt to increase the occurrence of desired behavior and/or decrease the frequency of undesired behavior. As reflected in Principle 2, intervention means changing external conditions of the behavioral context or system in order to make desirable behavior more likely than undesirable behavior.

When designing interventions, Principles 3 and 4 are critical: The most motivating consequences are soon, certain, and sizable (Principle 3); and positive consequences are preferable to negative consequences (Principle 4).

The process of observing and recording the frequency of desirable and undesirable behavior on a checklist is an opportunity to give individuals and groups valuable behavior-based feedback. When the results of a behavioral observation are shown to individuals or groups, they receive the kind of information that enables practice to improve performance.

Considerable research has shown that providing people feedback regarding their ongoing behavior is a very cost-effective intervention approach.[23] Chapter 3 details techniques for giving AC4P feedback effectively.

"T" for Test

The *test* phase of DO IT provides work teams or change agents with information they need to refine or replace an ABA intervention, and so improve the process. If observations indicate significant improvement in the target behavior has not occurred, the change agents analyze and discuss the situation, and refine the intervention or choose another intervention approach.

On the other hand, if the target reaches the desired frequency level, the change agents can turn their attention to another set of behaviors. They might add new critical behaviors to their checklist, expanding the domain of their behavioral observations. Alternatively, they might design a new intervention procedure to focus only on the new behaviors.

Every time participants evaluate an intervention approach, they learn more about how to improve targeted behaviors. They have essentially become AC4P behavioral scientists, using the DO IT process to: (a) diagnose a problem involving human behavior, (b) monitor the impact of a behavior-change intervention, and (c) refine interventions for continuous improvement. The results from such testing provide motivating consequences to sustain this learning process and keep the change agents and their participants involved.

7. Use Theory to Integrate Information, Not to Limit Possibilities

B.F. Skinner was critical of designing research projects to test theory.[24] This despite much, if not most, research is theory driven. Theory-driven research can narrow the perspective of the investigator and limit the extent of findings with the scientific method. Applying the DO IT process merely to test a theory can be like putting blinders on a horse. It can limit the amount of input gained from systematic observation.

Exploratory ABA investigation has resulted in many important findings. Systematic observations of behavior occurred before and after an intervention or treatment procedure to answer the question, "I wonder what will happen if...?," rather than "Is my theory correct?"

ABA researchers might be expecting or hoping for a particular result, but they are open to finding anything relevant to influencing behavior. Then they modify their research design or observation process according to their behavioral observations, not a particular theory. Their innovative research has been data driven rather than theory driven, which is an important perspective for behavior-change agents, especially when applying the DO IT process.

It's often better to be open to many possibilities for improving performance than to be motivated to support a certain process. Numerous intervention procedures are consistent with the ABA approach, and an intervention process that works well in one situation will not necessarily be effective in another setting.

Thus, it's usually advantageous to teach change agents to make an educated guess about what intervention procedure to use at the start of a behavior-change process, while being open to intervention refinement as a result of the DO IT process. Of course, Principles 1 to 4 should always be used as guidelines when designing intervention procedures.

Distinct consistencies will be observed after many systematic applications of the DO IT process. Certain procedures will work better in some situations than others, with some individuals than others, or with some behaviors than others. Summarizing functional relationships between intervention impact and specific situational or interpersonal characteristics can lead to developing a research-based theory of what works best under particular circumstances.

In this case, theory is used to integrate information gained from systematic behavioral observation. Skinner approved of this use of theory, but cautioned that premature theory development can lead to premature theory testing and limited profound knowledge.[24]

Examples of Applied Behavior Analysis Intervention

Most large-scale ABA interventions designed to improve behavior can be classified as either antecedent or consequence strategies. This section reviews four activator (or antecedent) strategies and three consequence strategies ABA change agents have applied effectively to change socially important behaviors. The success of these ABA interventions was evaluated with a DO IT scheme.

Activators

Activators or antecedent interventions include (a) education, (b) verbal and written prompts, (c) modeling and demonstrations, and (d) commitment procedures.

Education. Before attempting to improve a behavior, it's often important to provide a strong rationale for the requested change. Sometimes this process involves making remote, uncertain, or unknown consequences more salient to the relevant audience. For example, a curriculum change requiring all students to take a particular course should be accompanied with reasons for the change, especially the positive consequences students gain by taking the required course.

Educational antecedents can be disseminated through print or electronic media, or delivered personally in individual or group settings. Researchers have shown that education presented interpersonally is more effective when it's done in small, rather than large groups, and when it actively involves participants in relevant activities and demonstrations.[25]

Providing information and activating awareness of a problem are often important components of ABA intervention, but keep in mind information alone is seldom sufficient to change behavior, especially when the desired behavior is inconvenient.[26] Education or awareness antecedents are often combined with other intervention components, as discussed below.

Prompts. Prompting strategies are verbal or written messages strategically delivered to promote the occurrence of a target behavior. These activators are reminders to perform the target behaviors.

Geller, Winett, and Everett[27] identified several favorable conditions for the effectiveness of prompting antecedents. Prompts work best when: a) the target behavior is specifically defined by the prompt (e.g., "Buckle your safety belt" rather than "Drive safely"), b) the target behavior is relatively easy to perform (e.g., placing cafeteria food waste in a designated composting receptacle vs. collecting and delivering recyclables), c) the message is displayed where the target behavior can be performed (e.g., at the cafeteria where food waste can be separated on the spot vs. on the local news), d) when the message is stated politely (e.g., "Please clean your desk" vs. "You must clean your desk"), and e) when the activator implies a consequence, as discussed above.

Prompts are popular. They are simple to implement, cost relatively little, and can have considerable impact if used properly. Werner, Rhodes, and Partain increased dramatically the amount of polystyrene recycling in a university cafeteria by increasing the size of signs designed to prompt recycling, and placing them next to recycling bins.[28]

Geller, Kalsher, Rudd, and Lehman designed safety-belt reminders to be hung from the rear-view mirrors of personal vehicles.[29] In both of these successful applications, the prompts were displayed in close proximity to where the target behavior could be performed, and the behavior requested was relatively convenient to perform.

Modeling. Prompts can be effective for simple, convenient behaviors. Modeling is the more appropriate approach when the desired behavior is complex. Modeling involves demonstrating specific target behaviors to a relevant audience. This activator is more effective when the model receives a rewarding consequence immediately after the target behavior is performed.[30]

Modeling can be accomplished via an interpersonal demonstration, but reaches a broader audience through electronic media. However, as the illustration shows, we sometimes model and thus teach undesirable behavior.

Behavioral Commitment. Behavioral commitment is straightforward and easy to implement, and it can be very effective. Although all ABA interventions request behavior change, a behavioral commitment takes this process a step further.

Individuals are asked to agree formally to change their behavior. They make a behavioral commitment. Asking individuals to make a written or verbal commitment to perform a target behavior increases the likelihood that behavior will be performed.[31]

When individuals sign a pledge or promise card to increase a desirable behavior (e.g., complete homework, practice, exercise) or cease an undesirable behavior (e.g., talk while the teacher is lecturing, step in front of another student in line, chew gum in class, skip a class) they feel obligated to honor their commitment, and often do.[32] More examples of successful applications of this intervention strategy are explained in Chapters 4 and 5.

Commitment-compliant behavior is explained by ABA professionals with the notion of *rule-governed behavior*. People learn rules for behavior and through their experiences they learn that following the rule is linked to positive social and personal consequences (e.g., interpersonal approval), and breaking the rule can lead to the negative consequences of disapproval or legal penalties.

This tendency to follow through on a behavioral commitment is attributed by social psychologists to the social norm of *consistency*. This norm creates pressure to be internally and externally consistent. You'll read more about this in Chapter 5.

This behavioral commitment strategy can be conveniently added to many ABA interventions. At a time when vehicle safety-belt use was not the norm, my students and I combined commitment and prompting strategies by asking university students, faculty, and staff to sign a card promising to use their vehicle safety belts. Participants also agreed to hang the "promise card" on the rear-view mirror of their vehicles, which served as a proximal prompt to buckle up.

As you may have guessed, individuals who signed the "Buckle-Up Promise Card" were already using their vehicle safety belt more often than those individuals who did not; but after signing the pledge, these individuals increased their belt use significantly.[33]

Consequence Strategies

Consequences are the primary determinant of voluntary behavior, according to ABA researchers and practitioners. The most effective activators make recipients aware of potential consequences, either explicitly or implicitly. Let's consider three basic consequence strategies: penalties, rewards, and feedback.

Penalties. These interventions identify undesirable behaviors and administer negative consequences to those who perform them. Although favored by governments, ABA practitioners typically avoid this approach in community interventions for a variety of reasons. One practical reason: It usually requires extensive enforcement to be effective, and enforcement requires backing by the proper authority. An ordinance that fined residents for throwing soda cans in the garbage would need some reliable way to observe this unwanted behavior, which obviously, would not be easy.

The negative impact of the penalty approach on the attitudes of the target audience is the main reason ABA practitioners have opposed use of behavioral penalties. Most individuals react to punishment with negative emotions and attitudes.[34] Instead of performing a behavior because of its positive impact, they simply do it to avoid negative consequences. And when enforcement is not consistent, behaviors are likely to return to their previous state.

Astute readers will note the label "penalty approach" rather than "punishment." And next, the term "reward" is used instead of "positive reinforcement." This differentiates the technical and the application meanings of these consequence strategies. Reinforcement and punishment imply the consequence changed the target behavior. If punishment does not decrease behavior or reinforcement (positive or negative) does not increase behavior, the relevant consequences were not punishers or reinforcers.

Punishment and reinforcement procedures are defined by the effects of the consequence on the target behavior. Because large-scale or community-based applications of consequence strategies rarely identify the behavioral impact per individual, the terms penalty and reward are more appropriate. Regardless of behavioral impact, penalties are negative consequences and rewards are positive consequences.

Rewards. Because of the negative side-effects associated with punishment, ABA practitioners favor following a desirable behavior with a positive consequence or reward. Rewards include money, merchandise, verbal praise, or special privileges, given as a consequence of the desired target behavior.

Reward strategies have some problems of their own. Still, many community-based reward interventions have produced dramatic increases in targeted behaviors.

Because rewards follow behaviors, they are included in the consequence section of this chapter. However, as the illustration shows, rewards are often preceded by behavioral antecedents announcing the availability of the reward following a designated behavior.

This activator is termed an *incentive*. An activator announcing punitive consequences for unwanted behavior is termed a *disincentive*. Sometimes rewards or penalties are used without incentives or disincentives. In these cases, the positive or negative consequence follows the behavior without an advanced announcement of the response-consequence contingency. Examples are provided in Chapter 3.

While effective at increasing the frequency of desirable behavior in a variety of settings and circumstances, incentive/reward interventions have a few disadvantages. An obvious practical disadvantage of using rewards is they can be expensive to implement from both a financial and administrative perspective.

A second limitation: Target behaviors tend to decrease when the rewards are removed, almost as dramatically as they increase when the rewards are introduced. In fact, this effect is so reliable ABA researchers often use this effect to evaluate intervention impact. They first measure the pre-intervention (baseline) rate of a target behavior, then assess the increase in the frequency of the behavior while rewards are in place, and finally document a decrease in behavioral frequency when the rewards are removed.

When a target behavior occurs more often while an intervention is in place and returns to near baseline levels when the intervention is withdrawn, ABA researchers demonstrate *functional control* of the target behavior. The intervention caused the behavior change. An obvious solution to this reversal problem is to keep a reward strategy in place indefinitely. Bottle bills, which provide a refund of 5-10 cents when bottles and cans are returned, illustrate an effective long-term incentive/reward strategy.

Finally, some researchers criticize reward interventions by contending rewards diminish *intrinsic motivation*.[35] Instead of focusing on the positive aspects of completing a task for its own sake, individual's become *extrinsically motivated* to perform the behavior. In essence individuals reason, "If someone is paying me to perform a behavior, the activity must be unpleasant and not worth performing when the opportunity for reward is removed."

The overjustification effect, as this perspective of extrinsic rewards is termed, is depicted in the illustration.[36] The prior extrinsic reward for solving a math problem takes the student's attention away from intrinsic or natural consequences of the behavior – solving an important problem.

Effective interpersonal recognition and feedback interventions call attention to the target behavior and can enhance intrinsic motivation. This issue is entertained further in Chapter 3, including a rationale and intervention techniques for using behavior-based rewards and interpersonal recognition to increase self-motivation and improve performance.

Feedback. Feedback strategies provide information to participants about their behavior. They can make the consequences of desirable behaviors more salient (e.g., grade improvement after studying more often, money saved by taking the bus, amount of weight lost from an exercise program), and increase the frequency of behaviors consistent with desired outcomes. Chapter 3 details communication techniques for giving supportive and corrective behavior-based feedback effectively in order to improve performance.

Although I reviewed these six non-punitive ABA intervention techniques (education, prompts, modeling, commitment, rewards, and feedback) separately, in practice several are often combined in a single intervention process. Most interventions combine some sort of antecedent information component with a behavior-based consequence (e.g., reward and/or feedback). The reward or feedback can be based on participants' behavior (i.e., process-based) or based on the cumulative results of several behaviors from one individual or a team of individuals (i.e., outcome-based).

It's important to apply behavior-based and outcome-based consequences strategically. The behavior-consequence contingency defines an accountability system which in turn influences the participant's behavior.

Outcome-based feedback and reward programs to promote industrial safety are popular worldwide, because they are easy to implement and they decrease the reports of injuries. Employees receive rewards (e.g., gift certificates, lottery tickets, or financial bonuses) when the company-wide injury rate is reduced to a certain level.

The result: Rewards are received because the frequency of *reported* injuries decrease.

However, most of these outcome-based incentive/reward programs do more harm than good. Why? Because actual safety-related behaviors do not change – just the *reporting* of injuries.

When the factual reporting of injuries is stifled by outcome-based incentives and rewards, the opportunity for critical conversations about injury prevention is lost. The real-world examples show how rewards for outcomes can have a detrimental effect on behavior. Managers get what they reward.

Similarly, in some educational settings, the focus is on the students' final grade and test scores rather than on the critical thinking skills gained from the teaching/learning process. For example, the public posting of class scores on standardized tests, and concomitant peer pressure, could motivate some teachers to teach strategies for outcome achievement (i.e., answering test questions correctly) rather than teaching the methods and trials-and-tribulations that enabled the discovery of certain facts. Hence, students will memorize facts in order to test well, rather than appreciating the creative and often intriguing teaching/learning process that could most benefit their own lives.

These real-world examples show how rewards for outcome over process can have detrimental behavioral effects. Teachers get the behavior they reward.

The Challenge of Sustaining Behavior Change

The intervention approaches reviewed above will change behavior, but will the target behavior continue when the intervention is removed?

This is primarily a challenge of institutionalizing the ABC contingencies of the intervention process, contend some ABA professionals.[37] External and extrinsic activators and consequences need to be transferred from the behavior analyst or intervention agent to the indigenous personnel of the organizational setting in which the target behavior occurs. The intervention is not removed; rather those who deliver the intervention contingencies are changed.

Other behavior analysts claim this maintenance challenge, is about behavior continuing in the absence of the extrinsic intervention.[38] Some presume the objectives of the intervention need to be internalized. As indicated earlier, people act themselves into thought processes consistent with the new behavior. As such, personal change is viewed as a continuous spiral of behavior causing thinking, thinking inducing more behavior, and then this additional behavior influencing more thinking consistent with the behavior, and so on.

However, programmatic research indicates that some interventions do not facilitate an attendant change in thinking. This is reflected profoundly in Daryl Bem's classic theory of self-perception.

Behavioral Self-Perception

Bem prefaced his behavioral presentation of self-perception theory with " . . . individuals come to 'know' their own attitudes, emotions, and other internal states by inferring them from observations of their own overt behavior and/or the circumstances in which this behavior occurs".[39] We write mental scripts or make internal attributions about ourselves from our observations and interpretations of the various three-term or ABC contingencies that enter our life space.

And, " . . . if external contingencies seem sufficient to account for the behavior, then the individual will not be led into using the behavior as a source of evidence for his self-attributions".[40]

Children who had the excuse of a severe threat for not playing with a "forbidden toy" did not internalize a rule, and played with the forbidden toy when the threat contingency was removed.[41] Similarly, college students paid $20 for telling other students a boring task was fun did not develop a personal view that the task was enjoyable.[42] The reinforcement contingency made their behavior incredible as a reflection of their personal belief or self-perception.

In contrast, participants who received a mild threat or low compensation (only $1) to motivate their behavior developed a self-perception consistent with their behavior. The children avoided playing with the forbidden toy in a subsequent situation with no threat, and the college students who lied for low compensation decided they must have liked the boring task. In theory, these participants viewed their behavior as a valid guide for inferring their private views, since their behavior was not under strong contingency control. This theory and its practical implications are explained further and illustrated in Chapter 5 as the consistency principle of social influence.

The More Outside Control, the Less Self-Persuasion

According to substantial research, self-persuasion is more likely when the extrinsic control of the three-term contingency is less obvious or perhaps indirect. When there are sufficient external consequences to justify the amount of effort required for a particular behavior, the performer does not develop an internal justification for the behavior. There is no self-persuasion and performing the behavior does not alter self-perception.[43] Under these circumstances maintenance of the behavior is unlikely, unless it's possible to keep a sufficient accountability system (e.g., incentives or disincentives) in place over the long term, as was the case for a 13-year incentive process that successfully reduced injuries in an open-pit mine.[44]

Intervening to improve behavior over the long term is more complex than applying the three-term contingency. Not only is it necessary to consider whether the performer needs instruction, motivation, or only support to improve or maintain behavior,[45] it seems internal cognitive factors are important whenever external contingencies cannot remain in place to hold people accountable. This implicates self-persuasion and self-directed behavior, topics not typically considered in ABA. These concepts imply that indirect influence is more likely to lead to sustained behavior change than direct persuasion.

Direct Persuasion. Advertisers use direct persuasion. They show us actors enjoying positive consequences or avoiding negative consequences by using their products. They apply the three-term contingency or ABC paradigm to sell their goods and services. The activator announces the availability of a reinforcing consequence if the purchasing behavior is performed.

Advertisers also apply research-based principles from social psychology to make their messages more persuasive. Specifically, social scientists have shown advantages of using highly credible communicators, and of arousing their audience's emotions.[46] Sales pitches are often delivered by authority figures (celebrities, chief executives) who attempt to get viewers emotionally involved with product-related issues.

In today's social media world, one's friends can be influential if they indicate on Facebook, they "like" a certain product. Advertisers are spending more and more money on this "peer persuasion" tactic.

These attempts at direct persuasion are not asking for behavior that is inconvenient or difficult to execute. Normally, the purpose of an advertisement is to persuade a consumer to select a certain brand of merchandise they already use. This boils down to merely choosing one commodity over another at the retail store. This is hardly a burdensome change in lifestyle.

AC4P behavior is usually more inconvenient and requires more effort than switching brands at a supermarket. Long-term participation in the AC4P Movement is far more cumbersome and lifestyle-changing than the consumer behavior targeted by advertisers.

In fact, direct attempts to persuade people to make inconvenient changes in their lifestyle have often yielded disappointing results. Communication strategies have generally been unsuccessful at persuading smokers to quit smoking[47] drivers to stop speeding,[48] homeowners to conserve water[49] or insulate their water heaters,[50] bigoted individuals to cease prejudicial behavior, or sexually active people to use condoms.[43] Similarly, the "Just Say No to Drugs" campaigns have not influenced significant behavior change.

The direct approach can give the impression the target behavior is accomplished for someone else's benefit. This can cause a disconnection between the behavior and self-perception. Then there's no self-persuasion – and self-perception is the mindset needed for lasting change in the absence of incentives/rewards, disincentives/penalties, or another type of extrinsic and external accountability system.

The Indirect Approach. Self-persuasion is more likely to occur when the motivational strategy is less obvious. Compliments regarding a person's performance are often more powerful when they are more indirect than direct.[51]

Imagine you overhear a person tell someone else about your superb achievement on a particular assignment. Or suppose a friend gives you secondhand recognition by sharing what another person said about your AC4P behavior. Both of these situations reflect indirect commendation, and will likely have more influence on your self-perception than a direct statement of praise. Why? Because the direct approach is tainted by the possibility flattery is given for an ulterior motive.

Indirect persuasion deviates significantly from the standard "command and control" method of promoting compliance. Both approaches might be equally effective at motivating behavior change, but an indirect approach will be far more successful at enhancing the kind of internal dialogue needed to sustain behavior in the absence of an external motivator or accountability system.

Defining intervention conditions to make this happen is not easy. Start by asking, "Does the situation promote individual choice, ownership, and personal accountability?" "Does the context in which AC4P behavior is desired contribute to connecting or disconnecting the link between what people do and what they think of themselves?" "Are the AC4P activities only behaviors or do they stimulate supportive cognitive activity or self-persuasion?"

The role of psychological states or expectancies in facilitating AC4P behavior are reflected in these questions. If certain feelings or beliefs affect people's participation in the AC4P Movement, then enhancing these states can be a powerful indirect way to cultivate an AC4P culture of compassion. The next chapter explains this further by specifying both direct and indirect ways to increase the frequency and improve the quality of AC4P behavior.

In Conclusion

This initial chapter reviewed seven fundamental principles and related applications of ABA. These serve as the foundation of the AC4P Movement, from analyzing the behavioral components of social issues to implementing and disseminating practical, evidence-based strategies for large-scale behavior change. Some research-based examples of effective ABA interventions were presented, but the following chapters offer many more.

The need to consider self-talk and person-states when designing and implementing AC4P interventions was explained. This domain of self-persuasion or self-motivation (see Chapter 3) justifies the label *humanistic behaviorism,* as introduced in the Preface. It takes us beyond traditional ABA. The principles and applications in the book illustrate ways to make ABA methods more effective and durable by incorporating concepts from humanistic theory and therapy. Still, when all is said and done, we have only scratched the surface regarding the potential of ABA and the AC4P approach to mitigate numerous negative consequences resulting from the intimidating social and environmental problems we face every day.

Notes

1. Geller, E. S. (1998). *Understanding behavior-based safety: Step-by-step methods to improve your workplace* (2nd Edition). Neenah, WI: J. J. Keller & Associates, Inc; Geller, E. S., & Williams, J. (Eds.). (2001). *Keys to behavior-based safety from Safety Performance Solutions.* Rockville, MD: Government Institutes; Geller, E. S. (2005). *People-based safety: The source.* Virginia Beach, VA: Coastal training and Technologies Corporation; Geller, E. S., & Johnson, D. J. (2007). *People-based patient safety: Enriching your culture to prevent medical error.* Virginia Beach, VA: Coastal Training and Technologies Corporation.

2. Skinner, B. F. (1938). *The behavior of organisms: An experimental analysis.* Acton, MA: Copley Publishing Group; Skinner, B. F. (1953). *Science and human behavior.* New York, NY: Macmillan; Skinner, B. F. (1974). *About behaviorism.* New York, NY: Alfred A. Knopf.

3. Goldstein, A. P., & Krasner, L. (1987). *Modern applied psychology.* New York: Pergamon Press; Greene, B. F., Winett, R. A., Van Houten, R., Geller, E. S., & Iwata, B. A. (Eds.) (1987). *Behavior analysis in the community: Readings from the Journal of Applied Behavior Analysis.* Lawrence, KS: Society for the Experimental Analysis of Behavior, Inc.

4. Carnegie, D. (1936). *How to win friends and influence people.* New York, NY: Simon and Schuster.

5. Skinner, B. F. (1971). *Beyond freedom and dignity.* New York, NY: Alfred A. Knopf.

6. Atkinson, J. W. (1957). Motivational determinants of risk-taking behavior. *Psychological Review, 64,* 359-372; Atkinson, J. W. (1964). *An introduction to motivation.* Princeton, NJ: Van Nostrand; Atkinson, J. W., & Litwin, G. F. (1960). Achievement motive and test anxiety conceived as motive to approach success and motive to avoid failure. *Journal of Abnormal and Social Psychology, 60,* 52-63.

7. Berglas, S., & Jones, E. E. (1978). Drug choice as a self-handicapping strategy in response to noncontingent success. *Journal of Personality and Social Psychology, 36,* 405-417; Rhodewalt, F. (1994). Conceptions of ability achievement goals, and individual differences in self-handicapping behavior: On the application of implicit theories. *Journal of Personality, 62,* 67-85; Rhodewalt, F., & Fairfield, M. (1991). Claimed self-handicaps and the self-handicapper: The relations of reduction in intended effort to performance. *Journal of Research in Personality, 1991, 25,* 402-417.

8. Geller, E. S. (1991) (Ed.). *Social validity: Multiple perspectives.* Monograph Number 5. Lawrence, KS: Society for the Experimental Analysis of Behavior, Inc.

9. Covington, M.V. (1992). *Making the grade: A self-worth perspective on motivation and school reform.* Cambridge, MA: Cambridge University Press; Martin, A. J., & Marsh, H. W. (2003). Fear of failure: Friend or foe? *Australian Psychologist, 38,* 31-38.

10. Covington, M. V., & Roberts, B. W. (1994). Self-worth and college achievement: Motivational and personality correlates. In P. R. Pintrich, D. R. Brown, & C. E. Weinstein (Eds.). *Student motivation, cognition, and learning: Essays in honor of Wilbert J. McKeachie*, Hillsdale, NJ: Earlbaum.

11. Covington, M.V. (1992). *Making the grade: A self-worth perspective on motivation and school reform*. Cambridge, MA: Cambridge University Press.

12. Maier, S. F., & Seligman, M. E. P. (1976). Learned helplessness: Theory and evidence. *Journal of Experimental Psychology: General, 105,* 3-46.

13. Wiegand, D.M., & Geller, E.S. (2005). Connecting positive psychology and organizational behavior management: Achievement motivation and the power of positive reinforcement. *Journal of Organizational Behavior Management, Vol. 24,* 3-25.

14. Azrin, N. H., & Holz, W. C. (1996). Punishment. In W. K. Honig (Ed.). *Operant behavior: Areas of research and application* (pp. 380-447). New York, NY: Appleton-Century-Crofts.

15. Estes, W. K., & Skinner, B. F. (1941). Some quantitative properties of anxiety. *Journal of Experimental Psychology, 29,* 390-400.

16. Geller, E. S. (2001). *The psychology of safety handbook*. Boca Raton, FL: CRC Press; Geller, E. S. (2002). *The participation factor: How to get more people involved in occupational safety*. Des Plaines, IL: American Society of Safety Engineers; Geller, E. S. (2005). *People-based safety: The source*. Virginia Beach, VA: Coastal Training and Technologies Corporation.

17. O'Brien, D. P. (2000) *Business measurements for safety performance*. New York, NY: Lewis Publishers; Petersen, D. (2001). *Authentic involvement*. Itasca, IL: National Safety Council.

18. Geller, E. S., & Lehman, G. R., (1991). The buckle-up promise card: A versatile intervention for large-scale behavior change. *Journal of Applied Behavior Analysis, 24,* 91-94.

19. Wolf, M.M. (1978). Social validity: The case of subjective measurement or how behavior analysis is finding its heart. *Journal of Applied Behavior Analysis, 11,* 203-213.

20. Schwartz, I. S., & Baer, D. M. (1991). Social validity assessments: Is current practice state of the art? *Journal of Applied Behavior Analysis, 24,* 189-197.

21. Eckenfelder, D. J. (1996). *Values-driven safety*. Rockville, MD: Government Institutes, Inc.

22. Daniels, A. C. (2000). *Bringing out the best in people: How to apply the astonishing power of positive reinforcement* (2nd Edition). New York, NY: McGraw-Hill, Inc.

23. Alvero, A. M., Bucklin, B. R., & Austin, J. (2001). An objective review of the effectiveness and characteristics of performance feedback in organizational settings. *Journal of Organizational Behavior Management, 21,* 3-29; Balcazar, F., Hopkins, B. L., & Suarez, I. (1986). A critical, objective review of performance feedback. *Journal of Organizational Behavior Management, 7,* 65-89.

24. Skinner, B. F. (1974). *About behaviorism*. New York: Alfred A. Knopf.

25. Geller, E. S., & Hahn, H. A. (1984). Promoting safety-belt use at industrial sites: An effective program for blue-collar employees. *Professional Psychology: Research and Practice, 15,* 533-564; Lewin, K. (1958). Group decision and social change. In E. E. Maccoby, T. M. Newcomb, & E. L. Hartley (Eds.). *Readings in social psychology* (pp. 197-211). New York, NY: Holt, Rinehart & Winston.

26. Geller, E. S. (1992). Solving environmental problems: A behavior change perspective. In S. Staub & P. Green (Eds.). *Psychology and social responsibility: Facing global challenges* (pp. 248-270). New York, NY: New York University Press.

27. Geller, E. S., Winett, R. A., & Everett, P. B. (1982). *Environmental preservation: New strategies for behavior change*. New York, NY: Pergamon Press.

28. Werner, C. M., Rhodes, M. U., & Partain, K. K. (1998). Designing effective instructional signs with

schema theory: Case studies of polystyrene recycling. *Environment and Behavior, 30,* 709-735.

29. Geller, E. S., Kalsher, M. J., Rudd, J. R., & Lehman, G. (1989). Promoting safety belt use on a university campus: An integration of commitment and incentive strategies. *Journal of Applied Social Psychology, 19,* 3-19.

30. Bandura, A. (1977). *Social learning theory.* Englewood Cliffs, NJ: Prentice Hall.

31. Dwyer, W. O., Leeming, F. C., Cobern, M. K., Porter, B. E., & Jackson, J. M. (1993). Critical review of behavioral interventions to preserve the environment: Research since 1980. *Environment and Behavior, 25,* 485-505.

32. Geller, E. S., & Lehman, G. R. (1991). The buckle-up promise card: A versatile intervention for large-scale behavior change. *Journal of Applied Behavior Analysis, 24,* 91-94.

33. Geller, E. S., Kalsher, M. J., Rudd, J. R., & Lehman, G. (1989). Promoting safety belt use on a university campus: An integration of commitment and incentive strategies. *Journal of Applied Social Psychology, 19,* 3-19.

34. Sidman, M. (1989). *Coercion and its fallout.* Boston, MA: Authors Cooperative, Inc., Publishers.

35. Deci, E. L., & Ryan, R. M. (1985). *Intrinsic motivation and self-determination in human behavior.* New York: Plenum Publishers; Kohn, A. (1993). *Punished by rewards: The trouble with gold stars, incentive plans, A's, praise, and other bribes.* Boston, MA: Houghton Mifflin; Pink, D. H. (2009). *Drive: The surprising truth about what motivates us.* New York, NY: Penguin Group.

36. Lepper, M., & Green, D. (1978) (Eds.). *The hidden cost of reward.* Hillsdale, NJ: Erlbaum.

37. Malott, R. W. (2001). Occupational safety and response maintenance: An alternative view. *Journal of Organizational Behavior Management, 21*(1), 85-102; McSween, T., & Matthews, G. A. (2001). Maintenance in organizational safety management. *Journal of Organizational Behavior Management, 21*(1), 75-83.

38. Baer, D. M. (2001). Since safety maintains our lives, we need to maintain maintaining. *Journal of Organizational Behavior Management, 21*(1), 61-64; Boyce, T. E., & Geller, E. S. (2001). Applied behavior analysis and occupational safety: The challenge of response maintenance. *Journal of Organizational Behavior Management, 21*(1), 31-60; Geller, E. S. (2001). Dream – Operationalize – Intervene – Test: If you want to make a difference – Just DO IT. *Journal of Organizational Behavior Management, 21*(1), 109-121; Stokes, T. F., & Baer, D. M. (1977). An implicit technology of generalization. *Journal of Applied Behavior Analysis, 10,* 349-367.

39. Bem, D. J. (1972). Self-perception theory. In L. Berkowitz (Ed.). *Advances in experimental social psychology,* Vol. 6 (pp. 1-60). New York, NY: Academic Press, p.2.

40. Bem, D. J. (1972). Self-perception theory. In L. Berkowitz (Ed.), *Advances in experimental social psychology,* Vol. 6 (pp. 1-60). New York, NY: Academic Press, p.3.

41. Lepper, M., & Green, D. (1978). *The hidden cost of reward.* Hillsdale, NJ: Erlbaum.

42. Festinger, L., & Carlsmith, J. M. (1959). Cognitive consequences of forced compliance. *Journal of Abnormal and Social Psychology, 58,* 203-210.

43. Aronson, E. (1999). The power of self-persuasion. *American Psychologist, 54,* 875-884.

44. Fox, D. K., Hopkins, B. L., & Anger, W. K. (1987). The long-term effects of a token economy on safety performance in open-pit mining. *Journal of Applied Behavior Analysis, 20,* 215-224.

45. Geller, E. S. (2001). Dream – Operationalize – Intervene – Test: If you want to make a difference – Just DO IT. *Journal of Organizational Behavior Management, 21*(1), 109-121.

46. Aronson, E. (1999). The power of self-persuasion. *American Psychologist, 54,* 875-884; Hovland, C., & Weiss, W. (1951). The influence of source credibility on communication effectiveness. *Public*

Opinion Quarterly, 15, 635-650.

47. Elder, J. P., Geller, E. S., Hovell, M. F., & Mayer, J. A. (1994). *Motivating health behavior.* New York, NY: Delmar Publishers.

48. Geller, E. S. (1998). *Applications of behavior analysis to prevent injury from vehicle crashes* (2nd Edition). Monograph published by the Cambridge Center for Behavioral Studies, Cambridge, MA.

49. Geller, E. S., Erickson, J. B., & Buttram, B. A. (1983). Attempts to promote residential water conservation with educational, behavioral, and engineering strategies. *Population and Environment, 6,* 96-112.

50. Geller, E. S. (1981). Evaluating energy conservation programs: Is verbal report enough? *Journal of Consumer Behavior, 8,* 331-334.

51. Allen, J. (1990). *I saw what you did and I know who you are: Bloopers, blunders and success stories in giving and receiving recognition.* Tucker, GA: Performance Management Publications; Geller, E. S. (1997). Key processes for continuous safety improvement: Behavior-based recognition and celebration. *Professional Safety, 42*(10), 40-44.

CHAPTER 2

The Psychology of AC4P

E. Scott Geller

THE LARGE-SCALE, LONG-TERM health, safety, and welfare of people require us to routinely go beyond the call of duty on behalf of others. We call this Actively Caring for People or AC4P – the theme of this book. Usually actively caring involves *self-motivation*, as I explain in the next chapter. Often AC4P behavior requires a certain amount of *courage*, and this is clarified in the fourth chapter of Part I of this book.

Research in social psychology,[1] applied behavior analysis,[2] and person-based psychology[3] provides principles and practical strategies for increasing the occurrence and improving the quality of AC4P behaviors throughout a culture. These are reviewed in Part I of this book.

What is AC4P?

Figure 2.1 presents a simple flow chart summarizing a basic approach to culture change. We start a culture-change mission with a vision or ultimate purpose – for example, to achieve an AC4P culture of compassion. With group consensus supporting the vision, we develop procedures or action plans to accomplish our mission. These are reflected in process-oriented goals which denote goal-related behaviors.

The popular writings of Covey,[4] Peale,[5] Kohn,[6] and Deming[7] suggest behavior is activated and maintained by self-affirmations, internal motivation and personal principles or values. But, these authors as well as many motivational consultants miss a key component of human dynamics – the power of consequences.

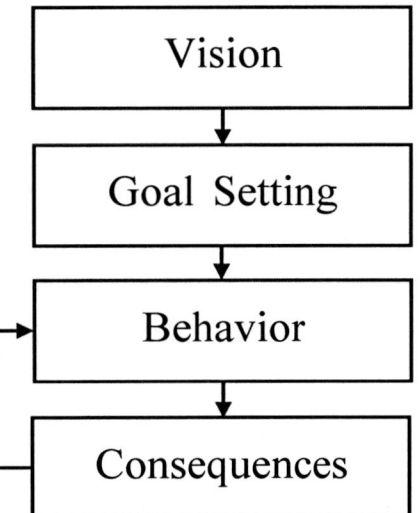

Figure 2.1. An AC4P culture requires vision and behavior management.

Consequences are Critical

Appropriate goal setting, self-affirmations, and a positive attitude can indeed activate behaviors to achieve goals and visions. But we must not forget one of B.F. Skinner's most important legacies – *selection by consequences*.[8] As depicted in Figure 2.1, consequences follow behavior and are needed to support the right behaviors and correct wrong ones.

Without support for the "right stuff," good intentions and initial efforts fade away. How long does a plan to complete homework more consistently as a New Year's resolution last if the student cannot see acknowledgement from the teacher and improved test scores (consequences) after the first several weeks of consistent homework completion (behavior) in an effort to ace the class (an outcome goal)?

In *How to Win Friends and Influence People*, Dale Carnegie affirms, "Every act you have ever performed since the day you were born was performed because you wanted something".[9] Sometimes natural consequences are available to motivate desired behaviors, but often extrinsic consequences (or external accountabilities) need to be managed to motivate the behavior needed to achieve a goal.

For example, I presume my students often have visions of earning an "A" in my university classes, and they set relevant process goals to study regularly in order to achieve that ultimate "A" grade (an outcome goal). I hold them accountable to study the material by giving exams periodically throughout the semester.

When the days for exams are announced in the course syllabus, students typically adjust their study behavior according to this accountability scheme. They increase their frequency of studying successively as the day of the exam approaches, performing most of their studying behaviors the night before an exam.

But when my assessment protocol is changed from announced to unannounced exams, most students change their study behavior dramatically. Under this accountability system, students feel compelled to prepare for every class, anticipating a possible exam on any class day. Although students uniformly dislike this second approach, they are substantially more prepared for class when the occurrence of an exam cannot be predicted.

Some students study the course material consistently to reach their learning goals, regardless of the external accountability agenda set by their teacher. These individuals are self-motivated and implement their own self-management procedures to keep them on track. I cover this special type of motivation in the next chapter, as well as ways to achieve this level of personal responsibility.

Students' post-exam, course-related behaviors are usually affected by their test scores – the consequences of their test-taking behavior. But for a number of reasons, it's difficult to predict how a particular exam grade will influence an individual's goal-setting or study behavior.

A high grade does not always motivate a higher rate of course-related studying, as expected from the principle of positive reinforcement; and a low grade does not necessarily lead to less studying as would be predicted from punishment theory. A sense of competence or confidence from a high grade could influence less study behavior; and fear of failure after receiving a low grade might affect more study behavior, including some self-management goal-setting and feedback strategies.

As you can see, the driving motivators are consequences. This is a key lesson to learn and use. The "pop psychology" notion that people can overcome their challenges and achieve whatever they want through positive thinking, self-affirmations, and relevant goal-setting before their behavior is just not true.

Without appropriate consequences to support the right behavior and correct the wrong behavior, goal-directed behavior will simply stop. People cannot reach their behavior-specific process goals unless they receive relevant feedback to keep them on track. I'm talking about behavior-based feedback to support desirable behavior and correct undesirable behavior.

Actively Caring is Critical

In Figure 2.2, a new box is added to the basic flow diagram in Figure 2.1. The point is simple but extremely important: Vision, goals and consequences are not sufficient for culture change. People need to *actively care* about the goals, action plans, and consequences. They need to believe in and own the vision.

They need to feel empowered and encouraged from peers to attain process goals that support the vision. And peers need to give them supportive and corrective feedback to increase the quantity and quality of behaviors consistent with vision-relevant goals.

Corrective feedback is critical for individuals to improve their future behavior. Supportive feedback is a powerful consequence for the maintenance of behavior, because it tells individuals what they are doing right.

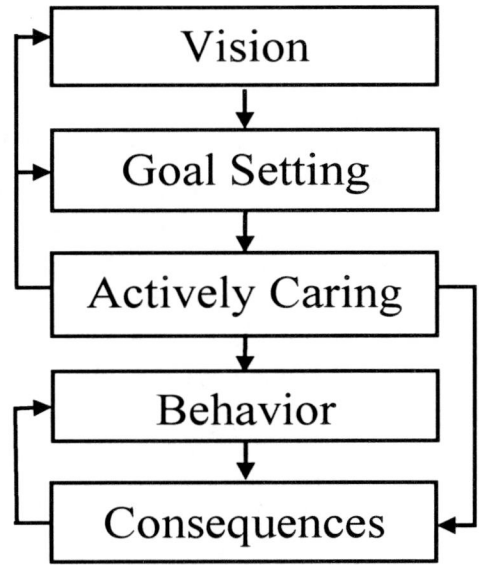

Figure 2.2. Continuous improvement requires actively caring.

In most relationships, supportive feedback is rare, so special attention is needed to increase this important feedback process. Corrective and supportive behavior-based feedback are essential for continuous improvement and for achieving an AC4P culture of people contributing to the well-being of each other. The next chapter details strategies for giving feedback to others effectively.

Three Ways to Actively Care

When individuals perform AC4P behaviors, they can improve environment factors, enhance person factors, or increase the frequency of others' AC4P behaviors. When people alter environmental conditions, or reorganize resources in an attempt to benefit others, they are AC4P from an environmental perspective. Examples of AC4P behaviors in this category include: organizing another student's study table or locker, posting a warning sign near a trip hazard, shoveling snow from a neighbor's sidewalk, washing another person's vehicle, helping a party host collect recyclables, and contributing money to a student's fund-raising effort.

Person-based AC4P occurs when people attempt to make others feel better. Often, it doesn't take much to improve an individual's emotions, attitudes, or mood states. Examples of person-based AC4P include: listening proactively to others, expressing concern for another person's difficulties, complimenting an individual's academic or athletic performance, sending a get-well card, and posting birthday wishes on a person's Facebook. These types of AC4P behavior will likely boost people's self-esteem, self-efficacy, personal control, optimism, and/or sense of belonging – thereby increasing their propensity to actively care (as explained below).

Also included here are *reactive* AC4P behaviors performed in crisis situations. For example, if you save someone from drowning, administer cardiopulmonary resuscitation (CPR), or give a drunk driver a ride home you're actively caring from a person-based perspective.

From a proactive perspective, behavior-focused AC4P is most beneficial, but is also the most challenging. This happens when people apply an instructive, supportive, or motivational intervention to improve another person's desirable behavior.

When we teach others how to promote AC4P behavior or provide supportive comments or possible improvements regarding observed behavior, we are actively caring from a behavioral focus. Teachers and athletic coaches do this when they help another person achieve a desired performance goal. Plus, recognizing the desirable AC4P behavior of others in a one-to-one conversation is also AC4P with a behavior focus.

Why Categorize AC4P Behaviors

Why go to the trouble of categorizing AC4P behaviors? Good question! Consider what these behaviors are trying to accomplish, and realize the relative difficulty in performing each of them. Environment-focused AC4P behavior might be the easiest approach for some people because it usually does not involve interpersonal interaction.

When people contribute financially to a charity, donate blood, or complete an organ donor card, they do not interact personally with the recipient of the contribution. These AC4P behaviors are certainly commendable and may represent significant commitment and effort, but the absence of personal encounters between giver and receiver is separate from other types of AC4P behavior.

Certain situations and dispositions might facilitate or inhibit one type of AC4P behavior and not the other. For example, communication skills are needed for AC4P on the personal or behavioral level. And different aspects of those communication skills usually come into play. Behavior-focused AC4P is more direct and usually more intrusive than person-focused AC4P.

It's more risky and potentially confrontational to intervene – to attempt to direct or motivate another person's behavior, in contrast to demonstrating concern, respect, or empathy for someone. Just consider the connotations of *intervention*. It's usually thought of as a form of confrontation, a negative interaction due to the frequent resistance of the person whose behavior is in question.

Helping someone in a crisis situation certainly takes effort and requires special skills, but there is rarely a possibility of rejection. On the other hand, attempting to step in to correct someone's behavior could lead to negative, even hostile, reaction. Effective behavior-based AC4P, as in interpersonal coaching, usually requires both interpersonal skills to gain the individual's trust, along with behavior-based skills to support desired behavior and/or correct undesired behavior.

Behavior-focused AC4P is actually expected from parents, teachers, supervisors, and coaches who are in charge of improving the behavior of individuals in certain situations. Thus, some behavior-focused AC4P is part of one's job and is expected. But here the question is whether you apply the best AC4P methods (e.g., supportive and corrective feedback that improve both behavior and attitude).

Suppose you observe a stranger not using a vehicle safety belt, or driving while talking on a cell phone, or riding a bicycle without a bike helmet. Would you say something to keep this person safe? Some people even hesitate to offer such proactive AC4P feedback for a friend, co-worker, or colleague.

Is it beyond the call of duty to look out for the well-being of a family member or friend? Most readers would say "No". But when AC4P becomes a social norm or the expected behavior in a culture, actively caring for a stranger will not stretch beyond one's normal routine.

As legislated in Australia, it's your "duty to care". AC4P behavior occurs whenever you look out for the well-being of another, but the degree of self-motivation and courage needed to actively care varies dramatically as a function of situational and dispositional factors.

A Hierarchy of Needs

Probably the most popular theory of human motivation is the hierarchy of needs proposed by humanist Abraham Maslow.[10] Categories of needs are arranged hierarchically, and it's presumed people don't attempt to satisfy needs at one stage or level until the needs at the lower stages are satisfied.

First, we are motivated to fulfill physiological needs. This includes basic survival requirements for food, water, shelter, and sleep. After these needs are under control, we are motivated by the desire to feel secure and safe from future dangers. When we prepare for future physiological needs, we are proactively working to satisfy our need for safety and security.

Next we have our social-acceptance needs – the need to have friends and feel like we belong. When these needs are gratified, our concern focuses on self-esteem, the development of self-respect and feeling worthwhile.

When I ask audiences to tell me the highest level of Maslow's Hierarchy of Needs, several people usually shout "self-actualization". When I ask for the meaning of "self-actualization," however, I receive limited or no reaction. You see, the concept of being self-actualized is rather vague and ambiguous.

In general terms, we reach a level of self-actualization when we believe we have become the best we can be, taking the fullest advantage of our potential as human beings. We labor to reach this level when striving to be as productive and creative as possible. Once accomplished, we feel a sense of brotherhood and affection for all human beings. We desire to help humanity as members of a single family – the human race.[11]

Perhaps it's fair to say these individuals are most ready to perform AC4P behavior.

Maslow's Hierarchy of Needs is illustrated in Figure 2.3. Note self-actualization is *not* at the top. Maslow[12] revised his renowned hierarchy shortly before his death in 1970, placing self-transcendence above self-actualization. Transcending the self means going beyond self-interest and is quite analogous to the AC4P concept.

According to Viktor Frankl,[13] self-transcendence includes giving ourselves to a cause or to another person and is the ultimate state of existence for the healthy individual. After satisfying our physiological needs, safety and security, acceptance, self-esteem, and self-actualization, people can be motivated to reach self-transcendence by reaching out to help others – to perform AC4P behavior.

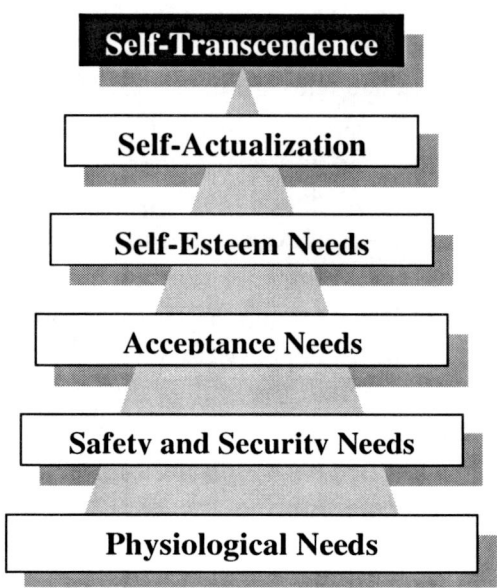

Figure 2.3. The highest need in Maslow's revised hierarchy relfects AC4P.

It seems intuitive that various self-needs require satisfaction before self-transcendent or AC4P behavior is likely to occur. But scant research supports ranking needs in a hierarchy. It's possible to think of many examples where individuals perform many AC4P behaviors before satisfying all their own needs. Mahatma Gandhi is a prime example of a leader who put the concerns of others before his own. He suffered imprisonment, extensive fasts, and eventually assassination in his 50-year struggle to help his poor and downtrodden compatriots.

I'm sure you can think of individuals in your life, including yourself perhaps, who reached the top level of self-transcendence before satisfying needs in the lower stages. Later in this chapter I'll show that satisfying lower-level needs might not be *necessary* for AC4P behavior, but people are generally more willing to actively care after satisfying the lower need levels in Maslow's hierarchy.

Psychological Science and AC4P

Walking home on March 13, 1964, Catherine (Kitty) Genovese reached her apartment in Queens, New York, at 3:30 A.M. Suddenly, a man approached her with a knife, stabbing her repeatedly, and then raped her. Kitty screamed, "Oh my God, he stabbed me! Please help me!" into the early morning stillness. Lights went on and windows opened in nearby buildings. Seeing the lights, the attacker fled. When he saw no one come to the victim's aid, he returned to stab her eight more times and rape her again.

The murder and rape of Kitty Genovese lasted more than 30 minutes, and was witnessed by 38 neighbors. One couple pulled up chairs to their window and turned off the lights so they could get a better view. Only after the murderer and rapist departed for good did anyone phone the police. When the neighbors were questioned about their lack of intervention, they couldn't explain it.

The reporter who first publicized the Kitty Genovese story, and later made it the subject of a book,[14] assumed *bystander apathy* was caused by big-city life. People's indifference to their neighbors' troubles was a conditioned reflex in crowded cities like New York, he reasoned.

After this horrific incident, hundreds of experiments were conducted by social psychologists to determine causes of this so-called *bystander apathy*.[15] This research discredited the reporter's common-sense conclusion. Several factors other than big-city alienation contribute to bystander apathy.

Lessons from Research

Professors Bibb Latané, John Darley, and their colleagues studied bystander apathy by staging emergency events observed by varying numbers of individuals. Then they systematically recorded the speed at which one or more persons came to the victim's rescue. In the most controlled experiments, the observers sat in separate cubicles and could not be influenced by the body language of other subjects. In the first study of this type, the participants introduced themselves and discussed problems associated with living in an urban environment.

In each condition, the first individual introduced himself and then casually mentioned he had epilepsy and the pressures of city life made him prone to seizures. During the course of the discussion over the intercom, he became increasingly loud and incoherent, choking, gasping, and crying out before lapsing into silence. The experimenters measured how quickly the participants left their cubes to help him.

When participants believed they were the only witness, 85 percent left their cubicles within three minutes to intervene. But only 62 percent of the participants who believed one other witness was present left their cubicle to intervene, and only 31 percent of those who thought five other witnesses were available attempted to intervene. Within three to six minutes after the seizure began, 100 percent of the lone participants, 81 percent of the participants with one presumed witness, and 62 percent of the participants with five other bystanders left their cubes to intervene.

The hesitancy of observers of an emergency to intervene and help a victim when they believe other potential helpers are available has been termed the *bystander effect*. It has been replicated in several situations.[16] Some researchers suggest ways to prevent bystander apathy – a critical barrier to achieving an AC4P culture.

Keep in mind this research only studied reactions in crisis situations; behaviors we categorize as reactive, person-focused AC4P behavior. It seems intuitive, though, the findings are relevant for both environment-focused and behavior-focused AC4P behaviors in proactive situations.

Diffusion of Responsibility. A key contributor to the bystander effect is the assumption that someone else should or could assume the responsibility. For example, many observers of the Kitty Genovese rape and murder assumed another witness would call the police, or attempt to scare away the assailant. Perhaps some observers waited for a witness more capable than they to rescue Kitty.

Does this factor contribute to lack of intervention when someone needs help? Do people ignore or deny opportunities to actively care for another person (i.e., a stranger) because they presume someone else will help? Perhaps some people assume, "If those who know the person seeking assistance don't care enough to help, why should I?"

Social psychology research suggests teaching people about the bystander effect can make them less likely to fall prey to it themselves.[17] Often, people have a "we-they" attitude or a territorial perspective ("I'm responsible for the people in this area; you're responsible for those in that area"). Eliminating this "we-they" perspective increases people's willingness to actively care for others.[18]

An AC4P Norm. Many, if not most, U.S. citizens are raised to be independent rather than interdependent. However, intervening for the benefit of others, whether reactively in a crisis situation or proactively to prevent potential crises, requires a sincere commitment toward interdependence.

Social psychologists refer to a *social responsibility norm* as the belief people should help those who need help. Subjects who scored high on a measure of this norm, as a result of upbringing during childhood or special training sessions, were more likely to intervene in a bystander intervention situation, regardless of the number of other witnesses.[16]

Knowing What to Do. When people know what to do in a crisis, they do not fear appearing foolish and do not wait for another, more skilled person to intervene. The bystander effect was eliminated when observers had certain competencies, such as training in first-aid treatment, which enabled them to take charge of the situation.[19] When observers believe they possess the appropriate tools to help, bystander apathy is decreased or eliminated.

Recognizing others for performing AC4P behaviors is critical for the development of an AC4P norm and an AC4P culture. But our field studies have shown this is easier said than done (see also Chapter 13). Participants in these studies agreed with the mission to recognize others for their AC4P behaviors. Still, the percentage who delivered such recognition in prescribed ways was always much lower than expected and desired. These percentages increased dramatically following role playing to develop relevant interpersonal skills, accompanied by meetings of AC4P support groups.[20]

Most proactive AC4P action requires self-motivation (Chapter 3) and moral courage (Chapter 4) in addition to relevant interpersonal skills. Much of our AC4P research, some of which is reviewed in this book, addresses ways to facilitate the occurrence and improve the effectiveness of AC4P behaviors and remove barriers that hold us back from thanking people for their AC4P behavior.

It's Important to Belong. Bystander apathy is reduced, according to research, when observers know one another and have developed a sense of belonging or mutual respect from prior interactions.[21] Most, if not all, of the witnesses to Kitty Genovese's murder did not know her personally. It's likely the neighbors did not feel a sense of community with one another. Situations and interactions that reduce a "we-they" or territorial perspective and increase feelings of relatedness or community will increase the likelihood people will actively care for each other.

Mood States. Several social psychology studies have found people are more likely to offer help when they are in a good mood.[22] And the mood states that facilitated helping behavior were created very easily, for example, by arranging for potential helpers to find a dime in a phone booth, giving them a cookie, showing them a comedy film, or providing pleasant aromas. Are these findings relevant for cultivating an AC4P culture?

Daily events can elevate or depress our moods. Some events are controllable, while others are not. Clearly, the nature of our interactions with others can have a dramatic impact on the mood of everyone involved. The research on mood and its effects on helping behavior might motivate those of us who want to facilitate an AC4P culture to interject more positivity and optimism into our interpersonal conversations with others.

Beliefs and Expectancies. Social psychologists have shown that certain dispositional characteristics or beliefs influence one's inclination to help a person in an emergency. Specifically, individuals who believe their world is fair and predictable, a place where good behavior is rewarded and bad behavior is punished, are more likely to help others in a crisis.[23] Also, people with a higher sense of social responsibility and the general expectancy that people control their own destinies showed a greater willingness to actively care.[24]

The beliefs and expectancies that influence AC4P behaviors are not developed overnight and obviously cannot be changed overnight. But a particular culture, including its policies, appraisal and recognition procedures, educational opportunities and approaches to discipline, can certainly increase or decrease perceptions or beliefs in a just world, social responsibility, and personal control, and in turn influence people's willingness to perform AC4P behavior.[25]

Deciding to Actively Care

As a result of their seminal research, Latané and Darley[26] proposed that an observer makes four sequential decisions before helping a victim. These four decisions (depicted in Figure 2.4) are influenced by the situation or environmental context in which an AC4P opportunity occurs, the nature of the crisis, the presence of other bystanders and their reactions, and relevant social norms and rules.

Although the model was developed to evaluate intervention in emergency situa-

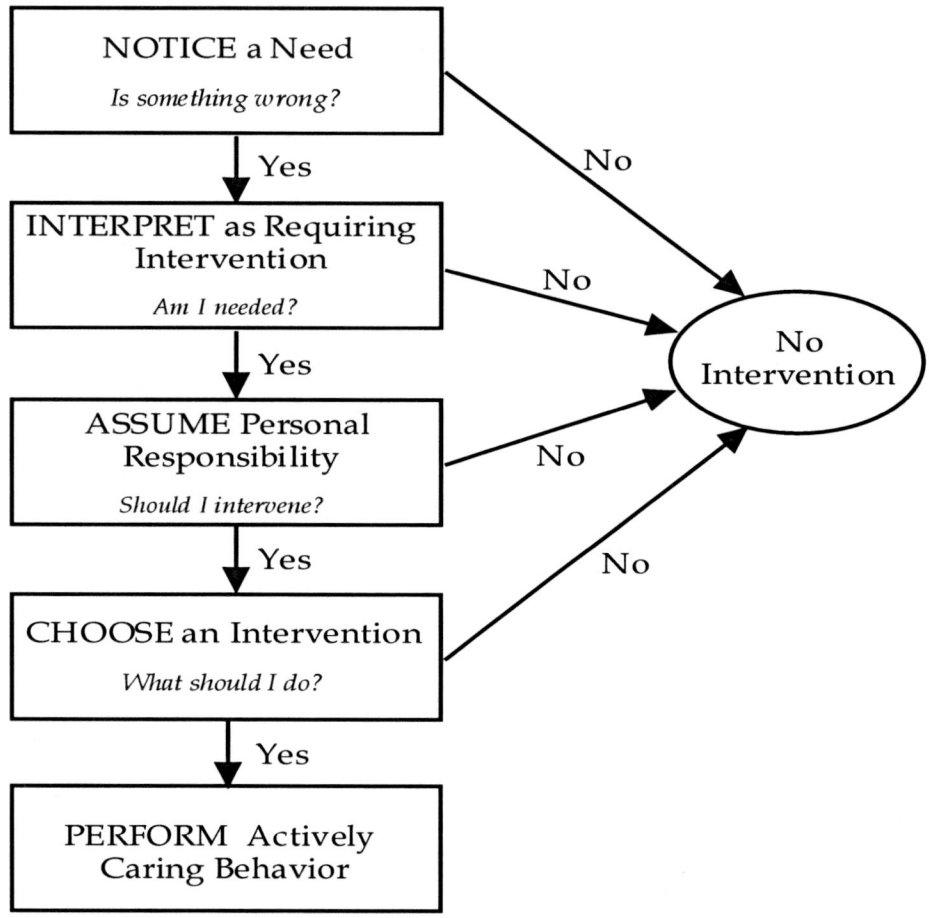

Figure 2.4. AC4P behavior requires four sequential decisions.

tions – where there's a need for direct, reactive, person-focused AC4P behavior – it's quite relevant for the other types of AC4P, as well.

Step 1: Is Something Wrong? The first step in deciding whether to intervene is simply perceiving something is wrong. Some situations or events naturally attract more attention than others. Most emergencies are novel and upset the normal flow of life. However, as shown by Piliavin et al.,[27] the onset of an emergency, such as a person slipping on ice or falling down a flight of stairs, will attract more attention and helping behavior than the aftermath of an "injury," as when a victim is regaining consciousness or rubbing an ankle after a fall. Of course, we should expect much less attention to potential problems in daily, nonemergency situations in school, at work, and at home.

In active and noisy teaching/learning environments, teachers and students narrow their focus to what is personally relevant. We learn to tune out irrelevant stimuli. In these situations, the ongoing behaviors of people around us are less noticeable and attention-getting. Yet these behaviors may need proactive AC4P support or correction.

But, even if the need for proactive participation is noticed, AC4P behavior will not necessarily occur. The observer must interpret the situation as requiring intervention. This leads us to the next question requiring a "Yes" answer for AC4P behavior to occur.

Step 2: Am I Needed? Of course we can come up with a variety of excuses for not helping. Distress cues, such as cries for help, and the actions of other observers can clarify an event as an emergency. When we are confused, we look to other people for information and guidance.

In other words, by watching what others are doing, we figure out how to interpret an ambiguous event and how to react accordingly. The behavior of others is especially important when stimulus cues are not present.[28]

In situations where the need for intervention or corrective action is not obvious, we usually seek information from others to understand what's going on and to receive direction. This is the typical state of affairs when it comes to noticing a need for AC4P behavior or recognizing another person's AC4P behavior. In fact, the need for *proactive* AC4P behavior is rarely obvious.

When I ask my students to look for AC4P behavior around them and then recognize the person with an "AC4P Thank-You Card," I typically receive less than 10% compliance. The most frequent excuse for not recognizing AC4P behavior is, "I didn't see actively caring worthy of a thank-you card."

Step 3: Should I Intervene? "Is it my responsibility to intervene?" The answer is clear if you are the only witness to a situation you perceive as an emergency. But you might not answer "Yes" to this question when you know other people are also observing the same emergency, or cry for help. You have reason to believe someone else will intervene, perhaps a person more capable than you. This perception relieves you of personal responsibility. But what happens when everyone believes the other guy will take care of it? This is likely what happened in the Kitty Genovese incident.

A breakdown at this stage of the decision model doesn't mean the observers don't care about the welfare of the victim. Actually, it's probably incorrect to call lack of intervention *bystander apathy*.[29] The bystanders might care very much about the victim, but defer responsibility to others because they believe other observers are more likely or better qualified to intervene.

Similarly, students might care a great deal about the well-being of another student, but feel relatively incapable of acting on their caring. People might resist taking personal responsibility to actively care because they don't believe they have the most effective tools to make a difference.

In addition to a "can do" attitude, people need to believe it's their personal responsibility to actively care for others. The challenge in achieving an AC4P culture is to convince everyone they have a responsibility to actively care for others. A social norm or expectancy needs to be established. All participants share equally in a daily assignment to keep everyone healthy and productive.

Plus, AC4P leaders need to accept the special responsibility of teaching others any techniques they learn at workshops or group meetings that could increase a person's perceived competence (or self-efficacy) to actively care more effectively. If we don't meet this challenge, many people are apt to decide AC4P is not for them.

Step 4: What Should I Do? This last step of the Latané and Darley decision model pinpoints the importance of education and training. Education gives people the rationale and principles behind a particular intervention approach. It gives people information to design or refine intervention strategies, leading to a sense of ownership for the particular tools they help to develop. Through training, people learn how to translate principles and rules into specific behaviors or intervention strategies.

Bottom line: People who learn how to intervene effectively through relevant education and training are more likely to be successful agents of an AC4P intervention.

This decision logic suggests certain methods for increasing the likelihood people will actively care. Specifically, the model supports the need to teach people how to recognize a need for AC4P behavior at the environment, person, and behavior levels and then determine what intervention strategies are available and most effective in each case. Plus, people need to learn how to give supportive feedback and genuine recognition for those who emit AC4P behavior.

It's also imperative to promote AC4P as a core value of the particular culture. This means everyone assumes responsibility for the health, safety, and well-being of others in their culture and never waits for someone else to act.

Cultivating an AC4P Culture

Culture influences and sustains one's propensity to actively care. A teaching/learning culture, for example, can incorporate an accountability system that encourages interpersonal helping. Plus, the daily interactions of people influence certain person-states that affect one's propensity to go beyond the call of duty for another person's well-being. The frequency of AC4P behavior varies *directly* with extrinsic-response contingencies and *indirectly* as a function of certain dispositional person-states.

The Direct Approach

For almost 30 years, I have promoted the use of a special "Actively-Caring Thank-You Card" at my University to recognize individuals for their AC4P behavior. The front of this brightly-colored card includes the mascot of our University and two University sponsors. The definition of AC4P behavior is given on the back of the card, along with specific examples of actively caring.

 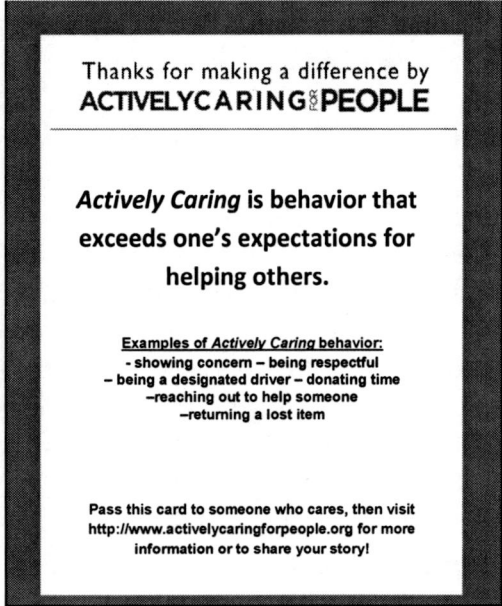

Several organizations have customized this thank-you card for their culture. I have seen this simple thank-you-card cultivate a sense of interdependence and belongingness throughout a work group, as well as help people feel good about their own AC4P behavior.

In their book, *Measure of a Leader*, Aubrey and James Daniels describe a creative device they have used successfully for years to motivate discretionary behaviors throughout an organization. Specifically, managers hang a chart in a conspicuous location that lists the names of all employees in a certain work area. Then they give each person a sticker identifying that individual. Whenever a worker is helped by a colleague, that person puts his or her identifying sticker on the chart, next to the name of the person who performed the AC4P behavior.

The Daniels brothers report dramatic culture change. "Not only does it give recognition for those who help, but it is an antecedent for others to take the initiative in finding ways they can help other team members."[30] This accountability system could readily be adopted for a school setting, analogous to assigning students gold starts for their successful academic performance.

In addition, for more than 20 years I've been promoting the use of a green wristband, embossed with the words "Actively Caring for People," to recognize people for their AC4P behavior. Over the years, I've distributed about 50,000 of these wristbands after my keynote addresses at conferences and organizations. My students have used this recognition approach to reduce bullying by promoting and rewarding AC4P behavior in various educational settings (see Chapter 6).[31]

For these latter applications, the AC4P wristbands were redesigned to include a different identification number per wristband, and the website (www.ac4p.org) was developed where people can: a) share their AC4P stories (with the number of the wristband they gave or received), b) track worldwide where a particular AC4P wristband has been, and c) order more AC4P wristbands to reward others for actively caring.

To date, more than 2,000 AC4P stories have been shared on this website, and more than 50,000 AC4P wristbands have been purchased with proceeds going to the Actively Caring for People Foundation, Inc. We believe this particular accountability system for activating and rewarding AC4P behavior has great potential for spreading the AC4P paradigm worldwide and inspiring the development of AC4P cultures in educational settings and beyond.

Genuine appreciation and recognition can have dramatic positive effects on a person's attitude, mindset, and disposition. A recognition system that directly acknowledges AC4P behavior can result in a spiraling cycle of favorable culture change. Positive regard for people's AC4P behaviors increases the frequency of the target behavior directly, while simultaneously feeding the five person-states that set the occasion for more AC4P behavior. These person-states are defined next, as well as ways to enhance them.

The Indirect Approach

Psychological science considers both the observable (outside) and non-observable (inside) aspects of individuals. Indeed, long-term behavior change requires people to change *inside* as well as outside. The promise of a positive consequence or the threat of a negative one can maintain desired behavior while the response-consequence contingencies are in place. But what happens when they are withdrawn? What happens when people are in situations, like at home, when no one is holding them accountable for their behavior?

If people do not *believe* in the AC4P way of doing something and do not *accept* AC4P as a value or a personal mission, they will not choose AC4P behavior when no one's watching. If people are not self-motivated to actively care, the frequency of AC4P behavior will be much less than desired. I explain self-motivation and illustrate ways to enhance this person-state in the next chapter.

Figure 2.5 illustrates how person factors interact with the basic activator-behavior-consequence (ABC) model of behavior-focused psychology, as introduced in Chapter 1.[32] Activators direct behavior and consequences motivate behavior, but as shown in Figure 2.5, these events are first filtered through the person. Numerous internal and

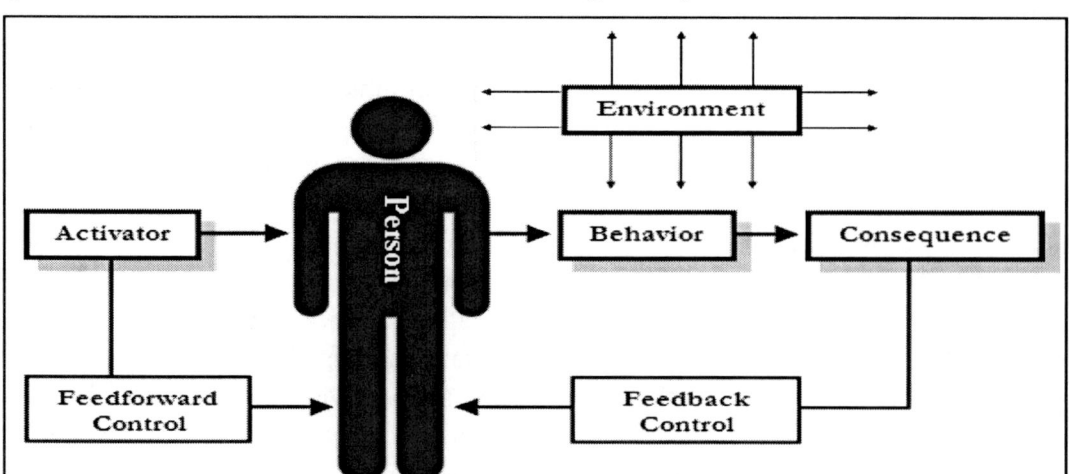

Figure 2.5. Activators and consequences are filtered through the person.

situational factors influence how we mentally process activators and consequences. If we see activators and consequences as schemes to control us, our attitude about the situation will likely be negative.

On the other hand, when we believe the external contingencies are genuine attempts to help us do the right thing, our attitude will be more positive. Personal or internal dynamics determine how we receive activator and consequence information. This can influence whether environmental events enhance or diminish what we do. Let's consider five states that influence one's propensity to perform AC4P behavior.

Self-Esteem (*"I am valuable"*). One's self-concept, or feeling of worth, is a central theme of most humanistic therapies.[33] According to Carl Rogers and his adherents, we possess both a real and an ideal self-concept.

We have notions or aspirations of what we would like to be (our ideal self) and what we think we are (our real self). Our self-esteem decreases as the gap between our real and ideal self-concepts increases. The mission of many humanistic therapies is to help a client reduce this gap.

Acting to help others raise their self-esteem has obvious benefits. Research shows people with high self-esteem report fewer negative emotions and less depression than people with low self-esteem.[34] Those with higher self-esteem also handle life's stresses better.[35]

Individuals who score higher on measures of self-esteem are: a) less susceptible to outside influences,[36] b) more confident of achieving personal goals,[37] and c) make more favorable impressions on others in social situations.[38] People with higher self-esteem also help others more frequently than those scoring lower on a self-esteem scale.[39]

Empowerment (*"I can make a difference"*). In management literature, empowerment typically refers to delegating authority or responsibility, or sharing decision-making.[40] In contrast, the AC4P perspective of empowerment focuses on *how a person reacts* after receiving more power or influence.

From a psychological perspective, empowerment is a matter of personal perception. Do you feel empowered or more responsible? Can you handle the additional assignment? This view of empowerment requires the personal belief that "I can make a difference".

Perceptions of personal control,[41] self-efficacy,[42] and optimism[43] strengthen the notion of empowerment. An empowered state is presumed to increase your motivation to "make a difference," perhaps by going beyond your normal routine on behalf of the well-being of another person. Empirical support exists for this intuitive hypothesis.[44] Let's look more closely at these three person states that affect our propensity to actively care.

Self-Efficacy. In other words, *"I can do it"* (or, *"You can do it."*). I'm talking about your self-confidence. This is a key principle in social learning theory, determining whether a therapeutic intervention will succeed over the long term.[45]

People who score relatively high on a measure of self-efficacy perform better at a wide range of tasks, and work harder to achieve a specific goal, according to dozens of studies. These "can do" believers also demonstrate greater ability and motivation to solve complex problems, have better health and safety habits, and are more successful at handling stressors.[46]

Self-efficacy contributes to self-esteem, and vice versa; but these constructs are different. Self-esteem refers to a general sense of self-worth; self-efficacy refers to feeling successful or effective at a particular task. Self-efficacy is task focused, and can vary markedly from one task to another. One's level of self-esteem remains relatively constant across situations.

Personal Control. This is the sense that *"I am in control"*. J. B. Rotter[41] used the term *locus of control* to locate the forces controlling a person's life. People with an *internal* locus of control believe they usually have direct personal control over significant life events as a result of their knowledge, skill, and abilities. They believe they are captains of their life's ship.

In contrast, persons with an *external* locus of control believe "outside" and random factors like chance, luck, or fate play important roles in their lives. Externals believe they are victims, or sometimes beneficiaries, of circumstances beyond their direct personal control.[47]

More than 2,000 studies have investigated the relationship between perceptions of personal control and other variables.[48] Internals are more achievement-oriented and health conscious than externals. They are less prone to distress, and more likely to seek medical treatment when they need it.[49]

Having an internal locus of control helps reduce chronic pain, facilitates psychological and physical adjustment to illness and surgery, and hastens recovery from some diseases.[50] Internals perform better at jobs that allow them to set their own pace, whereas externals work better when a machine controls the pace.[51]

Optimism. *"I expect the best"* sets the tone for optimism. It's the learned expectation that life events, including personal actions, will turn out well.[52] Optimism relates directly to achievement. Martin Seligman[53] reported, for example, that world-class swimmers who scored high on a measure of optimism recovered from defeat and swam even faster compared to those swimmers scoring low. Following defeat, the pessimistic swimmers swam slower.

Compared to pessimists, optimists maintain a sense of humor, perceive problems or challenges in a positive light, and plan for success. They focus on what they can *do* rather than on how they *feel*.⁵⁴ Optimists handle stressors constructively and experience positive stress more often than negative distress.⁵⁵ They essentially expect to succeed at whatever they do, and so they work harder than pessimists to reach their goals. Optimists are beneficiaries of the self-fulfilling prophecy.⁵⁶

Fulfilling an optimistic prophecy can enhance our perceptions of personal control, self-efficacy, and even self-esteem. Realizing this should motivate us to do whatever we can to make interpersonal conversations positive and constructive. This will

not only increase optimism in a certain culture, but also promote a sense of group cohesiveness or belonging – another person state that facilitates AC4P behavior.

Belonging (*"I am a team member"*). M. Scott Peck challenges us to experience a sense of true community with others in his best seller, *The Different Drum: Community making and peace*.⁵⁷ We need to develop feelings of belonging with one another regardless of our political preferences, cultural backgrounds, and religious beliefs.

We need to transcend our differences, overcome our defenses and prejudices, and develop a deep respect for diversity. Peck claims we must develop a sense of community or interconnectedness with one another if we are to accomplish our best and ensure our sustainability as human beings.

It's intuitive that building a sense of community or belonging among our friends and colleagues will increase the frequency of our AC4P behaviors. Improvement in behavior requires interpersonal observation, feedback, and recognition. For this to happen, people need to adopt a collective win-win perspective instead of the individualistic win-lose orientation so common in many educational settings.

A sense of belonging and interdependency leads to interpersonal trust and caring – essential features of an AC4P culture. In the next chapter, I explain how one's sense of community or relatedness to others affects self-motivation – a person's drive to do something without an external incentive or accountability system.

Figure 2.6 lists a number of special attributes prevalent in most families, where interpersonal trust and belonging are usually optimal. We are willing to actively care in special ways for the members of our immediate family. The result is optimal trust, belonging, and AC4P behavior for the health, safety, and welfare of our family members.

To the extent we follow the guidelines reflected in Figure 2.6 among members of our everyday peer group, we will achieve an AC4P culture. Following the principles implied in Figure 2.6 will develop trust and belonging among people, and lead to the quantity and quality of AC4P behavior expected among family members – at school, at home, at work, and everywhere in between.

- We use more rewards than penalties with *family* members.
- We don't pick on the mistakes of *family* members.
- We don't rank one *family* member against another.
- We brag about the accomplishments of *family* members.
- We respect the property and personal space of *family* members.
- We pick up after other *family* members.
- We correct the undesirable behavior of *family* members.
- We accept the corrective feedback of *family* members.
- We are interdependent with *family* members.
- We actively care because they're *family*.

Figure 2.6. A family perspective among teachers and students helps to cultivate an AC4P culture.

A Self-Supporting AC4P Cycle

The five person-states presented here as influencing people's willingness to actively care are shown in Figure 2.7 as an AC4P Model. Each of these person-states has a rich research history in psychology, and some of this research relates directly to the AC4P Model. Research that tested relationships between these person-states and actual behavior has supported this model,[58] although much more research is needed in this domain.

A particularly important question is whether the AC4P person-states are both antecedents and consequences of an AC4P act. It seems intuitive that performing an act of kindness that is effective, accepted, and appreciated could increase the helper's self-esteem, self-efficacy, personal control, optimism, and sense of belonging. This, in turn, should increase the probability of more AC4P behavior. In other words, one act of caring, properly appreciated, should lead to another and another. A self-supporting AC4P cycle is likely to occur.

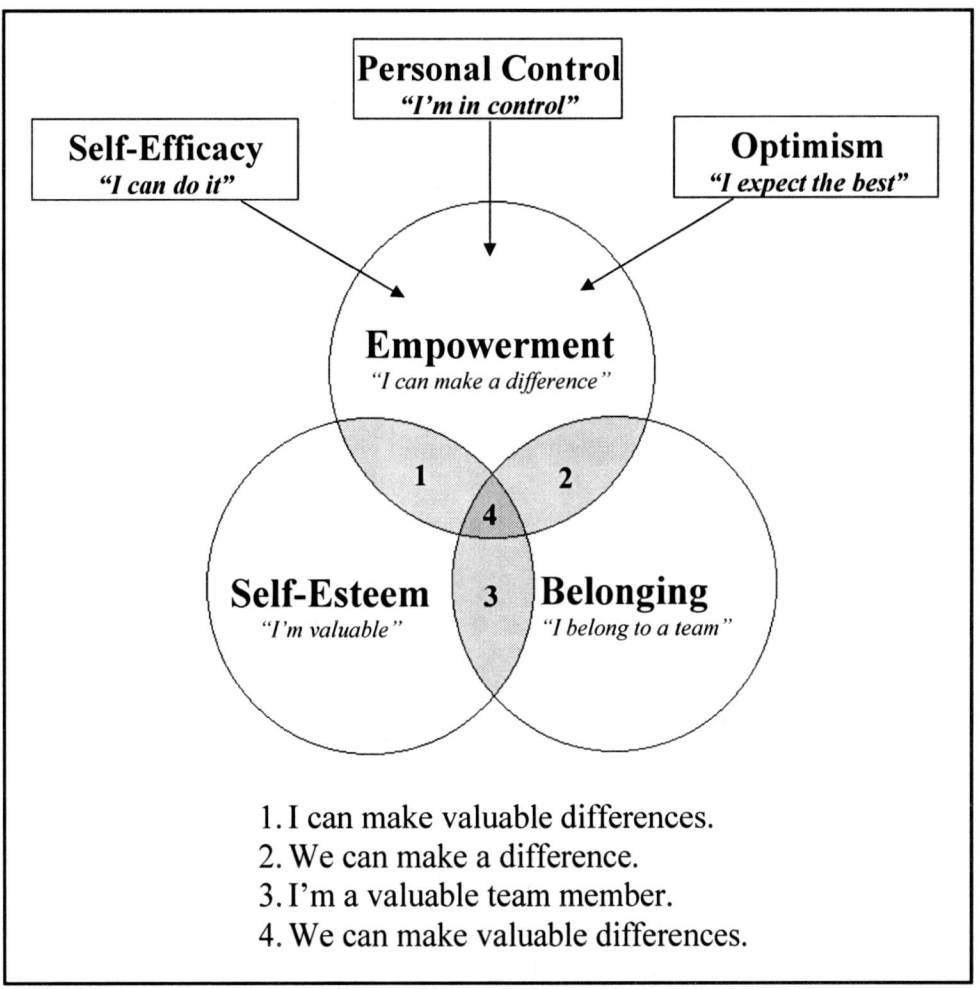

Figure 2.7. Five person-states influence a person's willingness to actively care.

Enhancing the AC4P Person-States

Sometimes participants at my workshops and seminars express concern the AC4P person-state model might not be practical. "The concepts are too soft or subjective," is a typical reaction. Teachers, parents, coaches, and work supervisors accept the behavior-based approach to performance improvement because it's straightforward, objective, and clearly applicable to educational, work, and family settings. But person-based concepts like self-esteem, personal control, optimism, and belonging appear ambiguous, "touchy-feely," and difficult to deal with. "The concepts sound good and certainly seem important, but how can we wrap our arms around these 'warm fuzzies' and use them to promote an AC4P culture?"

To be sure, person-states are more difficult to define, measure, and manage than behaviors. But we just can't ignore how people *feel* about a behavior-improvement process. For people to accept a behavior-change process and sustain the target behaviors for the long term, we must confront internal person-states when designing and implementing an intervention.

After introducing the AC4P Model (Figure 2.7) at my workshops on AC4P, I often divide participants into discussion groups. I ask group members to define events, situations, or contingencies that decrease and increase the person-state assigned to their group. Then I ask the groups to derive simple and feasible action plans to increase their assigned dispositional state. This promotes personal and practical understanding of the concept.

The AC4P Model may be soft, but feedback from these workshops shows it's not too hard to grasp. Action plans have been practical and quite consistent with techniques studied by researchers. Also, there has been substantial overlap of practical recommendations – workshop groups dealing with different person-states have come up with similar contributory factors and action plans. Let's take a look at what my workshop participants have proposed regarding factors and strategies related to each of these person-states.

Self-Esteem

Participants suggest a number of ways to build self-esteem, including: a) Provide opportunities for personal learning and peer mentoring; b) Increase recognition for desirable behaviors and individual accomplishments; and c) Solicit and follow up on a person's suggestions.

It's essential to give more positive (or supportive) than negative (or corrective) feedback. When offering corrective feedback, it's essential to focus on the act, not the actor. Emphasize an error only reflects behavior that can be corrected, not some deeper character flaw. Don't come off as a judge of character, implying a mistake suggests some subjective personal attribute like "carelessness," "apathy," "bad attitude," or "poor motivation".

Be a patient, active listener. Allow people to offer reasons for their error or poor judgment. Resist the temptation to argue about these. Giving a reason or excuse is just a way to protect one's self-esteem, and it's generally a healthy response. Remember, you already made your point by showing the error and suggesting ways to avoid the mistake in the future. Leave it at that.

If a person doesn't react constructively to corrective feedback, it might help to explore feelings. "How do you feel about this?" you might ask. Then listen empathically to assess whether self-esteem has taken a hit. You'll learn whether some additional communication is needed to place the focus squarely on what is external and objective, rather than subjective and internal.

Self-Efficacy

Self-efficacy is more situation-specific than self-esteem, so it fluctuates more readily. Feedback should be directed only at one's perception of what's needed to do a particular task successfully. It should not veer off in the nebulous direction of general self-worth.

Keep in mind that repeated negative feedback can have a cumulative effect, chipping away at an individual's perception of self-worth. Then it takes only one remark, perhaps one you would think is innocuous and insignificant, to "break the camel's back" and activate what seems like an overreaction.

Our communication may not be received as intended. We might do our best to come across positively and constructively, but because of factors beyond our control, the communication might be misperceived. One's inner state can dramatically bias the impact of interpersonal feedback. Note that self-efficacy reflects a perception of competence, and in the next chapter I explain how feeling competent leads to self-motivation.

Achievable Tasks. What makes for a "can do" attitude? Personal perception is the key. A teacher, coach, or parent might believe s/he has provided everything needed to complete a task successfully. However, the student or athlete might not think so. It's important to ask, "Do you have what you need? We're checking for feelings of self-efficacy." This is easier said than done, because people often hesitate to admit their incompetence. Who wants to concede, "I can't do it?" Instead, we try to maintain the appearance of self-efficacy.

Ask open-ended questions when you give assignments to assess whether those on the receiving end are prepared to get the job done. In large groups, though, this probing for feelings of self-efficacy is impossible. As a result, in the classroom many students get left behind in the learning process (frequently because they skipped classes or an important reading assignment). As they get farther and farther behind in my class, their low self-efficacy is supported by the self-fulfilling prophecy and diminished optimism. Sometimes this leads to "raise-the-white-flag-behavior" and feelings of helplessness.[59]

All too often, these students withdraw from my class or resign themselves to receiving a low grade. In the workplace, employees who cannot keep pace with new procedures might withdraw into themselves or put up defensive resistance.

Personal Strategies. Watson and Tharp[60] suggest the following five steps to increase perceptions of self-efficacy. First, select a task at which you expect to succeed, not one you expect to fail. Then, as your feelings of self-efficacy increase, you can tackle more challenging projects.

A cigarette smoker who wants to stop smoking, for example, might focus on smoking 50 percent fewer cigarettes per week rather than attempting to quit "cold turkey". With early success at reducing the number of cigarettes smoked, the individual could make the criterion more stringent (like smoking no cigarettes on alternate days). Continued success leads to more self-efficacy.

Second, it's important to distinguish between the past and the present. Don't dwell on past failures. Past failures are history – today is the first day of the rest of your life. Focus on a renewed sense of self-confidence and self-efficacy.

Third, it's important to keep good records of your progress toward reaching your goal. Our cigarette smoker should record the number of cigarettes smoked each day, and note when the rate of smoking is 50 percent less for a week. This should be noted as an achievement, and then a new goal should be set. Focusing on your successes (rather than failures) represents the fourth step in building self-efficacy.

The fifth step: Develop a list of tasks or projects you'd like to accomplish, and then rank them from easiest to most difficult to accomplish. Whenever possible, start with the easier tasks. The self-efficacy and self-confidence developed from accomplishing less demanding tasks will help you tackle the more challenging situations on your list.

Focus on the Positive. Many of the strategies I've presented for improving person-states include a basic principle – focus on the positive. Whether attempting to build your own self-efficacy or that of others, success needs to be emphasized over failure. Thus, whenever you have the opportunity to teach others or give them feedback, you must look for small-win accomplishments and give genuine approval before commenting on ways to improve. Again, this approach is easier said than done.

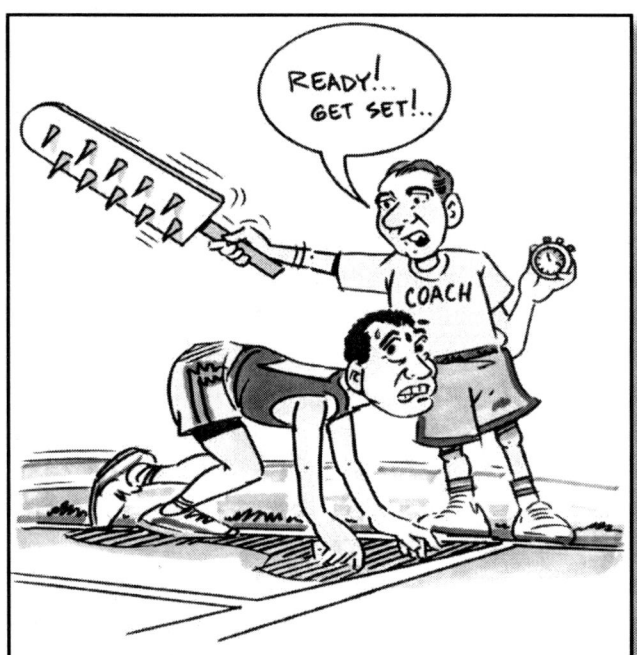

Failures are easier to spot than successes. They stick out and interrupt the flow. That's why most teachers are quick to give negative attention to students who disrupt the classroom, while giving only limited positive attention to students who remain on task and go with the flow. Plus, many of us have been conditioned (unknowingly) to believe negative consequences (penalties) work better than positive consequences (rewards) to influence behavior change.[61]

Personal Control

Participants at my seminars on AC4P have listed a number of ways to increase perceptions of personal control, including: a) set short-term goals and track progress toward long-term accomplishment; b) offer frequent rewarding and correcting feedback for process activities rather than only for outcomes; c) provide opportunities to set personal goals, teach others, and chart "small wins";[62] d) teach colleagues basic behavior-change intervention strategies (especially feedback and recognition procedures); e) provide time and resources for people to develop, implement and evaluate intervention programs; f) show change agents, teachers, coaches, and parents how to graph daily records of baseline, intervention, and follow-up data; and g) post response-feedback graphs of group performance.

The perception of personal control is analogous to perceptions of personal choice and autonomy. When people believe they are in control of a situation or challenge, they generally feel a sense of personal choice. "I choose to take charge of the mission which is within my domain of influence." Appreciate the similarity between these person-states. In the next chapter I discuss the connection between perceptions of choice and self-motivation.

Optimism

Optimism flows from thinking positively, avoiding negative thoughts, and expecting the best to happen. Anything that increases our self-efficacy should increase optimism. Also, when our personal control is strengthened, we perceive more influence over our consequences. This gives us more reason to expect the best. Again, we see how the person-states of self-efficacy, personal control and optimism are clearly intertwined. A change in one will likely influence the other two. Note also how these person-states relate to perceptions of choice and competence – determinants of self-motivation, as I explain in the next chapter.

Belonging

Here are common proposals given by my seminar discussion groups to create and sustain an atmosphere of belonging: a) decrease the frequency of top-down directives and "quick-fix" programs, b) increase opportunities for cooperative learning, interactive group discussions, group goal-setting and feedback, and group celebrations for both process and outcome achievements (see Chapter 3 for more on group celebrations), c) use self-managed or self-directed study/learning groups.

Feelings of empowerment and belonging can be enhanced when groups are given control over important matters like developing a constructive homework assignment or a particular AC4P initiative. When resources, opportunities, and talents enable team members to assert, "We can make a difference," feelings of belonging occur naturally. This leads to synergy, with the group achieving more than could be possible from participants working independently.

In Conclusion

Continuous improvement in any endeavor involving human dynamics requires people to actively care for others as well as themselves. The research-based principles reviewed here are relevant to increasing the frequency and improving the quality of AC4P behavior throughout a particular culture. Some practical intervention procedures benefit AC4P behavior indirectly by enhancing the person-states that facilitate one's willingness to actively care. Other strategies target AC4P behaviors directly, but often have an indirect positive effect on the person-states that increase one's propensity to actively care.

Any procedure that increases a person's self-esteem, self-efficacy, personal control, optimism, or sense of belonging or interdependence in a system will indirectly benefit

AC4P behavior. A number of communication techniques enhance more than one of these states simultaneously, particularly actively listening to others for feelings and giving genuine praise for other people's accomplishments.

Reflect on your own life to appreciate the power of personal choice, and how the perception of personal control makes you more self-motivated, involved, and committed to a particular mission. The perception of choice can help activate and sustain AC4P behavior.

Perceptions of belonging are important, too. They increase when groups are given some control over important decisions and receive genuine recognition for their accomplishments.

Synergy is the ultimate outcome of belonging and win-win interpersonal involvement. It occurs when group interdependence produces more than what's possible from going it alone.

AC4P behaviors are the building blocks of an AC4P culture. The more quality AC4P behaviors occurring among people in a given school, work, or family setting, the more likely will an AC4P culture evolve.

It usually takes self-motivation to initiate and sustain the kind of behavior needed for an AC4P culture, because people are rarely held accountable for performing AC4P behavior. The next chapter explains how to increase perceptions of self-motivation, thereby setting the stage for effective AC4P behavior. You'll see several direct connections between the person-states that increase one's propensity to actively care and those that enhance one's self-motivation.

Notes

1. Cialdini, R.B. (2001). *Influence: Science and practice* (4th Edition). Needham Heights, MA: Allyn & Bacon; Schroeder, D.A., Penner, L.A., Dovidio, J.F., & Piliavin, J.A. (1995). *The psychology of helping and altruism*. New York, NY: McGraw-Hill, Inc.

2. Geller, E.S. (1998). *Understanding behavior-based safety: Step-by-step methods to improve your workplace* (Revised Edition). Neenah, WI: J.J. Keller & Associates, Inc; Geller, E.S. (2001). *The psychology of safety handbook*. Boca Raton, FL: CRC Press; Geller, E.S. (2002). People-based safety: Seven social influence principles to fuel participation in occupational safety. *Professional Safety, 47*(10), 25-31; Geller, E.S., & Williams, J.H. (2001). *Keys to behavior-based safety*. Rockville, MD: ABS Consulting; McSween, T.E. (1995). *The values-based safety process: Improving your safety culture with a behavioral approach*. New York, NY: Van Nostrand Reinhold.

3. Geller, E.S. (1998). *Beyond safety accountability: How to increase personal responsibility.* Neenah, WI: J.J. Keller & Associates, Inc; Geller, E.S. (2001). Actively caring for occupational safety: Extending the performance management paradigm. In C.M. Johnson, W.K. Redmon, & T.C. Mawhinney (Eds.). *Organizational performance: Behavior analysis and management.* New York, NY: Springer.

4. Covey, S.R. (1989). *The seven habits of highly effective people.* New York, NY: Simon and Schuster; Covey, S.R. (1990). *Principle-centered leadership.* New York, NY: Simon & Schuster, Inc.

5. Peale, N.V. (1952). *The power of positive thinking.* New York, NY: Prentice-Hall.

6. Kohn, A. (1993). *Punished by rewards: The trouble with gold stars, incentive plans, A's, praise, and other bribes.* Boston, MA: Houghton Mifflin.

7. Deming, W.E. (1986). *Out of the crisis.* Cambridge, MA: Massachusetts Institute of Technology, Center for Advanced Engineering Study; Deming, W.E. (1993). *The new economics for industry, government, education.* Cambridge, MA: Massachusetts Institute of Technology, Center for Advanced Engineering Study.

8. Skinner, B.F. (1981). Selection by consequences. *Science, 213,* 502-504.

9. Carnegie, D. (1936). *How to win friends and influence people.* New York, NY: Simon & Schuster, Inc., p. 57.

10. Maslow, A.H. (1943). A theory of human motivation. *Psychological Review, 50,* 370-396; Maslow, A.H. (1954). *Motivation and personality.* New York, NY: Harper.

11. Schultz, D. (1977). *Growth psychology: Models of the healthy personality.* New York, NY: D. Van Nostrand.

12. Maslow, A.H. (1971). *The farther reaches of human nature.* New York. NY: Viking.

13. Frankl, V. (1962). *Man's search for meaning: An introduction to logotherapy.* Boston, MA: Beacon Press.

14. Rosenthal, A.M. (1964). *Thirty-eight witnesses.* New York, NY: McGraw-Hill.

15. Latané, B., & Darley, J.M. (1968). Group inhibition of bystander intervention. *Journal of Personality and Social Psychology, 10,* 215-221; Latané, B., & Darley, J.M. (1970). *The unresponsive bystander: Why doesn't he help?* New York, NY: Appelton-Century-Crofts.

16. Latané, B., & Nida, S. (1981). Ten years of research on group size and helping. *Psychological Bulletin, 89,* 308-324.

17. Beaman, A.I., Barnes, P.J., Klentz, B., & McQuirk, B. (1978). Increasing helping rates through informational dissemination: Teaching pays. *Personality and Social Psychology, 37,* 1835-1846.

18. Hornstein, H.A. (1976). *Cruelty and kindness: A new look at aggression and altruism.* Englewood Cliffs, NJ: Prentice-Hall.

19. Shotland, R.L., & Heinold, W.D. (1985). Bystander response to arterial bleeding: Helping skills, the decision-making process, and differentiating the helping response. *Journal of Personality and Social Psychology, 49,* 347-356.

20. McCarty, S.M., Teie, S., & Furrow, C.B. (2012). *Training students to observe and reward actively-caring behavior.* Technical Research Report, Center for Applied Behavior Systems, Department of Psychology, Virginia Tech, Blacksburg, VA.

21. Rutkowski, G.K., Gruder, C.L., & Romer, D. (1983). Group cohesiveness, social norms, and bystander intervention. *Journal of Personality and Social Psychology, 44,* 545-552.

22. Carlson, M., Charlin, V., & Miller, N. (1988). Positive mood and helping behavior: A test of six

hypotheses. *Journal of Personality and Social Psychology, 55,* 211-229.

23. Bierhoff, H.W., Klein, R., & Kramp, P. (1991). Evidence for the altruistic personality from data on accident research. *Journal of Personality, 59,* 263-280.

24. Schwartz, S.H., & Clausen, G.T. (1970). Responsibility, norms, and helping in an emergency. *Journal of Personality and Social Psychology, 16,* 299-310; Staub, E. (1974). Helping a distressed person: Social, personality, and stimulus determinants. In L. Berkowitz (Ed.), *Advances in experimental social psychology,* Vol. 7. New York, NY: Academic Press.

25. Geller, E.S. (1998). *Beyond safety accountability: How to increase personal responsibility.* Neenah, WI: J.J. Keller & Associates, Inc; Geller, E.S. (2001). Actively caring for occupational safety: Extending the performance management paradigm. In C.M. Johnson, W.K. Redmon, & T.C. Mawhinney (Eds.). *Organizational performance: Behavior analysis and management.* New York, NY: Springer.

26. Latané, B., & Darley, J.M. (1970). *The unresponsible bystander: Why doesn't he help?* New York, NY: Appleton-Century-Crofts.

27. Piliavin, J.A., Piliavin, I.M., & Broll, L. (1976). Time of arousal at an emergency and likelihood of helping. *Personality and Social Psychology Bulletin, 2,* 273-276.

28. Clark, R.D., III, & Word, L.E. (1972). Why don't bystanders help? Because of ambiguity? *Journal of Personality and Social Psychology, 24,* 392-400.

29. Schroeder, D.A., Penner, L.A., Dovidio, J.F., & Piliavin, J.A. (1995). *The psychology of helping and altruism.* New York, NY: McGraw-Hill.

30. Daniels, A.C., & Daniels, J.E. (2005). *Measure of a leader.* Atlanta, GA: Performance Management Publications, p. 158.

31. McCarty, S.M., & Geller, E.S. (2011, Summer). Want to get rid of bullying? Then reward behavior that is incompatible with it. *Behavior Analysis Digest International, 23*(2), 1-7.

32. Kreitner, R. (1982). The feedforward and feedback control of job performance through organizational behavior management (OBM). *Journal of Organizational Behavior Management, 4*(2), p. 3.

33. Rogers, C. (1957). The necessary and sufficient conditions of therapeutic personality change. *Journal of Consulting Psychology, 21,* 95-103; Rogers, C. (1977). *Carl Rogers on personal power: Inner strength and its revolutionary impact.* New York, NY: Delacorte.

34. Straumann, T.J., & Higgins, E.G. (1988). Self-discrepancies as predictors of vulnerability to distinct syndromes of chronic emotional distress. *Journal of Personality, 56,* 685-707.

35. Brown, J.D., & McGill, K.L. (1989). The cost of good fortune: When positive life events produce negative health consequences. *Journal of Personality and Social Psychology, 57,* 1103-1110.

36. Wylie, R. (1974). *The self-concept* (Vol. 1). Lincoln, NE: University of Nebraska Press.

37. Wells, L.E., & Marwell, G. (1976). *Self-esteem.* Beverly Hills, CA: Sage.

38. Baron, R.A., & Byrne, D. (1994). *Social psychology: Understanding human interaction* (7th Edition). Boston, MA: Allyn and Bacon.

39. Batson, C.D., Bolen, M.H., Cross, J.A., & Neuringer-Benefiel, H.E. (1986). Where is altruism in the altruistic personality? *Journal of Personality and Social Psychology, 1,* 212-220.

40. Conger, J.A., & Kanungo, R.N. (1988). The empowerment process: Integrating theory and practice. *Academy of Management Review, 13,* 471-482.

41. Rotter, J.B. (1966). Generalized expectancies for internal versus external control of reinforcement. *Psychological Monographs, 80,* No. 1.

42. Bandura, A. (1997). *Self efficacy: The exercise of control.* New York, NY: W.H. Freeman and Company

43. Scheier, M.F., & Carver, C.S. (1985). Optimism, coping and health: Assessment and implications of generalized outcome expectancies. *Health Psychology, 4,* 219-247; Scheier, M.F., & Carver, C.S. (1993). On the power of positive thinking: The benefits of being optimistic. *Current Directions in Psychological Sciences, 2,* 26-30; Seligman, M.E.P. (1991). *Learned optimism.* New York, NY: Alfred A. Knopf.

44. Bandura, A. (1986). *Social foundations of thought and action.* Englewood Cliffs, NJ: Prentice Hall; Barling, J., & Beattie, R. (1983). Self-efficacy beliefs and sales performance. *Journal of Organizational Behavior Management, 5,* 41-51; Ozer, E. M., & Bandura, A. (1990). Mechanisms governing empowerment effects: A self-efficacy analysis. *Journal of Personality and Social Psychology, 58,* 472-486; Phares, E.J. (1976). *Locus of control in personality.* Morristown, NJ: General Learning Press.

45. Bandura, A. (1990). Self-regulation of motivation through goal systems. In R.A. Dienstbier (Ed.). *Nebraska symposium on motivation,* Vol. 38. Lincoln, NE: University of Nebraska Press; Bandura, A. (1994). Self-efficacy. In *Encyclopedia of human behavior* (Vol. 4). Orlando, FL: Academic Press; Bandura, A. (1997). *Self efficacy: The exercise of control.* New York, NY: W.H. Freeman and Company.

46. Bandura, A. (1982). Self-efficacy mechanism in human agency. *American Psychologist, 37,* 122-147; Betz, N.E., & Hackett, G. (1986). Applications of self-efficacy theory to understanding career choice behavior. *Journal of Social and Clinical Psychology, 4,* 279-289; Hackett, G., Betz, N.E., Casas, J.M., & Rocha-Singh, I.A. (1992). Gender, ethnicity, and social cognitive factors predicting the academic achievement of students in engineering. *Journal of Counseling Psychology, 39,* 527-538.

47. Rotter, J.B. (1966). Generalized expectancies for internal versus external control of reinforcement. *Psychological Monographs, 80,* No. 1; Rushton, J.P. (1984). The altruistic personality: Evidence from laboratory, naturalistic and self-report perspectives. In E. Staub, D. Bar-Tal, J. Karylowski, & J. Reykowski (Eds.). *Development and maintenance of prosocial behavior.* New York, NY: Plenum.

48. Hunt, M.M. (1993). *The story of psychology.* New York, NY: Doubleday.

49. Nowicki, S., & Strickland, B.R. (1973). A locus of control scale for children. *Journal of Consulting Psychology, 40,* 148-154; Stickland, B.R. (1989). Internal-external control expectancies: From contingency to creativity. *American Psychologist, 44,* 1-12.

50. Taylor, S.E. (1991). *Health psychology* (2nd Edition). New York, NY: McGraw-Hill.

51. Eskew, R.T., & Riche, C.V. (1982). Pacing and locus of control in quality control inspection. *Human Factors, 24,* 411-415; Phares, E.J. (1991). *Introduction to personality* (3rd Edition). New York, NY: Harper Collins.

52. Peterson, C. (2000). The future of optimism. *American Psychologist, 55*(1), 44-55; Scheier, M.F., & Carver, C.S. (1985). Optimism, coping and health: Assessment and implications of generalized outcome expectancies. *Health Psychology, 4,* 219-247; Seligman, M.E.P. (1991). *Learned optimism.* New York, NY: Alfred A. Knopf.

53. Seligman, M.E.P. (1991). *Learned optimism.* New York, NY: Alfred A. Knopf.

54. Carver, C.S., Scheier, M.F., & Weintraub, J.K. (1989). Assessing coping strategies: A theoretically-based approach. *Journal of Personality and Social Psychology, 56,* 267-283; Seligman, M.E.P. (2011). *Flourish: A visionary new understanding of happiness and well-being.* New York, NY: Simon & Schuster, Inc.; Peterson, C., & Barrett, L.C. (1987). Explanatory style and academic performance

among university freshmen. *Journal of Personality and Social Psychology, 53,* 603-607.

55. Scheier, M.F., Weintraub, J.K., & Carver, C.S. (1986). Coping with stress: Divergent strategies of optimists and pessimists. *Journal of Personality and Social Psychology, 51,* 1257-1264.

56. Tavris, C., & Wade, C. (1995). *Psychology in perspective.* New York, NY: Harper Collins College Publishers.

57. Peck, M.S. (1979). *The different drum: Community making and peace.* New York, NY: Simon & Schuster, Inc.

58. Geller, E.S. (2001). Actively caring for occupational safety: Extending the performance management paradigm. In C.M. Johnson, W.K. Redmon, & T.C. Mawhinney (Eds.). *Organizational performance: Behavior analysis and management.* New York, NY: Springer; Geller, E.S. (2001). Sustaining participation in a safety improvement process: Ten relevant principles from behavioral science. *Professional Safety, 46*(9), 24-29.

59. Peterson, C., Maier, S.F., & Seligman, M.E.P. (1993). *Learned helplessness: A theory for the age of personal control.* New York, NY: Oxford University Press; Seligman, M.E.P. (1975). *Helplessness: On depression development and death.* San Francisco, CA: Freeman.

60. Watson, D.C., & Tharp, R.G. (1987). *Self-directed behavior: Self-modification for personal adjustment* (7th Edition). Pacific Grove, CA: Brooks/Cole Publishing Company.

61. Notz, W.W., Boschman, I., & Tax, S.S. (1987). Reinforcing punishment and extinguishing reward: On the folly of OBM with SPC. *Journal of Organizational Behavior Management, 9*(1), 33-46.

62. Weick, K.E. (1984). Small wins: Redefining the scale of social problems. *American Psychologist, 39,* 40-44.

CHAPTER 3

The Psychology of Self-Motivation

E. Scott Geller

EXACTLY WHAT IS an external accountability intervention? In the work world, these motivational tools include time sheets, overtime compensation records, peer-to-peer behavioral observations, public posting of performance indicators, group and individual feedback meetings, and performance appraisals.

In schools it's all about grades, and teachers attempt to keep students motivated by emphasizing the relationship between the quality of their school-work and the all-important grade. Psychologists call these "extrinsic motivators," and managers and teachers use them to keep employees and students on track, respectively.

Sometimes it's possible for people to establish conditions that facilitate self-accountability and self-motivation. When people go beyond the call of duty to actively care for the welfare of others they are self-motivated to an extent. Achieving an AC4P culture requires more people to be self-motivated at more times and in more situations. This chapter presents evidence-based ways to make this happen, as gleaned from research in behavioral and psychological science.

Self-Motivation for AC4P[1]

Without safety regulations, policies and external accountability systems, more students would be victimized in schools and many more employees would get hurt or killed on the job and on the road. All of us, including teachers, students, employers, police officers and safety professionals need extrinsic controls to hold us accountable to perform safe and AC4P behavior, while avoiding confrontational and risky behavior. Why do we need such extrinsic controls?

Desirable AC4P behaviors are relatively inconvenient, uncomfortable, and inefficient. The soon, certain, positive consequences (or intrinsic "natural" reinforcers) of many undesirable behaviors often overpower our self-motivation to be as careful and caring as possible.

Every driver knows it's risky to talk on a cell-phone or type a text message while driving, yet many drivers perform these behaviors regularly. Why?

The immediate and naturally-reinforcing consequences take priority over the low likelihood of a crash. These risky drivers are not self-motivated to actively care for the safety of themselves and others on the road.

Here's the key question: What can we do to overcome the human nature implied by these profound quotations from B.F. Skinner: "Immediate consequences outweigh delayed consequences" and "Consequences for the individual usually outweigh consequences for others".[2]

In other words, AC4P behavior is seemingly not rewarded by soon, certain, and positive consequences for the individual. Therefore, we need techniques to overcome this natural tendency to avoid AC4P behavior. Some practical solutions are derived from psychological science, especially research conducted by Edward Deci and Richard Ryan.[3]

Human Needs and Self-Motivation

We have three basic psychological needs, and when these needs are satisfied, we are self-motivated, according to Deci and Ryan. Specifically, self-motivation is supported by situational factors (e.g., environmental contexts and other people) that facilitate fulfillment of our needs for autonomy, relatedness, and competence. "Self-motivation, rather than external (or extrinsic) motivation, is at the heart of creativity, responsibility, healthy behavior, and lasting change."[4]

Autonomy

Autonomy is a matter of being self-governing or having personal control. In Chapter 2, I described this condition as a person-state related to one's propensity to actively care for the safety and well-being of others.[5] Autonomous behavior is self-initiated, self-endorsed, and authentic. It reflects one's true values and intentions. Geller and Veazie[1] refer to this attribute as "choice," and plenty of research shows people are more self-motivated when they have opportunities to choose among action alternatives.[5]

Early Laboratory Research. More than 40 years ago when I was conducting research in cognitive science, I conducted a very simple experiment and obtained very simple results. The implications of the findings, however, are relevant to self-motivation in numerous situations.

Half of the 40 participants in this experiment were shown a list of five three-letter words (i.e., cat, hat, mat, rat, and bat) and asked to select one. Then, after a warning tone, the selected word was presented on a screen in front of the participant, and s/he pressed a micro-switch as fast as possible after seeing the word.

The latency in milliseconds between the presentation of the word and the participant's response was a measure of simple reaction time. This sequence of warning signal, word presentation, and participant reaction occurred for 25 trials. If a participant reacted before the stimulus word was presented, the reaction time was not counted, and the trial was repeated. The session took less than 15 minutes per subject.

The word selected by a particular participant was used as the presentation stimulus for the next participant. Thus, this participant did not have the opportunity to choose the stimulus word. As a result, the word choices of 20 participants were assigned to 20 other participants.

This simple experiment had two conditions – a *Choice* condition (in which participants chose a three-letter word for their stimulus) and an *Assigned* condition (in which participants were assigned the stimulus word selected by the previous participant). To my surprise, the mean reactions of participants in the *Choice* group were significantly faster than those of participants in the *Assigned* group.

Although these results were explained by presuming the opportunity to choose their stimulus word increased the motivation of the participants to perform in the reaction time experiment, the large group differences were unexpected. How could the simple choice of a three-letter word influence faster responding in a simple reaction-time experiment? In fact, because I did not feel confident in a basic motivational explanation for these surprising results, I did not pursue publication of these data in a professional research journal. Only years later did I appreciate the real-world ramifications of those findings.[5]

From Laboratory to Classroom. About a year after the simple reaction-time study described above, I tested the theory of choice as a motivator in the college classroom. I was teaching two sections of Social Psychology; one at 8:00 A.M. Monday, Wednesday, and Friday, and the other at 11:00 A.M. on these same days. There were about 75 students in each class.

On the first day of class, I did not hand out a pre-prepared syllabus with weekly assignments, but distributed only a general outline of the course which introduced the textbook, the course objectives, and the basic criteria for assigning grades (i.e., a quiz on each textbook chapter and a comprehensive final exam on classroom lectures, discussions, and demonstrations).

In an open discussion and voting process, the 8:00 class was given the opportunity to choose the order in which the ten textbook chapters would be read for homework and discussed in class. They could also submit multiple-choice questions for me to consider using for the ten chapter quizzes, and they could hand in short-answer and discussion questions for possible application on the final exam.

The 11:00 class received the order of textbook chapters selected previously by the 8:00 class, and this class was not given an opportunity to submit quiz or exam questions.

Thus, I derived *Choice* and *Assigned* classroom conditions analogous to the two reaction-time groups I had studied one year earlier. Two of my undergraduate research assistants attended each of these classes, posing as regular students, and systematically counted the frequency of behaviors reflecting class participation. These observers did not know about my intentional *Choice* vs. *Assigned* manipulations.

From the day the students in my 8:00 class voted on the textbook assignments, this class seemed to be livelier than the later 11:00 class. My perception was verified by the participation records of the two classroom observers.

Furthermore, the ten quiz grades, final-exam scores, and my teaching-evaluation scores from standard forms distributed during the last class period were significantly higher in the *Choice* class than the *Assigned* class. (Although several students from the 8:00 class submitted potential quiz and final-exam questions, none were actually used. Each class received the same quizzes and final exam.)

I'm convinced the *Choice* versus *Assigned* manipulation was a critical factor. The initial opportunity to choose reading assignments increased students' motivation and class participation and this extra motivation and involvement led to more involvement, perceived choice, self-motivation and learning. The students' attitudes toward the class improved as a result of feeling more in control of the situation.

It's likely the "choice" opportunities in the 8:00 class were especially powerful because they were so different than the traditional top-down classroom atmosphere at the time, as typified by the organization of my 11:00 class. In other words, the contrast of the *Choice* class with the students' other courses made the "choice" opportunities in my 8:00 class especially salient, meaningful, and motivational.

We've All Been There. You need only reflect on your own life circumstances to realize how a *perception* of choice or personal control increases your self-motivation, involvement, and commitment. Please note we're talking about the *perception* of choice, as reflected in the illustration. We are not always in control of the critical events of ongoing circumstances, and thus we've experienced the frustration, discomfort, and distress of being at the mercy of environmental circumstances or other people's decisions.

And we've certainly experienced the pleasure of having alternatives to choose from and feeling in control of those factors critical for successful performance. How sweet the taste of success when we can attribute the achievement to our own choices.

Bottom Line: The message is clear. Whenever possible, give people opportunities to choose mission-relevant goals and the procedures to reach them. The result: increased self-motivation, engagement, and ownership.

This may require relinquishing some top-down control, abandoning a desire for a "quick fix," changing from focusing on outcomes to recognizing process achievements, and giving people opportunities to choose, evaluate, and refine their means to achieve the ends. The result: more people going beyond the call of duty on behalf of others when no one's watching.

Competence

Several researchers of human motivation have proposed that people naturally enjoy being able to solve problems and successfully complete worthwhile tasks[6]. In their view, people are self-motivated to learn, to explore possibilities, to understand what's going on, and to participate in achieving worthwhile goals. The label for this fundamental human motive is *competence*. "All of us are striving for mastery, for affirmations of our own competence."[7]

Motivation researchers assume the desire for competence is self-initiating and self-rewarding. Behavior that increases feelings of competence is self-directed and does not need extrinsic or extra reinforcement to keep it going. Feeling competent to do worthwhile work motivates continued effort. When people feel more successful or competent, their self-motivation increases. As one behavioral scientist put it, "People are not successful because they are motivated; they are motivated because they have been successful".[8]

The Power of Feedback. How do we know we are competent at something? How do we know this competence makes a valuable difference? You know the answer – feedback.

Feedback about our ongoing behavior tells us how we are doing and enables us to do better. That familiar slogan, "Practice makes perfect" is actually incorrect. Practice makes permanence and without appropriate feedback, well-practiced behavior can be wrong. We hone our skills through practice *and* behavior-focused feedback.

Some feedback comes naturally, like when we recognize our behavior has produced a desired result. But often behavioral feedback requires careful and systematic observation by another individual – a trainer or coach – who later communicates his or her findings to the performer. In each case, feedback enables development of perceived competence and self-motivation.

Feedback is essential to fulfill a basic human need – the need for competence. And helping people satisfy this need increases their self-motivation to perform the relevant behavior. But feedback regarding the *outcome* of a project or process does not reflect individual choices or competence, and thus can be ineffective. Only feedback that is behavior-focused and customized for the recipient can enhance an individual's perception of personal control and competence, and thus bolster self-motivation.

Is Feedback Reinforcing? Technically, a reinforcer is a behavioral consequence that maintains or increases the frequency of the behavior it follows. So, if behavior does not continue or improve after feedback, the feedback was not a reinforcer. Likewise, praise, bonus pay, or frequent flyer points are not reinforcers when they don't increase the frequency of behavior they target; and they often don't. However, interpersonal, behavior-based rewards can increase our perception of competence.

Can well-delivered supportive or corrective feedback increase our perception of competence and self-motivation? Absolutely, but it's not a payoff for doing the right thing. Rather, it's behavior-based information a person uses to feel more competent or to learn how to become more competent.

There is perhaps no other consequence with greater potential to improve competence, self-motivation, and individual performance than behavior-focused feedback. Behavioral feedback, delivered with an AC4P mindset, is usually a reinforcer because it maintains or increases a certain desired behavior.

A Paradigm Shift. This discussion of feedback, competence, and self-motivation calls for a paradigm shift – a change in perspective about AC4P behavior. We should assume people are naturally self-motivated to help others, instead of calling on guilt or sacrifice to get people involved to improve the health, welfare, or safety of other people.

Simply put, we hate feeling incompetent or helpless. We want to learn, to discover, to become more proficient at worthwhile tasks. We seek opportunities to ask questions, to study pertinent material, to work with people who know more than we do, and to receive feedback that can increase our competence and subsequent self-motivation.

AC4P behavior is not a thankless job requiring self-sacrifice, obligation, or a special degree of altruism. Participation in an AC4P process provides opportunities to satisfy a basic human need – the need for personal competence.[6] Effective and frequent delivery of behavior-based feedback provides a mechanism for improving the quality of an AC4P process, as well as cultivating feelings of competence and self-motivation throughout a culture.

Relatedness

The innate need for *relatedness* reflects "the need to love and be loved, to care and be cared for…to feel included, to feel related."[9] This is analogous to the state of belonging – a person-state influencing one's propensity to actively caring for the health, safety, and well-being of others. Geller and Veazie[1] use the term *community* to reflect this person-state because the concept of community is more encompassing than relatedness or belongingness.

A community perspective reflects systems thinking and interdependency beyond the confines of family, social groups, and work teams, as explicated by Peter Block[10] and M. Scott Peck.[11] Community is an AC4P mindset for human kind in general – an interconnectedness with others that transcends political differences and prejudices, and profoundly respects and appreciates diversity.

Systems Thinking and Interdependence. Focus your efforts on optimizing the system, W. Edwards Deming tells us in his best sellers on total quality management, *Out of The Crisis* and *The New Economics*.[12] Peter Senge stresses that systems thinking is *The Fifth Discipline*,[13] and key to continuous improvement. And Stephen Covey's discussion of interdependency, win-win contingencies, and synergy in his popular self-help book, *The Seven Habits of Highly Effective People*,[14] is founded on systems thinking and a community perspective.

Geller and Veazie propose and explicate in *The Courage Factor*[15] the amount of courage a person needs to intervene on behalf of another individual decreases as a function of the degree of connectedness between the two people. (See Chapter 4 for more on courage.)

Developing a community or interdependent spirit in an organization, a classroom, or a family unit leads to two primary human-

performance payoffs: a) individuals become more self-motivated to do the right thing, and b) people are more likely to actively care for the well-being of others. In their reality-based narrative, Geller and Veazie[1] illustrate the do's and don'ts of building an interdependent community perspective.

More Paradigm Shifts. A systems or community approach to improving people's welfare implicates a number of paradigm shifts from the traditional management of a school, a classroom, and yes, a family. We need to shift from trying to find one root cause of a problem (e.g., interpersonal bullying, sexual abuse, substance abuse, and truancy) to considering a number of potential contributing factors from each of three domains – environment, behavior, and person.

Interdependent systems thinking requires a shift from down-stream outcome-based measures of individual or group performance (grades, injury rates, familial acceptance) to a more proactive and diagnostic evaluation of process variables within the environment, behavior, and person domains.

Systems thinking enables a useful perspective on basic principles of human motivation, attitude formation, and behavior change. The influence of activators and consequences on behavior are thought to be linear, or so we believe. But systems-thinking implicates a circular or spiral perspective.

While an event preceding a behavior might direct it and a particular event following a behavior determines whether it will occur again, it's instructive to realize the consequence for one behavior can serve as the activator for the next behavior. With this perspective, behavior-based feedback can serve as a motivating consequence or a directive activator, depending on when and how it's presented.

Spiral causality and the consistency principle combine to explain how small changes in behavior can result in attitude change, followed by more behavior change and then more desired attitude change, leading eventually to personal commitment and total involvement in the process.[16] Similarly, the notion of spiral causality and the reciprocity principle explain why initial AC4P from a few individuals can result in more and more AC4P behavior from many individuals.

This *ripple effect* can eventually lead to families, school-project teams, and community groups AC4P regularly for the health, safety, and well-being of each other, with a win-win interdependent attitude and a proactive mindset. In the end we have AC4P synergy. It can all start with systems thinking and one intentional act of kindness from one person to another. (See Chapter 5 for more on this AC4P *ripple effect*.)

How to Increase Self-Motivation

The C-words of *Choice*, *Competence*, and *Community* are used by Geller and Veazie[1] in their narrative as labels for the three evidence-based person-states that determine self-motivation. Dispositional, interpersonal, and environmental conditions that enhance these states, presumed to be innate needs by some psychologists,[17] increase personal perceptions of self-motivation.

Researchers offer the following ten guidelines for increasing self-motivation by affecting one or more of the three person-states (or needs) defined above. Geller and Veazie[1] explain each of these with real-world examples from the schools, work sites, and families.

1. Explain Why

Rules and regulations should be accompanied with a meaningful explanation (i.e., why?) to provide a rationale for behavior that is not naturally reinforcing. Often, we tell people what to do (with rules and regulations) without including the rationale – the why?

In educational institutions, policies regarding student admissions, staff-evaluation, and student grading, as well as changes in textbooks, are often announced without a reasonable rationale.

In the community, some people may choose to ignore residential speed laws (e.g., 20 mph zone) because they don't understand how such a dramatic reduction in vehicle speed improves safety. In this case, it could help to know that pedestrians have an 85% chance of being killed when hit at 40 mph versus a 5% fatality rate when hit by a vehicle traveling 20 mph.[18]

If individuals were able to connect a speed restriction to saving a human life, as opposed to fear of a speeding ticket, there might be less speeding. Or at least those complying with the 20 mph speed limit would more likely perceive personal choice and more self-motivation regarding their decision to obey reduced mph mandates.

2. It's Not Easy

Acknowledge that "People might not want to do what they are being asked to do."[19] For example, admit certain behaviors (e.g., safety-related behaviors) are relatively inconvenient and uncomfortable, but given the reasonable rationale provided, the personal response cost is worthwhile.

And even though the value of AC4P coaching (i.e., giving a colleague interpersonal feedback to support right behavior and correct wrong behavior) is obvious, acknowledge it's natural to feel awkward in this situation, whether delivering or receiving the feedback. This justifies role-playing exercises to improve people's social skills at delivering and receiving behavior-based feedback. (See Chapter 4 for more on delivering and receiving feedback effectively.)

3. Watch Your Language

Your language should suggest minimal external pressure. The common phrases "safety is a condition of employment," "all accidents are preventable," "bullying is a rite of passage," or "random acts of kindness" reduce one's sense of autonomy. The slogan, "AC4P is a value of our organization, school, or community" implies personal authenticity, interpersonal relatedness, and human interaction.

In the workplace, injuries are typically referred to as "accidents," implying limited personal choice or control and making it reasonable to think, "When it's your time, it's your time."

In schools, some teachers believe "students are just cruel at this age," or "bullying just happens." As a result they exercise limited personal interaction to prevent bullying behavior. The problem is "beyond their control".

The common phrase "random acts of kindness"[20] has a disadvantage when describing AC4P behavior. Random implies the behavior happened by chance, which suggests it's beyond individual choice or control. A kind act may appear random to the recipient, but it's intentionally performed and is usually self-motivated. Our preferred alternative: *intentional* acts of kindness. Parts III and IV of this book illustrate numerous intentional acts of AC4P.

The language we use to prescribe or describe behavior influences our perceptions of its meaningfulness and its relevance to our lives. Language impacts culture, and vice versa.

4. Provide Opportunities for Choice

Participative management means employees have personal choice during the planning, execution, and evaluation of their jobs. People have a need for autonomy, regardless of dispositional and situational factors. In the workplace, managers often tell people what to do as opposed to involving them in the decision-making process.

In schools, students are often viewed as passive learners, because teachers plan, execute, and evaluate most aspects of the teaching/learning process. Students' perceptions of choice are limited. Yet cooperative teaching/learning – where students contribute to the selection and presentation of lesson material – has been shown to be most beneficial over the long term.[8]

5. Involve the Followers

Rules established by soliciting input from those affected by the regulation support autonomy.[9] Teachers are more likely to comply with regulations they helped to define. Shouldn't they have significant influence in the development of policy they will be asked to follow? Those on the "front line" know best what actions should be avoided versus performed in order to optimize the teaching and learning in their classrooms.

Before a rule or regulation is implemented in an educational system, those affected (i.e., faculty and/or students) should certainly be given opportunities to offer suggestions. In a family, as the children mature, certain rules should be open to discussion before being mandated. This takes more time, but the marked increase in effectiveness justifies any loss in efficiency.

6. Set SMARTS Goals

Customize process and outcome goals with individuals and work teams. The most effective goals are SMARTS: *Specific, Motivational, Achievable, Relevant, Trackable, and Shared.*[16]

Process goals reflect successive behavioral steps to achieve on route to accomplishing a significant outcome goal. In educational settings, completing certain homework assignments and studying a certain number of hours per week serve as process goals, leading to the outcome of an improved exam grade, and eventually a desirable grade in a particular course. Achieving such process goals and obtaining desirable grades leads to the more remote outcome goal of graduating with honors.

In family settings, goal-setting involving the participation of children may seem unreasonable, but at a certain point of their evolving maturity, full family involvement in defining the required individual and group behaviors (e.g., daily chores, school work, and budget management) to meet desired outcome goals (e.g., house and lawn maintenance, good school grades, and a family vacation) promotes mutual trust, perceived equity, and interdependent participation.

For optimal effectiveness, it's critical to apply the SMARTS acronym to the definition of a process goal. "S" for "specific" means the goal needs to be defined precisely with regard to the specific actions planned within a certain time period (e.g., study at least two hours per weeknight for one month; complete a certain two-hour exercise routine three times a week for five consecutive months; recognize and reward five AC4P behaviors per week.

Is Your Goal Motivating? "M" for "motivational" refers to the realization of the extrinsic and/or natural consequences acquired following goal attainment. For example, an individual could plan for a weekend at the beach after completing the weekly exercise routine for five months (extrinsic reward), and anticipate fitting well in a new bathing suit (intrinsic reinforcer). Moreover, it naturally feels good to reward the AC4P behavior of others with an AC4P wristband, and such action contributes to cultivating an AC4P culture.

The "A" for "attainable" simply means the participants believe they can achieve the process goal, although it will not be easy. Studying two hours every weeknight for a month, for example, might be considered challenging but feasible. And, sticking to a specified exercise routine for five months will be difficult but doable. Recognizing and rewarding AC4P behavior is easier said than done, but it does get easier with practice.

The "R" for "relevant" refers to a clear, rational connection between achieving the process goal and obtaining an eventual outcome. Participants need to believe working toward accomplishing the process goal is consistent with their mission to obtain an eventual outcome goal. Regular study behavior is relevant to performing well on exams and earning a high course grade; regular exercise will lead to improved fitness, health, and well-being; and recognizing people regularly for their AC4P behavior contributes to cultivating an AC4P culture of compassion.

The "T" for "trackable" reflects the need to track your progress toward attaining process goals. This implies, of course, goal-relevant behaviors can be counted successively as the participants get closer to realizing their goal. For example, students record the time they start and stop studying each weeknight; every two-hour exercise routine completed is marked on the calendar; and occurrences of AC4P behavior are indicated on a spread sheet that includes a space to specify the particular AC4P behavior rewarded.

Sharing Your Goal. Finally, the "S" for "share" means it's useful to share your process goal with others. Public announcement of a group or individual goal increases commitment to work toward reaching that goal. And when others know your laudable goal and realize value in accomplishing that goal, they will likely help to support your progress.

For example, you might anticipate friends asking you about your goal-directed behavior, and such expected social accountability could enhance your self-motivation. In fact, just seeing those individuals who know about your goal can serve as a reminder to stay on course. You anticipate the question, "How's your goal progress these days," and you want to answer, "Very well, thank you".

So it's beneficial: a) for a student to announce his or her study-time goal to other students; b) to tell others of a fitness-routine goal, and c) for leaders of an AC4P Movement to share their recognition goals with other advocates of an AC4P culture.

Observational learning is a positive side-effect of such goal sharing. When others interested in the mission implied by your goal learn about your goal setting and view your progress, they might consider setting a similar goal for themselves or their team. Your shared goal setting and progress sets an impressive example for others to follow. This was a beneficial result of the following goal-setting story.

Joanne's AC4P Story. Two years ago, my wife Joanne made a New Year's resolution to perform an AC4P behavior every day until her 60th Birthday on March 27th. She announced her goal to family and friends, including leaders of our campus AC4P Movement. She also described each of her AC4P behaviors on the website: ac4p.org. I hope it's obvious this was a SMARTS process goal. As Joanne reports in her personal story (Chapter 15), she did accomplish this goal; but it wasn't easy.

Joanne knew she was setting a "stretch goal," but it was actually more challenging than she had expected. It took significant planning, preparation, and time to achieve daily AC4P behaviors, which varied widely from cooking meals and shoveling snow for neighbors to giving gift certificates to individuals she observed providing noteworthy community service.

Daily sharing of her AC4P actions sustained social support for her commitment, and set an impressive example many AC4P advocates have attempted to emulate on a smaller scale.

For example, each semester we initiate the "AC4P Challenge" among the 50 to 60 research students in our Center for Applied Behavior Systems. We evaluate whether students can attain the goal of performing five intentional AC4P acts in one week. "If Joanne can do 60 in 60," we say, "then surely you can accomplish five AC4P acts in seven days".

Most students willingly sign an "AC4P Commitment Card" for the "AC4P Challenge," but less than 50% report meeting this seemingly easy goal. Actively caring on a daily basis is easier said than done when AC4P behavior is defined as going beyond the norm to benefit the health, safety, or well-being of others.

7. Use Behavior-Based Feedback

Teachers, supervisors, and parents are more likely to notice and reprimand undesirable behavior, than discern and acknowledge desirable behavior. This is why the term "feedback" carries negative connotations.

What is one to think if asked, "Can I give you some feedback about your behavior last night"? Likewise, how do you feel after receiving an email from the principal that he wants you to come to his office at the end of the day for some feedback? Has your day been ruined? For many of us, the illustration below rings true.

It's unfortunate but true: Most people expect feedback to be more negative than positive. Of course, that perception can be changed if teachers, supervisors, and parents verbalized more *supportive* than corrective feedback.

Suppose that teacher who asked to see you at the end of the day for a feedback session gives you only supportive feedback. She defines specific desirable behaviors she had observed you perform, and expresses genuine appreciation for the extra effort you consistently demonstrate in completing homework assignments and contributing to constructive classroom discussions.

As a student, how would that make you feel? Would "feedback" take on a more positive meaning, at least with this teacher? Would you share this positive experience with others and likely enhance others' perception of "feedback" and this teacher's caring for her students? That's the power of interpersonal recognition and approval in cultivating a self-motivated AC4P culture.

***If-Then* Rewards.** Use *if-then incentive/reward contingencies* when individuals are not already self-motivated to perform the desired behavior or intrinsic reinforcers are not available. This does not mean the *if-then incentive/reward contingencies* are bad or undesirable, as some uninformed authors have claimed.[21] Extrinsic rewards influence many behaviors and this is not detrimental to self-motivation; they just might not increase it.

For example, I choose certain airlines and hotels in order to earn "points" that can translate to material rewards or improved service. My awareness of this "manipulation tactic" does not impact my disposition in any negative way. In fact, I'm pleased to be extrinsically rewarded for making certain choices. Indeed, my sense of choice to select the airline or hotel that offers the "if-then" rewards has a beneficial impact on my overall self-motivation.

In the same view, it's not detrimental to reward students for performing certain behaviors relevant to their education, as authors uneducated in psychological science have claimed.[21] The student who doesn't choose to read books, for example, cannot experience the inherent enjoyment (i.e., intrinsic reinforcement) of reading. In this case, an *if-then contingency* can be invaluable.

The student is extrinsically rewarded for performing a behavior previously emitted only infrequently. Subsequently, the student may enjoy reading, especially after feeling competent at this worthwhile task. Then self-motivation takes control, and extrinsic incentives are no longer needed.

As I explained earlier, competence fuels self-motivation. People can help others feel competent by offering words of appreciation for behaviors that reflect their personal competence. Hence, genuine approval of a student's reading behavior from a teacher increases the student's perception of competence and self-motivation.

***Now-That* Rewards.** At times, special rewards of excellence are given to individuals and groups for excelling at performance in a given domain, from accomplishments in teaching and learning to winning an athletic competition. These extrinsic consequences are well received, often to the applause of an approving audience. Such acknowledgment does wonders to an individual's sense of personal competence, leading to more self-motivation to sustain or even enhance the relevant skill set.

It's noteworthy these latter examples of rewarding desirable behavior reflect a *now-that* contingency rather than *if-then*. These rewards do not include an incentive (i.e., the announcement of the availability of a reward if a designated behavior occurs). The behavior might be initiated for a variety of internal, intrinsic, or extrinsic reasons, but the unannounced *now-that* reward is given after the behavior occurs in order to support its occurrence.

In some cases, this rewarding consequence increases the probability the desirable behavior will recur. In most cases, a person's sense of competence increases following sincere *now-that* rewards, fueling self-motivation to continue the rewarded behavior.

Behavior-Based Recognition. In school, teachers' interpersonal praise of their students' work are invaluable to boosting self-competence, confidence, and self-motivation to continuously improve. And every parent knows through personal experience the motivational benefits of demonstrating enthusiastic approval of a child's dedication to do well at a particular task.

Words of approval, appreciation, and praise are relatively rare, especially when compared to the use of verbal reprimands, as experience has taught us. Mistakes or disruptive behaviors stick out and invite corrective action; but desirable behavior does not naturally attract attention and seemingly does not require intervention.

By now you certainly see the special advantages of supportive feedback in enhancing self-motivation, right? Still, there are times when it's necessary to correct undesirable behavior. How should this be done?

8. Give Corrective Feedback Well

Make use of empathy and compassion to correct undesirable behavior. Be nondirective, actively listen to excuses, and emphasize the positive over the negative. It can be uncomfortable to provide others with behavior-based corrective feedback, even when the recipient of your feedback is a family member or friend.

Remind yourself and the feedback recipient that only with specific behavioral feedback can performance be improved. Remember, practice does not make perfect unless the performer receives supportive feedback for right behavior and corrective feedback for wrong behavior.

Incorrect behavior is not an indictment of a person's attitude, values, or personality. Our unintentional mistakes do not reflect who we are. So it is critical to emphasize that your corrective feedback is only about behavior you have observed and not a judgment of the person.

Continuous improvement occurs when observers have the courage to give relevant behavior-based feedback, and when those observed have the humility to accept the feedback and make relevant behavioral adjustments. After all, we all want to improve behavior that's important to us, and this often requires behavioral feedback from others

How should you approach someone to give corrective feedback? Your initial words are critical. If you come on too strong when directing a person to improve in a certain way, the "victim" may get defensive and offer excuses for a mistake. Or, if the observer has relevant authority over the victim, which is often the case, the victim might make the behavioral adjustments called for; but the change will not stick if the victim does not agree with and accept the behavioral advice.

How can you get buy-in for the behavioral feedback you have the courage to offer? Your opening words should be inquisitive rather than accusative. If the feedback targets a person's unsafe behavior, my good friend John Drebinger recommends beginning with a question like, "Could I look out for your safety?"[22] Who could say "No" to a request like this?

Then following a "Yes, of course," the observer mentions the behavior that needs adjustment for injury prevention. Often it's best if the observer can mention some desirable behavior first, and then suggest where there's room for improvement.

An AC4P coach is nondirective when communicating corrective feedback. The coach provides specific behavior-based feedback for the person observed to consider. There is no pressure to change. The only accountability is self-accountability. Any adjustment in behavior is self-motivated, activated by the results of a behavioral observation. Recall the application of the critical behavior checklist (CBC) to monitor and improve my daughter's driving behavior, as discussed in Chapter 1.

9. Celebrate to Increase a Sense Community

Celebrations, when done correctly, can motivate teamwork and build a sense of belongingness and community among groups of individuals, boosting their self-motivation. Of course the key words in the preceding sentence are "when done correctly". Let's consider seven guidelines for celebrating group accomplishments:

Reward the Right Behavior. What behaviors are acknowledged at your school celebrations? Is the focus more on the outcome than the process? And, do you have more celebrations for athletic than academic performance? Yes, at graduation ceremonies the focus might be on success in the classroom, but who and what get celebrated attention throughout the school year?

Furthermore, is the focus of your school celebrations on individual or group performance? Your personal experience tells you a sense of community or belongingness can be stifled with an emphasis on individual over group performance. So, is it possible your school celebrations do more harm than good in cultivating an AC4P culture that is fueled by win/win interdependence and hindered by win/lose independence?

You need to consider these rhetorical questions along with the principle: You get the behavior you recognize at celebrations. If you want students to cooperate in a mutually- supportive teaching/learning environment, you need to establish the contingencies and celebrations that support interdependent teamwork for scholarship.

More groups than individuals need to be rewarded for academic success. More calls for celebration need to be for outcomes related to academic success than for the winning record of a sports team. Plus, the process of achieving an educational milestone needs to be identified and recognized, as discussed next.

Focus on the Journey. Most of the academic celebrations I've seen gave far too little attention to the journey – the processes that contributed to reaching the milestone. Typically, the focus was on the end result, the outcome measure, like achieving an outstanding grade-point average or winning a scholastic scholarship.

There was scant discussion about *how* the outcome was achieved. It's natural to toast the bottom line, but there's more to be gained from taking the opportunity to diagnose and recognize process success. Here we're talking about the success of a group, not an individual.

When you pinpoint the processes instrumental to reaching a particular milestone, you give valuable direction and motivation. Participants learn what to continue doing for an effective journey. Those responsible for the behaviors leading to the celebrated outcome receive a special boost in competence, personal control, and optimism. Plus, information is added to these individuals' internal recognition scripts which in turn enhances their self-motivation.

Perhaps the most important reason to acknowledge journey activities leading to a noteworthy group outcome is that it gives credit where credit is due. Focusing on the process endorses the people and their actions that made the difference, fueling self-motivation. This leads to the next guideline.

Recipients Should Be Participants. Rarely do participants in a celebratory event discuss the processes they supported in order to reach the outcome. And so a valuable "teaching moment" is missed. Instead, speeches from administrators or popular teachers often kick off a school celebration. Sometimes charts are displayed to compare the past with the improved present. "Our test scores in Math and Science are significantly higher this year than last year."

Often a sincere request for continuous improvement is made, and an administrator points out the schools academic ranking compared to "sister schools." Sometimes promises for a bigger celebration are made following continued success.

Occasionally a motivational speaker or humorist gives everyone a lift and some laughs. Often special rewards are given to individuals or team captains, along with a handshake from a school official. Certificates and trinkets might be handed out, along with a steak dinner.

In the typical school celebration, teachers and administrators give and the students receive – certainly an impressive show of support from the top. But the ceremony would be more memorable and beneficial as both a learning and motivational experience if students were more participant than recipient.

Teachers should listen more than speak, and students should talk more about their experiences than listen to teachers' pleasure with the bottom line. And again, the focus should be more on team or group success than individual achievement.

Relive the Journey. Teachers should facilitate discussion of the activities that led to the celebrated accomplishment. Relive the procedures that made the journey successful. This "reenactment" strengthens students' internal scripts that direct and motivate their ongoing support of the effective teaching/learning process. Teachers who listen to these discussions with genuine interest and concern are rewarding the participation that enabled the success, and they are empowering students to continue their journey toward higher-level accomplishment.

Discuss Successes and Failures. Consider a school celebrating higher "standards of learning" test scores this year than last year, or a greater percentage of high-school seniors accepted into colleges or universities. What kind of celebration would you suggest?

I hope you would follow these guidelines, starting with a focus on the process and recognizing the variety of teacher, staff, and student behaviors that enabled this success. This should include discussions, perhaps among teachers and students at dinner tables, about both successes and failures--displaying the positive results and recalling disappointments, dead ends, and frustrations.

Pointing out the highs and lows make presentations realistic, and underscore the amount of dedication needed to complete educational assignments and develop the critical thinking needed for true academic success.

Presentations that point out hardships along the journey to success justify the celebration. The celebrated bottom line was not a matter of luck. It took hard work by many teachers, students, and staff going beyond the call of duty. The payoff: small-win contributions, constructive interdependence, win-win collaboration, and unique synergy.

Make it Memorable. Goal attainment is meaningful and memorable when people discuss the difficulties in reaching a goal. When teachers listen to students' presentations with sincere interest and appreciation, the event becomes even more significant and credible. And when a tangible reward is distributed appropriately at such an occasion, a mechanism is established to sustain the memory of this occasion and promote its value.

Ideally, the memento should include words, perhaps a theme or slogan that reflects the particular celebration. The tangible reward should be something readily displayable or usable at school – from drink mugs, placards, and pencil holders to caps, shirts, and umbrellas, for example.

When delivering these keepsakes, it should be noted they were selected "to help you remember this special occasion and what it has meant to all of us. This small token of our appreciation will remind us how we got here."

One week after a memorable celebration I attended several years ago, every participant received a framed group photograph of everyone who attended the event. That picture hangs in my office today, and every time I look at it, I'm reminded of the time several years ago when teachers did more listening than talking in a most memorable and educational group celebration.

Don't Neglect Your Leaders. In every group project, some individuals take charge and champion the effort, while others sit back and "go with the flow".

Some people exert less effort when working with a group than when working alone. Psychologists call this phenomenon "social loafing".[23]

Recognize the champions of a group effort one-on-one, and let them know you realize the importance of their leadership in a team accomplishment. You appreciate their extra-effort, AC4P contributions. This adds substantially to the self-motivation these individuals had already received from the earlier group celebration. As a result, you've increased the likelihood of their continued leadership for attaining further goals.

Solicit Ideas. When I mentioned to my graduate students I was writing a book chapter on how to celebrate, one of them quickly responded, "That's easy, a $100 bottle of cognac, a $6 cigar, and a special friend". I had to tell him, of course, my focus was on a different kind of celebrating.

But it occurred to me that everyone has his or her own way of celebrating. And when it comes to group celebration, we often inadvertently impose our prejudices on others. We usually don't take the time to ask potential participants what kind of celebration party they would like.

When it comes to organizing a group celebration, many people don't know how to celebrate. Ask people what they want for their celebration, and the discussion likely focuses on tangible rewards. "What material commodity should we receive for our efforts?" This puts the celebration in a payoff-for-behavior mode and is not the real purpose of a group celebration. You want a meaningful and memorable event that increases a sense of belonging and community, and can serve as a stepping stone to even greater achievements.

10. Build Interpersonal Trust

To cultivate an AC4P culture, interpersonal trust is absolutely fundamental. Trust is the foundation for building a community of people who go beyond the call of duty to give each other behavior-based support and relevant corrective feedback.

Seven C-words capture the essence of building interpersonal trust and interdependence: communication, caring, candor, consistency, commitment, consensus, and character. Let's consider how each of these C-words implicates interpersonal trust and community-building. The phrase associated with the following C-words summarizes the key definitions given in my *American Heritage* and *New-Merriam-Webster* dictionaries.[24]

Communication – *exchange of information or opinion by speech, writing, or signals*. What people say and how they say it influences our trust in both their capability and their intentions.

I'm sure you've heard many times the way something is said, including intonation, pace, facial expressions, hand gestures, and overall posture, has greater impact than what was actually said. And, you've certainly experienced personal feelings of trust toward another person change as the result of how that individual communicated information.

Often we trust certain information because we respect the credentials of the communicator or we like the way the message is displayed. Personal opinion or "common sense" is relied on if the message sounds good to us and if the presentation is given well – with Clarity, Confidence, and Charisma.

Those three C-words suggest how we get others to trust our knowledge, skill, or ability. But what about trusting one's intentions? Do you know people who have impressive credentials and communicate elegantly, but something makes you suspicious about their intentions?

You believe they know what to do, but you're not convinced they will do what they say. They have the right talk, but give the impression they don't walk it. This critical issue is reflected in each of the subsequent C-words for trust-building.

However, before moving on to the other C-words, let's consider the most powerful communication strategy for increasing trust in one's intentions – AC4P listening. There is probably no better way to earn someone's trust in your intentions than by listening attentively to that person's communication with an AC4P mindset.

When you listen to others first before communicating your own perspective, you not only increase the chance they will reciprocate and listen to you, you also learn how to present your message for optimal understanding, appreciation, and buy-in.

Caring – *showing concern or interest about what happens.* When people believe you sincerely care about them, they will care about what you tell them. They trust you will look out for them when applying your knowledge, skills, or abilities. They trust your intentions because they believe you care.

You communicate AC4P and build interpersonal trust when you ask questions. I'm referring to inquiry about a particular task or set of circumstances. Questions targeting a specific aspect of a student's ongoing challenges send the signal you care about him or her. This communication is more credible than the general, "How ya doing?" greeting.

Take the time to learn what others are doing. Listen and observe. Here I'm talking about "listening to the talk, and walking the talk". You want to "talk the walk" so people trust your intentions.

Candor – *straightforwardness and frankness of expression; freedom from preju-*

dice. We trust people who are frank and open with us. People who don't beat around the bush.

When they don't know an answer to our questions, they tell us outright they don't know and they'll get back to us with an answer.

You have reason to mistrust individuals if their interactions with you reflect prejudice or the tendency to judge blindly. You question their ability to evaluate others and their intentions to treat people fairly.

When people give an opinion about others because of their race, religion, gender, or birthplace, you should doubt these individuals' ability to make people-related decisions. And, you should wonder whether their intentions to perform on behalf of another individual will be biased or tainted by a tendency to pre-judge people on the basis of overly simple and usually inaccurate stereotypes.

Consistency – *agreement among successive acts, ideas, or events.* Consistency is a key determinant of interpersonal trust. Perhaps the *fastest* way to destroy interpersonal trust is to not follow through on an agreement. This is also the *easiest* way to stifle trust.

How often do we make a promise we don't keep? Most promises are *if-then* contingencies. We specify a certain consequence will follow a certain behavior. Whether the consequence is positive or negative, trust decreases when the behavior is not rewarded or punished as promised.

When my daughters were young, I frequently caught myself impulsively making promises (or policy statements) I didn't keep. For example, when they misbehaved while their mom and I were packing the car for a trip, it was not uncommon for one of us to say, "Stop doing that right now or we're not going". Often our daughters stopped the undesirable behavior. The "policy maker" was then reinforced for making the promise.

But what happened when my daughters didn't stop their misbehavior or resumed the undesirable behavior after a brief hiatus? Sure, we still made the trip. The punishment contingency might be shouted a few more times, but regardless, we eventually piled into our car and took off. What did these empty threats teach our daughters?

We would have been far better off promising a less severe negative consequence we could implement consistently, such as delaying the trip until the behavior stops. "We can't go until you stop fighting," would have been much better than a more severe *if-then* threat with inconsistent consequences.

Commitment – *bound emotionally or intellectually to a course of action.* When you follow through on a promise or pledge to do something, you tell others they can count on you. You can be trusted to do what you say you will do.

The consistency principle reflects a spiral of causality and explains how behavior influences attitude, and vice verse. When we choose to do something, we experience internal pressure to maintain a personal belief system or attitude consistent with that behavior. And when we have a certain belief system or attitude toward something, we tend to behave in ways consistent with such beliefs or attitudes. More about this critical AC4P principle is discussed in Chapter 5.

Commitment and total involvement result from a causal spiraling of action feeding attitude, then attitude feeding more action, which strengthens the attitude and leads to more behavior.

Researchers have found three ways to make an initial commitment to do something lead to the most causal spiraling and total involvement.[30] First, people live up to what they write down, so ask for a signed statement of a commitment. Second, the more public the commitment, the greater the relevant attitude and behavior change, presumably because social pressures are added to the personal pressure to be consistent in word and deed.

Third, and perhaps most importantly, for a public and written commitment to initiate causal spiraling of behavior supporting attitude (and vice versa), the commitment must be viewed as a personal choice. When people believe their commitment was their idea, the consistency principle is activated. But when people believe their commitment was unduly influenced by outside factors, they do not feel a need to live up to what they were coerced to write down. (You'll read more about this principle in Chapter 5.)

Consensus – *agreement in opinion, testimony, or belief.* Whenever the results of a group decision-making process come across as "win-lose," some mistrust is going to develop. A majority of the group might be pleased, but others will be discontented and might actively or passively resist involvement.

And even the "winners" could feel lowered interpersonal trust. "We won this decision, but what about next time?" And without solid back-up support of the decision, the outcome will be less than desired. "Without everyone's buy-in, commitment and involvement, we can't trust the process to come off as expected."

How can group consensus be developed? How can the outcome of a heated debate be perceived as a win-win solution everyone supports? Consensus-building takes time and energy, and requires candid, consistent and caring communication among all members of a discussion or decision-making group. When people demonstrate the C-words discussed above for building trust in interpersonal dialogue, they also develop consensus and more interpersonal trust regarding a particular decision or action plan.

There's no quick fix to doing this. It requires plenty of interpersonal communication, including straightforward opinion sharing, intense discussion, emotional debate, active listening, careful evaluation, methodical organization, and systematic prioritizing. But on important matters, the outcome is well worth the investment.

When you develop a solution or process every potential participant can get behind and champion, you have cultivated the degree of interpersonal trust needed for total involvement. Involvement in turn builds personal commitment, more interpersonal trust, and then more involvement.

Character – *the combined moral or ethical structure of a person or group; integrity; fortitude.* Generally, a person with "character" is considered honest, ethical, and principled. People with character are credible or worthy of another person's trust because they display confidence and competence. They know who they are; they know where they want to go; and they know how to get there.

All of the strategies discussed here for cultivating a trusting culture are practiced by a person with character. Individuals with character are willing to admit vulnerability. They are humble and realize they aren't perfect and need behavioral feedback from others. They know their strengths and weaknesses, and find exemplars to model.

By actively listening to others and observing their behaviors, individuals with character learn how to improve their own performance. And if they're building a high-performance team, they can readily find people with knowledge, skills, and abilities to complement their own competencies. They know how to make diversity work for them, their group, and the entire organization.

Having the courage to admit your weaknesses means you're willing to apologize when you've made a mistake, and to ask for forgiveness. There is probably no better way to build trust between individuals than to own up to an error that might have affected another person.

Of course you should also indicate what you will do better next time or ask for specific advice on how to improve. This kind of vulnerability enables you to heed the powerful enrichment principle I learned from the late Frank Bird, "Good better best, may we never rest until good is better and better is best".[26]

While admitting personal vulnerability is a powerful way to build interpersonal trust, the surest way to reduce interpersonal trust is to tell one person about the weakness of another. In this situation it's natural to think, "If he talks that way about her, I wonder what he says about me

behind my back". It's obvious how criticizing or demeaning others in their absence can lead to interpersonal suspiciousness and mistrust.

Back-stabbing leads to more back-stabbing, and eventually you have a work culture of independent people doing their own thing, fearful of making an error, and unreceptive to any kind of behavior-based feedback. Key aspects of continuous performance improvement – team-building, interpersonal observation, and AC4P coaching – are extremely difficult or impossible to implement in such a culture.

Start to build interpersonal trust by implementing a policy of no back-stabbing. People with character, as defined here, always talk about other people as if they can hear you. In other words, to replace interpersonal mistrust with trust, never talk about other individuals behind their backs unless you're willing to say the same thing directly to them.

A Summary

The seven C-words offer distinct directives for AC4P trust-building behavior. *Communicating* these guidelines to others in a *candid* and *caring* way opens up the kind of dialogue that starts people on a journey of AC4P trust-building. Then people need to give each other *consistent* and *candid* feedback regarding those behaviors that reflect these trust-building principles.

With *character* and *commitment*, they need to recognize others for doing it right and offer corrective behavior-focused feedback when there's room for improvement. And of course it's critical for the recipient of such *candid* feedback to accept it with *caring* appreciation and a *commitment* to improve.

Then, the feedback recipient needs to show the *character* to thank the observer for the feedback, even when the *communication* is not all positive and is not delivered well. S/he might offer feedback on how to make the behavior-based feedback more useful. Dialogue like this is necessary to build *consensus* and sustain a journey of continuous AC4P trust and community-building.

In Conclusion

An AC4P culture requires people to do the right thing on behalf of other people when no other person is holding them accountable. Such self-accountability to perform AC4P behavior usually requires self-motivation. This research-based chapter introduced a number of practical ways to facilitate the self-motivation needed to achieve and sustain an AC4P culture.

This book offers a number of real-world examples of the self-motivation principles and leadership lessons reviewed here, as well as practical ways to apply these principles and lessons for enhancing people's self-motivation to actively care for the health, education, safety, and well-being of others.

Notes

1. Geller, E.S., & Veazie, R.A. (2010). *When no one's watching: Living and leading self motivation.* Newport, VA: Make-A-Difference, LLC.

2. Chance, P. (2007). The ultimate challenge: Prove B.F. Skinner wrong. *The Behavior Analyst, 30,* 153-160.

3. Deci, E.L. (1975). *Intrinsic motivation.* New York, NY: Plenum; Deci, E.L., & Flaste, R. (1995). *Why we do what we do: Understanding self-motivation.* New York, NY: Penguin Book; Deci, E.L., & Ryan, R.M. (1995). *Intrinsic motivation and self-determinism in human behavior.* New York, NY: Plenum; Ryan, R.M., & Deci, E.L. (2000). Self-determinism theory and the foundation of intrinsic motivation, social development, and well-being. *American Psychologist, 55,* 68-75.

4. Deci, E.L., & Flaste, R. (1995). *Why we do what we do: Understanding self-motivation.* New York, NY: Penguin Books, p.9.

5. Geller, E.S. (2001). *The psychology of safety handbook.* Boca Raton, FL: CRC Press; Ludwig, T.D., & Geller, E.S. (2001). *Intervening to improve the safety of occupational driving: A behavior-change model and review of empirical evidence.* New York, NY: The Haworth Press, Inc.; Monty, R.A., & Perlmuter, L.C. (1975). Persistence of the effect of choice on paired-associate learning. *Memory & Cognition, 3,* 183-187; Perlmuter, L.C., Monty, R.A., & Kimble, G.A. (1971). Effect of choice on paired-associate learning. *Journal of Experimental Psychology, 91,* 47-58; Steiner, I.D. (1970). Perceived freedom. In L. Berkowitz (Ed.). *Advances in experimental social psychology* (Vol. 5). New York, NY: Academic Press.

6. White, R.W. (1959). Motivation reconsidered: The concept of competence. *Psychological Review, 66,* 297-321.

7. Deci, E.L., & Flaste, R. (1995). *Why we do what we do: Understanding self-motivation.* New York, NY: Penguin Books, p.66.

8. Chance, P. (2008). *The teacher's craft: The 10 essential skills of effective teaching.* Long Grove, IL: Waveland Press, Inc.

9. Deci, E.L., & Flaste, R. (1995). *Why we do what we do: Understanding self-motivation.* New York, NY: Penguin Books, p.88.

10. Block, P. (2008). *Community: The structure of belonging.* San Francisco, CA: Berrett-Koehler Publishers.

11. Peck, M.S. (1979). *The different drum: Community making and peace.* New York, NY: Simon & Schuster, Inc.

12. Deming, W.E. (1986). *Out of the crisis.* Cambridge, MA: Massachusetts Institute of Technology, Center for Advanced Engineering Study; Deming, W.E. (1993). *The new economics for industry, government, education.* Cambridge, MA: Massachusetts Institute of Technology, Center for Advanced Engineering Study.

13. Senge, P.M. (1990). *The fifth discipline: The art and practice of the learning organization.* New York, NY: Doubleday.

14. Covey, S.R. (1989). *The seven habits of highly effective people.* New York, NY: Simon and Schuster, Inc.

15. Geller, E.S., & Veazie, R.A. (2009). *The courage factor: Leading people-based culture change.* Virginia Beach, VA: Coastal Training and Technologies Corporation.

16. Geller, E.S. (2005). *People-based safety: The source.* Virginia Beach, VA: Coastal Training Technologies Corp., pp. 95-98.

17. Deci, E.L. (1975). *Intrinsic motivation.* New York, NY: Plenum; Deci, E.L., & Flaste, R. (1995). *Why we do what we do: Understanding self-motivation.* New York, NY: Penguin Book; Deci, E.L., & Ryan, R.M. (1995). *Intrinsic motivation and self-determinism in human behavior.* New York, NY: Plenum; Ryan, R.M., & Deci, E.L. (2000). Self-determinism theory and the foundation of intrinsic motivation, social development, and well-being. *American Psychologist, 55,* 68-75.

18. United Kingdom Department of Transport (1987). *Killing speed and saving lives.* London, England: Department of Transport.

19. Deci, E.L., & Flaste, R. (1995). *Why we do what we do: Understanding self-motivation.* New York, NY: Penguin Books, p. 104.

20. Conari Press (1993). *Random acts of kindness.* Emeryville, CA.

21. Kohn, A. *Punished by Rewards: The trouble with gold stars, incentive plans, A's, praise, and other bribes,* Boston, MA: Houghton Mifflin; Pink, D.H. (2009). *Drive: The surprising truth about what motivates us.* New York, NY: Penguin Group.

22. Drebinger, J. W. (2011). *Would you watch out for my safety? Helping others avoid personal injury.* Galt, CA: Wulamoc Publishing.

23. Latane, B., Williams, K., & Harkins, S. (1979). Many hands make light the work: The causes and consequences of social loafing. *Journal of Personality and Social Psychology, 37,* 822-832.

24. *The American Heritage Dictionary,* (1991). Boston, MA: Houghton Mifflin Company; *New-Merriam-Webster Dictionary* (1989). Springfield, MA: Merriam-Webster Publishers.

25. Cialdini, R.B. (2001). *Influence: Science and practice* (4th Edition). New York, NY: Harper Collins College.

26. Bird, Jr., F.E., & Davies, R. J. (1996). *Safety and the bottom line.* Loganville, GA: Febco.

CHAPTER 4

The Courage to Actively Care

E. Scott Geller

IT'S OFTEN NOT ENOUGH to know what to do in order to actively care effectively (i.e., competence) and to be motivated to perform AC4P behavior (i.e., commitment). The missing ingredient is *courage*. The same five person-states introduced in Chapter 2 as determinants of AC4P behavior are discussed here as precursors to courage.

The simple AC4P intervention strategies presented in this chapter are practical for large-scale application and evidence-based benefits. But, none have been adopted on a broad scale. Why not? Is it lack of compassion, courage, commitment, competence, self-motivation, or something else? Exploring answers to this question will help us determine the next steps in achieving an AC4P culture of compassion.

Interpersonal Intervention and Courage

As with any program designed to improve behavior, people could claim they lack the resources and/or time to implement the intervention. They could doubt the effectiveness of the AC4P technique and wonder whether the time to implement the interpersonal intervention is worth the effort.

However, these excuses are irrelevant for the techniques described here. Why? Because they are straightforward and easy to accomplish with minimal effort. More importantly, empirical research (as cited below) has demonstrated the beneficial impact of these simple interpersonal approaches to promote human welfare and/or prevent harm to people.

Standard excuses for inaction cannot work here. So what is the barrier to large-scale implementation of simple-to-use interpersonal methods that clearly benefit everyone involved?

The key word is "interpersonal". Each effective intervention method requires personal interaction with other people. It is likely many people lack the courage to intervene as an agent of change. This chapter discusses the level of courage needed, and suggests ways to develop that courage in ourselves and others.

Bottom line: What does it take for more people to become interpersonal change agents on behalf of the welfare of others? Effortless evidenced-based techniques to help people prevent harm to themselves and others are available, but at this time it seems too few people have the courage to use them.

What is Courage?

The American Heritage Dictionary[1] defines courage as "the state or quality of mind or spirit that enables one to face danger with self-possession, confidence, and resolution." This denotation is consistent with the two-page description of courage in *Wikipedia* (http://en.wikipedia.org/wiki/courage), except Wikipedia distinguishes between *physical courage* – when confronting physical pain, hardship, or threat of death, and *moral courage* – in the face of possible shame, embarrassment, or discouragement.[2]

Leaders certainly need competence and commitment to be effective change agents.[3] But, interpersonal intervention to prevent possible harm to a person (i.e., proactive AC4P behavior) takes *moral courage*. A person could have both competence and commitment in a particular situation, but not be courageous. Consider the following two authentic incidents related to AC4P, the first was dramatic and reactive while the other was temperate and proactive.

Responding to an Emergency

In the midst of a safety meeting, Joanne Dean, the safety director of a large construction firm in New Jersey is notified of a horrendous "accident." The operator of an industrial equipment truck with an attached auger was pulled into the auger by the weed mesh under the mulch on which he was standing. The worker chose not to stand on the safety platform provided for this task.

Joanne runs to help the bloody victim whose body is severed in half. She assists the on-site nurse with the AED (automated external defibrillator), covers the body parts with a blanket, and stays at the scene until the local EMS (emergency medical service) and coroner arrive.

It took commitment to step up and intervene in this horrible casualty. It's likely Joanne's competence as an emergency-response instructor contributed to her propensity to actively care, but her AC4P behavior took more than commitment and competence.

Indeed, three key safety professionals of the company that hired the construction firm chose not to intervene. They stood at a distance and watched Joanne and the other responders. We can assume these experienced, professional bystanders possessed both the competence and commitment required for their leadership positions. But on this day they appeared to lack moral courage.

Responding to a Risky Situation

While waiting in the lobby of a Fortune-500 company, Bob Veazie, a safety consultant and former culture-change agent for a Fortune-100 company, observes an at-risk behavior. A maintenance worker has climbed to the top of an eight-foot step-ladder to change a light bulb. Because the ladder is not long enough for this job, the individual is standing with one foot on the top step of the ladder. A co-worker is looking up and talking to the man on the ladder, but he's not holding the ladder steady.

Imagining a serious injury from a fall to the hard marble floor of the lobby, Bob walks to the ladder and calls up to the at-risk worker. Holding the bottom of the ladder, he requests the man to come down because, "It doesn't seem safe to stand on the top of that ladder". Then he asks whether a longer ladder is available.

Bob Veazie showed moral courage by intervening with this at-risk stranger. Bob could have faced an unpleasant confrontation, and been publicly embarrassed or humiliated. Bob's competence and commitment as a safety trainer and consultant certainly contributed to his inclination to speak up. But competence and commitment were not sufficient for the moral courage he showed. In fact, Bob's training partner who has extensive competence and intense commitment for safety saw the same at-risk behavior, but she chose not say or do anything about it.

How Can Courage Be Encouraged?

Courage is a human characteristic distinct from competence and commitment. But these three qualities of leadership are interdependent to a degree. Individuals with greater competence and commitment in a given situation are more likely to demonstrate courage. One's propensity to demonstrate courage in certain circumstances is increased whenever relevant competence or commitment is augmented.

Developing Competence

As discussed in Chapter 3, behavior-focused training increases one's competence at a particular task. This involves: a) describing and demonstrating a desirable behavior or skill-set, b) giving specific behavior-based feedback during a participant's role-playing of designated target behavior(s), c) practicing the desired behavior(s) with both corrective and supportive feedback, and d) implementing the new competency in real-world situations.[4]

When learners teach this skill-set to others, their perception of competence increases further, along with their personal commitment.[5] And as I commented above, greater feelings of competence and commitment are more likely to support acts of courage.

Developing Commitment

Motivation or commitment to do something is determined by the intrinsic and extrinsic consequences of a task, as well as one's personal interpretation of those consequences.[6] While many tasks are performed for expected soon, certain, and significant consequences, we use self-talk to avoid impulsive reactive behavior and work for long-term goals.[7] Self-talk is also a potential means of overcoming anxiety and reinforcing a commitment to step up and be courageous when called upon.

Cultivating Courage

The moral courage of Joanne and Bob was due to many factors. This suggests cultivating courage is more complex and less straightforward than developing competence and commitment. For example, both Joanne and Bob are extraverts. They gain energy from interacting with people. Both are naturally outgoing and inclined to communicate with others. They would be described as having excellent "people skills."

Another of the Big Five personality traits that facilitated the courage of Joanne and Bob is conscientiousness.[8] I know each of them very well and it's obvious they each carry an AC4P mindset with them at all times – both on and off the job.

Beyond personality *traits*, certain person-*states* increase one's propensity to show AC4P courage. These person-states – self-esteem, self-efficacy, personal control, optimism, and sense of belongingness – were introduced in Chapter 2, along with ways to enhance these dispositions to increase the probability an individual will perform AC4P behavior.

Culture and the Courage to Actively Care

Many of the factors that influence one's propensity to demonstrate AC4P courage can be filed under the general label – culture. Certain cultural factors related to the development and cultivation of courage are exhibited daily by people around us. Another real-life story not only illustrates physical courage, but also demonstrates some practical strategies for promoting the moral courage needed for the kind of interpersonal intervention needed to achieve an AC4P culture.

Physical Courage to Actively Care

On January 16, 2007, Dr. Kevin Brothers, executive director of the Somerset Hills Learning Institute, was wheeled into St. Barnabas' Renal Surgery Center. He was in top physical and mental health, and had never before "gone under the knife" and experienced surgery. He received a three-hour surgical procedure – not for himself but for someone else.

Dr. Brothers donated his kidney to his mentor and professional colleague – Dr. Patricia Krantz, Executive Director of the Princeton Child Development Institute. Seven months earlier Dr. Brothers had learned Dr. Krantz was in severe kidney failure. Without a transplant, she would require dialysis within a few months.

Dr. Krantz was not aware that Dr. Brothers and several other colleagues had agreed to donate one of their kidneys to her. Among all of Dr. Krantz's family, friends, and colleagues who received extensive blood work and tissue sampling, there was only one viable match – Kevin Brothers.

The difference between physical and moral courage is evident in the three real-world incidents I have described here. When we risk social embarrassment or interpersonal confrontation on behalf of another person's welfare, we show *moral* courage. In contrast, when we risk physical harm to ourselves when looking out for another person's well-being, we demonstrate *physical courage*.[2] While Joanne Dean and Bob Veazie demonstrated moral courage, Kevin Brothers' elective surgery exemplifies physical courage.

The AC4P courage of Dr. Brothers was extraordinary. Beyond a number of person factors, including Dr. Brothers' self-esteem, self-efficacy, personal control, optimism and sense of belongingness, a number of cultural factors facilitated this display of courage. Let's consider these cultural factors as potential guidelines for promoting AC4P courage in your culture.

A Group Commitment. Dr. Brothers' first courageous act was to pledge to give one of his kidneys to Dr. Krantz. When Kevin talked with me prior to his surgery, he admitted it was relatively easy to muster the courage to sign the donor pledge. The probability of him being the best antigen match was seemingly low. Surely one of Dr. Krantz's family members would be a better match.

Although surprised he was the best match, Dr. Brothers affirmed strong motivation to honor his commitment to the group of potential donors. He acknowledged the value of this two-part approach to motivate his AC4P behavior – first the promise and then the action. This two-step approach is applicable to many situations.

Suppose each student in a class signed a group declaration to give each other corrective feedback wherever they saw behavior that could be perceived as bullying. This commitment could be called a "Declaration of Interdependence." In fact, this was the label on a large poster at a leadership seminar for supervisors, safety leaders, and maintenance personnel of Delta Airlines.[9] The commitment poster was signed by more than 100 Delta employees, and is prominently displayed in the maintenance workers' break room at the Hartsfield-Jackson International Airport in Atlanta, GA. (This practical AC4P intervention is explained further in the next chapter, along with the theoretical foundation.)

This group obligation, given voluntarily and publicly within a supportive social context, helps to sustain the moral courage required to give behavior-based feedback. A "Declaration of Interdependence" could be introduced to a class as the group commitment: "We're all on board together to reduce interpersonal conflict and bullying behavior." After group consensus and commitment to this reasonable declaration, students have increased courage to deliver behavioral feedback relevant to supporting AC4P behavior and preventing bullying-related behavior.

Group Support. Both before and after his surgery, Dr. Brothers received substantial social support for his physical courage. This is often crucial in deciding to move forward in a courageous way. His wife Debbie, a registered nurse, and their four daughters totally supported Kevin's decision "to move ahead to give *our* kidney as soon as possible". Dr. Brothers said, "*Our* kidney, because this was a well-informed family decision made with the support of Debbie and our girls." Dr. Brothers' courage was also aided by the dedicated support group of friends and colleagues who pledged to donate a kidney.

Two weeks after a successful surgery, Kevin Brothers returned to work. "What an outpouring of support our family received from our school's parents and staff," reported Debbie Brothers. The parents and staff of the Princeton Child Development Institute were also extremely supportive, sending thank-you cards to Dr. Brothers for helping to prolong Dr. Krantz's life and enable her to continue her important work worldwide.

Substantial research reports verify the beneficial impact of social support on human performance, from enhancing motivation to engage in a challenging task to facilitating recovery from physical illness and injury[10] (e.g., see my cancer story in Chapter 17). This factor relates directly to the person-state of belongingness.

If you feel you belong to a social network or circle of friends or peers, this increases your inclination to actively care for another individual's health, safety, or general well-being. If that AC4P behavior requires an act of courage, strong feelings of belonging create a sense of responsibility or obligation to not disappoint the group. Cultivating social support throughout a particular culture is extremely beneficial to increasing the courage factor and the frequency of AC4P behavior.

Various interpersonal activities can enhance social support and courage, including team goal setting, interpersonal coaching, collaborative work projects, and group celebrations (as described in Chapter 3). Relationship-building conversations are also critical. Methods for cultivating and increasing social support are reflected in the various AC4P applications discussed in Parts II and III of this book.

A Trusting Culture. When Kevin Brothers honored his pledge to give Patricia Krantz one of his kidneys, his courage was bolstered by his feeling that all of the others in his special donor group would follow through on their commitment if they had the best antigen match. He also trusted the expert medical staff at St. Barnabas Medical Center would give Dr. Krantz and him the very best healthcare. He expected a successful kidney transplant.

The topic of interpersonal trust, including the need to distinguish between trusting an individual's ability vs. his/her intentions, is addressed in Chapter 3, as well as in other publications.[11] In Chapter 3, I explained specific ways to increase interpersonal trust. In addition, you might consider asking colleagues and/or students how specific events, policies, or communications impact their trust levels, and their courage to speak up about interpersonal conflict or other undesirable behavior they observe.

Solicit ideas to eliminate barriers to interpersonal trust and nurture courage. Add policies and/or procedures that could enhance people's perception they can trust the intentions and abilities of their colleagues and students. A number of practical action plans will likely result from this process, many similar to those suggested in Chapter 2. Still, just the process of soliciting ways to impact interpersonal trust will have a positive trust-building and courage-building effect.

A Common Worthwhile Purpose. Dr. Brothers and his colleagues in the kidney-donor group admired and greatly appreciated the teaching and research of Dr. Patricia Krantz. Indeed, Dr. Krantz has pioneered the application of behavioral science for the treatment of autism, and she mentored Dr. Brothers while he was a research intern and Ph.D. student. In Dr. Brother's words, "Dr. Krantz gave me the opportunity to learn science, and her teachings continue to be the underpinnings of my career... (and) her guiding me into the field of autism treatment has given more children a chance for a better life".

The group that pledged to donate a kidney for Dr. Krantz had a common and commendable purpose. Likewise, advocates for an AC4P culture have a common and worthwhile mission. In fact, there is perhaps no more esteemed purpose than to actively care for others health, safety, and general welfare.

A Family Mindset

It certainly takes more courage to actively care for a stranger than a colleague. In fact, attending to the welfare of a family member is usually not even considered courageous but rather an obligation. As I proposed in Chapter 2 (see Figure 2.6), when teachers and students think of each other as "family," actively caring for the well-being of these individuals becomes more an act of commitment than courage.

The probability of AC4P behavior is increased whenever interpersonal behavior supports a family mindset among students, teachers, and staff. Figure 4.1 illustrates this proposed relationship between the degree of courage needed for interpersonal AC4P behavior and the degree of relatedness or interpersonal connection between the person needing help and the observer.

It's unlikely many readers would undergo elective surgery to give a kidney to a stranger. Fortunately, AC4P does not require the *physical courage* shown by Dr. Brothers.

Indeed, proactive AC4P behavior doesn't require any physical courage – only the *moral courage* to face possible embarrassment, rejection or conflict when giving feedback or advice to improve another person's behavior, or rewarding the AC4P behavior of another person. A supportive *family* mindset among people removes the fear of negative consequences from such proactive and behavior-focused AC4P.

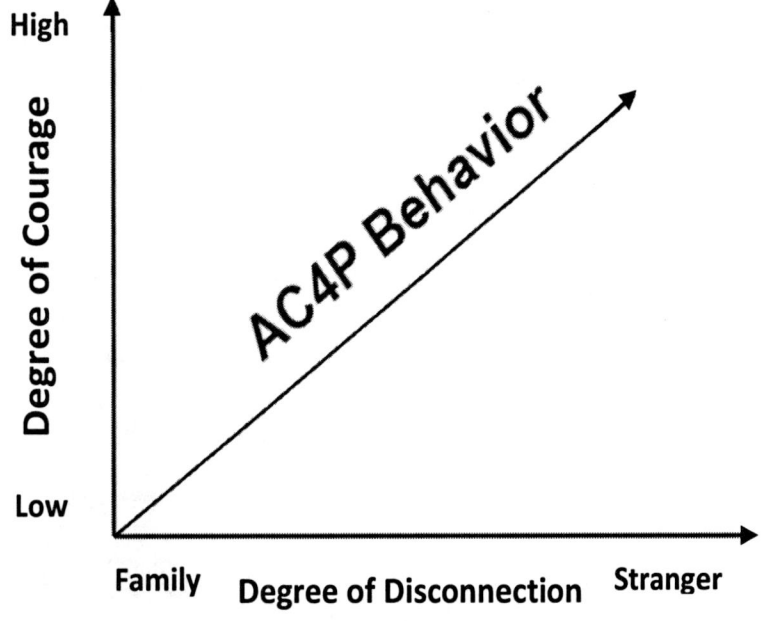

Actually, many AC4P actions do not require courage; they only present an inconvenience.

Figure 4.1. *The amount of courage needed to actively care increases directly with the degree of disconnection between the observer and the person in need of assistance.*

If you saw a member of your immediate family get behind the steering wheel of a vehicle and neglect to buckle up, you would not hesitate to intervene. Courage would hardly enter the picture.

But what would you do if you got in a hotel shuttle van at the airport and noticed the driver and several passengers did not buckle up? Would you offer some proactive AC4P corrective feedback? Would you have the moral courage to intervene on behalf of these at-risk strangers?

You have several excuses for not speaking up, right? It's only a short trip to the hotel and the probability of a crash is miniscule. These folks are adults, and if they want to travel at-risk, that's their choice. Plus, if you say something about this, another occupant might be offended by your meddling and call you a "safety nerd".

So why actively care in this situation? Here's a thought: Consider that your moral courage sets a memorable leadership example. Such behavior could start a constructive AC4P conversation and initiate a ripple effect of AC4P behavior.

Contemplating one's lack of moral courage can activate some disconcerting tension between what an individual thinks s/he *would* do in this and similar situations versus what the person knows s/he *should* do. The more one holds AC4P as a personal value, the greater the tension or cognitive dissonance.[12] Following through with moral courage relieves such tension and exemplifies AC4P leadership.

The AC4P intervention strategies discussed next are simple, convenient, and effortless, and they exemplify the kind of AC4P leadership needed to cultivate an AC4P culture.

Question: Do you have the moral courage to apply any of these, and encourage others to do the same? Implementing these on a large scale would move us one step closer to achieving our vision of an AC4P culture of compassion. And for the most part, they really do not require a great amount of courage.

The Flash-for-Life

Developed initially in 1984 and replicated in several other situations, this rather intrusive but effective intervention merely involves the change agent holding up a card to request a certain safety-related behavior (i.e., vehicle safety-belt use); and if the target individual complies, the "flasher" flips the card over to reveal "Thank You". The top illustration shows my daughter, Karly, at age 3 1/2 holding up the 11

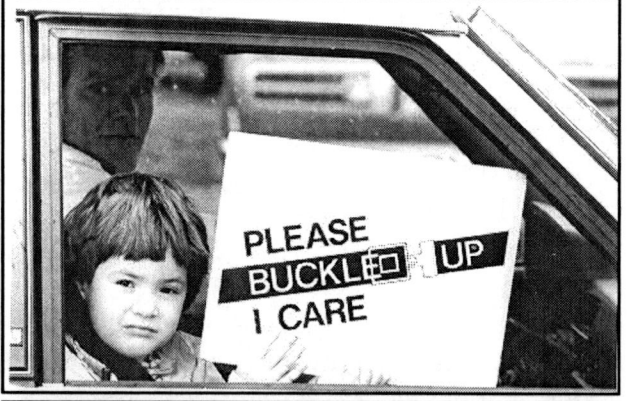

by 14 inch sign to an unbuckled driver at an intersection. When the driver buckled up, she turned over the bright yellow sign with bold black lettering to say "Thank you". Note the ABC (activator-behavior-consequence) contingency of this intervention.

Here the courage factor is minimized by the physical distance between the actions taking place. In our first study, the "flasher" was positioned in the passenger seat of a vehicle stopped in the left lane at an intersection.[13] Table 4.1 depicts the impact of this simple intervention by specifying the percentage of vehicle drivers who buckled up after viewing the flashcard.

As shown in Table 4.1, seven different vehicle passengers of varying ages, ranging from 3.5 to 23 years of age, "flashed" a total of 787 unbuckled drivers in Blacksburg, Virginia, home of Virginia Tech; whereas only two of these passengers (i.e., Tim and Hollie) showed the Flash-for-Life card to 300 passengers in the adjacent rural town of Christiansburg, Virginia.

Some drivers did not turn their head to look at the sign, and therefore the compliance percentages are based on only those unbuckled drivers who looked directly at the sign. It's noteworthy this prompting intervention was more successful in the university town than in Christiansburg (i.e., an average of 24.6 vs. 13.7 percent compliance, respectively). The age of the "flasher" did not have a reliable effect on the driver's compliance with the buckle-up prompt.

It's worth noting that this intervention did not result in any verbal or physical harassment. Although the "flasher" did get a few hand signals which didn't mean right or left turn. When my daughter asked, "What do they mean, Daddy," I told her they were signaling, "You're number one, they're just using the wrong finger." Incidentally, none of these one-finger hand signals came from females.

The first applications of the "Flash for Life" occurred before safety-belt use laws, when only about 20% of U.S. drivers buckled up. Twenty years later, with about 80% of U.S. drivers using their vehicle safety belts, my students and I compared the impact of a positive reminder ("Please Buckle Up I Care") with the more common negative-reinforcement prompt (i.e., "Click it or Ticket") on both behavioral compliance and body language.[14]

Table 4.1. Summary of "Flash for Life" Results[13]					
Flasher (Name & Age)	Number of Observations	Number Who looked	Number Who buckled	Percentage Who Looked	Percentage Who Buckled
Blacksburg, VA					
Karly *age 3 ½*	179	154	37	86.0	24.0
David *age 5*	31	21	5	67.7	23.8
Abby *age 7*	68	47	16	69.1	34.0
Carrie *age 7*	64	48	9	75.0	18.8
Dane *age 10*	56	43	6	76.8	14.0
Hollie *age 22*	206	177	43	85.9	24.3
Tim *age 23*	183	148	41	80.3	27.6
Total	787	634	157	80.9	24.6
Christiansburg, VA					
Tim *age 22*	145	123	19	84.8	15.4
Hollie *age 23*	155	133	16	85.8	12.0
Total	300	256	35	85.3	13.7

Table 4.2 (on the next page) reveals the percentage of unbuckled drivers who buckled up after viewing one of the two types of cards. This table also shows the percentage of drivers giving positive vs. negative hand signals and facial expressions per type of prompt. It's noteworthy the positive "I Care" prompt was not only more effective at activating buckle-up behavior than the threatening reminder, it also prompted more positive and less negative body language than did the negative-reinforcement prompt (all p's < .05).

Intervention Sign	Percentage who Buckled-Up	Percentage of Positive Hand Gestures	Percentage of Negative Hand Gestures	Percentage of Positive Expressions	Percentage of Negative Expressions
Flash for Life n=895	33.6%	13.2%	.9%	25.0%	3.9%
Click it or Ticket n=927	25.6%	7.8%	2.6%	18.9%	9.2%

Table 4.2. Summary of Results from Positive vs. Negative Buckle-Up Prompting[15]

The AC4P-Behavior Promise Card

This nonintrusive and straightforward strategy is suitable for numerous circumstances and target behaviors.[15] It requires little in the way of courage. It has been used effectively to increase the occurrence of specific safety-related behavior (e.g., the use of safety glasses, gloves, and vehicle safety belts)[16] as well as to promote an interdependent AC4P paradigm or mindset.[17]

Based on the powerful social-influence principle of consistency,[18] this behavior-change tactic merely asks participants to sign an individual "promise card" or a "group pledge" that declares an explicit commitment to regularly perform a particular AC4P behavior for a specified period of time.

For maximum behavioral impact, the pledge-card signing should be public and voluntary. A generic promise card is depicted below that can be used to increase the occurrence of a number of AC4P behaviors.

AC4P Promise Card

I promise to _____

_____

From _____ until _____

_____
signature   date

The AC4P Polite Light

Taking on the negative emotions of road-rage driving would seem to call for a greater degree of courage. But not so in this case. It involves the use of a vehicle light to signal a simple "Courtesy Code" under relevant conditions. Specifically, one flash means "Please," two flashes reflect "Thank You," and three flashes are used to signal "I am sorry". Vehicle emergency lights can be used to flash this "1-2-3 code," or a small green light as shown here can be affixed to the vehicle's rear window and operated with the convenient push of a button.

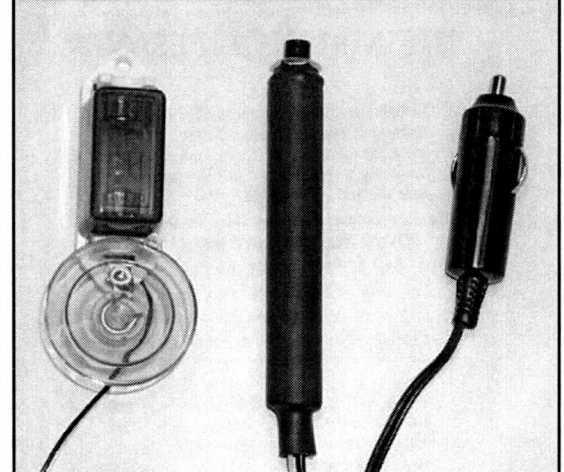

In a community-wide evaluation of this intervention strategy, the polite-driving code was promoted on radio stations and billboards throughout the town of Christiansburg, Virginia, and "polite lights" were distributed at various workshops. Results were encouraging, but the idea was not adopted.

The success of this intervention relied not on courage but on marketing and outreach, and then for people to use the Courtesy Driving Code. Marketing and the minor inconvenience of flashing the Courtesy Code were key barriers that prevented this AC4P behavior from large-scale use. So far, anyway.

The Airline Lifesaver

Flying in an airplane requires courage for some people to the degree they need medication to reduce anxiety. Others never think of the risks involved in flying.

For this particular AC4P intervention, courage is needed for one-on-one interaction with a stranger. The 3 X 5 inch card depicted on the next page can be handed to the flight attendant when boarding an airplane. It requests the following announcement be made after landing: "Now that you have worn a seat belt for the safest part of your trip, the flight crew would like to remind you to buckle up during your ground transportation".

To intervene with busy flight attendants by handing them this card and requesting they add on an announcement at the flight's conclusion doesn't require much in the way of courage. Of course there is the fear of possible rejection. "No, I don't have the time." But what this exercise demonstrates is the more committed you are to AC4P and the more passionate you feel about it, the easier it is to risk rejection and go ahead with this simple and convenient intervention. It's also easier if you have extroverted

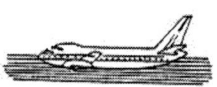

THE AIRLINE LIFESAVER

Airlines have been the *most effective* promoters of seat belt use. Please, would someone in your flight crew consider announcing a statement like the following near the end of the flight.

"Now that you have worn a seat belt for the safest part of your trip -- the flight crew would like to remind you to buckle-up during your ground transportation."

This announcement will show that your airline cares about transportation safety. And who knows -- you might start the buckle-up habit for someone and help save a life! Thank you.

people skills, such as Joanne and Bob in the stories told earlier.

The first Lifesaver Card shown here is the first one I used, beginning in 1985. In 1994, I began using an incentive card that offered the flight attendants a prize if they read the announcement. The back of this card is depicted below, which specifies an *if-then reward contingency*. Later, I alternated the distribution of these two types of reminders to determine the impact of an incentive intervention.

A 17-year study demonstrated substantial compliance with this Airline Lifesaver request,[19] but no current airline has adopted this simple safety-based intervention. And, I know of no individual using this technique consistently when boarding an airplane.

When the request was made without an incentive (i.e., prompt only), 35.5% of 798 recipients read the message. However, when the flight attendant was offered a prize for delivering the buckle-up reminder, 53.3% of 245 recipients complied with the request.

Of course, showing that many flight attendants read the buckle-up reminder when asked to do so does not reveal behavior change directly related to people's welfare. Indeed, it is rare to see such direct benefits of proactive efforts to prevent personal injury.

However, two behavior-change benefits of the Airline Lifesaver have been documented.[20] In one case, a passenger who heard the buckle-up reminder asked the driver of the airport commuter van to buckle up, claiming "If a flight attendant can request safety-belt use, so can I".

After you read the "buckle-up reminder," a passenger will give you a coupon redeemable for various prizes.

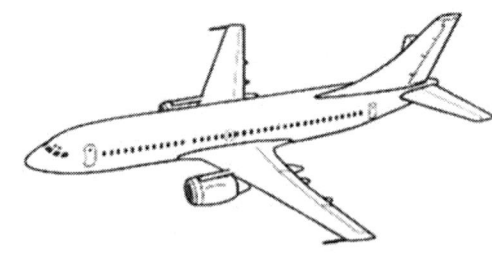

1 coupon .... $5.00 *
2 coupons $15.00
3 coupons $30.00
(* Prize equivalent)

For more information call (703) 231-8145
Center for Applied Behavior Systems

For a second testimony, I received a letter from a passenger who said he used the back-seat safety belt in a taxi cab because he had just heard the buckle-up reminder at the end of his flight. Traveling over 70 mph, the taxi hydroplaned on a wet road and struck the guardrail. Serious injuries were prevented because this person had buckled up. The actual letter from this individual is printed in my first book on the psychology of safety.[21]

The Driver-Training Score Card

As mentioned earlier, it often requires less moral or physical courage to actively care for family members than for strangers. But here is an intervention that has been successful in both applications.

More than 15 years ago, I documented an effective behavior-change intervention for driver training, which led to numerous adaptations in work settings.[21] Specifically, I worked with my 15-year-old daughter to develop a critical behavior checklist (CBC) for driving. As detailed in Chapter 1, this CBC lists a number of driving-related behaviors, along with columns to record whether each behavior is safe or at-risk, and a column to write comments relevant for a follow-up feedback session (see Figure 1.3).

While much research and even common sense indicates this process works to improve safety-related behaviors, I am unaware of a single adoption of this technique for driver education/training. However, this behavior-change technique is the foundation of behavior-based safety (BBS), and there is much empirical support for the BBS approach to increasing safety-related behaviors and preventing injuries.[22]

The Taxi-Cab Feedback Card

At keynote addresses to large audiences, I have proposed that safety leaders record the safety-related driving behaviors of cab, bus, and limo drivers on a simple observation-feedback card; and after the trip, show the results to the driver for valuable behavior-based feedback.[23]

A sample feedback card, applicable in numerous driving situations, is shown on the next page. The top half of the card is given to the driver, while the bottom half has a return address and stamp on the back. This enables tracking of the driver behaviors observed by the passengers of public-transport vehicles.

This observation-and-feedback technique reflects another adaption of a basic process of BBS, applied in industries worldwide with remarkable improvements in injury statistics. However, I know of no large-scale application of this evidence-based process for public transportation. It does take substantial moral courage to use this proactive AC4P strategy in taxi cabs, limos, and buses.

The AC4P Thank-You Card

For many years, I have promoted the use of a simple thank-you card for delivery to people following their performance of AC4P behavior.[24] In fact, "thank-you cards" have been customized for particular industrial sites and educational settings. For example, I have distributed the "Virginia Tech Thank-You Card" depicted in Chapter 2 (p. 45) for more than 20 years.

Every semester I make these cards available for my students to use to acknowledge the AC4P behavior of others, but relatively few students take them. Student leaders in our Center for Applied Behavior Systems (CABS) have regularly used this recognition technique for more than two decades, because this recognition process has been institutionalized in our CABS culture. However, beyond applications in CABS, university use of a thank-you card is rare.

Given the power, generic applicability and relative convenience of one-to-one recognition, it's appropriate to end this chapter with evidence-based details about how to give and receive interpersonal recognition. Each of the three prior chapters in Part I on the theoretical and research foundation of AC4P refer to one-to-one recognition.

In Chapter 2, "Actively Caring Thank-You Cards" were introduced as a mechanism to cultivate a sense of connectedness and AC4P throughout an organization. In Chapter 3, I discussed interpersonal recognition within the context of supportive feedback to sustain and potentially increase the occurrence of AC4P behavior. Here I offer specific behavioral strategies for delivering and receiving recognition. First, it's critical to understand and believe in the importance of giving quality AC4P recognition.

In terms of the courage factor, it's worth noting many people are uncomfortable communicating rather intimately on a one-to-one, face-to-face basis. But the value of this sort of interaction makes it important to use whatever means you have at your disposal to overcome fears of interpersonal interaction. Ask for coaching on this critical skill-set. Observe others competent at up-close-and-personal interaction and model techniques that fit your style.

We Learn More from Success

"We can't learn unless we make mistakes." How many times have you heard this? This might make us feel better about the errors of our ways, and provide an excuse for focusing more on people's failures than on their successes, but in reality nothing could be further from the truth.

Behavioral scientists have shown convincingly that success – not failure – produces the most effective learning.[25] Edward Lee Thorndike, for example, studied intelligence at the start of the last century by putting chickens, cats, dogs, fish, monkeys, and humans in situations that called for problem-solving behavior. He then systematically observed how these organisms learned. He coined the "Law of Effect" to refer to the fact that learning depends upon behavioral consequences.

When a behavior is followed by a "satisfying state of affairs" the probability of that behavior occurring again is increased. But, if an "*annoying* state of affairs" follows a behavior, that behavior (considered an error) is less likely to recur.[26]

Which kind of consequence – positive or negative – leads to the most learning? Does an error have to occur in order to solve a problem? We can reflect on our own experiences to answer these questions. A pleasant consequence gives us direction and motivation to continue the behavior. We know what we did to receive the reward, and are thus motivated to earn another.

In contrast, a negative consequence following a mistake only tells us what not to do. It provides no specific direction for problem solution. An overemphasis on a mistake can be frustrating and discouraging, and de-motivate us to continue the learning process.

Errors are not necessary for learning to occur. In fact, when training results in no errors, made possible with certain presentation techniques, learning occurs most smoothly and is most enjoyable. Errors disrupt the teaching/learning process and can lead to a negative attitude, especially if negative social consequences accentuate the mistake. Even subtle reactions to an error – a disappointed face or verbal tone – can increase feelings of helplessness or despair and turn a person off to the entire learning process.

From the courage perspective, the less focus and talk of errors, the less courage is called for. Offering positive consequences (e.g., supportive feedback) requires substantially less courage, right?

The antidote to depressed learning from the negative consequences of incorrect behavior is to provide positive consequence for correct behavior. And the most powerful positive consequence to support a learning process is interpersonal recognition – the theme of this discussion. Below I offer seven guidelines for giving quality AC4P recognition.

Before leaving this topic of learning from success versus failure, it's noteworthy that Thorndike referred to the type of learning discovered in his problem-solving situations as "trial and accidental success."[26] Many textbook authors have used the term "trial-and-error learning" when describing Thorndike's research, even though Thorndike himself opposed the term because of its inaccurate implications. But let's not focus on this error; rather consider the need to support AC4P behavior with quality recognition.

1. Be Timely

In order for recognition to provide optimal direction and support, it needs to be associated directly with the desired behavior. This is not necessarily an act of courage, but recognition should be delivered promptly. People need to know what they did to earn the appreciation. Then they might be motivated to continue that behavior.

If it's necessary to delay the recognition, the conversation should relive the activity deserving recognition. Talk specifically about the behavior warranting special acknowledgement. Don't hesitate to ask the recipient to recall aspects of the situation and the commendable behavior. This enables direction and motivation to continue the desired behavior.

2. Make It Personal

Recognition is most meaningful when it's perceived as personal. Recognition should not be generic, fit for any situation, as in "Nice job". Rather, it needs to be customized to fit a particular individual and circumstance. This happens naturally when the recognition is linked to *designated behavior.*

When you recognize someone, you are expressing personal thanks. Sometimes it's tempting to say "*we* appreciate" rather than "*I* appreciate," and to refer to group gratitude rather than *personal appreciation*. Speaking for the school can come across as impersonal and insincere.

Of course, it's appropriate to reflect value to the school or college/university when giving recognition, but the focus should be personal. "I saw what you did to support our AC4P process and I really appreciate it. Your example illustrates the kind of leadership we need around here to achieve an AC4P culture." This second statement illustrates the next guideline for quality recognition. Again, being positive and proactive shouldn't require that much courage, but some people are not at ease delivering interpersonal praise.

3. Take It to a Higher Level

Recognition is most memorable and inspirational when it reflects a higher-order quality. Adding a universal attitude like leadership, integrity, trustworthiness, or AC4P to your recognition statement makes the recognition more meaningful and thus rewarding. It's important to state the specific behavior first, and then make an obvious linkage between the behavior and the positive attribute it reflects.

Our attempts to get college students to recognize others for their AC4P behavior have been less successful than desired. Many claim they didn't observe AC4P behavior worthy of special recognition, whereas others admit lack of courage to present a thank-you card or a Hershey PayDay candy bar (labeled "Pay-It-Forward") as a reward for AC4P behavior.

Some say, "It's unnatural or silly," while others resist because it could come across as manipulative. A sincere verbal "Thank You" is okay, they declare, "But giving someone a material reward could be seen as a ploy to control them."

One of my graduate students claimed he's more comfortable rewarding a stranger with a candy bar or a thank-you card than a friend because, "The embarrassment of using a behavior modification technique would be more personal and aversive among close friends than strangers."

My comeback is, "It's all in the delivery." My students hear this and review the seven steps given here for giving quality AC4P recognition, but the use of thank-you cards and candy bars to recognize AC4P behavior has not markedly increased. However, we have found less resistance to passing on an AC4P wristband when the wristband is viewed as more than a reward for behavior.

More specifically, when the wristband is presented as a symbol of AC4P leadership and worn to show membership in an elite group of individuals dedicated to cultivating an AC4P culture of compassion, my students show more interest and willingness to participate in such a recognition process. The AC4P wristband is given to not only reward AC4P behavior, but to signify membership in a Movement to cultivate AC4P cultures of compassion.

This connection brings the interpersonal recognition to a higher level, enabling positive impact on this recipient's self-esteem, competence, and sense of interdependency and belongingness. As mentioned earlier, courage should not be a significant issue here, but the depth of commitment and passion regarding AC4P can make a difference in "taking it to a higher level".

4. Deliver It Privately

Because quality recognition is personal and indicative of higher-order attributes, it needs to be delivered in private and one-on-one. This requires a certain degree of courage for those not comfortable in private, one-on-one conversations; especially with people they don't know well. But consider this: The recognition is special and only relevant to one person. So, it will mean more and seem more genuine if it's given from one individual to another.

It seems conventional to recognize individuals in front of a group. This approach is typified in athletic contests and reflected in the pop psychology slogan, "Praise publicly and reprimand privately". Many managers take the lead from this common-sense statement and give individuals recognition in group settings.

Indeed, isn't it maximally rewarding to be held up as an exemplar in front of one's peers? Not necessarily, because many people feel embarrassed when singled out in front of a group. Part of this embarrassment could be due to fear of subsequent harassment by peers. Some peers might call the recognized individual an "apple-polisher" or "brown-noser," or accuse him or her of "sucking up to the teacher".

When I was in fifth grade, my teacher recognized me in front of the class for doing "an excellent job" on my homework. As depicted in the illustration, I was so embarrassed. Then after school, a gang of boys beat me up on the playground. Unfortunately, that teacher never found out the negative side-effect of her public recognition.

In athletic events the participants' performance is measured fairly and the winners are objectively determined. However in educational and work settings it's usually impossible to assess everyone's relevant behaviors objectively and obtain a fair ranking for individual recognition.

Therefore, praising one individual in public may lead to perceptions of favoritism from individuals who feel they did equally well, but did not get praised. Plus, such ranking sets up a win-lose atmosphere – perhaps appropriate for sporting events but not in settings where interdependent teamwork is needed to achieve group goals.

It's beneficial, of course, to recognize teams of students for their accomplishments, and this can be done in a group setting, as I discussed in Chapter 3. Since individual responsibility is diffused or dispersed across the group, there is minimal risk of individual embarrassment or later peer harassment.

However, as I indicated in the prior chapter, it's important to realize that group achievement is rarely the result of equal input from all team members. Some take the lead and work harder, while others "loaf" and count on the group effort to make them look good. Thus, it's important to deliver personal and private recognition to those individuals who went beyond the call of duty for the sake of their team.

5. Let It Sink In

In this fast-paced age of trying to do more with less, we try to communicate as much as possible when we finally get in touch with a busy person. After recognizing an individual's special AC4P effort, we are tempted to tag on a bunch of unrelated statements, even a request for additional behavior. This comes across as, "I appreciate what you've done, but I need more".

It does take a certain amount of courage, or "guts" to tell someone "I need more out of you". All the more reason to drop the request and let the praise sink in.

Resist the temptation to do more than praise the AC4P behavior you saw. If you have additional points to discuss, it's best to reconnect later, after the rewarding recognition has had a chance to sink in and become a part of the individual's self-talk for self-recognition and self-motivation.

By giving quality AC4P recognition, we give people a script they can use to reward their own behavior. In other words, our quality recognition strengthens the other person's self-reward system. And, positive self-talk (or self-recognition) is critical for long-term maintenance of AC4P behavior. Thus, by allowing our recognition communication to stand alone and soak in, we enable the internalization of rewarding words that can be used later for self-motivation of additional AC4P behavior.

6. Use Tangibles for Symbolic Value

Tangible rewards can detract from the self-motivation aspect of quality recognition. If the focus of an AC4P recognition process is placed on a material reward, the words of appreciation can seem less significant. In turn, the beneficial impact on one's self-motivation is lessened.

On the other hand, tangible rewards can add to the quality of interpersonal recognition if they are delivered as tokens of appreciation. Rewards that include a relevant AC4P slogan, as on the AC4P wristband, can help to promote the desired behavior. But how you deliver a tangible reward will determine whether it adds to or subtracts from the long-term benefit of your praise.

The benefit of interpersonal recognition is weakened if the tangible is viewed as a payoff for the AC4P behavior. However, if the reward is seen as symbolic of going beyond the call of duty for another person's well-being, it strengthens the praise. Have the courage to tell it like it is: The AC4P wristband or another tangible reward is a token of appreciation or a symbol of going beyond the call.

7. Consider Secondhand Recognition

Up to this point, I've been discussing one-on-one verbal communication in which one person recognizes another for a particular AC4P behavior. It's also possible to recognize a person's outstanding efforts indirectly, and such an approach can have special advantages. Suppose, for example, you overhear me talk to another person about your outstanding presentation about the AC4P Movement. How will this secondhand recognition affect you? Will you believe my words of praise were genuine?

Sometimes people are suspicious of the genuineness of praise when it's delivered face-to-face. Is there an ulterior motive? Perhaps a favor is expected in return. Or maybe the recognition is seen merely as an extension of a communication exercise and thus devalued as sincere appreciation. Secondhand recognition, however, is not as easily tainted with these potential biases. Therefore, its genuineness is less suspect.

Suppose I tell you someone else in your workgroup told me about the superb job you did leading a certain group meeting. What will be the impact of this type of secondhand recognition? Chances are you'll consider the recognition authentic because I was only reporting what someone else said. Because that person reported your success to me rather than you, there was no ulterior motive for the indirect praise.

Such secondhand recognition can build a sense of belongingness or group cohesion among individuals. When you learn someone was bragging about your behavior, your sense of friendship with that person will likely increase.

As I emphasized in Chapter 3 when discussing trust-building, gossip can be beneficial – *if it's positive*. When we talk about the achievement of others in behavior-specific terms, we begin a cycle of positive communication that can support desired behavior, as well as activate self-talk for self-recognition and self-motivation.

Have the courage to initiate this cycle of positivism. We also set an example for the kind of interpersonal communication that enhances self-esteem, self-efficacy, personal control, optimism, and group cohesion. As explained in Chapter 2, these are the very person-states that increase the potential for AC4P behavior and the achievement of an interdependent culture of compassion.

A Summary

Referring to classic learning research, I made the case that success is more important than failure in developing and maintaining desired behaviors. This emphasis on success rather than corrective feedback should lessen the need for courage. It's usually more important to recognize people for their correct behaviors than to criticize them for their mistakes. But how we recognize people dramatically influences the impact of our interpersonal interaction. I offered seven basic guidelines to consider when planning to recognize others for their AC4P contributions.

This list of guidelines is not exhaustive, but it does cover the basics. Following these guidelines will increase the positive impact of interpersonal recognition. The most important point is that more recognition for AC4P behavior is needed, whether given firsthand or indirectly through positive gossip. It only takes a few seconds to deliver quality AC4P recognition.

Start giving AC4P recognition today – even for behaviors that occurred yesterday. Delayed recognition is better than no recognition. And, quality recognition does not need to occur face-to-face. Leaving a behavior-based and personal recognition message on phone-mail, e-mail, or in a written memo (formal or informal) can make a person's day. It shows you appreciate what you saw and helps to build that person's self-recognition script for later self-motivation. This behavior takes minimal courage and can reap benefits far greater than the little inconvenience required.

Perhaps realizing the positive impact we can have on people's behaviors and attitudes with relatively little effort will be self-motivating enough for us to muster the courage, if that is what is needed, to do more recognizing. Even more important, however, are the social consequences we receive when attempting to give quality recognition.

The reaction of the people who are recognized can have a dramatic impact on whether AC4P recognition increases or decreases throughout a culture. We need to know how to respond to recognition in order to assure quality AC4P recognition continues. This is our next and final topic of this chapter.

Accept Recognition Well

Most of us get so little recognition from others we are caught completely off guard when acknowledged for our commendable actions. We don't know how to accept recognition when it finally comes. Don't shy away when it does come; have the courage to embrace it.

Remember the basic behavioral-science principle: Consequences influence preceding behaviors. Thus, quality recognition increases the probability the behavior recognized will continue, and one's reaction to the recognition influences whether the behavior of recognizing someone will be attempted again. It's crucial to react appropriately when we receive recognition from others. Let's consider seven basic guidelines for receiving recognition.

1. Don't Deny or Disclaim

Often when I attempt to give quality AC4P recognition, I get a reaction that implies I'm wasting my time. I get disclaimer statements such as, "It really was nothing special" or, "Just doing my job." The most common reply: "No problem." This implies the commendable behavior is not special and should not have been recognized.

We need to accept recognition without denial and disclaimer statements, and without deflecting the credit to others. It's okay to show pride in our small-win accomplishments, even if others contributed to the successful outcome. After all, the vision of a compassionate AC4P culture includes everyone going beyond the call of duty for the well-being of others. In this context, numerous people deserve recognition daily.

Accept that recognition will be intermittent at best for everyone; and when your turn comes, accept the recognition for your most recent AC4P behavior and for the many prior AC4P behaviors you performed that went unnoticed. Keep in mind your genuine appreciation of the recognition will increase the chance that more recognition will be given by others.

2. Listen Actively

Listen actively to the person giving you recognition. You want to learn what you did, right? Plus, you can evaluate whether the recognition is given well. If the recognition does not pinpoint a particular behavior, you might ask the person, "What did I do to deserve this?" This will help to improve that person's method of giving recognition.

Of course, it's important not to seem critical but rather to show genuine appreciation for the special attention. Consider how difficult, yes how courageous, it is for many people to go out of their way to recognize others. So, revel in the fact you're receiving some recognition, even if its quality could be improved.

3. Use It Later for Self-Motivation

Most of your AC4P behaviors will go unnoticed. You perform many of these when no one else is around to observe you. Even when other people are available, they will likely be so preoccupied with their own routines they won't notice your extra effort. So when you finally do receive recognition for AC4P behavior, take it in as well-deserved.

Don't hesitate to relive this moment later by talking to yourself. Such self-recognition can motivate you to continue going beyond the call of duty on behalf of other people's well-being. As mentioned earlier, self-talk can help you muster the courage to perform more AC4P behavior.

4. Show Sincere Appreciation

You need to show sincere gratitude with a smile, a "Thank You," and perhaps special words like, "You've made my day." Your reaction to being recognized can determine whether similar recognition is apt to occur again. So be prepared to offer a sincere

"Thank You" and words that reflect your pleasure in the memorable interaction. And consider the courage the other person might have needed to give you your recognition.

I find it natural to add, "You've made my day" to the "Thank-You" because it's the truth. When people go out of their way to offer me quality recognition, they *have* made my day. I often relive such situations to improve a later day.

5. Reward the Recognition

When you accept recognition well, you reward the person for their appreciation. This can motivate that individual to do more recognizing, especially if the person is more of an introvert and requires courage to step out and speak up to give recognition.

Sometimes, you can do even more to assure the occurrence of more quality recognition. Specifically, you can recognize the person for recognizing you. You might say, for example, "I really appreciate you noticing my AC4P behavior and calling me a leader of the AC4P Movement." Such rewarding feedback provides direction and motivation for those aspects of the AC4P recognition process that are especially worthwhile and need to become routine.

6. Embrace the Reciprocity Norm

Some people resist receiving recognition because they don't want to feel obligated to give recognition to others. This is the reciprocity norm at work. If we want to achieve an AC4P culture, we need to embrace this norm. When you are nice to others, as when providing them with special praise, you increase the likelihood they will reciprocate by showing similar behavior. You might not receive the returned favor, but someone will.[27] See Chapter 5 for more on the cascading effect of reciprocity.

It's important to realize your genuine acceptance of quality recognition will activate the reciprocity norm; and the more this norm is activated from positive interpersonal communication, the greater the frequency of interpersonal recognition and AC4P behavior.

So accept recognition well, and embrace the reciprocity norm. The result will be more interpersonal involvement consistent with the vision of an AC4P culture of compassion. Again, interpersonal involvement does not come easy to all of us. The quality of AC4P interactions can go a long way to easing one's resistance to involvement.

7. Ask for Recognition

If you feel you deserve recognition, why not ask for it? In terms of courage, yes, asking for praise is easier if you are an extrovert compared to an introvert.

Your request might result in recognition viewed as less genuine than if it were spontaneous, but the outcome from such a request can be quite beneficial. You might receive some words worth reliving later for self-motivation. Most importantly, you will remind the other individual in a nice way that s/he missed a prime opportunity to offer quality recognition. This could be a valuable learning experience for that person.

Consider the possible beneficial impact from your statement to another person that you are pleased with a certain result of your extra effort, including your performance of particular AC4P behavior. With the right tone and affect, such verbal behavior will not seem like bragging but rather a declaration of personal pride in a small-win accomplishment – something more people should feel and relive for self-motivation. The other person will support your personal praise with supportive testimony, and this will bolster your self-motivation. Plus, you will teach the other person how to support the AC4P behaviors of others.

Many years ago, I instituted a self-recognition process among my research students that increased our awareness of the value of receiving praise, even when it's self-initiated. I told my students during class or group meetings they could request a standing ovation at any time. All they had to do was specify the behavior they felt deserved recognition and then ask for a standing ovation. Obviously, such recognition is not private, personal, and one-to-one, and therefore it's not optimal. Plus, the public aspect of this process inhibited many personal requests for a standing ovation.

However, over the years a number of my students have requested a standing ovation, and the experience has always been positive for everyone. Each request has included a solid rationale. Some students express pride in an exemplary grade on a project; others acknowledge an acceptance letter from a graduate school, internship, or journal editor. The actual ovation is fun and feels good, both on the giving or receiving end. Plus, we all learn the motivating process of behavior-based recognition, even when it doesn't follow all of the quality principles.

The Craving

William James, the first renowned American psychologist, wrote, "The deepest principle in human nature is the craving to be appreciated".[28] A little later John Dewey, the famous American educator who developed the field of school psychology, claimed, "The deepest urge in human nature is the desire to be important".[28] Then in 1936, Dale Carnegie advocated the key to winning friends and influencing people is to "always make the other person feel important".[28] How can we readily fulfill the human need to feel appreciated and important? The answer, of course, is to give and receive recognition well.

In Conclusion

Many excuses and barriers can be offered for the lack of large-scale application of effective AC4P interventions analogous to those described in this chapter. I explained three C-words reflecting the leadership qualities needed to achieve an AC4P culture of compassion: Competence, Commitment, and Courage.

Many people are competent and committed regarding the achievement of an AC4P culture. In other words, they know what to do, and are motivated to do whatever it takes to increase the quantity and quality of AC4P behaviors in educational, work, and community settings.

However, I suggest the missing link is often *moral* courage, or the audacity to step up, take an *interpersonal risk* and go beyond one's predictable routine on behalf of the well-being of other people, especially complete strangers.

Beyond competence (or self-efficacy), four person-states that influence courage in this context were discussed in Chapter 2 (i.e., self-esteem, belongingness, personal control, and optimism), and guidelines for cultivating an AC4P culture have been entertained in the first three chapters of this book.

The chapters in Parts II and III, authored by a variety of AC4P leaders, specify cost-effective techniques for increasing the frequency and effectiveness of AC4P behaviors in particular settings and for a designated meaningful purpose. Many of the AC4P applications describe the profound personal and interpersonal advantages of a particular AC4P intervention. These are the special reinforcing consequences that keep all of us in pursuit of an AC4P culture of compassion.

Test your *moral courage* as an AC4P leader by using these various intervention techniques. You can log on to ac4p.org and download airplane lifesaver cards, feedback cards, thank-you cards, and more.

Notes

1. *The American Heritage Dictionary* (1991) (2nd College Edition). New York, NY: Houghton Mifflin Company, p.333.
2. McCain, J., & Salter, M. (2004). *Why courage matters: The way to a braver life.* New York, NY: Random House, Inc.
3. Blanchard, K.P., Zigarmi, P., & Zigarmi, D. (1985). *Leadership and the one minute manager.* New York, NY: William Morrow and Company, Inc.
4. Geller, E.S. (1996). *The psychology of safety: How to improve behaviors and attitudes on the job.* Radnor, PA: Chilton Book Company; Geller, E.S. (1998). *Practical behavior-based safety: Step-by-step methods to improve your workplace.* Neenah, WI: J.J. Keller & Associates, Inc.; Geller, E.S. (2001). *The psychology of safety handbook.* Boca Raton, FL: CRC Press.
5. Kouzes, J.M., & Posner, B.Z. (2006). *A leader's legacy.* San Francisco, CA: John Wiley & Sons, Inc.
6. Geller, E.S. (1996). *The psychology of safety: How to improve behaviors and attitudes on the job.* Radnor, PA: Chilton Book Company; Geller, E.S. (2001). *The psychology of safety handbook.* Boca Raton, FL: CRC Press; Geller, E.S. (2005). *People-based safety: The source.* Virginia Beach, VA: Coastal Training Technologies Corporation; Geller, E.S. (2006). Reinforcement, reward, & recognition: Critical distinctions and a reality check. *Industrial Safety & Hygiene News, 40(3),* pp. 12,14; Geller, E.S. (2007). Why do people act that way? *Industrial Safety & Hygiene News, 41(10),* 21-22.
7. Mischel, W. (2004). Toward a integrative model for CBT: Encompassing behavior, cognition, affect, and process. *Behavior Therapy, 35,* 185-203.
8. Geller, E.S. (2008). *Leading people-based safety: Enriching your culture.* Virginia Beach, VA: Coastal Training Technologies Corporation; Geller, E.S., & Weigand, D.M. (2005). People-based safety: Exploring the role of personality in injury prevention. *Professional Safety, 50 (12),* 28-36.
9. Geller, E.S. (2001). *The psychology of safety handbook.* Boca Raton, FL: CRC Press., p. 378.
10. Reif, C.D, & Singer, B. (2000). Interpersonal flourishing: A positive health agenda for the new millennium. *Personality & Social Psychology Review, 4,* 30-44; Sarasson, B.R., Sarasson, I.G., &

Gurung, R.A.R. (1997). Close personal relationships and health outcome : A key to the role of social support. In S. Duck (Ed.) *Handbook of personal relationships* (2nd Edition) (pp.547-573). New York, NY: Wiley; Sarasson, B.B., Sarasson, I.G., & Pierce, G.R. (1990). *Social support: An interactional view*. New York, NY: Wiley.

11. Geller, E.S. (1999). Interpersonal trust: Key to getting the best from behavior-based safety coaching. *Professional Safety, 44(4),* 16-19; Geller, E.S. (2002). *The participation factor: How to increase involvement in occupational safety*. Des Plaines, IL: American Society of Safety Engineers.

12. Festinger, L. (1957). *A theory of cognitive dissonance.* Stanford, CA: Stanford University Press.

13. Geller, E.S., Bruff, C.D., & Nimmer, J.G. (1985). The "Flash for Life": A community prompting strategy for safety-belt promotion. *Journal of Applied Behavior Analysis, 18*, 145-159.

14. Cox, M.G., & Geller, E.S. (2011). Community prompting of safety-belt use: Impact of positive versus negative reminders. *Journal of Applied Behavior Analysis, 43(2),* 321-325; Farrell, L.V., Cox, M.G., & Geller, E.S. (2007). Prompting safety-belt use in the context of a belt-use law: The "Flash-for Life" revisited. *Journal of Safety Research, 38, 407-411.*

15. Geller, E.S., & Lehman, G.R. (1991). The buckle-up promise card: A versatile intervention for large-scale behavior change. *Journal of Applied Behavior Analysis, 24*, 91-94.

16. Streff, F.M., Kalsher, M.S., & Geller, E.S. (1993). Developing efficient workplace safety programs: Observations of response covariation. *Journal of Organizational Behavior Management, 13(2),* 3-15.

17. Geller, E.S. (2001). *The psychology of safety handbook.* Boca Raton, FL: CRC Press.

18. Cialdini, R.B. (2001). *Influence: Science and practice* (4th Edition). New York, NY: Harper Collins College Publishers.

19. Geller, E.S., Hickman, J.S., & Pettinger, C.B. (2004). The Airline Lifesaver: A 17-year analysis of a technique to prompt safety-belt use. *Journal of Safety Research, 35,* 357-366.

20. Geller, E.S. (2005). *People-based safety: The source.* Virginia Beach, VA: Coastal Training Technologies Corporation.

21. Geller, E.S. (1996). *The psychology of safety: How to improve behaviors and attitudes on the job.* Radnor, PA: Chilton Book Company, p. 148.

22. Sulzer-Azaroff, B., & Austin, J. (2000). Does BBS work? Behavior-based safety and injury reduction: A survey of the evidence. *Professional Safety, 45(7),* 19-24.

23. Geller, E.S. (1998). *Practical behavior-based safety: Step-by-step methods to improve your workplace.* Neenah, WI: J.J. Keller & Associates, Inc.

24. Geller, E.S. (1998). *Practical behavior-based safety: Step-by-step methods to improve your workplace.* Neenah, WI: J.J. Keller & Associates, Inc.; Geller, E.S. (2005). *People-based safety: The source.* Virginia Beach, VA: Coastal Training Technologies Corporation.

25. Chance, P. (1999). *Learning and behavior* (4th Edition). Belmont, CA: Wadsworth.

26. Thorndike, E.L. (1911). *Animal intelligence: Experimental studies.* New York, NY; Hafner, p. 174; Thorndike, E.L., (1931). *Human learning.* Cambridge, MA: MIT Press.

27. Cialdini, R.B. (2001). *Influence: Science and practice* (4th Edition). New York, NY: Harper Collins College Publishers; Gouldner, A.W. (1960). The norm of reciprocity: A preliminary statement. *American Sociology Review, 25,* 161-167.

28. Carnegie, D. (1936). *How to win friends and influence people* (1981 Edition). New York, NY: Simon & Schuster, p. 19.

CHAPTER 5

Nudging AC4P with Social Influence:
Practical Applications for Schools

Cory Furrow and E. Scott Geller

FOR AN AC4P CULTURE to thrive over the long term, self-motivation is essential (see Chapter 3). However, people sometimes need a slight extrinsic nudge to actively care for others, especially strangers. The social influence principles, founded on over 50 years of research by social psychologists, offer practical techniques to help make this happen – strategies to activate and/or support occurrences of AC4P behavior.

Social influence is perceived pressure or support from others that creates notable change in an individual's behavior. Do not confuse this with persuasion. We are not seeking to persuade a change in opinion or attitude. Persuasion does not necessarily change overt behavior.[1]

In this chapter we define practical behavior-change techniques derived from six basic social-influence principles – consistency, liking, reciprocity, social proof, authority, and scarcity. We illustrate how these principles and related techniques have been (or could be) used to nudge others to perform AC4P behaviors or to increase the probability certain AC4P behavior will continue.[2] Appropriate interventions based on these principles can help cultivate an AC4P culture of compassion, and propel the expansion of AC4P worldwide.

Before defining the social-influence principles and their applications, let's review the concepts relevant for appreciating the applicability of these principles – three types of behavior change and their connection to the Activator-Behavior-Consequence (ABC) Model of Applied Behavior Analysis, as explained in Chapter 1.

Three Types of Behavior Change

Conformity, compliance, and obedience are three types of behavior change that result from social influence. Note that conformity occurs when the social pressure is relatively low, whereas obedience follows the perception of high social pressure.[1]

Conformity

Conformity is an attempt to "fit-in." We conform when we alter our behavior to match the behavior of others.[1] To "fit in" students wear school colors or clothes to match the current fashion trend.

Compliance

Compliance comes about when we are directly or indirectly requested to change a behavior.[1] A direct request emanates from a interpersonal interaction, usually verbal communication. An indirect request uses a message or sign to solicit compliance. A professor personally asking a student to visit during office hours is a direct request to gain compliance. A sign posted on the professor's office door stating, "Please visit during these office hours," is an indirect request.

Obedience

When a perceived authority figure requests (or orders or commands) a change in behavior, obedience occurs to appease the authority.[1] Obedience reduces a follower's sense of personal control or choice. This in turn reduces self-motivation, as explained in Chapter 3. This de-motivating effect of obedience occurs whether the authority's request is direct (i.e., interpersonal) or indirect.

The ABC Model

How activators and consequences influence behavior is exemplified by the ABC Model of Applied Behavior Analysis (ABA). Simply stated, behavior is directed by activators and motivated by consequences.[3] As illustrated in Chapter 1, activators can be education/training programs, written/verbal prompts, online webinars, and modeling/demonstrations.[4] In a chemistry laboratory, an eye-washing station includes a sign with how-to-use instructions. This is a written instructional prompt.

Announcing the availability of a consequence makes for the most influential activators. Incentives activate behavior by announcing a certain reward will follow a designated behavior. In contrast, a disincentive warns people of the negative consequence or a penalty if certain undesired behavior occurs (e.g., "Miss class and your parents will be notified." "Bully a classmate and you'll be suspended.").

Consequences vary from rewards to penalties, social approval to disapproval, and to more severe outcomes.[4] Failing to brake and stop at a stop sign can produce irritating but temporary social disapproval (e.g., other drivers angrily honking their car horn), the more permanent financial cost of a penalty if the behavior is observed by a police officer, or a severe, even fatal crash – colliding with a pedestrian or another vehicle.

Social or interpersonal consequences are desirable to the extent they: a) offer an accurate perception of reality, b) contribute to developing or maintaining meaningful social relationships, or c) contribute to a desirable self-concept, according to Robert Cialdini and Noah Goldstein.[5]

Making an accurate, reality-based decision can have the consequence of helping to attain a goal. Develop meaningful relationships with classmates can make a course more enjoyable and also cultivate support for cooperative learning. A favorable self-concept increases self-esteem and perhaps one's confidence to perform AC4P behavior.[6]

Accuracy, social affiliation, and a favorable self-concept – motivating characteristics of consequences from social interaction – connect to three of the five person-states proposed in Chapter 2 to increase one's propensity to actively care – self-efficacy/competence (accuracy), belongingness (affiliation), and self-esteem (a positive self-concept).

One behavior can produce three desirable consequences. After hearing a convincing and engaging presentation, you observe your peers fundraising for a special school event. You pitch in to help. This environment-based AC4P behavior (see Chapter 2) is supported by each of three motivating consequences. Your behavior is an "accurate" consequence of a persuasive speech and reflects relevant and meaningful compliance. You gain social approval and avoid social disapproval from your peers by helping them solicit financial support for a worthwhile school function. Such meaningful behavior enhances your self-esteem or sense of self-worth.

Social-influence principles and related techniques can be understood and executed within the framework of the ABC Model of ABA. The six principles and techniques covered in the remainder of this chapter are essentially activators. But each infers desirable or undesirable consequences following relevant behavior. Most of these consequences relate to conformity, compliance and obedience either in combination or alone – the three consequence categories defined by Cialdini and Goldstein.[5]

The Consistency Principle

The first of the six social-influence principles is consistency. Here is how it can work: After a university class, Mike and Dan walk together to their next class. Dan lights up a cigarette. During the walk, Dan says he'd like to quit smoking for his health. He seems to feel guilty about smoking. However, Dan verbalizes a convincing rationalization: "Cigarettes relieve my stress." Before entering the next classroom, any guilt about smoking is dissipated. Dan's self-talk convinced him reducing stress by smoking a cigarette overshadowed any future and uncertain costs to his personal health.

The well-known Theory of Cognitive Dissonance was developed by Leon Festinger.[7] Cognitive Dissonance rattles people when they realize their behaviors are inconsistent with their beliefs, attitudes, or values. The smoker experienced dissonance when he said cigarettes are bad while continuing to smoke one. To ease this disturbing dissonance, he identified what he perceived as a soon and certain health benefit from smoking (i.e., stress relief).

Self-Perception Theory, an extension of Cognitive Dissonance Theory, was proposed ten years later by Daryl Bem.[8] According to Self-Perception Theory we validate our values, attitudes, or beliefs (internal attributes) by observing our own behaviors. For example, Tim is passionate about sports (e.g., football, basketball, and baseball) and fitness. He believes these passions emanate from his dedicated participation in sports since elementary school. As an athlete in high school, he trained in a gym and lettered in three sports. Tim includes fitness as a personal value and he *chooses* to perform behavior consistent with that value.

Note the critical word *chooses*. Self-perception is only influenced by behavior perceived to be personally chosen. Behavior perceived to be influenced entirely by external contingencies (e.g., incentives/rewards or disincentives/penalties) does not come to define personal values, attitudes, or beliefs. Likewise, cognitive dissonance is absent when attitude-discrepant behavior is perceived to be controlled by extrinsic consequences (e.g., financial compensation).

The techniques explained below – foot-in-the-door, social labeling and commitment – apply the *Consistency* principle to influence the behavior of others. Remember the critical role of choice. When we believe our inconsistent behavior or attitude was controlled by outside factors, we are not disrupted by cognitive dissonance and do not feel compelled to adjust our behavior, attitude, or perception of self.[9]

Foot in the Door

The *Foot-in-the-Door* (FITD) technique gains compliance with a relatively large request by first obtaining compliance to a smaller, related request.[10] In preparing for a group presentation, ask a group member to develop the title slide. After completing this task to your approval, ask this team member to develop several more slides for the class presentation.

Jonathan Freedman and Scott Fraser empirically demonstrated the FITD technique with a seminal field study.[10] The researchers went door-to-door and asked homeowners to post a large sign on their front lawn. For the Large-Request-First condition, homeowners were shown a picture of a large obtrusive sign stating "Drive Carefully," and asked if they would allow the researchers to place the same sign in their yard. Of these homeowners (n=24), only 16.7% complied.

In contrast, another group of homeowners were asked if they'd be willing to place a small 3" X 3" sign in their window that stated, "Be a Safe Driver," as a Small-Request-First (or FITD) condition. Two weeks later, those homeowners who complied with the small-sign request were asked if they would place the same large sign used in the Large-Request-First condition in their front yard. Of the 25 homeowners who agreed with the small request first, 76% permitted the large sign in their yard.

Social Labeling

When an individual is assigned a desired attribute, attitude, or belief and is then asked to comply with a behavior related to that label, social labeling has occurred.[11] If the social label is desirable, the individual wants to behave consistent with it.

Cory applied the social-labeling technique when managing the data entry/verification process for the Center for Applied Behavior Systems at Virginia Tech. During initial training, Cory gave new researchers supportive and corrective feedback as they practiced the data-processing task. Afterward, he gave especially competent students two positive labels by commenting, "You seem to be detail-oriented and obviously care about doing quality work."

After 15 minutes or so, Cory returned and asked the competent student researchers how things were going as he spot-checked their work. These new researchers were highly focused on their work and asked many thoughtful questions. They appeared to do their best work in order to match the social label Cory had given them.

Supportive Research. To increase charitable donations, Robert Kraut applied a similar social-labeling technique.[12] Homeowners were asked to make a charitable donation for the American Heart Association by a research assistant (RA) acting as a door-to-door volunteer. Participants were split into two conditions, depending on whether they agreed to make a donation (i.e., the Charitable or Uncharitable condition). In both conditions, participants received the same leaflet supporting the charity.

Participants in the Charitable condition were randomly assigned to one of two groups. One group received the leaflet with a card stating, "Charitable people give generously to help a good cause and those less fortunate than themselves. Are you one?"[13] The other received the same leaflet and card, but the RA added the personal statement, "You are a generous person. I wish more of the people I met were as charitable as you."[13]

Similarly, those who didn't make a donation were randomly assigned to one of two groups. One group received the same leaflet given to those in the Charitable condition, but the attached card stated, "Uncharitable people give excuses and refuse to help others. Are you one?"[14]

The second group in the Uncharitable condition, received the same leaflet and card, but a personal label was added: "Let me give you one of our health leaflets anyway. We've been giving them to everyone, even people like you who are uncharitable and don't normally give to these causes."[14]

One to two weeks after the leaflets, cards, and personal labels had been distributed, the same homeowners were asked by a different RA, posing as a door-to-door volunteer, whether they would like to donate to help raise money for multiple sclerosis. Individuals in the Charitable condition (n=37) who had received the personal label donated an average of $.70 (equivalent to approximately $3.67 in 2013), whereas those in the Charitable condition who had not received the personal label (n=62) donated an average of $.41 (equivalent to approximately $2.15 in 2013).[15]

Interestingly, individuals in the Uncharitable condition who received the uncharitable label (n=27) donated significantly less money (p<.05) than did those who had not received the uncharitable label (n=27). Those who got the uncharitable label donated an average of $.23 (equivalent to approximately $1.20 in 2013). Those in the group without the personal statement that implied an uncharitable label donated an average of $.33 (equivalent to approximately $1.73 in 2013).

These results suggest people behave consistently with reasonable labels given to them. Participants who received a charitable label through a personal statement donated more than participants who did not receive the label. Similarly, participants who received a label reflecting uncharitability donated less than uncharitable participants who had not received a personal statement implying uncharitability.

Consider the disadvantage of giving someone a negative label. A person might behave undesirably to be consistent with a negative label such as being lazy, a poor reader, or an underachiever. A negative label like "underachiever" can be an excuse to put less effort into achieving a personal or group goal. A positive label might activate and/or support desirable behaviors such as being energetic, conscientious, or a diligent worker. However, the type of positive label is critical, according to programmatic research by Carol Dweck.[16]

Ability vs. Effort Labels. Dr. Dweck and her colleagues gave hundreds of early adolescents a set of ten fairly difficult problems from the nonverbal portion of an IQ test. Afterward, all participants were praised individually for their performance on the test, but the nature of the praise was varied systematically. For half of the students, the praise was based on their *ability*. They were each told: "Wow, you got eight right. That's a really good score. You must be smart at this".[17]

The other students were each praised with a positive social label for their *effort* with these words, "Wow, you got eight right. That's a really good score. You must have worked really hard."[18]

Both groups scored equivalently on the IQ test. But researchers noted significant differences in students' behavior following their *ability* vs. *effort* label. All students had the choice to work on a challenging new task they could learn from. Most of those with the ability label rejected this opportunity. Apparently "they didn't want to do anything that could expose their flaws and call into question their talent".[18] In contrast, 90 percent of the students praised for their *effort* welcomed the opportunity of a challenging new task from which they could learn.

Later, when all of these students performed less effectively on some additional more difficult problems, their reaction to failure feedback was influenced by the prior label given them (i.e., ability vs. effort). The *ability* kids felt like failures. They believed they did not live up to their ability; and they rated the task as "not fun anymore."

The *effort* group saw in their failure a need to try harder. They did not perceive any indictment of their intellect, and they did not indicate a lack of enjoying the problem-solving task. "Many of them said that the hard problems were the most fun."[18]

After experiencing these difficult problems, the researchers gave the adolescents some easier problems to solve. The performance of the *ability*-labeled students plummeted. The *effort*-labeled students performed increasing more effectively. In the profound words of Dr. Dweck, "Since this was a kind of IQ test, you might say that praising ability lowered the students' IQs. And that praising their effort raised them."[19]

A final difference showed up when the adolescents were asked to write down their opinions of the problem-solving tasks they completed for students at other schools. A space was provided on the survey form for the students to report the personal scores they received on the problems. To the researchers' surprise and disappointment, 40 percent of the *ability*-labeled students reported higher grades than they actually earned. In the author's words, "We took ordinary children and made them into liars by telling them they were smart."[19]

Bottom line: Focus on the process (or effort) rather than the outcome (or results) when praising another person's performance. Cory focused on the process behaviors of the research students rather than giving them an ability label. He did not praise students for being highly competent, but rather for being highly task-focused and for asking thoughtful questions.

Commitment

In 2008, Maureen took out a small loan to help pay for college. The loan officer reviewed different loan options and payment plans with Maureen and her dad. After reviewing the various options, Maureen selected the loan that best fit her current financial situation. Then, Maureen signed the loan agreement in front of the loan officer and her dad, committing Maureen to make monthly payments for a year.

Maureen's experience epitomizes the three components that increase one's propensity to honor a commitment – choice, active, and public.[20] Maureen chose to actively sign the commitment document in the presence of her dad and the loan officer.

Perceived Choice. As a teacher, imagine telling your students the final exam will be in multiple-choice format. This comes across as top-down control, with no perceived choice. Now consider an alternative approach: Select two test formats (e.g., essay or multiple-choice) and let the students choose between the two. The students will perceive some personal choice in this situation which could facilitate self-motivation (as discussed in Chapter 3). In most cases, the majority of students will vote for multiple-choice, the format you prefer.

When a decision-maker perceives a sense of choice, his or her decision is considered authentic and self-endorsed.[21] People who make a commitment without perceiving some choice are less likely to honor it.[7]

Back to the student-loan example: Maureen felt personal choice when selecting her student loan. There was really no rational alternative to that particular loan. Maureen had to get the loan if she wanted to pay tuition. But because Maureen was able to choose from various loan options, she perceived her decision as self-directed and self-endorsed.

Active. The second component to increasing one's propensity to honor a commitment is to make it active. Signing a document, shaking hands, or succumbing to fraternity hazing are active commitments involving behavior. Maureen actively signed the student loan that committed her to make monthly payments. Without such action, a commitment is passive and less binding. It's like verbally making a promise without any active assurance.[22]

Public. Making a commitment in front of others also increases the propensity to honor that commitment. Social consequences are anticipated from behaviors consistent or inconsistent with a public commitment. A public commitment implies possible social approval or disapproval following behavior consistent or inconsistent with the commitment, respectively.[23]

Figures 5.1 and 5.2 depict a public commitment intervention applied at an AC4P safety seminar for safety leaders, supervisors and maintenance personnel at Delta Airlines. After giving a half-day workshop on the AC4P principles and applications for the safety and well-being of others, Scott Geller walked to the back of the auditorium and signed his name to a "Declaration of Interdependence" as a public commitment to look out for the safety and well-being of others (Figure 5.1). Then, Scott requested the audience to follow suit.

Figure 5.1 Scott makes a commitment.

Social context was probably critical in influencing most of the workshop participants to sign this declaration (Figure 5.2), which is displayed in the break-room for the maintenance employees of Delta Airlines at the Hartsfield-Jackson Atlanta International Airport, Atlanta, Georgia. Scott's request was both public and voluntary in nature, contributing to the effectiveness of an active exercise designed to inspire awareness of the AC4P concepts and the development of relevant action plans. This real-world example of obtaining group commitment is applicable to a number of circumstances in elementary, middle, and high schools, as well as colleges and universities.

Figure 5.2. The workshop participants make a commitment.

Consider the discussion of SMARTS goal setting in Chapter 3. The final "S" in the SMARTS acronym represents Shared – making a public commitment. Sharing goals with others creates internal and external accountability. Not only are people motivated to make their behavior consistent with their commitment to achieve a specific goal (i.e., internal accountability), they also want others to see them living up to their commitment (i.e., external accountability).

AC4P Applications

The *Consistency* principle offers a plethora of AC4P applications. The FITD technique can increase the occurrence of AC4P behavior among friends, colleagues, and even strangers. First, start with a small request like "Please wear the AC4P wristband to signify your intention to join the AC4P Movement." Then, follow with a larger request for this person to give another person supportive and/or corrective feedback regarding behavior related to AC4P.

Note these requests can be interpersonal (e.g., from a student to a teacher, a teacher to another teacher, or a parent to a child) or intrapersonal (i.e., self-talk to perform more AC4P behavior). Compliance with the second larger request makes it reasonable to appeal for more effortful behavior (e.g., "Would you watch another person perform that task with a behavioral checklist, and determine the percentage of optimal vs. suboptimal behavior?").

Social labeling is a subtle way to promote AC4P behaviors. Simply give a person a particular desirable and suitable social label (e.g., "You seem to be someone who really cares about the well-being of others") and then follow with a request, "Would you mind providing behavior-based feedback to individuals regarding the quality of their AC4P behavior?"

The AC4P label will increase the probability the targeted individual will comply with your AC4P request. Of course, the first request in the FITD example (i.e., to wear an AC4P wristband) reflects social labeling. Those who wear the AC4P wristband display an AC4P label, and this will likely increase their propensity to perform AC4P behavior.

Leaders of the AC4P Movement have used the social labeling tactic to cultivate an AC4P culture in elementary schools. As detailed in Chapter 6, teachers rewarded two students daily with an AC4P wristband to wear for the day after performing or writing an AC4P story. These two students were labeled publically as the "Actively Caring Heroes of the Day," and they proudly wore the AC4P wristband. Systematic evaluations indicated these students performed more AC4P behavior on the days they wore the AC4P wristband, presumably to live up to the positive social label they had received for one day.

A commitment strategy to promote AC4P behavior for environmental conservation was used recently by research students in the Center for Applied Behavior Systems (CABS). Customers leaving a large grocery store were asked by researchers if they'd like to increase their use of reusable grocery bags for purchased groceries. When customers gave a positive response, the research assistant offered a hangtag to hook on a vehicle's rearview mirror as a reminder. Then, the customers were asked to sign the back of the hangtag as a part of their commitment to use reusable grocery bags.

Notice how this social-influence strategy applied the commitment techniques to enhance compliance. First, customers chose to use reusable grocery bags. Then, they signed the hangtag in front of the research assistant, making the commitment active and public. Subsequently, they were reminded of their pro-environment commitment whenever they looked at the card hanging from the rear-view mirror.

The Liking/Ingratiation Principle

We like to be liked, asserts the *Liking* principle.[24] Naturally, people are more likely to comply with a request from others they like, and to actively care for the well-being of these individuals. Ingratiation refers to attempts to get others to like you.[1] Relatively convenient strategies for getting others on board with the AC4P Movement are provided by this social-influence principle of Liking.

Similarity

We tend to like people who are similar to us, and we are more likely to comply with requests from these individuals. Similarities can vary from comparable opinions and attitudes to backgrounds and past experiences, attire, and notable behaviors.[25] It's more likely "birds of a feather flock together" than "opposites attract."

Gaining compliance through similar attire was tested in a field study conducted at Purdue University in 1971. Research assistants (dressed in either collegiate or hippy attire) randomly asked for a dime to make a long-distance phone call from either collegiate or hippy-dressed students (n=384) they encountered in a hallway near a dining facility. Participants were more likely to give a research assistant (RA) a dime when the RA wore similar attire (i.e., collegiate or hippy attire).[26]

In a related study, the experimenter told a RA and the participant they shared a similar fingerprint type. In the Common-Fingerprint condition, the participant and RA were told they shared a common fingerprint type; while in the Rare-Fingerprint condition, the shared fingerprint type was considered rare.

In a Control condition, the experimenter did not comment on the relative uniqueness of their shared fingerprint type. After the experimenter dismissed the two individuals, the RA asked the participant to review a document for a class and provide feedback.[27]

Of 29 participants in the Control-Fingerprint condition, 48.3% complied with the RA's request. In the Common-Fingerprint condition, compliance increased to 54.8% of 31 participants. In the Rare-Fingerprint condition, 82.1% of 28 participants complied with the RA's request.

Interestingly, a person can gain favor or compliance by faking or claiming a false similarity. In the fingerprint study, for example, the RA and participant didn't really share the same fingerprint type. But this false similarity was enough to gain compliance.

Now consider this true story: Stephanie's task was to convince county residents to make a donation to fund the construction of a new high school, following the collapse of the roof on the old high school. Stephanie was the best at convincing others to make large donations. Her secret: "Appear to be like them." When Stephanie heard a southern accent over the phone, she faked a southern accent. If the person stated a personal opinion or interest, Stephanie faked similarity: "I feel the same" or "I do that too." Stephanie's ability to create a fake similarity enabled her to gain more donations than her co-workers. Of course, it's critical the apparent similarity is believable, which is not the case in the illustration.

Compliments

Who doesn't like to receive a compliment? Complimenting people is a quick and easy way to gain their favor.[28] You increase the target's self-esteem and perhaps a sense of competence (see Chapter 3). You also set the stage for reciprocity (as discussed later in this chapter). Interestingly, even if the target is aware of an ulterior motive behind the flattery, the target still views the person giving the compliment as favorable.[24]

Professors are suckers for flattery. Many undergraduates seeking a letter of recommendation or acceptance into a graduate program flood professors with compliments and flattery. A student approached Scott and said, "Dr. Geller, your inspirational teaching of the introductory psychology course convinced me to change my major to psychology!" A few weeks later the same student came to Scott with a request: "Dr. Geller, would you write me a letter of recommendation for a summer internship program?"

Even if Scott suspected an ulterior motive behind the prior compliment, the undergraduate still increased the probability of receiving a letter of recommendation. Since students seldom give these kinds of "life-changing" compliments to their professors, the compliment in this case was rare and impacted by the Principle of Scarcity, as explained later in this chapter.

Compliments from a student to a classmate, a teaching assistant, or a teacher might be viewed as uncommon and perhaps insincere. Still, individuals who receive a compliment are extremely pleased and are more likely to comply with a request.

Bottom line: When people say, "Flattery will get you everywhere," they are probably more right than wrong.

Mere-Exposure Effect

When a new song is first played on the radio, it may not get a positive review from listeners. As the song continues to be played, it may "grow on" the listeners. From mere exposure, listeners can develop a positive attitude toward a song. The impact of repeated exposure was demonstrated in a series of studies conducted by Robert Zajonc.[29]

In one of his experiments, each participant was shown a series of photos. The relative frequency of showing each photo varied among participants. After viewing the photos, participants rated how much they liked each photo. Higher favorability ratings went to those photos viewed more frequently.[29]

Advertisers use the mere-exposure effect constantly to sell their products. We see Coca-Cola products on bill boards, vending machines, in TV commercials, in restaurants, and on the sides of trucks. Does such excessive exposure increase sales of Coke products? Apparently the Coca-Cola Company believes so, given the amount of money spent to promulgate these exposures.

The mere-exposure effect can apply to interpersonal relationships. Initially, one's attitude toward a teacher, classmate, or school administrator might be neutral. Through frequent interaction, one's impression of another person can become positive. This exposure can then influence one-on-one communication and relationship building. Now we have the possibility of true friendship and increased potential for interpersonal AC4P behavior.

AC4P Applications

The AC4P interventions accomplished by Virginia Tech (VT) students at Chardon High School (CHS) exemplify the influential power of claiming similar backgrounds (see Chapter 10). Both educational settings were sites of tragic school shootings. After the shootings at CHS in 2012, student leaders contacted AC4P leaders at VT to help recover and move forward.

When the AC4P leaders talked with leaders and students at CHS, they discussed their "common background" to make critical connections. Also, when giving workshops and coaching CHS staff and students, the AC4P leaders wear blue jeans and an AC4P T-shirt customized for CHS, approximating the common attire of most high-school students.

The SAPS process (see Chapter 6) rewards others for their AC4P behavior and promotes exposure of AC4P through the social media. Briefly, the four-step process includes the following components:

See: Observe an AC4P behavior; ***Act:*** Thank the person for actively caring and reward the individual with an AC4P wristband embossed with a unique ID number; ***Pass:*** Ask the AC4P person to look for AC4P behavior from another individual and then pass on the wristband to reward him/her for the AC4P behavior observed; and ***Share:*** Ask the AC4P person to share their AC4P story at ac4p.org, including the ID number of the wristband received for particular AC4P behavior.

Typically, a compliment is given in the "Act" step of the SAPS process (e.g., "Thank you for actively caring; that was really nice of you"). This initial compliment helps to gain favor from the AC4P individual, and this is supported by the gift of an AC4P wristband. This gained favor increases the AC4P person's propensity to share the AC4P story at the ac4p.org website, and to look for opportunities to reward another individual with the AC4P wristband.

The AC4P Movement gains favorable exposure to expand and grow through the mere-exposure effect, like advertising agencies trying to sell a product. Leaders of the AC4P Movement are already using various techniques to gain favorable exposure, including Facebook.com pages, the ac4p.org website, scholarship (such as this book), t-shirts, media exposure (e.g., radio interviews and local/national television stations), keynote addresses at professional conferences, webinars, as well as the AC4P wristband.

The Reciprocity Principle

Ricky, a father and a husband, suffered a severe stroke that forced him to go on disability. Community members heard about this and came to the rescue. Almost every day for a few months, church members took turns cooking dinner for the family of four. Neighbors and friends transported Ricky to therapy. Financial collections were made to help with the bills. In fact, one relative paid all of the bills for the entire year.

Support wasn't limited to these AC4P behaviors. Community members gathered their resources to construct a new roof on Ricky's home, install heating and air-conditioning systems, and remodel the home to make it handicapped assessable.[30]

These AC4P individuals are certainly caring people and their AC4P behavior is noteworthy, but it's likely the Norm of Reciprocity played a role.

While all of these individuals went above and beyond the call of duty, some of their AC4P behavior could have been influenced by a "pay-back" mindset.

Ricky, who is Cory Furrow's father, had dedicated much of his time actively caring for others in their community, from leadership at church to Boy Scouts of America. So when Ricky's family needed help, the community stepped to the plate and provided the much-needed support.

Norm of Reciprocity

The Norm of Reciprocity was identified by Alvin Gouldner in 1960 as an obligation to help individuals who have provided you with help, and to retaliate against those who have caused you harm.[31] Many laws and governing societies originated from the Norm of Reciprocity (e.g., Babylon's Code of Hammurabi[32]).

Many human interactions, exchanges, and traditions existing on a smaller scale involve this social norm. In the western culture, gift exchanges occur on special occasions such as birthdays, weddings, baby showers, and holidays. Other reciprocal behaviors develop as families take turns preparing holiday dinners or alternating as host. After being a dinner guest at a friend's home, a couple typically reciprocates with a dinner at their home.

Exchanging holiday cards in December is an enduring tradition in the American culture. Many families go to great lengths to ensure they send holiday cards, including Christmas, Hanukkah, Kwanzaa to important individuals/families in their lives. Plus, when a family receives a holiday card from people to whom they originally failed to send a card, they typically send one in return or at least put the sender on their "holiday-card list" for the following year.

This Norm of Reciprocity was tested by two social psychologists, Philip Kunz and Michael Woolcott. They sent 578 Christmas cards to a random group of Chicago residents they didn't know. To their surprise, 20% of the 578 recipients responded by either calling the researchers to reestablish a lost connection or sending them a Christmas card. Some recipients continued to send these researchers Christmas cards for a number of consecutive years after the first year the experiment was conducted.[33]

The Norm of Reciprocity occurs in two forms: 1) direct reciprocity, and 2)

indirect reciprocity. Direct reciprocity (DR) is the exchange of helpful or harmful behavior between two individuals.[34] It's helpful when one AC4P act begets another; it's harmful when an individual seeks revenge or "pay back" for an unkind act directed toward him/her.

As shown in the illustration, a time delay may exist between these behavioral exchanges. Still, the initial exchange can lead to repeated interactions and/or exchanges in the future. Indeed, it's common to experience these repeated interactions between friends, families, and acquaintances.

If exchanges are consistently harmful, the two individuals can easily become long-term enemies, like the Hatfields and the McCoys feuding over old grudges. Even though the negative side of reciprocity is noteworthy, here we focus on the positive side of reciprocity and its connection to AC4P behavior.

Direct Reciprocity

As depicted in Figure 5.3, and explained previously in the Christmas-card study, the first AC4P behavior is initiated by Person A. Person B's reciprocation is based upon the initial behavior from Person A. For example, direct reciprocity (DR) can occur when you give a pencil to a friend and at a later time, she willingly complies with your request for notebook paper.

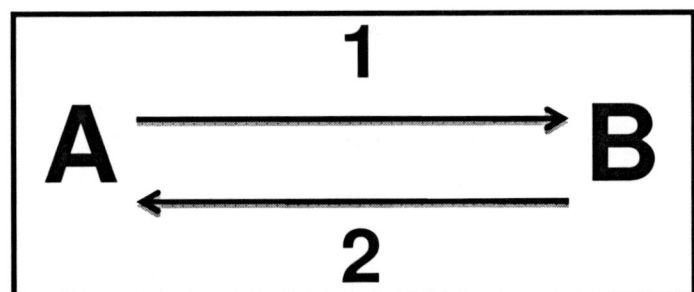

Figure 5.3. Each letter represents an individual, and "1" represents the intial AC4P behavior, whereas "2" is the reciprocal AC4P behavior.

Make the First Move. Reciprocity is a powerful activator that influences compliance. For this to occur, though, it's important to make the first move (e.g., be the first to give a gift, provide help, or make a donation); then follow with a request for AC4P behavior from the recipient.

One study found students who *received* gifts (e.g., t-shirt and travel mug) *before* a request to reward people's pro-environment behaviors with thank-you cards were more likely to pass out the thank-you cards than were students who were *promised* the same gifts *after* passing out five thank-you cards.[35]

Helping or gift-giving prior to a request is one way to increase compliance from others. Making a concession is another way to obtain agreement with a request.

"Door-in-the-face" is the term for this influence technique as discussed below.

In another study, The Norm of Reciprocity was used to increase the reuse of towels in a hotel to save energy, financial costs, and help protect the environment.[36] Researchers gained 30% participation in the reuse of hotel towels with the following "if-then" contingency: "Partner with us to help save the environment. In exchange for your participation in this program, *we at the hotel will donate* a percentage of the energy savings to a nonprofit environmental protection organization. The environment deserves our combined efforts. You can join us by reusing your towels during your stay."[37]

Participation grew to 42.5% with the following Reciprocity message: "We're doing our part for the environment. Can we count on you? Because we are committed to preserving the environment, *we have made a financial contribution* to a nonprofit environmental protection organization on behalf of the hotel and its guests. If you would like to help us in recovering the expense, while conserving natural resources, please reuse your towels during your stay."[38]

This study suggests the Norm of Reciprocity is more effective at gaining participation in a hotel towel-reusing program than an "if-then" contingency. Again, being the first to perform an AC4P behavior can activate the Norm of Reciprocity and gain compliance to a follow-up request.

Door-in-the-Face. "Can I have ten dollars?" a person asks you. More than likely you will turn down this plea, unless it comes from a friend who gave you money in the past. After you reject this first request, the person asks, "Could I have one dollar instead?" If you have the dollar, you might honor this request. Here's the critical question: Would you be more inclined to give up one dollar after your refusal to give up ten dollars than if you had never received the first request?

The answer is "yes," according to empirical research. People are more likely to comply after rejecting a request that is more costly, in terms of time, effort, or money. This is called Door-in-the-Face (DITF).[39] The DITF technique increases compliance to a small request by first making a larger related request that is expected to get rejected.

In a seminal study by Cialdini et al., the DITF was used to get college students to volunteer two hours of their time to serve as a chaperon for juveniles.[39] As expected, a low number of college students (16%) agreed to volunteer. But when the same request followed a larger request to chaperon a group of juveniles for two hours a week for a minimum of two years, significantly more students (i.e., 50%) volunteered for the smaller request.

Now, what if someone asks you for a thousand dollars and then follows up with a request for one dollar. Would you give up the dollar? A small request is likely to be declined if the initial request is too large, research evidence suggests. The request may seem manipulative and illegitimate, and the credibility of the requester is impaired, rationalized Joseph Schwarzwald et al.[40]

Indirect Reciprocity

Indirect reciprocity (IR) occurs when the behavior of a third individual is activated following awareness of a previous AC4P interaction between two other individuals.[41] Figure 5.4 illustrates two types of IR: 1) vicarious reciprocity, and 2) pay-it-forward reciprocity.[42]

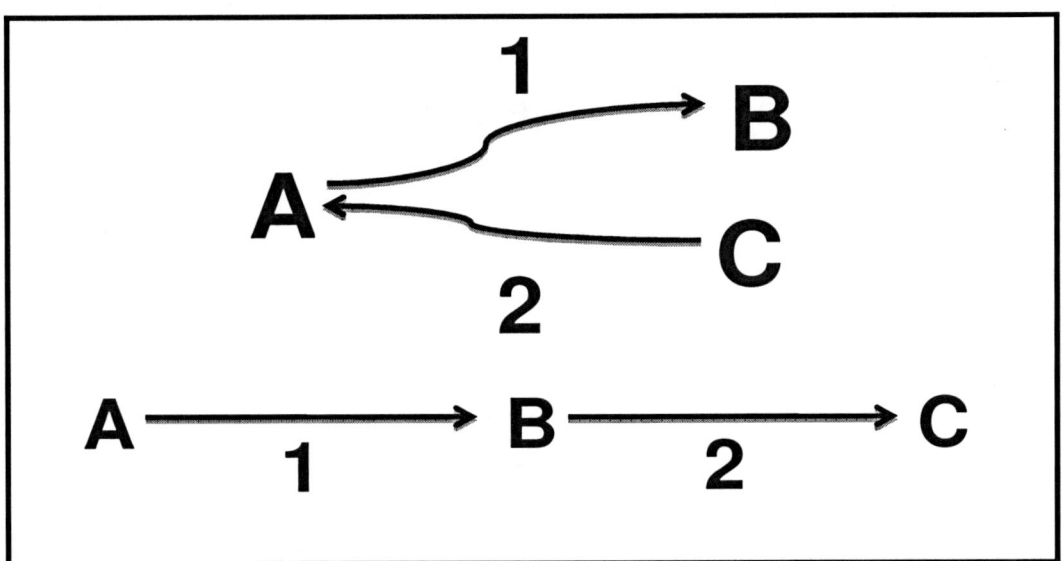

Figure 5.4, Top: Vicarious reciprocity: Person A helps Person B and then Person C helps Person A. Bottom: Pay-it forward reciprocity: Person A helps Person B, then Person B then helps Person C.

Vicarious Reciprocity. Vicarious reciprocity occurs when Person C observes Person A helping Person B, and then Person C chooses to help Person A as a result. For example, in a bullying situation, Person C (the bystander) might defend Person B (the victim) from Person A (the bully) by fighting back or reporting the conflict to an authority figure.

Recall the previously mentioned study from Goldstein et al. that increased the reuse of hotel towels. In their reciprocity condition, the researchers induced vicarious reciprocity. That is, the hotel (A) made a financial contribution to an environmental-protection organization (B), and the hotel guest (C) is asked to help the hotel recover financially from its donation by reusing towels.

Pay-it-Forward Reciprocity. The third individual's behavior (Person C) differentiates pay-it-forward reciprocity from vicarious reciprocity. Unlike vicarious reciprocity where Person C rewards Person A, in pay-it-forward reciprocity, Person C is a recipient of the helpful act.[41] Suppose at a cafeteria, Person A purchases the next customer's coffee (Person B); then Person B performs a similar AC4P behavior for Person C by purchasing his/her ice cream. Additionally, Person C might continue this linear chain of reciprocity by paying-it-forward to another individual.

Analogously, the Center for Applied Behavior Systems conducted an observational field study of pay-it-forward reciprocity at a university cafeteria.[42] To enter the buffet-style cafeteria, students pay a $6.00 admission fee. Due to the high volume and a rather slow financial transaction process, a long entrance/payment line was common. Periodically, a RA entered this line.

For all conditions, an 8 ½" X 11" sign (illustrated in Figure 5.5) was posted at the cash register, suggesting diners pay for the next person's meal. In the No-Reciprocity condition, the RA entered the line, paid for his/her meal and did not interact with any of the diners standing in line.

Figure 5.5. The sign at the cash register during all four phases of the study.

In the No-Interaction Reciprocity condition, the RA did not interact with the next diner but paid for his/her meal. In the Interaction-Reciprocity condition, the RA turned to the person behind him/her, pointed to the sign and said, "I just read this sign and I want to support the Actively Caring for People Movement, so I'm going to buy your meal," and then paid for the meal of this next diner.

In the No-Reciprocity condition, only 6.8% of 148 diners paid for the next person's meal. In the No-Interaction Reciprocity condition, 15.6% of 122 diners paid for the next person's meal; and in the Interaction-Reciprocity condition, 24.6% of 183 diners paid for the next person's meal. In this setting, pay-it-forward reciprocity was most likely to occur when the Norm of Reciprocity was activated with both a prompt (indirect request) suggesting how to reciprocate and a supportive verbal exchange (a direct request).

AC4P Applications

Reciprocity is a fundamental influence tactic in the SAPS process of the AC4P Movement. To clarify: A person rewards another person with an AC4P wristband for performing an AC4P behavior. Once the wristband has been accepted, the recipient may feel a sense of indebtedness. The rewarding individual asks the wristband recipient to use the wristband to reward someone else for his/her AC4P behavior. Such pay-it-forward behavior will alleviate any sense of indebtedness. Compliance with the request to pass on the wristband for AC4P behavior is increased through reciprocity.

The door-in-the-face technique can be used to activate others to actively care. You could challenge people to perform an AC4P act every day for a month. For most people, this would be a difficult task. When this request is rejected, follow with an easier request like: "Perform an AC4P act three times a week for a month." Of course, this same technique can be used to request others to reward observed AC4P behavior or provide behavior-based feedback to benefit another person's health, safety, or welfare.

Let's say you actively cared for an individual and this individual wants to reciprocate. Reciprocation may take place in the form of money, a free meal, or a promise to help you in the future. Regardless, as a result of your AC4P behavior, this individual feels a sense of indebtedness to return the favor. We recommend specifying how this sense of indebtedness can be relieved: "Simply pay it forward by actively caring for another person." Your suggestion may nudge pay-it-forward reciprocity, enabling your one AC4P behavior to have a ripple effect that spreads AC4P behavior.

The Social Proof Principle

John accompanies a group of friends in his school's à la carte lunch line. For a few minutes the group exchanges opinions on which items seem to be the most appetizing. From their discussions, John assumes a wide variety of items would be selected. Brittany is first and selects the grilled chicken salad. Next is Megan, who also selects the grilled chicken salad. Then, Joanne does the same. Each of the girls in the line selects the grilled chicken salad.

We look to others for guidance about which behaviors are appropriate or inappropriate in a particular situation, especially in an unfamiliar setting, according to the *Social Proof* principle. For instance, the individuals in the opening example discussed which item seemed the best to order and then each ordered the same item.

People apply the *Social Proof* principle through conformity. Conformity occurs when people imitate or copy the behavior of one or more persons.[43] Brittany selecting the grilled chicken salad influenced Megan's decision to select the same item. Of course, after Brittany and Megan selected the grilled chicken salad, the remaining girl in line conformed by selecting the same item.

Conforming behaviors are more likely to occur in uncertain or unfamiliar situations.[44] Having never been trained in formal dining etiquette, Cory

observes and imitates behaviors of others to learn what behaviors are appropriate. Cory is inclined to observe the behavior of the most senior person at the table because he assumes this person is most likely to be correct. This reflects the role of credibility in determining who is selected to imitate.

Laser-Dot Experiments

Social norms are rules or guidelines for appropriate/inappropriate behaviors.[45] Social approval results from behaviors consistent with a social norm. Behaviors inconsistent with a social norm risk social disapproval. When riding in an elevator, the social norm (in the U.S.) is to face the elevator door for the duration of the ride. Don't believe us? Break this social norm by turning and facing the back wall of the elevator. We guarantee the reactions from the passengers will be priceless.

Muzafer Sherif conducted a series of classic conformity experiments when studying the development of social norms.[46] There have been many variations of Sherif's paradigm, but the basic procedure was as follows. Each participant sat in a dark room. A laser dot was displayed on the wall across from the participant who was instructed to tell the researcher how far the laser dot moved on each trial. Unbeknownst to the participant, the laser dot was stationary.

With a dark room eliminating a visual frame of reference and occasional rapid eye movements, a stationary laser dot appears to move. Perceived movement of the laser dot is an illusion called the autokinetic effect.

In the first experiment, each participant evaluated the distance the laser dot appeared to move.[47] The participants' responses ranged from 0.4 inches to 9.6 inches. The wide range of responses allowed Sherif to conduct the next two studies to measure conformity.

The second experiment consisted of four trials per participant.[45] The first trial followed the same procedure as in the first experiment. Then, participants were placed in groups of two or three participants and three additional trials followed. On the second trial, the group members announced their response publically, and their responses varied quite a bit from each other. But on Trials 3 and 4, the variation in the group members' responses decreased significantly. Each group member's response was within one inch of each other's response.

Interestingly, the groups' responses varied across groups. Toward the end of each group's trial, a norm was developed regarding the observed distance the dot moved. For one group, the laser dot moved one inch; for another group, the norm was established at five inches. This showed how group behavior can determine different social norms, and how these norms can affect perception.

When a participant was removed from the group, Sherif found the group's social norm still existed.[48] In this study, a participant and RA reported the distance a laser dot moved for 50 trials and a social norm was established (i.e., the distance the laser dot moved). After the first 50 trials, the RA left and the participant continued to evaluate the distance the laser dot moved for another 50 trials. Sherif found each participant's responses given in the second set of 50 trials were similar to the responses in the first 50 trials. This suggests the social norm established in the first 50 trials remained after the RA left.

Because there wasn't a correct response in Sherif's experiments, participants might question their perception after hearing a conflicting view. As a result, perceptions were apparently altered to conform with those of others. Question: Will people conform to a group's incorrect response when the correct answer is obvious? The answer is "yes," according to research conducted by Solomon Asch.

Matching Line Length Experiments

In a series of studies analogous to those by Sherif, participants in Solomon Asch's studies selected one of three lines to match the length of a specified line – the standard.[49] The correct answer was always obvious. On successive trials, a participant publicly selected the line that matched the standard after several RAs publicly announced their judgments one by one.

The RAs made correct selections for the first few trials. Then, the RAs gave uniformly incorrect judgments for the remaining trials. Even though the correct answer was obvious, for all 12 trials the judgments for only 23% of 123 participants remained completely independent from the group's response. Most participants (i.e., 77%) denied reality in order to conform to the unanimously incorrect judgment of others.

Normative and Informational Influence

Other people's judgments can have dramatic impact on an individual's decisions, as demonstrated by the Sherif and Asch studies. In Sherif's experiments, participants' reports of the movement of a stable dot were influenced by the reported observations of others. In Asch's studies, participants denied their comparative judgments of line lengths to conform with the inaccurate judgments of a group. Why did these participants choose to conform?

People conform in anticipation of two possible consequences (i.e., social approval or social disapproval). People conform to gain approval from others and/or avoid disapproval of others. They also gain information by observing the behavior of others. This is considered normative influence.[44] In Sherif's laser-dot studies, conforming participants modified their perceptions after becoming aware of another participant's reported perception. In Asch's line-judgment studies, incorrect information from others influenced most participants to deny their own perceptions.

Back to the individuals in the lunch line exchanging opinions about which items seemed best. As in Sherif's experiments, the judgments of others were used by individuals to be correct in their decisions and/or to gain a sense of social affiliation. These benefits reflect two of the three motivating consequences proposed by Cialdini and Goldstein: accuracy/competence and affiliation/community.[5]

Changing behavior to gain social approval (or peer support) or to avoid social disapproval (typically viewed as peer pressure) results from normative influence. In contrast, changing behavior for accuracy or competency is referred to as informational influence.

Informational and normative influence can occur simultaneously. At the à la carte line, diners sought information from each other about their opinion on which was the best item. When Brittany and Megan selected grilled chicken salads, the other girl might have selected the same item because of both normative and informational influence.

Strength in Numbers

The more people performing a certain behavior, the more likely others will imitate the same behavior. Makes sense, doesn't it? But this is not always the case. To test the impact of group size on conformity, Stanely Milgram, Leonard Bickman, and Lawrence Berkowitz conducted a simple field study.[50] A number of RAs (i.e., 1, 2, 3, 5, 10, or 15 people) simultaneously looked toward the sky at a busy sidewalk in New York City.

Observers noted 42% of 1424 pedestrians looked up when one research assistant looked up. When three RAs looked up, the percentage of pedestrians who looked up averaged about 60%. When five RAs looked skyward nearly 86% of the pedestrians followed suit. But as the number of RAs increased beyond five, the percentage of pedestrians who looked up remained at approximately 80%.

In the line-judgment studies, Solomon Asch found a participant's conformity to a group's decision increased as the group size increased to three people.[49] But the percentage of conforming people remained the same as the group size increased beyond three people. What does this mean?

Results from these studies suggest the increase in people performing the same specific behavior can prompt others to conform. However, as the number of people observed performing the same behavior increases beyond a certain point, one's propensity to conform is only slightly increased, if at all.[51]

Similarity

A person is more likely to conform to someone if the individual is similar to that person with regard to gender, age, career/education, and cultural background.[26] Being of the same age and gender could explain why all of the girls at the restaurant chose the grilled chicken salad.

Injunctive and Descriptive Norms as Activators

Recall a social norm is a rule or guideline for performing or avoiding a certain behavior. Social norms are injunctive or descriptive. An *injunctive norm* defines desirable and/or undesirable behavior. An injunctive norm is what one "ought to do," as Robert Cialdini put it.[52] In the U.S., driving on the right side of the road is an injunctive norm. Strong disapproval is expressed (e.g., via shouting, horn honking, and/or hand gestures) when a driver is observed driving on the left side of the road.

A *descriptive norm* reflects the behavior of others. Are people hiking, running, or biking on a trail? In this case, whichever activity is occurring by the most people would be considered a descriptive norm.

Behavior change can be activated by changing one's perception of the injunctive and/or descriptive norm.[52] A credible person performing a certain behavior can alter one's perception of the descriptive norm. One student surfing the internet during class can prompt onlookers to also surf the internet.

Of course, the opposite scenario is possible: Students do not see others surfing the internet in class and follow suit. In this example, refraining from surfing the internet during class is an injunctive norm, but in some classes surfing the internet is a descriptive norm.

A sign is a low-cost way to inform people of the injunctive norm. Messages stating "no food or drink" are commonly found in office areas and classrooms. The message describes the desirable social norm for that setting. If most people comply, then a descriptive norm is created. As depicted in the illustration, a descriptive norm can put social pressure on a person to conform even when the norm is not injunctive.

AC4P Applications

Large-scale behavior change is influenced through the *Social Proof* principle. Many people conform to fashion trends or fads because others are doing it. Seeing others wearing the AC4P wristband encourages others to do the same. This demonstrates social approval of the AC4P Movement, and perhaps awareness of how this wristband gets passed on among individuals. Such social proof could activate interpersonal conversation about the AC4P Movement and requests to get involved. For example, a common reaction following our passing of the AC4P wristband is, "Oh thank you, I've seen these around campus and have always wanted one of my own."

The AC4P T-Shirt. The *Social Proof* principle is one of many social-influence techniques used by the leaders of the AC4P Movement. During the early stages of the AC4P Movement, the original AC4P t-shirt included the line "Join the Movement". The phrase, "Join the Movement" implies other people are already a part of the AC4P Movement – a descriptive norm. This message is more influential in getting others to join the AC4P Movement than a message like "Actively Care for People".

After the AC4P Movement gets established in a particular culture, the general "Join the Movement" t-shirt is often customized for the situation. See, for example, the illustration of the t-shirt developed by the AC4P leaders at Chardon High School in Chardon, Ohio. Chapter 10 presents particulars regarding the implementation of AC4P principles and applications at this high school following their tragic school shooting on February 27, 2012.[53]

The AC4P Website. The AC4P website applies the *Social Proof* principle in different ways. It offers a way for others to see the number of wristbands that have been registered and how the wristbands are traveling around the world. During AC4P presentations, AC4P leaders show a map of the world and tell AC4P stories connected to particular AC4P wristbands that have traveled across several countries.⁵⁴ See Part IV of this book for representative AC4P stories reported at ac4p.org.

A second way the *Social Proof* principle is used to promote the AC4P Movement is linking the AC4P website to Facebook.com. Through Facebook pages, individuals share their AC4P stories with friends and others. Here we have the influence of both the interpersonal *Liking* principle and a descriptive norm. In this case, the descriptive norm matches the injunctive norm.

Injunctive and Descriptive Norms. Many would agree with an injunctive norm like, "I should actively care for the well-being of others." But behavioral manifestations of this injunctive norm (i.e., performing AC4P behavior) occurs less often than desired, given there can never be too much AC4P behavior.

Negative gossip is promulgated through the news (perceived as a descriptive norm), whereas the AC4P website spreads positive gossip (an injunctive norm). Our vision is to see AC4P behavior become a descriptive norm.

Some schools and communities have organized an AC4P Day to align the injunctive and descriptive norm. Leaders in Newton, Connecticut (site of a tragic school shooting spree) implemented an "Acts of Kindness" day on September 14th, 2013. Community leaders gave speeches and distributed materials to initiate and maintain an AC4P buzz.

Similarly, thousands of students at Virginia Tech (VT) participate annually in "The Big Event" – a day when students volunteer their AC4P service for homeowners throughout the University community. They assist residents with a variety of projects, from planting trees and grooming gardens to cleaning home garages and basements.

Also, VT and many other universities are major financial contributors to cancer research through the annual "Relay-for-Life" event. AC4P behavior is becoming a descriptive norm at VT, partly as a result of the organization of special AC4P days that illustrate the social proof of actively caring.

The Authority Principle

The *Authority* principle reflects compliance to a request coming from an authority figure.²⁴ The term "authority" has negative connotations because many historical examples and studies have illustrated the top-down coercive influence of people abusing their authority.⁵⁶ Still, many people with authority (e.g., physicians, ministers, teachers, and parents) set the stage for desirable behavior.

Obedience to authority can lead to undesirable behavior. This was shown by Stanley Milgram in a series of seminal experiments in the 1970s.⁵⁷ Ordinary people will administer an electrical shock to another person at the request of a perceived authority figure, Milgram discovered. Note the participant's body language in the illustration of Milgram's experiment. She's visibly distressed, as was the case for many participants, while following the anti-AC4P instructions from an authority figure.

In the first study, all 40 participants administered at least 300 volts before refusing to continue administering an electrical shock.[58] Surprisingly, 65% of the 40 participants administered the maximum voltage of 450 volts, even after the shock recipient (a stranger to the shock administrator) pounded on the wall and shouted "Ouch, this hurts!" Fortunately, the shock recipient in these studies was a RA and never actually received a shock.

There's a flip side to Milgram's horrific findings. Ordinary people will help others at the request of a perceived authority figure, according to a 1988 study.[58] A female RA (the requester) dressed as a perceived authority figure and requested a passerby give a nickel to a second RA (the recipient). The recipient posed as if he needed a nickel to pay for a parking meter.

The three conditions in this study were defined by the requester's outfit. In the Common-Clothes condition, the requestor was dressed as a panhandler, wearing an old t-shirt, tattered pants and shoes. Well-tailored business attire was worn by the requestor in the Business-Attire condition. Thirdly, the requester in the Uniform condition wore an official but ambiguous uniform with a patch and badge.

Individuals were much more likely to give the recipient a nickel in the Uniform condition compared to the other two conditions. Of the 150 participants in the Uniform condition, 72% complied with the request. In contrast, compliance in the Business-Attire and Common-Clothes conditions was 48% and 52%, respectively.

In addition to recording the number of participants who gave a nickel per each condition, the participant's verbal behavior accompanying the gift was recorded and classified into four categories: a) altruism, b) unquestioned obedience, c) compliance, and d) ambiguous.

Altruistic responses reflected a desire to help (e.g., "I saw you were in need of a nickel and I wanted to help"). The unquestioned obedience responses lacked the desire to help (e.g., "That person told me to give you a nickel"). A mixture between unquestioned obedience and altruistic responses were categorized as compliance (e.g.,

"I was told to help you, and I figured why not"). Finally, vague responses for helping were categorized in the ambiguous category.

The results demonstrate 27% of 26 participants viewed their gift of a nickel *as more altruistic* when the requester wore common clothes compared to tailored business attire (12.5% of 24 participants) and a uniform (14% of 36 participants).

On the other hand, 62.5% of 24 participants in the Business-Attire condition and 72% of 36 participants in the Uniform condition gave unquestioned obedience responses while giving a nickel to the "beggar." In contrast, only 27% of 26 participants in the Common-Clothes condition gave *unquestioned obedience responses*.

Why do people obey an authority figure? In childhood, obeying a parent's decision is supported through positive and negative consequences, Stanley Milgram proposed.[56] Even in adulthood, consequences are often controlled by an authority figure (e.g., teachers or school administrators). In fact, authority is often defined by the person who controls the most consequences for others in a given situation.

Complying with a teacher's instructions can lead to a higher grade on an assignment, at least from the student's perspective. Not following the teacher's directions can lead to a lower grade.

Bottom line: Human behavior is motivated by consequences and people are likely to comply with requests from those in control of those consequences – the authority figure.

Harsh vs. Soft Factors

Authority figures can gain compliance through situational or person factors. These factors are categorized as harsh versus soft factors.[59] An authority figure who gains obedience from others based on a hierarchical position within a particular social structure represents the *harsh factor* approach. Teachers, event staff, and administrators employ harsh factors to gain obedience. A staff member at a football game can instruct a fan to empty a cooler full of alcoholic beverages before entering the stadium.

In contrast, the *soft factor* approach applies person factors (e.g., experience, education, and credibility) to gain obedience. Physicians, professors, and ministers typically can use their person factors to gain obedience within the relevant environmental context. Because of their education and experience, we usually don't question the medicine and dosage amounts prescribed by a physician.

Authority Heuristics

Matt was recently duped by a car salesman. Before purchasing a car, the car salesman agreed to have it inspected at Matt's request. The car salesman took the car to the onsite mechanic. After the car passed inspection, Matt purchased the car.

Within a week, the motor seized up and prevented the car from running. Matt immediately went back to the car salesman to return the car and get a refund. When Matt addressed the issue he discovered the mechanic was a relative of the car salesman who shares the profits for each vehicle sold. Their ploy caused Matt to lose several thousand dollars, and he still was without a functional vehicle.

In this real-life example, Matt became a victim of heuristics. *Heuristics* are mental shortcuts used to make a decision.[60] These shortcuts can save a lot of time and effort in making a decision. For instance, we often don't question a prescription from a medical doctor. After all, the physician is the expert and is looking out for our best interests.

In the car salesman example, Matt made two heuristic mistakes. First he allowed the car salesman to find a mechanic. This saved Matt the trouble of finding a mechanic and an inspection station. The second mistake: assuming the mechanic was a nonbiased third party, as is usually the case.

Bottom line: Individuals can gain obedience from others by creating the perception they are an authority. Bearing titles and wearing certain clothes are two methods people can use to influence the perception they warrant authority influence.[24]

Attire. A uniform can gain more obedience to a request than regular clothes.[61] To empirically test the impact of attire on onlookers' behavior, a RA dressed differently in two conditions.[62] In the Low-Status condition, the RA wore common clothes. In the High-Status condition, the same RA wore a finely pressed suit. In both conditions, the RA was the first of a number of pedestrians to disobey the pedestrian traffic signal by crossing the street when it displayed "wait." Observers recorded the number of people who illegally crossed the street with the RA and the individuals who waited to cross the street legally.

Significantly more people (14% of 290) illegally crossed the street when the confederate's clothes suggested high status than when the attire of the illegal pedestrian reflected low status (4% of 288).

Titles. Titles define a level of authority because they offer insight into the background of the individual (e.g., education, experience, and leadership). The military uses titles/ranks to signify the chain of command. A doctor's title (e.g., cardiologist, surgeon, and dentist) provides insight to his/her educational background and expertise.

Even when a title is not authentic, bearing one can impact one's decision.[63] Recall Matt getting duped by a car salesman and mechanic. The mechanic may not have been a mechanic at all. Because the individual held the title of mechanic, Matt trusted his decision regarding the condition of the vehicle.

Matt's trusting of the mechanic's credentials through titling relates to an instructive study. Over the phone a researcher claimed he was a medical doctor and instructed different nurses to give a patient a specific drug s/he did not need.[64] The results were terrifying. Almost all (95%) of the 22 nurses studied complied with the researcher's request. Fortunately, a RA stopped each nurse before the medicine was administered and informed them about the study.

That study was conducted in 1966. We wonder whether the same results would be found today, given the current context of frequent internet scamming and phone-call solicitation.

AC4P Applications

Leaders of the AC4P Movement have used various strategies from the *Authority* principle to spread the AC4P Movement. Soft-Factor approaches are commonly used by the AC4P leaders. Examples of experience, education, and credibility are often found in resources like the AC4P brochure and on the AC4P website (ac4p.org):

> *"Actively Caring, coined by Dr. E. Scott Geller, refers to any behavior going above and beyond the call of duty for others. For decades, Dr. Geller, alumni-distinguished professor at Virginia Tech, has applied behavioral science to keep people safe at work and on the road."*

To gain credibility via a title, the AC4P leaders are introduced as college students and campus leaders to an assembly of students, from elementary to high-school students. The same leaders wear AC4P t-shirts to display their involvement in the AC4P Movement. To enhance the leaders' credibility, they could add the title: "AC4P Leader" to their shirts.

The Scarcity Principle

In the mid 1800's, Napoleon III invited the royal family to a banquet. To show off, Napoleon III permitted the royal family to use special aluminum utensils; silver and gold utensils were used by ordinary folk.

Today, allowing the royal family to use aluminum utensils over silver and gold seems preposterous. But in Napoleon's era, aluminum was actually valued higher than silver and gold because it was more difficult to process. Near the end of the 19th century, aluminum's value dropped substantially, as more effective processing systems were discovered.[65]

According to the *Scarcity* principle, we value things that are rare or becoming rare.[24] People valued aluminum more than silver or gold in the 1850's because it was more difficult to obtain. The value of aluminum dropped when it became abundant. Our attraction to limited numbers and our attempts to preserve personal control reflect the *Scarcity* principle.

Limited Numbers

Having a limited quantity of a certain product, and increasing one's awareness of the limited availability, increases one's propensity to purchase the product.[24] Advertising companies implement the limited-number technique to sell their products. They claim the item is a "limited release," "limited edition," or "one of a few left in stock." In this latter example, the *Scarcity* principle works in conjunction with the *Social Proof* principle. That is, the message "one of a few left in stock" implies the product is in high demand and becoming scarcer.

Psychological Reactance

We behave to regain our personal control when we perceive a restriction or limitation to our freedom or individuality, according to *psychological reactance* theory.[66] Top-down control tactics can backfire for this reason. A young boy might "fight back" when his parents insist he wear certain clothes to school. The "fighting back" behavior presumes an attempt to regain some personal control. The boy in the illustration is "fighting back" or demonstrating counter-control.[67]

Recall from the section on the *Authority* principle that a harsh tactic is one way to gain obedience from others. Due to psychological reactance, though, a top-down approach can be counterproductive.[4] The university students getting most intoxicated on Thursday and Friday nights were those whose parents had used the most punitive strategies to stop their children from consuming alcohol, according to field research conducted by the VT Center for Applied Behavior Systems.[68]

It's called "The Forbidden Fruit Phenomenon." Restricting use of an item makes it scarce, and so the item seems more valuable when one can avoid the restrictions.

AC4P Applications

The *Scarcity* principle can be used to increase the perceived value of the AC4P wristband. For example, at conferences the AC4P leaders inform audience members they brought a limited number of wristbands to the conference. And, the AC4P wristbands can *only* be purchased at the ac4p.org website.

Of course, a social proof message can be added as an explanation for the limited number of AC4P wristbands. For instance, the scarcity of wristbands can be accounted for by explaining a large number of people wanted the wristband prior to the presentation.

Whenever t-shirts are customized for a particular school or community, both *Scarcity* and *Social Proof* are activated. Students and teachers want to purchase and wear the special t-shirts because it reflects the common AC4P spirit at their site – a descriptive and injunctive norm. *Scarcity* is implicated because the number of these customized t-shirts is necessarily limited. And this special t-shirt cannot be purchased anywhere except from the local AC4P leaders or on the website: ac4p.org.

In Conclusion

The six social influence principles and strategies described and illustrated here can help initiate and sustain the AC4P Movement at your school, at home, and throughout your neighborhood. Throughout this chapter we suggest ways to apply the social-influence principles and techniques to increase another person's propensity to perform AC4P behavior.

The method of delivering an influence technique can be more important than the technique itself. This is worth remembering. A top-down application can actually do more harm than good by activating psychological reactance or counter-control. That's why we call the AC4P approach to cultivate compassion on a large-scale – *humanistic behaviorism*.

We incorporate evidence-based principles of behavioral science to activate and sustain beneficial change. We also use person-centered principles of humanism to assure personal ownership and perceived empowerment. In other words, behavior-change methods are taught, coached, and implemented so both the benefactors and the beneficiaries believe in their effectiveness and want to support the AC4P Movement.

Notes

1. Kenrick, D. T., Neuberg, S. L., & Cialdini, R. B. (2002). *Social psychology: Unraveling the mystery* (2nd Edition). Boston, MA: Pearson.
2. Thaler, R. H., & Sunstein, C. R. (2009) *Nudge: Improving decisions about health, wealth, and happiness*. New York, NY: Penguin Group.
3. Geller, E. S. (1996). *The psychology of safety: How to improve behaviors and attitudes on the job*. Radnor, PA: Chilton Book Company; Geller, E. S. (2001). *The psychology of safety handbook*. Boca Raton, FL: CRC Press.
4. Lehman, P. K., & Geller, E. S. (2008). Applications of social psychology to increase the impact of behavior-focused intervention. In L. Steg, A. P. Buunk, & T.Rothengatter (Eds.) (2008). *Applied social psychology: Understanding and managing social problems* (pp. 117-136). Cambridge, MA: Cambridge University Press.
5. Cialdini, R. B., & Goldstein, N. J. (2004). Social influence: Compliance and conformity. *Annual Review of Psychology, 55*, 591-621.
6. Geller, E. S. (2001). *The psychology of safety handbook*. Boca Raton, FL: CRC Press; Geller, E. S., Roberts, D. S., & Gilmore, M. R. (1996). Predicting propensity to actively care for occupational safety. *Journal of Safety Research, 27*, 1-8.
7. Festinger, L. (1957). *A theory of cognitive dissonance*. Stanford, CA: Stanford University Press.
8. Bem, D. J. (1967). Self-perception: An alternative interpretation of cognitive dissonance phenomena. *Psychological Review, 74*, 183-200.
9. Bem, D. J. (1972). Self-perception theory. In L. Berkowitz (Ed.). *Advances in experimental psychology* (Vol. 6) (pp. 1-62). New York, NY: Academic Press.
10. Freedman, J. L., & Fraser, S. C. (1966). Compliance without pressure: The foot-in-the-door technique. *Journal of Personality and Social Psychology. 4*, 195-202.
11. Cialdini, R. B., Eisenberg, N., Green, B. L., Rhoads, K., & Bator, R. (1998). Undermining the

undermining effect of reward in sustained interest: When unnecessary conditions are sufficient. *Journal of Applied Social Psychology, 28,* 249-63; Tybout, A. M., & Yalch, R. F. (1980). The effect of experience: A matter of salience? *Journal of Consumer Research, 6,* 406-413.

12. Kraut, R. E. (1973). Effects of social labeling on giving to charity. *Journal of Experimental Social Psychology. 9,* 551-562.

13. Kraut, R. E. (1973). Effects of social labeling on giving to charity. *Journal of Experimental Social Psychology. 9,* 551-562, p. 554.

14. Kraut, R. E. (1973). Effects of social labeling on giving to charity. *Journal of Experimental Social Psychology. 9,* 551-562., p. 555.

15. Retrieved from: www.bls.gov/cgi-bin/cpicalc.pl

16. Dweck, C.S. (2006). *Mindset: The new psychology of success.* New York: Ballotine Books.

17. Dweck, C.S. (2006). *Mindset: The new psychology of success.* New York: Ballotine Books., p. 71.

18. Dweck, C.S. (2006). *Mindset: The new psychology of success.* New York: Ballotine Books., p.72.

19. Dweck, C.S. (2006). *Mindset: The new psychology of success.* New York: Ballotine Books., p. 73.

20. Cialdini, R. B. (2001). *Influence: Science and practice* (6th Edition). Boston, MA: Pearson Education; Lehman, P. K., & Geller, E. S. (2008). Applications of social psychology to increase the impact of behavior-focused intervention. In L. Steg, A. P. Buunk, & Rothengatter, T. (Eds.) (2008). A*pplied social psychology: Understanding and managing social problems* (pp. 117-139). Cambridge, MA: Cambridge University Press.

21. Geller, E. S. (2001). *The psychology of safety handbook.* Boca Raton, FL: CRC Press; Geller, E. S, & Veazie, B. (2010). *When no one's watching: Living and leading self-motivation.* Newport, VA: Make-A-Difference, LLC; Ludwig, T. D., & Geller, E. S. (2001). *Intervening to improve the safety of occupational driving: A behavior-change model and review of empirical evidence.* New York, NY: The Haworth Press, Inc.; Monty, R. A., & Perlmuter, L. C. (1975). Persistence of the effect of choice on paired-associate learning, *Memory & Cognition, 3,* 183-187; Perlmuter, L. C., Monty, R. A., & Kimble, G. A. (1971). Effect of choice on paired-associate learning. *Journal of experimental psychology, 91,* 47-58; Steiner, I. D. (1970). Perceived freedom in L. Berkowitz (Ed.). *Advancements in experimental social psychology* (Vol. 5). New York, NY: Academic Press.

22. Fazio, R. H., Sherman, S. J., & Herr, P. M. (1982). The feature-positive effect in the self-perception process. Does not doing matter as much as doing? *Journal of Personality and Social Psychology, 42,* 404-411.

23. Schlenker, B. R., Dlugolecki, D. W., & Doherty, K. (1994). The impact of self-presentations on self-appraisals and behavior. The power of public commitment. *Personality and Social Psychology Bulletin, 20,* 20-33; Tedeshi, J. T., Schlenker, B. R., & Bonoma, T. V. (1971). Cognitive dissonance: Private ratiocination or public spectacle? *American Psychologist, 26,* 685-695.

24. Cialdini, R. B. (2001). *Influence: Science and practice* (6th Edition). Boston, MA: Pearson Education.

25. Cialdini, R. B. (2001). *Influence: Science and practice* (6th Edition). Boston, MA: Pearson Education, p. 148.

26. Emswiller, T., Deaux, K., & Willits, J. E. (1971). Similarity, sex, and requests for small favors. *Journal of Applied Psychology, 1,* 284-291.

27. Burger, J. M., Messian, N., Patel, S., Prado, A., & Anderson, C. (2004). What a coincidence! The effects of incidental similarity on compliance. *Personality and Social Psychology Bulletin, 30,* 35-43.

28. Berscheid, E., & Walster, E. (1978). Interpersonal attraction. Reading, MA; Addison-Wesley; Howard, D. J., Gengler, C., & Jain, A. (1995). What's in a name? A complimentary means of persuasion. *Journal of Consumer Research, 22,* 200-211; Howard, D. J., Gengler, C., & Jain, A.

(1997). The name remembrance effect. *Journal of Social Behavior and Personality, 12,* 801-810.

29. Zajonc, R. B. (1968). Attitudinal effects of mere exposure. *Journal of Personality and Social Psychology, 9,* 1-27.

30. Cory thanks all of the individuals who supported his family during this challenging time. Your AC4P behavior enabled us to heal and move forward.

31. Gouldner, A. (1960). The norm or reciprocity: A preliminary statement. *American Sociological Review, 25*(2), 161-178.

32. Babylon's Code of Hammurabi is one of the earliest known laws. These laws were based upon lextalionis (eye for an eye), which means for every crime committed an equitable punishment should be issued.

33. Kunz, P.R., & Woolcott, M. (1976). Season's greetings: From my status to yours. *Social Science Research, 5*(3), 269-278.

34. Trivers, R.L. (1971). The evolution of reciprocal altruism. *Quarterly Reviews of Biology, 46*(1), 35–57.

35. Boyce, T. E., & Geller, E. S. (2001). Encouraging college students to support pro-environmental behavior: Effects of direct versus indirect rewards. *Environment and Behavior, 33,* 107-125.

36. Goldstein, N. J., Griskevicius, V., & Cialdini, R. B. (2007). Invoking social norms: A social psychology perspective on improving hotel's linen-reuse programs. *Cornell Hotel and Restaurant Administration Quarterly, 48(*2), 145-150.

37. Goldstein, N. J., Griskevicius, V., & Cialdini, R. B. (2007). Invoking social norms: A social psychology perspective on improving hotel's linen-reuse programs. *Cornell Hotel and Restaurant Administration Quarterly, 48*(2), p. 146.

38. Goldstein, N. J., Griskevicius, V., & Cialdini, R. B. (2007). Invoking social norms: A social psychology perspective on improving hotel's linen-reuse programs. *Cornell Hotel and Restaurant Administration Quarterly, 48*(2), pp. 147-148.

39. Cialdini, R. B., Vincent, J. E., Lewis, S. K., Catalan, J., Wheeler, D., & Darby, B. L. (1975). Reciprocal concessions procedure for inducing compliance: The door-in-the-face technique. *Journal of Personality and Social Psychology, 31,* 206-215.

40. Schwartzwald, D., Raz, M., & Zwibel, M. (1979). The applicability of the door-in-the-face technique when established behavior customs exit. *Journal of Applied Social Psychology, 9,* 576-586.

41. Nowak, M. A., & Sigmund, K. (2005). Evolution of indirect reciprocity. Nature, 437(7063), 1291-1298; Stanca, L. (2009). Measuring indirect reciprocity: Whose back do we scratch? *Journal of Economic Psychology, 30*(2), 190-202.

42. Furrow, C. B., Geller, E. S., & McCarty, S. M. (2013). A ripple effect from actively caring. In E. S. Geller (Ed.). *Actively caring for people: Cultivating a culture of compassion* (1st Edition) (pp. 93-101). Newport, VA: Make-A-Difference, LLC.

43. Brecker, S. J., Olson, J. M., & Wiggins, E. C. (2006). S*ocial psychology alive.* Belmont, CA: Thomson Wadsworth.

44. Deutsch, M., & Gerard, H. B. (1955). A study of normative and informational social influences upon individual judgment. *Journal of Abnormal and Social Psychology, 51,* 629-636.

45. Sherif, M. (1936). *The psychology of social norms.* Oxford, UK: Harper.

46. Sherif, M. (1935). A study of some social factors in perception. *Archives of Psychology, 27*(187), 1-60; Sherif, M. (1936). The psychology of social norms. Oxford, UK: Harper; Sherif, M. (1937). An experimental approach to the study of attitudes. *Sociometry, 1,* 90-89.

47. Sherif, M. (1935). A study of some social factors in perception. *Archives of Psychology, 27*(187), 1-60.

48. Sherif, M. (1937). An experimental approach to the study of attitudes. Sociometry, 1, 90-89.

49. Asch, S. E. (1951). Effects of group pressure upon the modification and distortion of judgments. In H. Guetzkow (Ed.) *Groups leadership and men* (pp. 177-190). Pittsburgh, PA: Carnegie Press; Asch, S. E. (1952). *Social psychology.* New York, NY: Prentice-Hall; Asch, S. E. (1956). Studies of independence and conformity: A minority of one against a unanimous majority. *Psychological Monographs: General and Applied, 70*(9), 1-70.

50. Milgram, S., Bickman, L., & Berkowitz, L. (1969). Note on the drawing power of crowds of different size. *Journal of Personality and Social Psychology, 13,* 79-82.

51. Latane, B. (1981). The psychology of social impact. *American Psychologist, 35*(4), 343-356.

52. Cialdini, R. B., Kallgren, C. A., & Reno, R. R. (1991). A focus theory of normative conduct: A theoretical refinement and reevaluation of the role of norms in human behavior. *Advances in Experimental Social Psychology. 24*, 201-234.

53. Generic and customized AC4P t-shirts can be ordered on the website ac4p.org.

54. Case studies are available on ac4p.org.

55. Examples are the Stanford Prison Experiment, Milgram Studies, Rape of Rwanda, and the Holocaust.

56. Milgram, S. (1974). *Obedience to authority: An experimental view.* New York, NY: Harper & Row.

57. Milgram, S. (1963). Behavioral study of obedience. *Journal of Abnormal and Social Psychology, 67,* 371-378.

58. Bushman, B. J. (1988). The effects of apparel on compliance: A field experiment with a female authority figure. *Personal and Social Psychology Bulletin, 14,* 459-467.

59. Koslowsky, M., Schwarzwald, J., & Ashuri, S. (2001). On the relationship between subordinates' compliance to power sources and organizational attitudes. *Applied Psychology: International Review. 50,* 455-476; Raven, B. H., Schwarzwald, J., & Koslowsky, M. (1998). Conceptualizing and measuring a power/interaction model of interpersonal influence. *Journal of Applied Social Psychology. 6,* 161-168.

60. Kahneman, D., Slovic, P., & Tversky, A. (1982) (Eds.). *Judgments under uncertainty: Heuristics and biases.* New York: Cambridge University Press.

61. Bickman, L. (1974). The social power of a uniform. *Journal of Applied Social Psychology, 4,* 47-61.

62. Lefkowitz, M., Blake, R. R., & Mouton, J. S. (1955). Status factors in pedestrian violation of traffic signals. *Journal of Abnormal and Social Psychology, 51,* 704-706.

63. Cialdini, R. B. (2001). Influence: Science and practice (6th Edition). Boston, MA: Pearson Education; Hofling, C. K., Brotzman, E., Dalrymple, S., Graves, N., & Pierce, C. M. (1966). An experimental study of nurse-physician relationships. *Journal of Nervous and Mental Disease, 143,* 171-180.

64. Hofling, C. K., Brotzman, E., Dalrymple, S., Graves, N., & Pierce, C. M. (1966). An experimental study of nurse-physician relationships. *Journal of Nervous and Mental Disease, 143,* 171-180.

65. Venetski, S. (1969). Silver from clay. *Metallurgist.* 13(7), 451-453.

66. Brehm, J. W. (1966). *A theory of psychological reactance.* New York, NY: Academic Press.

67. Skinner, B. F. (1971). *Beyond freedom and dignity.* New York, NY: Alfred A. Knopf.

68. Smith, R. C., & Geller, E. S. (2013). Actively caring to prevent alcohol abuse among college students: Research-based lessons from the field. In E.S. Geller (Ed.). *Actively caring for people: Cultivating a culture of compassion* (1st Edition) (pp. 273-290). Newport, VA: Make-A-Difference, LLC.

Part II: Applications of AC4P in Schools

Shane M. McCarty

ON APRIL 16th, 2007, a gunman took the lives of 32 Hokies and injured 17 more on the Virginia Tech (VT) campus before turning the gun on himself. This event marks the deadliest school shooting on a college campus in U.S. history.

A time of great uncertainty, reflection, and vulnerability immediately followed for the Hokie nation. By the next evening, those most affected by the tragedy were not thinking about themselves, but rather acting to help a classmate, friend, or stranger.

Following the tragedy, students searched for the means to stimulate and sustain a spirit of belongingness, long the hallmark of the Hokie community. We wrote inspiring notes in chalk on sidewalks outside of dining halls, used hundreds of Hershey's "Pay It Forward" candy bars in a management class to promote giving over receiving, and left "Random Acts of Kindness" notes throughout campus. But, all of these attempts seemed to have only a temporary effect.

One Intentional Act of Kindness

In the fall of 2008, I trekked in the early morning across campus from my dorm in Pritchard Hall to the VT Inn for the Pamplin Leadership Conference. My best friend Brandon called me from a Blacksburg bus stop a few miles away. "I've been waiting forever and no buses are in sight, so just go without me," said Brandon. I thought, "If Brandon isn't going, then I'm not".

So, I started walking back to my residence hall when my cell phone rings and the caller ID showed "Brandon". "Meet me at the Inn," he said. "A student saw me at the bus stop in my business suit; she stopped her car to ask if I was going to the Leadership Conference and now she's giving me a ride."

This act might have appeared *random*, but it wasn't. The driver was *intentional* – she noticed a need, and then accepted personal responsibility to offer a ride. Her intentional act of kindness allowed Brandon and me to attend the conference, which in turn led to the most influential lunch of my life.

Meeting Professor Geller

I walked into the crowded ballroom for lunch and immediately noticed the names of various companies on each of the tables. Brandon noticed the one table without a company name: There was a place tag for Professor Scott Geller. "We have to sit with him," insisted Brandon. Confused, I replied "Sit with a professor instead of leaders from global companies?" "We won't regret it. Trust me," he said.

Brandon was right. For the entire lunch, we conversed with Dr. Geller about the problems plaguing our current culture – a culture of entitlement, apathy, and negativity. "We need more actively caring for people" said Dr. Geller.

After lunch, Dr. Geller took to the podium and enthusiastically delivered remarks about the need for more compassion in our culture, using key points from our lunchtime discussion. Brandon and I were quite surprised to see our lunch companion as the keynote speaker, but we were even more surprised when we heard him draw from our dialogue in his presentation.

The Actively Caring for People Movement

Only a few days later Brandon and I arrived at Dr. Geller's office to learn more about the AC4P concept. After learning even more about the evidence-based principles of AC4P and successful applications in the workplace, we became convinced AC4P was the means to enhance a community spirit and sustain a culture of compassion after our tragedy.

Later, Scott Geller, Joanne Dean Geller, Brandon Carroll, Joey Zakutney, David Dorsett, Hunter Bradshaw, and I met to explore ways to cultivate an AC4P culture with a simple process: Recognize people for the AC4P behavior they exhibit.

In the fall of 2008, we distributed 2,000 green AC4P wristbands to University faculty, students, and staff as a "thank you" for their actively caring. But it didn't stop there. With a pay-it-forward mindset, wristband recipients passed on their wristbands to recognize the AC4P behavior of others. These wristbands affected individuals in profound ways, initiating a Movement that would eventually spread worldwide.

Reflecting on the Virginia Tech Tragedy

After seeing the positive impact of the AC4P Movement, spawned from the VT massacre, we began to explore explanations. We rejected the notion of a single root cause of that tragedy, and wondered what situational and dispositional factors contributed to Seung-Hui Cho's decisions that fateful morning.

Any number of factors may have influenced Cho, including mental illness and being a victim of bullying throughout his school years. Although school records showed no specific incidents of bullying, his classmates reported seeing him victimized by peers.[1]

Was he a victim of verbal ridicule or physical attacks from classmates? Or, was he a victim of social exclusion and isolation, rarely receiving AC4P behavior from others?

We will never know which factors contributed most to Cho's aberrant behavior on April 16th, 2007. But we are certain he could have been the recipient of more AC4P behaviors, potentially preventing the tragic shootings. By increasing the quality and quantity of actively caring in elementary schools, middle schools, high schools, and universities, we hope an AC4P approach will prevent interpersonal bullying and future tragedies caused by violence.

Introduction

The AC4P Approach in Schools

With the same AC4P principles that guide people-based safety (PBS) in industry and the practical wristband-recognition process, Scott Geller, Taris Mullins and I developed an AC4P approach to prevent bullying in schools. Rather than ubiquitous top-down and punitive-approaches to prevent bullying, we aimed to increase prosocial behavior, develop a belief in an AC4P social norm, and enhance the five person-states among elementary-school students.

Chapter 6 demonstrates the effectiveness of this AC4P approach to prevent bullying in elementary schools, along with the supporting theory and empirical results. We conclude that chapter with three inspirational stories from a parent, principal, and school counselor who experienced the beneficial consequences of this approach.

In Chapter 7, a middle-school teacher, representative of many educators, shares the challenges of cultivating a caring classroom within an education system focused on academic test performance in lieu of character development.

A New Direction for U.S. Education

There's little debate about the substandard quality of education in the U.S. In fact, nearly 50% of Americans gave a mediocre grade of "C" to our nation's schools.[2] Test scores and rankings corroborate our citizens' perceptions.

Students in eleven countries are making academic gains twice the rate of U.S. students.[3] And the U.S ranks 25th in math, 17th in science, and 14th in reading.[3] Additionally, 32 states and Washington, DC failed to achieve "No Child Left Behind" objectives and received waivers from the U.S. Department of Education.[4]

Are U.S. schools failing? Not completely, and not yet. But as long as increasing students' scores on standardized tests consume teachers' time and energy, student learning will certainly suffer. We need a renewed focus on the human dynamics of teaching and learning, as explained further in Chapter 14.

Schools need to emphasize interdependence, reward interpersonal compassion, and encourage healthy relationships that lead to a more positive and optimistic school climate. Research has shown that classrooms with a positive school climate had higher scores on standardized tests.[5] Moreover, a sense of belonging along with emotional and social intelligence are correlates of academic achievement (i.e., Grade Point Average).[6]

It's critical to note the importance of *equifinality* – different processes achieve the same outcome. Focusing on the test ("teaching to the test") and enhancing test-taking skills is one route to achieving the desired test outcome. But, this approach will not meet the long-term social and emotional needs of students. It won't develop character and citizenship. It doesn't facilitate relationships and excite students to be self-motivated.

A more compassionate AC4P school culture will contribute to character development, reduce destructive antisocial and bullying behavior, and build meaningful relationships. A byproduct will be improved academic performance. So, how can we achieve this?

Cultivating an AC4P School Culture

First, we need research-based AC4P interventions to increase prosocial behavior and enhance well-being among all school personnel and students. But, increasing prosocial behavior is not enough to reduce bullying, because bullying is maintained by a potent consequence – social support from peers.

Bullying differs from other forms of violence, because it involves a perceived *power imbalance* between a victim and a bully. Even adults, such as teachers and support staff, experience power differentials when top-down administrators direct them to implement programs and enforce policies with limited opportunities for their participation in decision-making processes.

The AC4P approach deviates from traditional top-down command-and-control strategies that implicate a *power imbalance.* Founded on Applied Behavior Analysis (see Chapter 1), it applies a model of *empowerment,* equipping teachers and support staff with the knowledge, tools, and rationale underpinning the intervention.

The aim is to cultivate an AC4P culture in which students, educators, and parents work together as a cohesive AC4P team, and feel *empowered* to develop AC4P strategies that fit their unique school cultures.

Three chapters in Part III highlight the empowerment-based pedagogy guiding the teaching of AC4P principles in various educational settings. Chapter 8 details how a day-long workshop was planned and delivered to educators and students, enabling them to develop practical strategies from AC4P principles to increase the occurrence of AC4P behaviors in middle schools, high schools, and universities.

Chapter 9 explains how ten VT student-athletes learned the AC4P principles in a psychology course and applied them to teach sports skills to children in a poverty-stricken area of the Dominican Republic.

Chapter 10 reviews how VT and Chardon High School students applied the AC4P principles in the aftermath of tragic school shootings to sustain compassion throughout their cultures.

Chapters 11 and 12 are personal stories from AC4P leaders who were profoundly affected by the VT tragedy. Victoria Stone reveals her AC4P behavior as a massage therapist immediately after the tragedy, and the inspirational story from Rohan Cobb-Ozanne illustrates how a student, who entered VT four years after the shooting, uses that horrific event to remind himself to promote the AC4P spirit. You will be inspired by the AC4P actions of Victoria and Rohan, and perhaps activated to follow their lead.

Chapter 13 explains how a university course on applied behavioral science facilitated the spread of AC4P throughout the University of Kansas. You will certainly be impressed by the positive and active reactions of university students to the AC4P Movement. But the students' AC4P behavior did require some nudging by the activator-behavior-consequence contingency (as detailed in Chapter 1).

Supporting the need for AC4P contingency management, Chapter 14 reveals how misplaced reinforcement contingencies hinder the quality of education in public schools, colleges, and universities.

In Conclusion

The current educational paradigm in U.S. schools seems to be more about "the blame game" and finding fault for mistakes rather than focusing on successes. Standardized test outcomes take precedence over learning processes; disincentives and penalties trump positive consequences for improving behavior.

This negatively affects how teachers teach, students learn, administrators lead, and parents interact with their children and school personnel. We need flourishing positive relationships, a *we* over *me* mindset, and a norm of AC4P behavior.

Educators, students, parents, and community members can *empower* each other to use the AC4P applications shared in the following chapters. Together, we can enhance students' self-esteem, self-efficacy, personal control, optimism, and sense of belonging, thereby helping to cultivate interpersonal compassion throughout our schools.

Notes

1. Johnson, A., Cahil, P., Dedman, B., Williams, P., Popkin, J., & Handelsman, S. (2007, April 19). High school classmate say gunman was bullied. *MSNBC*. Retrieved from http://www.msnbc.msn.com/id/18169776/ns/us_news-crime_and_courts/t/high-school-classmates-say-gunman-was-bullied; Mental Health History of Seung Hui Cho. (2007). *Virginia Governor's Report*. Retrieved from http://www.governor.virginia.gov/tempcontent/techPanelReport-docs/8%20CHAPTER%20IV%20LIFE%20AND%20MENTAL%20HEALTH%20HISTORY%20OF%20CHOpdf.pdf

2. What Americans said about the public schools. (2012). *Highlights of the 2012 PDK/ Gallup Poll*. Retrieved from http://www.pdkintl.org/poll/docs/2012-Gallup-poll-full-report.pdf

3. Hanushek, E.A., Peterson, P.E., & Woessmann, L. (2012). Achievement growth: International and U.S. state trends in student performance. Harvard's program on education policy and governance & education next. Retrieved from http://www.hks.harvard.edu/pepg/PDF/Papers/PEPG12-03_CatchingUp.pdf; U.S. students still lag behind foreign peers, schools make little progress in improving achievement. (2012, July 23). *Huffington Post*. Retrieved from http://www.huffingtonpost.com/2012/07/23/us-students-still-lag-beh_n_1695516.html

4. Resmovits, J. (2012, July 19). No child left behind waivers granted to 33 U.S. states, some with strings attached. *Huffington Post*. Retrieved from http://www.huffingtonpost.com/2012/07/19/no-child-left-behind-waiver_n_1684504.html

5. Lacey, A., & Cornell, D. (2011, August). *The impact of a bullying climate on schoolwide academic performance.* Poster session presented at the American Psychological Association meeting, Washington, DC.

6. Drake, B.M. (2011). Predictive modeling of first-year student success factors. Retrieved from http://irt2.indstate.edu/ir/assets/sem/Modeling1.pdf; Faircloth, B.S., & Hamm, J.V. (2005). Sense of belonging among high-school students representing four ethnic groups. *Journal of Youth and Adolescence, 34*(4), 293-309; Parker, J.D.A., Creque, R.E., Barnhart, D.L., Harris, J.I., Majeski, S.A., Wood, L.M., Bond, B.J., & Hogan, M.J. (2004). Academic achievement in high school: Does emotional intelligence matter? *Personality and Individual Differences, 37*(7), 1321-1330.

CHAPTER 6

AC4P to Prevent Bullying:
Activating and rewarding prosocial behavior in elementary schools

Shane M. McCarty and E. Scott Geller

BULLYING BEHAVIOR and its negative consequences have made national news: A thirteen-year-old student hanged himself due to homophobic teasing;[1] a college freshman jumped to his death after his roommate streamed a video of his sexual encounter online;[2] groups of students experience physical and emotional abuse daily because they just don't "fit in".[3]

Interpersonal bullying is intentional aggressive behavior that involves an imbalance of power, and occurs repeatedly over time.[4] It includes name calling, verbal or written abuse, exclusion from social situations, physical aggression, and coercion.

Bullying is widespread. It occurs in diverse locations, from the workplace to the home, and even virtually over the Internet. It's experienced among all ages, from young children to adults. In schools, nearly 30 percent of U.S. students have been moderately or frequently involved in bullying as bullies, victims, or both.[5] In the U.S. workplace, 37% of employees report being bullied on the job.[6]

Bullying negatively impacts both physical and mental health. Most bullied individuals' experience low psychological well-being, poor social adjustment, aversion to social environments, psychological distress and various physical disorders.[7] Victimization from bullying has been linked specifically to a variety of negative outcomes, including poor academic performance,[8] anxiety,[9] depression,[10] suicidal ideation,[11] suicide attempts and completions.[12]

Childhood bullying has been linked to future violence. According to the *Final Report and Findings of the Safe School Initiative* that studied 41 individuals involved in 37 school-based attacks between 1974 and 2000, "many attackers felt bullied, persecuted, or injured prior to their attack (on others)".[13]

For example, *Payback Time* was the theme of Eric Harris' suicide note after Dylan Klebold and he killed 12 classmates and a teacher before killing themselves at Columbine High School. This payback was for his years of school-based torment. Students had poured ketchup on him in the cafeteria, and had verbally assaulted and alienated him in various school situations.[14]

On April 16th, 2007, 33 Virginia Tech students and faculty lost their lives in the deadliest shooting on a U.S. college campus in history. There is evidence the shooter had been ostracized by his peers and bullied. "Long before the shooting, Seung-Hui Cho was bullied by fellow high-school students who mocked his shyness and the strange way he talked," reported his former classmates.[15]

Why Does Bullying Occur?

Social learning theory explains many occurrences of interpersonal bullying. Bandura[16] found the likelihood of modeling the behavior of others increases when three conditions are evident: 1) the role model is viewed as powerful; 2) the model's behavior is rewarded; and 3) the observer shares overt characteristics with the role model. These conditions occur frequently for bystanders observing bullying and may explain why some students choose to model the bullying of others. In other words, bullying is maintained by supportive consequences, such as perceived power and/or social rewards.

The social-learning processes of modeling and interpersonal approval among peers may shape bullying as normative behavior and accepted as such. Using naturalistic observations of children's play, Patterson, Littman, and Bricker[17] highlighted social-learning processes during aggressive interactions, indicating peers intentionally or inadvertently reinforce the aggressive behaviors of bullies with social attention. Plus, Craig and Pepler[18] observed teachers intervening to stop bullying in only 20% of classroom bullying episodes. Despite the social rewards supporting bullying behavior, interventions often do not target or alter reward systems related to interpersonal bullying.

Intervening to Prevent Bullying

Colvin, Tobin, Beard, Hagan, and Sprague[19] provide specific criteria for educators selecting a bullying-prevention program. Specifically, they advise the intervention to be: 1) supported by research, 2) based on behavioral principles, and 3) emphasize the teaching of prosocial behavior to replace bullying behavior.

To the contrary, many American schools have attempted to curb bullying by turning to rule enforcement and punitive measures. School psychologists reported the three most frequently used intervention strategies: 1) discussions between school personnel and bullies after bullying incidents; 2) negative consequences (e.g., suspension) for bullying; 3) heightened supervision in less structured places (e.g., the playground).[20]

A meta-analysis identified the most frequently-used program elements were classroom rules, teacher training, and improved classroom management.[21] Unfortunately, traditional anti-bullying interventions have a poor history of effectiveness.[22] Additionally, punitive approaches to behavior change have a number of serious disadvantages over both the short and long term.[23] Thus, it seems a different and positive approach is needed to prevent interpersonal bullying.

The AC4P Approach to Prevent Bullying

As detailed in Chapters 1 and 2, the behavior-based components of AC4P interventions focus on: a) improving observable behavior, b) using activators to direct behavior, and c) applying positive consequences to motivate behavior.

In addition, AC4P interventions use: a) supportive feedback and recognition as positive consequences to reward AC4P behavior and increase perceived competence to fuel self-motivation; b) evidence-based strategies to enhance perceived empowerment and self-motivation; and c) interpersonal communication to boost self-esteem, self-efficacy, personal control, optimism, and belongingness.

Our AC4P approach to prevent bullying includes the behavior-based framework and recommendations of Colvin et al.[19] and Whitted and Dupper.[24] Specifically, Whitted and Dupper[24] emphasized a successful bullying-prevention program should include: a) a school-level approach to change school culture; b) tangible and social rewards; c) clear behavioral expectations; and d) social-competence building.

Tangible and Social Rewards

Students who bully seek power and coercive dominance, find satisfaction in causing injury and suffering to other students, and are often recognized for their aggressive behavior with tangible or social rewards.[25] Given the responsiveness of these students to rewards, it seems an anti-bullying intervention should include an incentive/reward contingency that promotes behavior contrary to bullying.

In fact, a widely-practiced and effective way to eliminate an undesirable behavior is to reward desirable behavior incompatible with the undesirable behavior.[26] This translates to rewarding prosocial behavior in lieu of bully-related behavior.

Any action that benefits another person is *prosocial behavior*.[27] It can include sharing, helping, cooperating, donating, and volunteering. Research suggests a school-based approach that focuses on modeling prosocial behavior has potential as an anti-bullying intervention.

For example, Honig and Pollack[28] demonstrated that one month of daily discussions with second graders sharing their prosocial actions between themselves and others increased the number of prosocial actions observed among students, compared to classrooms without these daily discussion sessions. In fact, Demaray and Malecki[29] specifically recommended social support as a program-enhancing component for bullying prevention.

Behavioral Expectations

Whitted and Dupper[24] suggest establishing clear behavioral norms by "developing classroom and school-wide rules that prohibit bullying, as well as adult modeling of respectful and nonviolent behavior".[30] School-wide and classroom policies are frequently established to set behavioral expectations in schools.[21]

But it's more effective to set success-seeking objectives (i.e., goals with positive consequences) rather than failure-avoiding policies to avoid a specific behavior (e.g., rules against bullying).[31] The AC4P approach introduces prosocial/AC4P behaviors as expectations to facilitate a new social norm of interpersonal actively caring among peers.

Students are strongly influenced by their peer group. Students are more likely to become prosocial when they have prosocial peers.[32] Hoglund and Leadbeater[33] found fewer problems among first graders from unstable homes if they were in classrooms with a relatively high frequency of prosocial behavior. Given the benefits of a prosocial approach, we expected a reduction in bullying to occur when an intervention increases the frequency of prosocial behaviors.

Enhancing Social Competence

Whitted and Dupper[24] recommend enhancing social competence through interactive teaching techniques. Social competence refers to one's assessment of his or her ability to interact effectively with others.[34] Most students could potentially benefit from prosocial interactions aimed at enhancing social competence. Individuals lacking social competence are more likely to be victims of bullying and to bully others.[35]

Unfortunately, students are rarely provided with opportunities to develop their social skills within existing bullying-prevention programs. School psychologists indicated top-down approaches, such as classroom rules against bullying, were implemented frequently (89.6%), compared to alternative bullying-reduction strategies that could foster social competence, such as student peer counseling for victims (26.4%), student-led anti-bullying activities (34.9%), and formal participation of students in decision-making about bullying (36.3%).[20]

Our approach aimed to involve all students, beyond just bullies and victims, and provide opportunities for them to model and recognize AC4P behaviors performed by classmates.

The bullying-prevention intervention evaluated in this research was consistent with the AC4P principles, and was introduced as an "Actively Caring for People" process. This AC4P intervention communicated modeling and rewarded desired AC4P behavior.

The approach was based on humanism and applied behavior analysis – *humanistic behaviorism*. Tangible rewards and social approval were used to promote prosocial behaviors incompatible with bullying, aligning with the intervention guidelines recommended by Colvin et al.[19] and Whitted and Dupper.[24]

Field Study 1

Method

Participants and Setting. The participants were 199 fourth, fifth, and sixth-grade students from eight classrooms at an elementary school in northeast Virginia. The bullying-prevention committee of the school had requested the opportunity to conduct this AC4P program for the second time, approximately one year after piloting an initial version of the program in September 2009.

Intervention Plan. To increase prosocial behavior, the intervention program established an "if-then" contingency to motivate the AC4P behavior of students. To be eligible to wear a green wristband embossed with the message, "Actively Caring for

People," students had to write a story of a specific AC4P behavior they observed, or perform an AC4P behavior themselves and have it documented in a story written by another student.

At the start of each day, the classroom teacher selected three AC4P stories to read aloud to the class, publically recognizing the students in each story. From these three stories, one was selected and the pair of students involved – the good-deed performer and the observer – were each given a green AC4P wristband. These two students wore the AC4P wristband for the entire day, as the "Actively-Caring Heroes of the Day". This cycle of sharing AC4P stories and recognizing certain AC4P observers and performers was repeated each day for five consecutive weeks.

The teacher's selection of stories to read each day and the one story to use for the wristband reward was not random. During the five intervention weeks, every student was given an opportunity to be recognized at least once as the AC4P observer and once as the AC4P performer. To increase the likelihood the class would meet the team goal of every student participating at least once as both an observer and a performer, researchers instructed teachers to pick stories from students who rarely submit them.

Each week from Weeks 2 to 6, the teacher facilitated relationship-building and belongingness among classmates by randomly pairing students for interpersonal discussions.

At these weekly sessions, students discussed one of the following statements or questions: a) What do you want to be when you grow up?; b) Share a secret talent you have or something you do really well; c) What is your greatest fear, and why?; d) What do you like most about school, and why?; and e) Share something new about yourself.

The purpose of this exchange was to foster new relationships among the students and potentially make interpersonal AC4P behavior easier to perform and observe throughout the five-week intervention phase. Students were told everyone would receive their own AC4P wristband at the end of program if everyone contributes at least one AC4P story and is observed performing at least one AC4P behavior.

Evaluation Plan. An ABA time-series design was implemented, consisting of a Baseline phase during Week 1, an Intervention phase during Weeks 2 to 6, and a Withdrawal phase at Week 7.

Every Friday, students completed the same survey that addressed both the AC4P and bully-related behaviors observed, received and performed. Other questions related to personal perceptions and attitudes toward AC4P. Students completed the surveys anonymously and had the choice to answer all, some, or none of the questions. Informed consent was implied by the return of a survey.

Results

Bullying Behavior. After reading the definition of bullying included at the top of the survey, "Bullying is when someone hurts another person on purpose and more than once," students reported frequencies of observed bullying behavior, being bullied, and bullying others.

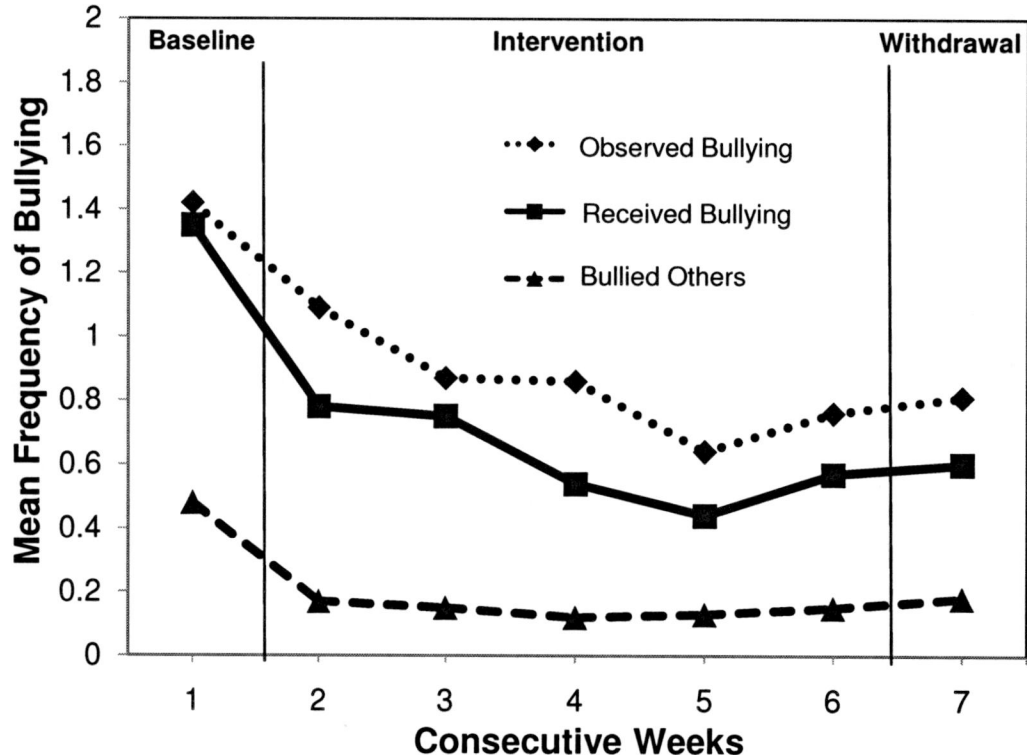

Figure 6.1. Mean frequency of observed bullying, being bullied, and bullying others over seven consecutive weeks.

Figure 6.1 depicts a consistent decrease in bullying behavior for: a) observed bullying, b) being bullied, and c) bullying others, as indicated respectively by their responses to the following questions: 1) In the past week, how many times have you seen someone else bullied?; 2) In the past week, how many times have you been bullied by someone else?; 3) In the past week, how many times have you bullied someone else?

The mean weekly frequency of observed bullying decreased every week from Weeks 1 to 5, until a slight increase occurred from Weeks 5 to 7. A similar trend occurred for victimization (i.e., the mean frequency of being bullied), and for interpersonal bullying (i.e., the mean frequency of bullying others). For each dependent variable the most dramatic decrease occurred from Baseline to Week 2 (the first week of the intervention).

Figure 6.2 on the next page depicts the percentage of students categorized as "victim only," "bully only," and "bully-victim" each week. If a participant self-reported his/her frequency of interpersonal bullying as zero and exceeded zero for victimization, the student was classified in the "victim only" group. If a student self-reported his/her frequency of interpersonal bullying as exceeding zero and equating to zero for victimization, the participant was classified in the "bully only" group. If a student reported his/her frequency as exceeding zero for both interpersonal bullying and victimization, s/he was classified in the "bully-victim" group.

Before the intervention began (i.e., during Week 1), there were 48 victimized students (24.1% of 199 students), 16 bullies (8%), and 15 bully-victims (7.5%). At the

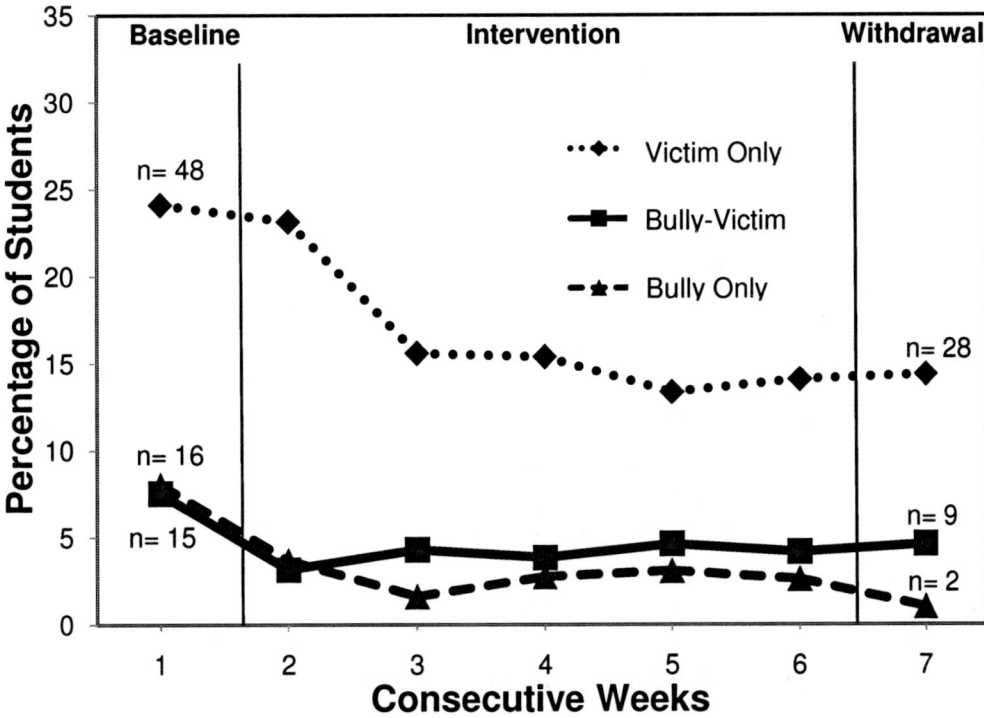

Figure 6.2. Percentage of students self-identified as Victim Only, Bully-Victim, and Bully Only over seven consecutive weeks.

end of the study (i.e., during Week 7), there were 28 victims (14.4%), two bullies (1%), and nine bully-victims (4.6%). During Baseline, 79 students (39.7%) were affected by bullying in some way as victims, bully-victims, or as bullies. By Week 7, only 39 students were included in one of these three categories (20%).

Prosocial Behavior. Each Friday, students responded on a rating scale (from 0 to 10+) to this question: "In the past week, how many times have you shared something (for example: a pencil, paper, book) with a classmate?" Student responses differed significantly as a function of whether a student had received an AC4P wristband during that week.

Specifically, wristband recipients for Week 2 reported a mean of 7.28 for frequency of interpersonal sharing behaviors during the first intervention week, compared to a frequency mean of 5.60 for non-recipients of a wristband. This difference was even greater during Week 6 when wristband recipients reported an average of 8.0 sharing behaviors compared to a mean of 5.96 for non-recipients of a wristband that week.

Perception of Helping. Students answered this question about their perception of helping: "My classmates help each other," which ranged from 1 (Strongly Disagree) to 5 (Strongly Agree) per individual response. Helping perceptions were significantly higher among wristband recipients (i.e., 4.37 mean score) than non-wristband recipients (i.e., 4.05). Thus, the differences in the students' perceptions of their classmates' helping varied as a function of whether the student had received the AC4P wristband that week.

Discussion

Our AC4P bullying-prevention intervention followed closely the criteria specified by Colvin et al.[19] and Whitted and Dupper.[24] Prosocial behavior was targeted instead of bullying. In fact, bullying was never mentioned as part of the intervention protocol. The entire focus was on increasing prosocial behavior. By intervening to increase a desirable behavior incompatible with the target undesirable behavior, it was assumed bullying would decrease.

After the intervention weeks, every student in all eight classrooms (n=199) submitted at least one AC4P story and performed a minimum of one AC4P behavior, achieving the classroom goal needed for all students to receive an AC4P wristband to keep. The effectiveness of this tangible recognition tool was demonstrated by the significant differences between those receiving an AC4P wristband versus those who did not, as reported on the weekly surveys for frequency of sharing behavior and perceptions of their classmates' helping behaviors.

Given bullies receive social approval or rewards for their actions,[25] the AC4P approach should have had the most influence on the "Bully Only" category, and that was indeed the case. Specifically, the 88% decrease (from 8% in Week 1 to 1% at Week 7) demonstrates the effect of systematically rewarding desirable prosocial behavior with a tangible AC4P wristband, peer attention, and teacher recognition, while giving no attention to bullying behavior.

The effectiveness of our prosocial approach, using the AC4P wristband as both an incentive and a reward, increased AC4P behavior as expected; it also affected students' perceptions in positive directions. After students performed AC4P behavior and received recognition and a wristband to wear for a day, they reported a higher perception of helping among classmates for the particular week. When a change in behavior has occurred, a change in attitudes is likely to follow.[36]

Bottom-Up vs. Top-Down. The AC4P approach evaluated in this report differed markedly from the popular Olweus Bullying Prevention Program (OBPP). The individual components of OBPP encourage more top-down supervision of students in "hot spots," and discussions with bullies, victims, and their respective parents after an incident.[37] In contrast, our bottom-up AC4P approach focused entirely on positive consequences for writing AC4P stories and performing AC4P behaviors.

At the classroom level, the OBPP establishes rules against bullying and encourages discussions about bullying.[37] In contrast, our AC4P intervention used class meetings for teachers to share AC4P stories and recognize AC4P heroes. The issue of bullying was assessed via a weekly survey, but never mentioned by teachers.

Bully-Free Virginia[38] highlighted the efficacy of the Olweus program at reducing the percentage of students being bullied (i.e., victims only and bully-victims) from 42.3% to 33.9% after one year of implementation. At the same school, five years later, our AC4P approach reduced the percentage of students being bullied from 31.6% to 19% after only seven weeks.

Thus, a year-long OBPP approach achieved a reduction of 8.4 percentage points compared to a reduction of 12.6 percentage points after our seven-week AC4P approach. However, the marked difference in intervention duration (i.e., one year versus seven weeks) limits the validity of these comparisons.

Regardless, it's notable the same outcome metrics were used to compare victimization due to bullying. The OBPP reports up to 50% self-reported reductions of students being bullied and bullying others.[39] The results of this study show a 56% decrease in being bullied and a 63% decrease in bullying others.

However, the pre-intervention percentage of students being bullied prior to the AC4P program was much lower (i.e., 31.6%) than the OBPP (i.e., 42.3%). Thus, both intervention approaches (i.e., OBPP vs. AC4P) had similar bullying reductions, despite the sharp contrast between the methods of AC4P (positive and prosocial-focus) and OBPP (rule enforcement and bullying-focus).

Limitations. This field study had several limitations, which could be overcome in follow-up research. Most Baseline-Intervention-Withdrawal (ABA) time-series designs involve several consecutive weeks of Baseline and stable levels of the target behavior(s) before implementing an intervention. Our ABA design was severely limited by using a single week of Baseline, five Intervention weeks, and only one week of Withdrawal.

Additionally, the Withdrawal phase was contaminated for classes exceeding 25 students, because every student needed to be recognized twice to meet the group contingency. In some cases, this required continuing the intervention on the first days of Withdrawal. Unfortunately, adding another week of Withdrawal was not feasible due to the school's schedule. Thus, we have no data on the durability of the intervention.

Self-report scales are the preferred[40] and most popular method[41] for assessing bullying in schools. But self-reported behavior from children is limited without more objective indices, such as disciplinary referrals and observations from teachers and field researchers.

Additionally, there's no objective assurance the teachers followed the daily protocol exactly as prescribed beyond their verbal reports of adhering to our instructions. We did not assess teachers' behavior; therefore, we have no information on any changes of their bully-related behavior, helping behavior, disciplining, and referral writing.

"Bullying" was never mentioned by teachers or students as part of the research protocol. However, it was mentioned in the survey each Friday. By defining "bullying" on the survey and asking questions that included the word "bullying," prior research shows students under-report the actual occurrence of bullying.[42]

Field Study 2

Field Study 1 was limited by sample size (n=199), thereby disallowing separate analysis by grade. This second field study occurred at a different school and expanded on the intervention used in Field Study 1. Also, this study included a larger sample size to enable an evaluation of grade level, from 2 to 6. Plus, the weekly survey added an estimate of the students' self-esteem.

Bullying Correlates

Bullying has many correlates, including: a) individual factors, such as age[43] and gender,[44] b) relational factors, such as family relationships[45] and social support from peers[29] and teachers,[46] and c) school factors, such as classroom climate.[47]

Age and Maturation. Research from human development and adolescent psychology has demonstrated the frequency of aggressive and prosocial behaviors differ as a function of maturation levels of school-aged children. A cross-sectional study of 12,292 Canadian adolescents found levels of physical aggression decreased over time for girls, but not for boys, as the age of students increased from five to 11.[48]

A longitudinal study found more prosocial intentions and behavior toward friends coming from fourth graders than first graders.[49] Regarding later development, a multiple-informant longitudinal study of Canadian and Italian children between ten and 14 years of age found the levels of prosocial behavior remained stable or declined as the age of children increased.[50]

Based on prior research, Baseline mean differences in bullying and prosocial behavior may vary as a function of school grade. However, no prior intervention research suggests differing levels of success for the AC4P approach as a function of grade level.

Self-Esteem. Self-esteem, or one's perception of self-worth, is a dispositional factor influencing bully-related behavior in educational settings. Children's scores on the Rosenberg Self-Esteem scale correlated negatively with victimization due to bullying.[51] Despite role distinctions between bullies and victims, both have relatively low self-worth or self-esteem.[52] Therefore, O'Moore and Kirkham[53] recommend increasing self-esteem among students in order to reduce the negative effects of bullying.

Geller[31] considered self-esteem to be a critical person-state or "establishing operation"[54] when proposing certain dispositions increase one's propensity to exhibit AC4P behavior, Indeed, relevant research has shown positive correlations between self-esteem and AC4P behavior.[55] Those scoring relatively high on measures of self-esteem were more likely to actively care in both reactive[56] and proactive situations.[57]

Method

Participants and Setting. The participants were 404 second (n=107), third (n=100), fourth (n=54), fifth (n=89), and sixth-grade (n=54) students from 16 classrooms at an elementary school in northeast Virginia. School administrators requested the AC4P intervention after hearing about its success at a nearby elementary school.

Intervention Plan. The AC4P intervention included three components not included in Field Study 1: 1) a one-hour teacher-training workshop by the senior author to describe the specific research protocol and show evidence-based support for the AC4P approach to prevent bullying; 2) a motivational AC4P presentation to students by the senior author; and 3) the modeling of AC4P behaviors among school personnel.

After Baseline assessments, every teacher participated in the one-hour training workshop. The senior author explained the background of the AC4P Movement, reviewed evidence-based principles underlying the AC4P approach, and showed results from the prior application of AC4P at a nearby elementary school. Teachers were given a five-page handout with specific instructions to follow throughout the intervention phrase.

Next, the senior author gave 45-minute presentations of the AC4P Movement at two separate student assemblies (i.e., Grades K to 3 and 4 to 6). Students were provided the definition of AC4P and shown the AC4P wristband.

Then they engaged in a "AC4P Caring Chat". They turned to a partner and shared a time when a classmate had helped him/her. Afterward, the AC4P program was explained in detail, along with the same individual and group if-then contingencies used in Field Study 1.

Teachers, administrators, and supporting staff were instructed to recognize and reward AC4P behavior of colleagues and/or co-workers with an adult-size AC4P wristband.

They were specifically instructed to follow the SAPS process by observing the AC4P behavior of an adult in the school building (*See*), thanking the person for actively caring (*Act*), passing the AC4P wristband to another colleague observed performing AC4P behavior (*Pass*), and sharing the story from the AC4P wristband exchange with their students (*Share*). The senior author gave one wristband to the Principal for circulation among teachers and support staff.

Evaluation Plan. In Field Study 2, an AB time-series design was implemented, consisting of a Baseline phase during Week 1 and an Intervention phase during Weeks 2 to 6.[58] Students completed the same bullying-related questionaire used in Field Study 1. Additionally, the students responded to a single-item estimate of self-esteem.

Results

Bullying Behavior. Bullying behavior was averaged for each grade, resulting in a mean weekly score of bullying frequency per each grade. Figure 6.3 on the next page shows a significant overall decrease in the frequency of observed bullying behavior for each grade from Baseline to Week 6.

The frequency of bullying behavior for each grade trends downward for four of the five Fridays with some inconsistency for Grade 5 (i.e., a slight increase in observed bullying from Weeks 3 to 5). Additionally, observed bullying was significantly less for Grade 6 than Grades 2, 3, 4, and 5.

Figure 6.4 on page 165 depicts the mean weekly reported frequency of being bullied, and shows a dramatic decrease from Baseline to Week 2, and a general downward trend across grades for the following Intervention weeks. The reported frequency of being bullied was significantly lower for Grade 6 than Grades 2 and 3.

Although the frequency of being bullied is a key metric, the percentage of students victimized may be more relevant. Students experiencing at least one act of bullying per week were categorized as "victims" (i.e., victims only and bully-victims). The mean percentage decrease in victims from Baseline to Week 6 was:

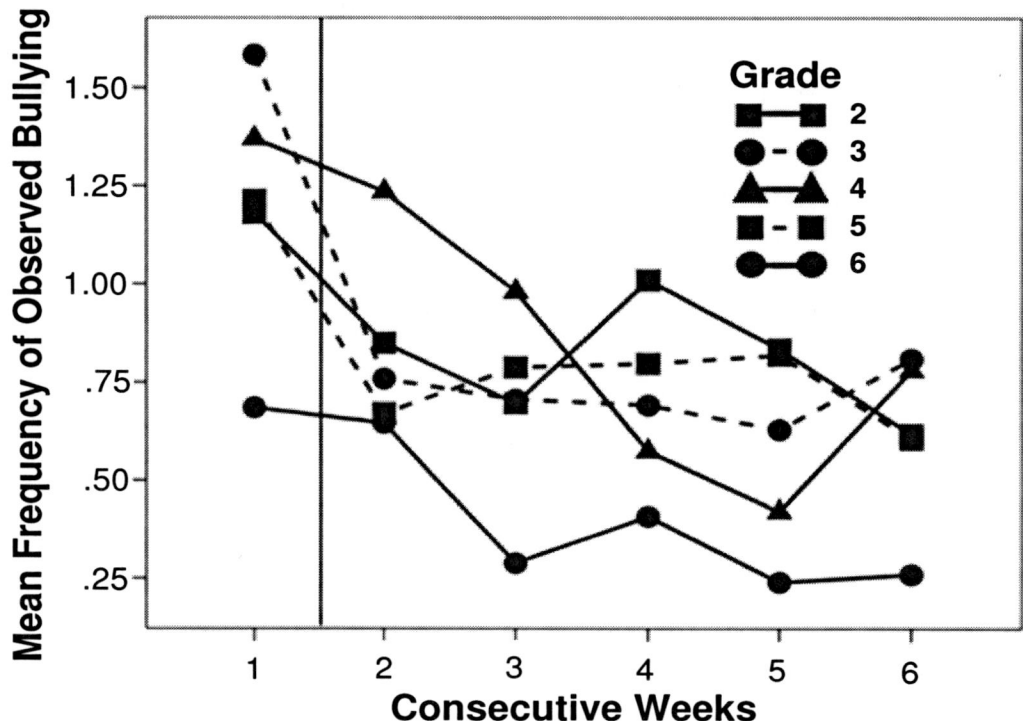

Figure 6.3. Mean frequency of observed bullying behavior per grade over six consecutive weeks.

43.7% for Grade 2, 38.7% for Grade 3, 6.5% for Grade 4, 65.5% for Grade 5, and 49.6% for Grade 6.

Self-Esteem. Students responded to a single face-valid item to measure self-esteem, "I feel good about myself," from the ten-item Rosenberg Self-Esteem (RSE) scale.[59] To respond to this statement, students circled one of five alternatives: Strongly Disagree, Disagree, Neutral, Agree, or Strongly Agree. As depicted in Figure 6.5 on page 166, the mean scores for the self-esteem item increased significantly from Baseline to Week 6 for each Grade.

Discussion

This follow-up study to Field Study 1 included three additional program components: 1) Teachers were educated for one hour on program implementation and the psychological principles underlying AC4P; 2) Students received a motivational AC4P presentation; and 3) Teachers, administrators, and support staff modeled the components of the AC4P intervention (i.e., SAPS).

From Baseline to Week 6 and across all grades, the frequencies of observed bullying behavior decreased significantly by 50.4%, and being bullied significantly decreased by 52.3%. This is consistent with Field Study 1, which found significant reductions in bullying others (63%) and being bullied (56%) from Baseline to Withdrawal.

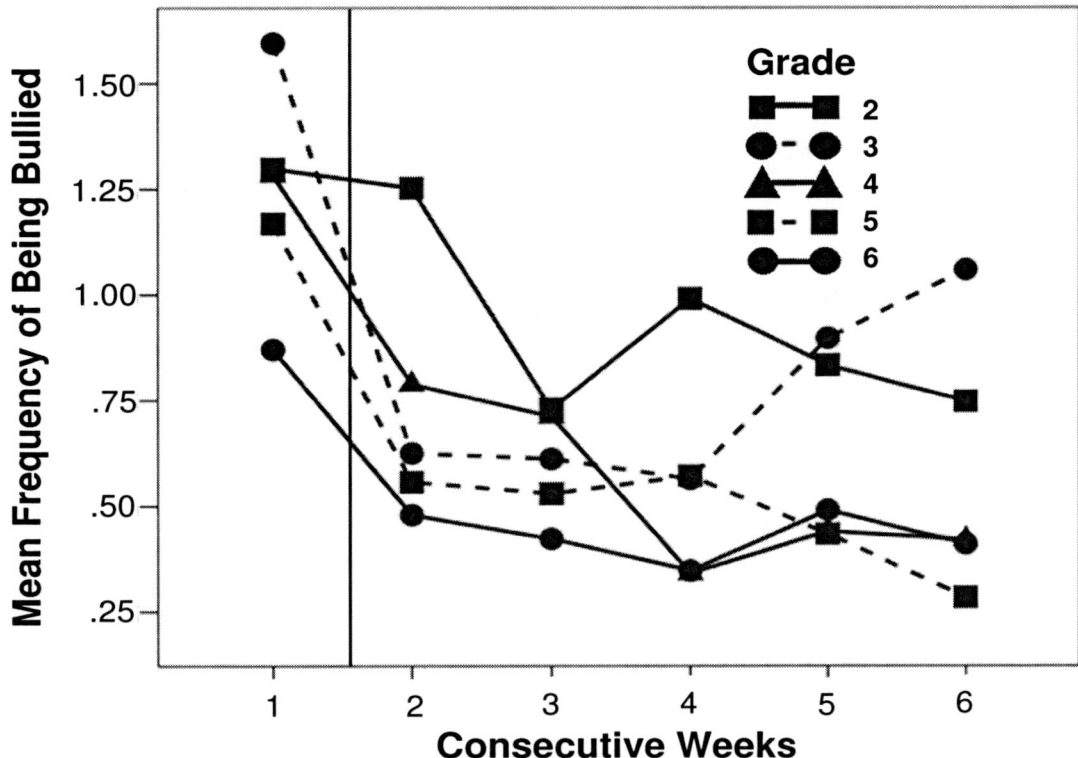

Figure 6.4. Mean frequency of being bullied per grade over six consecutive weeks.

As expected, bullying differed by grade level. At Baseline, observed bullying behavior was highest for Grade 3 and lowest for Grade 6. Similarly, victimization was highest at Baseline for Grade 3 and lowest for Grade 6.

The mean bullying differences as a function of grade are consistent with some but not all prior research. While Espelage and Holt[60] found students bully more frequently as grade-level increases, Olweus[4] and Ma[61] found higher rates of bullying occur for lower grade levels, as we demonstrated here.

Impact of Incentive/Reward Contingencies. A number of researchers and journalists suggest *if-then* contingencies are ineffective and harmful.[62] In fact, Kohn states, "Incentives do not alter the attitudes that underlie our behaviors… further, not receiving a reward one had expected to receive is also indistinguishable from being punished".[63] This was not the case in the research reported here. Indeed, for every grade the mean score of self-esteem increased throughout the Intervention phase.

Each week, a majority of students in the classroom did not receive the wristband reward, because a maximum of only ten students could be recognized weekly. Yet, marked increases in self-esteem occurred for each grade. Hence, a positive side-effect of the significant decline in bullying for all grades was a concomitant increase in a one-item estimate of self-esteem.

Toward an AC4P School Culture. Students appreciated the AC4P approach. At the conclusion of the AC4P intervention in the elementary school from Field

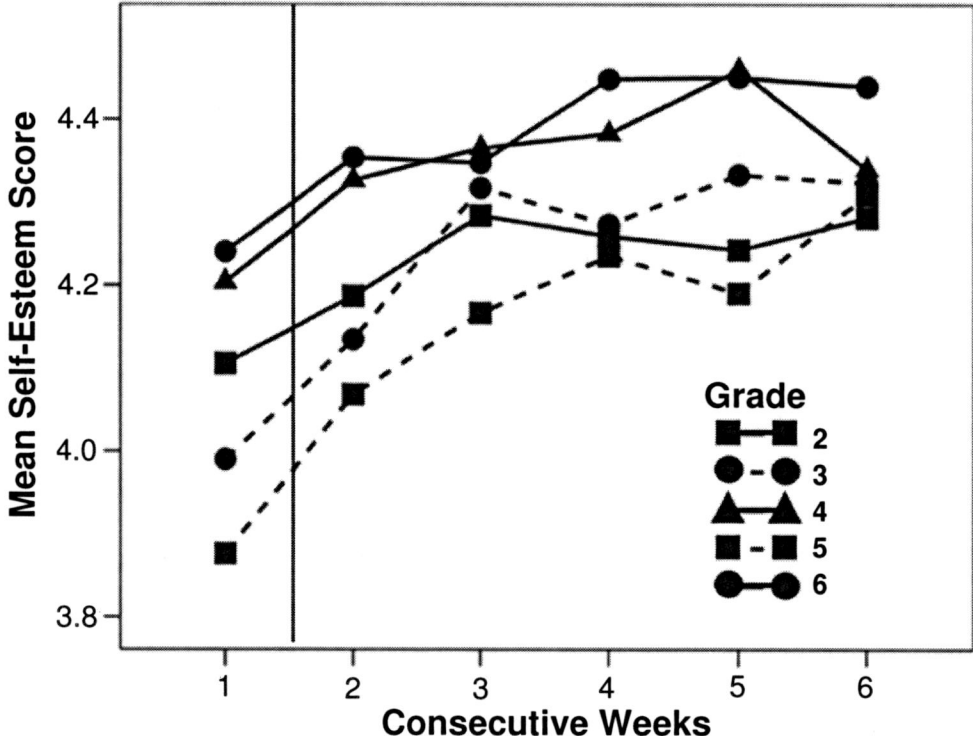

Figure 6.5. Mean self-esteem scores per grade over six consecutive weeks.

Study 2, the first author received a phone call from the Principal with a request to use the phrase "Actively Caring for People" on a stained-glass window.

The photograph on the following page depicts the special stained-glass window displayed prominently in the school cafeteria. The sixth-grade students had voted for this window as their class gift to the school.

This choice for an AC4P stained glass window and the students' marked increase in self-esteem throughout the intervention suggests a prosocial incentive/reward intervention can be effective and appreciated among the stakeholders most influenced by the intervention.

The Principal told a news reporter, "I think it struck a chord with our students, and would at any school. Actively Caring for People has become part of our language, part of our school."[64]

These reactions from the Principal and students reflect strong support for the social validity of this AC4P approach to prevent bullying.

Limitations. The limitations for Field Study 1 are the same here, requiring a need for follow-up evaluation of the AC4P approach to prevent bullying in elementary schools. Most significantly, both schools had schedules that disallowed a longer-term study of our AC4P bullying-prevention approach, and without an appropriate Withdrawal phase, the functional control of the intervention could not be demonstrated.

The large sample size (n=403) was adequate for assessing grade-level differences

in bullying behavior, but the sample sizes ranged markedly from second grade (n=107) to sixth grade (n=54). Therefore, empirical support for the same grade differences observed by Olweus[4] and Ma[61] should be considered with caution.

Additionally, these findings were observed among students with high socio-economic status (SES) and low ethnic diversity. Follow-up research is needed to determine whether generalization to other populations is warranted.

In Conclusion

These two field studies demonstrated promise of a teacher-directed AC4P approach to prevent bullying that targeted desirable prosocial behavior incompatible with interpersonal bullying. The tangible AC4P wristband served as an effective incentive/reward to increase prosocial behavior. Additionally, students' AC4P behaviors were more frequent and their related perceptions more positive after receiving an AC4P wristband.

Follow-up research is needed to determine the relative impact of the four components of the AC4P intervention: 1) teachers' public recognition and social support of students' AC4P behaviors; 2) weekly conversations to facilitate interpersonal friendships; 3) an individual if-then contingency to wear the AC4P wristband for a day; and 4) a group if-then contingency to keep the wristband after all classmates are recognized twice as AC4P heroes.

Marked reductions in bullying are the most relevant evaluation metric for a school-wide intervention to decrease bullying. Still, a measure of social validity is critical. As emphasized by Schwartz and Baer,[65] social validity refers to the acceptability and usability of an intervention program by assessing its impact on relevant stakeholders.

Social validity was high in both schools implementing the AC4P intervention, and the second school chose the words and symbols of AC4P for a stained-glass window.

Every student participated in the AC4P intervention, writing at least one AC4P story and performing at least one AC4P behavior. All of the teachers integrated the AC4P intervention into their daily morning routines. Additionally, administrators benefitted from the low financial cost of the program (i.e., $199 for 199 wristbands in Field Study 1 and $405 for the 404 student wristbands and one adult-size wristband used in Field Study 2).

Future research of the AC4P approach to prevent bullying will continuously improve and evaluate variations of the intervention.[66] For example, future program components will include: a) participation of stakeholders (e.g., parents) in the AC4P Movement by passing wristbands and sharing stories; b) a video-curriculum of AC4P stories and lessons from AC4P leaders; and c) an extension of the AC4P approach from elementary schools to middle schools,[67] high schools, and university settings.

From one perspective, the field studies reviewed here merely demonstrate the potential of a positive AC4P approach to preventing interpersonal bullying without ever mentioning bullying or using punitive measures with negative consequences. However, our initial experience with the AC4P approach suggests this intervention to prevent bullying is more than another incentive/reward contingency program.

The wristband reward was valued by students as a special recognition from their teacher for heroic behavior, and can readily spread beyond the classroom. Consider, for example, the following three email-stories received from a parent, principal and school counselor regarding the profound impact of the AC4P approach at their elementary school.

The Impact of the AC4P Wristband

My son's elementary school has a wonderful program where the children are able to submit in writing a kind act by another classmate. All submissions are evaluated on a daily basis and two children are selected to wear the wristband for an entire day. All of the teachers and children are aware of the significance of wearing a wristband.

Last week, my son, Jacob, assisted a child who was hurt on the playground and helped him to the nurse's office. The injured child submitted Jacob's kind act and on Friday, he became the proud recipient of the green "Actively Caring for People" wristband for the day. At the conclusion of the school day, he couldn't wait to come home and tell me about what had happened; however, he forgot to return the wristband to his teacher and it came home with him.

Jacob has a younger sister and she was as proud of him as his dad and I were. Unfortunately, she was playing with the wristband and pulled it to see how far it would stretch, and it broke. Jacob was devastated and although we have tried to super glue the wristband back together, he is distraught that the one item each child is trying very hard to earn the right to wear, is now broken. What should we do?!

The AC4P team sent a replacement wristband to the classroom teacher and they continued with the process. Jacob's story suggests this wristband represents more than a reward; rather it's an esteemed token of appreciation and a symbol of the students' shared vision to cultivate a more compassionate classroom.

A Student's Note to the Principal

A gym teacher met with a student after he bullied another student. They discussed why it was wrong and the student owned up to his behavior, but his next gesture was a surprise. The student wrote a note to the Principal to apologize for his actions. The end of the note said, "I am sorry for what I did, that was not actively caring".

Some people feel guilty when they don't live up to AC4P. At times, we may use guilt and shame interchangeably, but these terms are distinctly different.[68] After performing non-AC4P behavior (i.e., bullying), some might feel guilt, "My behavior was bad" while others feel shame, "I am a bad person". Prior research has shown children with higher scores on guilt also scored higher on prosocial behavior.[69]

The student who apologized via a note to the Principal may recognize the discrepancy between his actual behavior (non-AC4P) and ideal behavior (AC4P). While some may feel guilty, the student's response focused on his negative behavior being wrong (guilt), not labeling himself a bad person (shame). This reflects the AC4P principle of targeting behavior not the person when giving corrective feedback (see Chapter 3).

The AC4P approach established prosocial behavior as an expectation for students, thereby facilitating guilt for a student who failed to live up to the school-wide expectations. In other words, when we perceive our behavior as contrary to our values or ideal-self, we feel guilt or cognitive dissonance[36] and usually attempt to resolve this discrepancy by changing our behavior.

A Trip to the Pumpkin Patch

Most students loved the AC4P approach and the process of recognizing each other's classroom behavior with a wristband. We had a variety of AC4P stories from the students, but few compare to the following story.

We took our elementary students on a field trip to the Pumpkin patch a few days before Halloween. After some time, they noticed a college-age student working and spotted a wristband. One student had the courage to ask the worker what words were on the green wristband. "Actively Caring for People," said the worker.

The students were in awe. At that moment, they realized AC4P went beyond them, beyond the school and into the community. AC4P is not just a program in schools, but a Movement spreading beyond Virginia Tech to a pumpkin patch and communities worldwide.

These unsolicited email reports provide additional support for this AC4P approach to prevent bullying beyond our statistically significant research results. We are working tirelessly to improve this AC4P approach, so schools nationwide can begin the journey of cultivating an AC4P school culture.

Notes

1. Alexander, B. (2010, October 2). *The bullying of Seth Walsh: Requiem for a small-town boy*. Retrieved from www.time.com/time/nation/article/0,8599,2023083,00.html
2. Foderaro, L. (2010, September 29). Private moment made public, then a fatal jump. *The New York Times*.
3. Hirsch, L. (Director). (2011). *Bully*. [Motion Picture] The Weinstein Company.
4. Olweus, D. (1993). *Bullying at school: What we know and what we can do*. Malden, MA: Blackwell Publishing.
5. Nansel, T.R., Overpeck, M., Pilla, R.S., Ruan, W.J., Simons-Morton, B., & Scheidt, P. (2001). Bullying behaviors among U.S. youth: Prevalence and association with psychosocial adjustment. *The Journal of the American Medical Association, 285*(16), 2094-2100.
6. Riggio, R.E. (2010, February 2). Cutting-edge leadership. *Psychology Today*. Retrieved from http://www.psychologytoday.com/blog/cutting-edge-leadership/201002/workplace-bullying-applying-psychological-torture-work.
7. Limber, S.P. (2002). Addressing youth bullying behaviors. *Proceedings from the American Medical Association Educational Forum on Adolescent Health: Youth Bullying. Chicago, IL: American Medical Association*. Retrieved from http://www.ama-assn.org/ama1/pub/upload/mm/39/youthbullying.pdf.
8. Glew, G.M., Fan, M.Y., Katon, W., Rivara, F.P., & Kernic, M.A. (2005). Bullying, psychosocial adjustment, and academic performance in elementary school. *Archives of Pediatrics and Adolescent Medicine, 159*(11), 1026-1031.
9. Salmon, G., James, A., & Smith, D.M. (1998). Bullying in schools: Self-reported anxiety, depression, and self esteem in secondary school children. *British Medical Journal, 317*, 924-925.
10. Klomek, A.B., Marrocco, F., Kleinman, M., Schonfeld, I.S., & Gould, M.S. (2007). Bullying, depression, and suicidality in adolescents. *Journal of American Academy of Child Adolescent Psychiatry, 46*(1), 40-49.
11. Kaltiala-Heino, R., Rimpela, M., Marttuenen, M., Rimpela, A., & Rantanen, P. (1999). Bullying, depression, and suicidal ideation in Finnish adolescents: school survey. *British Medical Journal, 319*, 348-351.
12. Klomek, A.B., Sourander, A., Niemela, S., Kumpulainen, K., Piha, J., Tamminen, T., Almqvist, F., & Gould, M.S. (2009). Childhood bullying behaviors as a risk for suicide attempts and completed suicides: A population-based birth cohort study. *Journal of the American Academy of Child and Adolescent Psychiatry, 48*(3), 254-261.
13. Borum, R., Fein, R., Modzeleski, W., Reddy, M., & Vossekuil, B. (2002). United States Secret Service and United States Department of Education. *The final report and findings of the safe school initiative*. Retrieved from http://www.secretservice.gov/ntac/ssi_final_report.pdf.
14. Coloroso, B. (2008). *The bully, the bullied, and the bystander*. New York, NY: HarperCollins.
15. Johnson, A., Cahil, P., & Dedman, B, (2007, April 19). High school classmates say gunman was bullied. *MSNBC news*. Retrieved from http://www.msnbc.msn.com/id/18169776/ns/us_news-crime_and_courts/
16. Bandura, A. (1977). *Social learning theory*. Englewood Cliffs, NJ: Prentice-Hall.
17. Patterson, G., Littman, R., & Bricker, W. (1967). Assertive behavior in children: A step toward a theory of aggression. *Monographs of the Society for Research in Child Development*, 32 (5, No.113).
18. Craig, W., & Pepler, D. (2000). Observations of bullying in the playground and in the classroom. *School Psychology International, 21*(1), 22-36.
19. Colvin, G., Tobin, T., Beard, K., Hagan, S., & Sprague, J. (1998). The school bully: Assessing the problem, developing interventions, and future research directions. *Journal of Behavioral Education,*

8(3), 293-319.

20. Sherer, Y.C., & Nickerson, A.B. (2010). Anti-bullying practices in American schools: Perspectives of school psychologists. *Psychology in the Schools, 47*(3), 217-229.
21. Ttofi, M.M., & Farrington, D.P. (2010). Effectiveness of school-based programs to reduce bullying: A systematic and meta-analytical review. *Journal of Experimental Criminology, 7*(1), 27-56.
22. Swearer, S.M., Espelage, D.L., Vaillancourt, T., & Hymel, S. (2010). What can be done about school bullying?: Linking research to educational practice. *Educational Researcher, 39*, 38-47.
23. Sidman, M. (1989). *Coercion and its fallout*. Boston, MA: Authors Cooperative.
24. Whitted, S., & Dupper, R.D. (2005). Best practices for preventing or reducing bullying in schools. *Children & School, 27*(3), 167-175.
25. Roland, E. (2002). Aggression, depression, and bullying others. *Aggressive Behavior, 28*, 198-206.
26. Miltenberger, R.G. (1997). *Behavior modification: Principles and procedures*. Pacific Grove, CA: Brooks-Cole; Ogier, R., & Hornby, G. (1996). Effects of differential reinforcement on the behavior and self-esteem of children with emotional and behavioral disorders. *Journal of Behavioral Education, 6*(4), 501-510.
27. Simpson, B., & Willer, R. (2008). Altruism and indirect reciprocity: The interaction of person and situation in prosocial behavior. *Social Psychology Quarterly, 71*(1), 37-52.
28. Honig, A.S., & Pollack, B. (1990). Effects of a brief intervention program to promote prosocial behaviors in young children. *Early Education and Development, 1*(6), 438–444.
29. Demaray, M.K., & Malecki, C.K. (2006). A review of the use of social support in anti-bullying programs. *The Journal of School Violence, 5*(3), 51-70.
30. Whitted, S., & Dupper, R.D. (2005). Best practices for preventing or reducing bullying in schools. *Children & School, 27*(3), p.169.
31. Geller, E.S. (2001). *The psychology of safety handbook*. Boca Raton, FL: CRC Press.
32. Wentzel, K.R., Barry, C.M., & Caldwell, K.A. (2004). Friendships in middle school: Influences on motivation and school adjustment. *Journal of Educational Psychology, 96*(2), 195-203.
33. Hoglund, W., & Leadbeater, B. (2004) The effects of family, school, and classroom ecologies on changes in children's social competence and emotional and behavioral problems in first grade. *Developmental Psychology, 40*(4), 533-544.
34. Feldman, R.S., Philippot, P., & Custrini, R.J. (1991). In R.S. Feldman & B. Rime (Eds.). *Fundamentals of nonverbal behavior* (pp. 329-350). Cambridge, MA: Cambridge University Press.
35. Cook, C.R., Williams, K.R., Guerra, N.G., Kim, T.E., & Sadek, S. (2010). Predictors of bullying and victimization in childhood and adolescence: A meta-analytical investigation. *School Psychology Quarterly, 25*(2), 65-83.
36. Festinger, L. (1957). *A theory of cognitive dissonance*. Stanford, CA: Stanford University Press.
37. Olweus, D., & Limber, S.P. (2010). Bullying in school: Evaluation and dissemination of the Olweus bullying prevention program. *American Journal of Orthopsychiatry, 80*(1), 124-134; Olweus, D., & Limber, S.P. (2009). The Olweus bullying prevention program: Implementation and evaluation over two decades. In S. Jimerson, S. Swearer, & D. Espelage (Eds.). *Handbook of bullying in schools: An international perspective* (pp. 377-401). New York, NY: Routledge.
38. Bully-Free Virginia. (2012). *Spotlight on Virginia schools*. Retrieved from http://www.bullyfreevirginia.org/spotlight.html
39. Olweus, D. (1991). Bully/victim problems among schoolchildren: Basic facts and effects of a school-based intervention program. In D.J. Pepler & K.H. Rubin (Eds.). *The development and treatment of childhood aggression* (pp. 411-448). Hillsdale, NJ: Lawrence Erlbaum.
40. Crothers, L.M., & Levinson, E.M. (2004). The assessment of bullying: A review of methods and instruments. *Journal of Counseling and Development, 82*(4), 496-503.

41. Smith, P.K. (2004). Bullying: Recent developments. *Child and Adolescent Mental Health, 9*(3), 98-103.

42. Kert, A.S., Codding, R.S., Tryon, G.S., & Shiyko, M. (2010). Impact of the word "bully" on the reported rate of bullying behavior. *Psychology in the Schools, 47*(2), 193-204.

43. Scheithauer, H., Hayer, T., Petermann, F., & Jugert, G. (2006). Physical, verbal, and relational forms of bullying among German students: Age trends, gender differences and correlates. *Aggressive Behavior, 32*(3), 261-275.

44. Underwood, M.K., & Rosen, L.H. (2011). Gender and bullying. In D.L. Espelange & S.M. Swearer (Eds.), *Bullying in North American schools* (2nd Edition) (pp. 13-22). New York, NY: Routledge.

45. Duncan, R.D. (2011). Family relationships of bullies and victims. In D.L. Espelange & S.M. Swearer (Eds.), *Bullying in North American schools* (2nd Edition) (pp. 199-204). New York, NY: Routledge.

46. Flaspohler, P.D., Elfstrom, J.L., Vanderzee, K.L., Sink, H.E., & Birchmeier, Z. (2009). Stand by me: The effects of peer and teacher support in mitigating the impact of bullying on quality of life. *Psychology in the Schools, 46*(7), 636-649.

47. Doll, B., Song, S., Champion, A., & Jones, K. (2011). Classroom ecologies that support or discourage bullying. In D.L. Espelage & Swearer, (Eds.). *Bullying in North American schools* (2nd Edition) (pp. 147-158). New York, NY: Routledge.

48. Lee, K.H., Baillargeon, R.H., Vermunt, J.K., Wu, H.X., & Tremblay, R.E. (2007). Age differences in the prevalence of physical aggression among 5–11-year-old Canadian boys and girls. *Aggressive Behavior, 33*(1), 26-37.

49. Berndt, T.J. (1981). Age changes and changes over time in prosocial intentions and behavior between friends. *Developmental Psychology, 17*(4), 408-416.

50. Nantel-Vivier, A., Kokko, K., Caprara, G.V., Pastorelli, C., Gerbino, M.G., Paciello, M., Côté, S., Pihl, R.O., Vitaro, F., & Tremblay, R.E. (2009). Prosocial development from childhood to adolescence: A multi-informant perspective with Canadian and Italian longitudinal studies. *Journal of Child Psychology and Psychiatry, 50*(5), 590-598.

51. Rosenberg, M. (1979). *Conceiving the self.* New York, NY: Basic Books.

52. O'Moore, A.M., & Hillery, B. (1991). What do teachers need to know? In M. Elliott (Ed.). *Bullying: A practical guide to coping for schools.* Harlow: Longman Group.

53. O'Moore, M., & Kirkham, C. (2001). Self-esteem and its relationship to bullying behavior. *Aggressive Behavior, 27*(4), 269-283.

54. Michael, J. (1982). Distinguishing between discriminative and motivational functions of stimuli. *Journal of the Experimental Analysis of Behavior, 37*(1), 149-155.

55. Batson, C.D., Bolen, M.H., Cross, J.A., & Neuringer-Benefiel, H.E. (1986). Where is altruism in the altruistic personality? *Journal of Personality and Social Psychology, 50*(1), 212-220; Bierhoff, H.W., Klein, R., & Kramp, P. (1991). Evidence for altruistic personality from data on accident research. *Journal of Personality, 59*(2), 263-279; Wilson, J.P. (1976). Motivation, modeling, and altruism: A person X situation analysis. *Journal of Personality and Social Psychology, 34*(6), 1078-1086.

56. Michelini, R.L., Wilson, J.P., & Messe, L.A. (1975). The influence of psychological needs on helping behavior. *The Journal of Personality, 91*(2), 253-258.

57. Geller, E.S., Roberts, S., & Gilmore, M. (1996). Predicting propensity to actively care for occupational safety. *Journal of Safety Research, 27*(1), 1-8.

58. An ABA design was originally planned, but the pre-existing school schedule did not enable us to extend the study beyond six weekly assessments.

59. Rosenberg, M. (1965). *Society and the adolescent self-image.* Princeton, NJ: Princeton University Press.

60. Espelage, D.L., & Holt, M.K. (2001). Bullying and victimization during early adolescence: Peer

influences and psychosocial correlates. *Journal of Emotional Abuse, 2*(2-3), 123-142.

61. Ma, X. (2002). Bullying in middle school: Individual and school characteristics of victims and offenders. *School Effectiveness and School Improvement, 13*(1), 63-89.

62. Kohn, A. (1993). *Punished by rewards*. Boston, MA: Houghton-Mifflin; Pink, D.H. (2009). *Drive: The surprising truth about what motivates us*. New York, NY: Riverhead Books; Schwartz, B. (2010). Using our practical wisdom. *TED*. Retrieved from http://www.ted.com/talks/barry_schwartz_using_our_practical_wisdom.html

63. Kohn, A. (1993). Why incentive plans cannot work. (pp. 2-3). *Harvard Business Review, 71*(5), 54-61

64. Raboteau, A. (2011, July 25). Psychology professor, students say recognizing daily acts of kindness makes a huge impact. *Virginia Tech: Spotlight*. Retrieved from http://www.vt.edu/spotlight/impact/2011-07-25-caring/movement.html

65. Schwartz, I.S., & Baer, D. (1991). Social validity assessments: Is current practice state of the art? *Journal of Applied Behavior Analysis. 24*(2), 7-22.

66. We are grateful to the numerous school leaders who have led research efforts and provided feedback for us to continuously improve this AC4P approach, including Cynthia Brown, Jamey Chianetta, Janet Funk, Stephen Hockett, Lynda Jesukiewicz, Margo Kernen, Marsha Lawler, Ray Lonnett, Jane Manning, Janet Mitchell, Pamela Moody, Cathy Mullins, Abigail Rainie, Mary Therrell, Pamela Spinner, Philomena Vincente, Janie White, and the teachers, support staff, students, and parents from each of these outstanding schools.

67. We are grateful to the American Psychological Foundation for providing funding to study the effectiveness of the AC4P approach in middle schools.

68. Erickson, E.H. (1950). *Childhood and society*. New York, NY: Norton.

69. Krevans, J., & Gibbs, J.C. (2008). Parents' use of inductive discipline: Relations to children's empathy and prosocial behavior. *Child Development, 67*(6), 3263-3277.

CHAPTER 7

AC4P in a Middle School:
A teacher's journey

Andrea Langston

WITH SO MUCH attention and focus on state tests and federal indicators of adequate yearly progress, it has become increasingly difficult to provide engaging learning experiences and build relationships in my classroom. I've spent years attempting to increase AC4P behavior among my students.

Building a Caring Middle School

The solution can't be to fill some gap in the school curriculum like plugging the hole in a dike. We must understand the school as a community, identify the community's strengths, resources, and needs, and be purposeful to ensure lessons throughout the entire school day promote healthy relationships, respectful problem-solving, and a learning community of interdependence, compassion, and optimism. For this, we need a culture shift.

A Personal AC4P Encounter

In April 2011, I learned about the AC4P mission and vision from Shane McCarty and Sophia Teie when we drove to Cleveland, Ohio together for a conflict resolution conference. Armed with new knowledge and a green AC4P wristband, my journey to bring AC4P to my classroom began with my own AC4P experience after the conference.

I take a cab downtown to catch a bus to Pittsburgh, Pennsylvania to spend time with my family. The cab driver drops me off on the corner to wait with a father and daughter who, with suitcases, must also be waiting for the bus. It has been a long day. My presentation was on this last day of the conference, and I'm frazzled. I gather my luggage to wait the few minutes before the bus is scheduled to depart.

A man in a uniform, possibly a hotel worker, comes across the street and asks if we are waiting for the bus. He tells us the stop had been moved to the next block. We thank him and as he turns to leave I remember the green band on my wrist. I had noticed his name tag and call for him to come back. I thank George for actively caring for us, give him my wristband, and ask him to pass the gesture on.

I still see the expression on his face – the shine in his eyes when he reached out his hand for mine, asked me my name, and told me it was a "pleasure and an honor" and he would definitely pass it on. I had goose bumps and a smile that couldn't be erased. I also had something of a revelation: AC4P is not just what my classroom needs or my school needs, this is what the world needs!

As soon as I got settled on the bus, I called Sophia to share my story. We then committed to make AC4P happen at Blacksburg Middle School.

In the fall, we set out to build an AC4P model process that could work in our middle-school environment. I convinced my team teachers to help design this exemplar and implement a pilot program during our advisory time.

Shane and Sophia coordinated classroom coaches from their pool of student research assistants from the Center for Applied Behavior Systems (CABS) at Virginia Tech (VT). And so our middle-school AC4P process began.

Building Relationships by Moving Mountains

One of the most powerful moments of the AC4P implementation happened early on. I had worked with student coaches to plan weekly AC4P lessons. We started with the theme of "Courage". This was to acknowledge the fact that performing and recognizing acts of caring is easier said than done. The classroom activity to demonstrate courage was simple, but the result was nothing short of astonishing.

All participants, including teachers and staff, receive a ticket with a direction on it. We are instructed not to look at our tickets until one of the coaches finishes counting to three. On three, we look at our ticket, and then we all sit down. I know one ticket did not have the sit-down instructions. Clearly, something is wrong.

Swiftly, one of the coaches asks us all to look at our tickets again as he makes his way to the student he knows has the exception. I feel my stomach drop and perhaps even the blood drain from my face. Since the beginning of the year, this particular student had disrupted every community-building activity I had attempted. I am certain today will be no exception.

I want to salvage this lesson on AC4P courage and protect the coaches, but what can I do? I am even more worried when this student approaches me at the front of the room.

I suppress my urge to intervene even though I know he isn't following the direction on the ticket, which I presume had instructed him to give one of the VT coaches a compliment. I cringe and wait.

Then the student faces the classroom, looks at me and says, "Ms. Langston, thank you for teaching us every day and for believing in all our dreams".

I look at him, frozen, waiting for him to laugh, to make it a joke, to do something obnoxious. I sit stunned, wondering how this had happened. It was so touching to hear *him* thank *me*. The rest of the students must think he was sincere because no one is laughing.

It seems like a long time before I respond with a heartfelt, "You're welcome," and an appreciative, "Thanks for your kind words". He returns to his seat and the lesson continues.

I conclude the coaches had changed the statement on the "courage ticket" and had given the student more explicit directions in order to reduce the level of social risk. I seek out that ticket by collecting all of them from the students as they exit the classroom. When I turn over the exception, the ticket simply reads, "Thank your teacher".

A mountain has just been moved in our relationship. I later surmise this was a critical juncture in his personal growth and acceptance in the entire group. Ever since that courageous "thank you," this student returns to my room at the end of the school day to get his things; and he always takes the time to say goodbye and wish me a good evening.

Planting AC4P Seeds in a Learning Community

I've learned so much from the AC4P project. While many students struggled with writing AC4P stories about other students, especially when stepping beyond their friendship zones, eventually everyone received an AC4P wristband. Not all students continued to wear their bands, however. Those who did were those I had given the AC4P wristband during the first weeks of the process in order to create an AC4P "buzz".

The weekly AC4P lessons presented by the coaches from VT are great ways to inspire students to act and notice AC4P behavior in their school community, but sharing these on Fridays limited the carryover into practice during the week. After all, adolescents live very much in the present.

Students with whom I had been struggling to make connections started to become more of a family, especially my Advisory Group with whom I met each day for 20 minutes after their lunch period. While I didn't necessarily notice more acts of kindness among these students, I did sense less meanness.

Wearing the AC4P wristband has power. It's difficult to act unkindly or bully someone when you have the AC4P band on your wrist. People, even young people, choose to wear these wristbands because they believe in the AC4P mission and want to honor its meaning.

It's important to incorporate AC4P into the routine language of the classroom, not just during advisory time or on coaching days. It's amazing how seamlessly AC4P integrated into my History class.

My students now recognize leaders of the Progressive Era as people who actively cared in their communities; they see the absence of AC4P among the bystanders of the Holocaust; and they look for opportunities to recognize AC4P behavior as we discuss current events in our global community. AC4P has become part of their vocabulary and part of their world.

There continue to be challenges helping students expand their zones of compassion and caring – getting them to act outside of their friendship circles, and pushing them to recognize AC4P behavior among their peers.

Spending just one school year with my students, I have not yet seen the long-term effects of AC4P or the impact of the rest of my teaching. However, I have faith I have planted seeds that will grow. The harvest hinges on how those seeds are nourished.

I look forward to planting many more AC4P seeds among students with whom I am so fortunate to build relationships. With AC4P, I believe I can meet the challenge of cultivating and sustaining compassion in my classroom culture.

CHAPTER 8

Empowering People to Prevent Bullying:
Applying the AC4P principles in workshops[1]

Jenna McCutchen, Shane M. McCarty, and Brittany Tarzia

"*WE CAN DO IT.*" At first, we believed those words. Our team of 12 AC4P coaches from the Center for Applied Behavior Systems (CABS) at Virginia Tech (VT) was invited to the 2012 *Bullying Summit: Changing School and University Climate and Culture* at Cuyahoga Community College in Highland Hills, Ohio.

Our coaches were asked to lead workshops on the theory and application of the AC4P approach for three educational settings: a) middle schools, b) high schools, and c) universities. The participants would be students, teachers, school counselors, university professors and school administrators.

We were excited to teach the AC4P principles to people from different communities, but after reflection, we began to doubt our ability to meet this challenge.

Empowering Coaches to Teach AC4P

Representative of our doubts: In our preparation meeting, Brittany Tarzia spoke up and asked for guidance, "How can we empower others to actively care and meet the needs of their unique cultures?" No one could answer this question, because none of us felt empowered.

From a management perspective empowerment means, "Get more done with fewer resources". We didn't want to *be* empowered; we wanted to *feel* empowered. This would require us to answer "Yes" to three questions: 1) *Can I do it?* 2) *Will it work?* and 3) *Is it worth it?*[2]

Self-efficacy ("*I can do it*") is the belief you can organize and perform the procedures needed to achieve a desired goal.[3] This requires training to develop the skills and abilities to perform task-specific behaviors.

Response-efficacy ("*It will work*") explains why a process is useful for achieving a certain mission.[3] You must believe the intervention will have a desirable impact, and this belief can be acquired through education.

Outcome expectancy ("*It's worth it*") is the belief the consequences of the behaviors you perform are worth the effort required to perform them. Such outcome-expectancy not only motivates you, but also the collective group. This in turn fuels self-efficacy and response-efficacy.[2]

We needed to acquire each of these three beliefs to feel empowered and self-motivated to develop and deliver effective workshops on the AC4P approach for bullying prevention.

High Response-Efficacy and Outcome-Expectancy

We believed the principles underlying the AC4P approach could be applied effectively to prevent bullying, because we had observed firsthand the success of AC4P applications in elementary-school, middle-school, high-school and university settings.

And we knew it would be worthwhile to spread the AC4P theory and applications to the participants at the *Bullying Summit,* because learning these principles and applications could lead to compassionate relationships, safer schools, and AC4P communities.

Lacking Self-Efficacy

Individuals with general self-efficacy believe they are competent to perform various behaviors in a variety of situations. However, Bandura[3] conceptualized self-efficacy as task-specific. For example, some people believe in their ability to perform well in educational situations (academic self-efficacy), while others communicate effectively with strangers (social self-efficacy).

Our team lacked the specific self-efficacy to teach the AC4P approach. We did not feel empowered to develop and deliver effective AC4P workshops to teachers, students, and administrators.

Gaining Self-Efficacy (*"I can do it"*)

Our coaches met at Make-A-DiffRanch to develop a plan for the *Bullying Summit*, with guidance from Joanne and Scott Geller. Our mission was to develop self-efficacy among the AC4P coaches and strengthen the belief that we can do it.

In addition, the AC4P pedagogy extends beyond empowerment and uses strategies from evidence-based principles to enable people to believe they contribute, belong, achieve, choose, and are appreciated and heard.[4]

Icebreakers to Facilitate Learning[5]

The day began with an icebreaker to build self-efficacy and develop relationships among the AC4P coaches. Each coach read aloud to the group a meaningful lesson on the AC4P principles of interdependence, courage, compassion, or continuous learning.

Reflecting on a particular lesson, we discussed connections to our personal beliefs, values, and experiences. This uncomfortable but shared situation improved our public speaking skills and facilitated a sense of belonging among the coaches.

Participation Enhances Belonging[6]

After the icebreaker, we participated in open dialogue about what holds people back from having the courage to perform AC4P behavior (see Chapter 4). A critical question resulted: "Is it easier to pass an AC4P wristband to a stranger or to a friend?"

Each person in the group contributed answers based on their interpersonal exchanges of giving and receiving AC4P wristbands. Some coaches believed it's easier to pass a wristband to a friend; other coaches were challenged to explain AC4P and its purpose.

We shared personal stories and listened with empathy to the perspectives of fellow coaches. These discussions allowed us to be *heard* and *contribute* to conversations, enhancing *belongingness* within the group.

Strategies for AC4P Applications

After our discussions, Dr. Geller spent the next several hours educating us on strategies for applying the relevant AC4P principles in various educational settings. Now, we had the tools for applying our knowledge and the teaching strategies to empower the participants at the *Bullying Summit*, who would use these strategies to empower other leaders in their communities to perform AC4P behaviors and thereby prevent bullying.

The *Bullying Summit*

On the morning of the summit, Shane McCarty delivered a two-hour presentation on the behavioral and psychological science underlying the AC4P Movement and related strategies to prevent bullying. For audience members to believe the AC4P-based methods would work to prevent bullying, they needed to hear the empirical evidence supporting the AC4P approach and its potential to create an AC4P culture of compassion.

Shane shared evidence-based ways to increase the occurrence of AC4P actions directly with behavior-focused interventions and indirectly with practical strategies to enhance the five person-states that increase one's propensity to perform AC4P behavior (see Chapter 2).

Shane showed evidence of the success of specific AC4P applications in elementary schools (see Chapter 6), middle schools (see Chapter 7), high schools (see Chapter 10), and universities (see Chapters 9 & 13). Then, he proceeded to explain the indirect approach, which aims to increase the five person-states of self-esteem, self-efficacy, personal control, optimism, and belonging.

Will It Work?

Immediately following Shane's presentation, a first-grade teacher asserted, "This approach would be extremely effective in my classroom, even with my young students".

Other AC4P coaches heard similar stories from other teachers and students who seemed convinced the AC4P approach *will work* in their schools. After participating in the *Bullying Summit*, college professor Treena Rhodes gave the following testimony in an email:

> *The presentation on the empirical evidence was enlightening. Bullying behaviors have always existed in our schools, but only in recent years have concerted efforts to address bullying been widely publicized. However, many of the bullying-prevention campaigns focus on the bully alone.*
>
> *The Virginia Tech researchers considered the role of bullies, victims, and students unaffected by bullying, because their intervention influenced caring behaviors among all students. The AC4P approach was never presented as a "bullying-prevention" intervention, yet the results showed significant increases in caring behaviors and reductions in bullying behaviors.*

Is It Worth It?

More than 200 students and educators traveled from several school districts surrounding Cleveland, Ohio to attend the *Bullying Summit*. A high-school participant voiced a representative opinion: "The bullying-prevention program at my school doesn't work and so many of my friends need it to work".

A school counselor added, "I see students bullied frequently and I even get bullied myself; it's painful to see and we must stop it now".

Our presentation aimed to change the paradigm from *preventing* bullying to *promoting* actively caring. If we create an

AC4P culture, AC4P behavior will become normative and bullying behavior won't fit. *It's worth it* to initiate a culture shift towards AC4P, but this requires participants to be committed, competent, and courageous.[3]

Can We Do It?

The afternoon workshops gave the participants knowledge and tools to bring the AC4P Movement to their communities. We provided engaging activities to enhance perceptions of empowerment and self-motivation.

The Middle-School Workshop. The middle-school workshop was designed to raise the self-efficacy of student participants who volunteered to train their peers to be AC4P coaches and deliver AC4P lessons in middle schools. We also aimed to raise the self-efficacy of teachers who wanted to develop AC4P-related lesson plans in their respective schools.

Our focus was to build self-efficacy ("*I can do it*") when training high-school and university students to be AC4P coaches because this is a key component of the AC4P pedagogy. Participants were asked to develop creative ways of teaching the AC4P principle of belonging in their lesson plans.

Lesson-Plan Ideas from Students. Some bullying-prevention programs focus on identifying the "hot spots" – the locations in a school where bullying occurs most often.[6] The participants identified four popular locations in their schools (e.g., cafeteria, hallway, school bus, and gym). Instead of focusing on catching the bullying in a "hot spot," participants thought it beneficial for students to develop ideas to enhance the sense of belonging in these locations.

Targeting bullying "hot spots" in schools may create negative connotations with these particular locations. But brainstorming positive strategies for each location activates a beneficial community spirit, which should lead to more AC4P behavior among students in these "hot spots," and beyond.

Lesson-Plan Ideas from Educators. First, the educators articulated their negative attitudes toward discipline-focused and top-down methods to reduce bullying, such as relationship-detracting conversations with bullies and enforcement of school rules. They asserted that students' needs for belonging and autonomy are not met with current procedures in their schools.

A culture shift is more likely to occur with high-involvement and synergy from educators. Their new paradigm is to provide students with a choice to lead school-wide AC4P

activities among their peers. Additionally, educators found innovative ways to connect the AC4P principles with existing school initiatives (e.g., character development, student clubs, advisory times, parent-teacher conferences).

Educators envisioned students creating AC4P posters in art class; teachers discussing the courage and AC4P of legendary leaders in history class; promoting trust and belonging *within* teams during gym class while remaining competitive *between* teams, and so forth. They firmly believed the aforementioned strategies could cultivate a positive school climate, leading to higher performance on standardized tests.[8]

The High-School and College Workshop. Participants' in this workshop defined specific behaviors currently existing in their schools that enhance versus detract from the five person-states. Next, participants developed practical strategies to enhance these person-states:

Self-esteem. Teachers could: a) ask students for advice on how to present certain material, b) give students one-on-one genuine appreciation for their extra effort on a homework assignment or class project.

Self-efficacy. Teachers could: a) ask students for feedback on their lectures to help students' feel more competent, and b) pair students of differing skills and abilities to share personal strategies they used to develop their unique skill sets.

Personal control. Teachers could: a) offer students choice between two or more class activities, b) allow students to teach the class an interesting fact or story of their choice, and c) allow students to submit ideas for homework or test questions.

Optimism. Teachers could: a) lead a review game before a test and give rewards for correct answers, b) model positive words, such as "can," "will learn," "help me," and remove negative words, such as "can't," "too hard," and "hate".

Belonging. Teachers could: a) ask students for ideas that facilitate a sense of belonging and post them as class expectations in lieu of rules, b) create a class circle and share AC4P stories, and c) celebrate the achievement of class goals (see Chapter 3 on effective group celebrations).

In Conclusion

Our workshops provided evidence-based principles and practical strategies for immediate application in participants' educational cultures. We didn't give participants a manual with step-by-step procedures.

Rather, we taught the audience principles and showed sample applications, encouraged them to teach others, and then facilitated the process of transforming and customizing the principles into practical strategies for their school cultures.

The AC4P coaches developed successful workshops to empower the 200 participants at the *Bullying Summit*. Comments from workshop participants suggested: 1) They believed it was worthwhile to pursue a compassionate culture (*"It is worth it"*); 2) AC4P behavior could reduce bullying (*"It will work"*); and 3) The workshops had helped them develop the self-efficacy necessary to increase AC4P behavior in their respective educational cultures (*"We can do it"*).

At the end of the session, workshop participants' used language consistent with the AC4P principles: "I can *contribute* to help my community become a more compassionate place"; "We all want to feel *appreciated,* and now we really know how to show it"; "Conversing with others in an open-discussion gave me a chance to really be *heard*".

The AC4P pedagogy extends beyond empowerment. It uses strategies from evidence-based principles to enable people to believe they contribute, belong, achieve, choose, and are appreciated and heard.[4]

Participants had *choice* to create their own strategies based on the AC4P principles, *contributed* strategies for others to use and share, felt a sense of *belonging* among the participants who shared a similar vision for more compassion in their schools, and felt *appreciation* when they received an AC4P wristband from the coaches for their *accomplishment* of an action plan that could facilitate the achievement of an AC4P culture of compassion at their school.

Notes

1. We are grateful to Beech Brook, Cleveland State University, Cuyahoga Arts & Culture, Facing History and Ourselves, Office of the Ohio Attorney General, Ohio Department of Education, Orange Schools, University of Akron, and Elizabeth Wuerz and Jennifer Batton of the Global Issues Resource Center at Cuyahoga Community College for sponsoring a conference to improve school climate and culture.
2. Geller, E.S. (2005). *People-based safety: The source*. Virginia Beach, VA: Coastal Training and Technologies Corporation.
3. Bandura, A. (1997). *Self-efficacy: The exercise of control*. New York, NY: W.H. Freeman and Company.
4. Geller, E.S., & Veazie, R.A. (2010). *When no one's watching: Living and leading self-motivation*. Newport, VA: Make-A-Difference, LLC.
5. Kavanagh, M., Clark-Murphy, M., & Wood, L. (2011). The first class: Using icebreakers to facilitate transition in a tertiary environment. *Asian Social Science, 7,* 84-92.
6. Geller, E.S. (2002). *The participation factor: How to increase involvement in occupational safety*.

Des Plaines, IL: American Society of Safety Engineers.

7. Limber, S.P., Nation, M., Tracy, A.J., Melton, G.B., & Vlerx, V. (2004). Implementation of the Olweus bullying prevention programme in the Southeastern United States. In P. K. Smith, D. Pepler, & K. Rigby (Eds.). *Bullying in schools: How successful can interventions be?* (pp. 55–79). Cambridge, England: Cambridge University Press.

8. Lacey, A., & Cornell, D. (2011, August). *The impact of a bullying climate on schoolwide academic performance.* Poster session presented at the American Psychological Association meeting, Washington, DC.

CHAPTER 9

Pedagogy for AC4P:
From the university classroom to servant leadership in the Dominican Republic[1]

Shane M. McCarty, E. Scott Geller, Nick Smirniotopoulos, Danny White, Katie DeTuro, and Joanne Dean Geller

"THE PURPOSE OF OUR LIVES is to be happy."[2] A meaningful life of happiness requires *PERMA*: Positive emotion, Engagement, Relationships, Meaning, and Achievement,[3] proposes Martin Seligman, past president of the American Psychological Association and Founder of Positive Psychology.

At Virginia Tech (VT), our university motto and core value of *Ut Prosim* (That I May Serve) extends beyond personal happiness to the happiness we create for others through service. We call this Actively Caring for People (AC4P).

Our university motto, AC4P mindset, AC4P principles, and PERMA formed the foundation for our pedagogy applied in a university course – *Ut Prosim: Self-Motivation and Leadership Discovery*. This chapter highlights the AC4P Pedagogy of this psychology course that included a service-learning trip to the Dominican Republic.

We connected the AC4P principles and our pedagogical philosophy with factors that facilitate happiness and service teaching/learning.

Our Teaching Paradigm

The current teaching/learning system in higher education does not effectively meet some essential teaching/learning needs. Our U.S. colleges and universities have created a mass of aimlessly wandering students, believe sociological researchers Richard Arum and Josipa Roksa. Their book, *Academically Adrift,* highlights a study that shows 45% of college students do not show measurable gains in critical thinking, complex reasoning, and writing skills by their sophomore year.[4]

Thus, we deviated substantially from the typical lecture-based approach, and applied AC4P principles and PERMA to engage students in course material while impacting their personal growth.

Positive psychologists have shown financial stability of up to $75,000 annual income increases happiness, and then other factors become increasingly important.[5] Yet, educational institutions continue to perpetuate the perspective that employability and earning power are the key metrics for a successful college/university experience.[6]

In contrast, we believe a successful undergraduate education should include the development of an AC4P or *Ut Prosim* mindset. This perspective informed the development and application of the exercises, lessons, and assessments used in this course.

A Special Service/Learning Course

"Tell me and I'll forget; show me and I'll remember; involve me and I'll understand."[7] This Chinese proverb reflects an effective approach to teaching and learning.[8] Professor Scott Geller and his two teaching assistants followed this principle throughout their course, designed to teach the human dynamics of real-world problem solving.

Students read *When No One's Watching: Living and Leading Self-Motivation*,[9] listened to lectures on psychological theories and applications, and participated in open discussions on the evidence-based AC4P principles highlighted in Part I of this book.

Next, the ten student-athletes in this class applied these lessons directly to teach various sports activities to 60 children in the developing areas of Veròn and Punta Cana in the Dominican Republic (D.R.).

The students were also introduced to leadership principles relevant to preventing HIV/AIDS and cultivating an AC4P culture in this developing region. Throughout their insightful journey, the ten student-athletes in this course explored their personal values, developed leadership skills for effective teaching, collaborated to present HIV/AIDS prevention information with Deportes Para la Vida ("Sports for Life"), and demonstrated *Ut Prosim* by performing AC4P behavior throughout the trip.

Expectations Preceding Our Journey

Os Guinness once observed, "Contrast is always the mother of clarity".[10] We anticipated our trip to the D.R. would provide contrasts on multiple fronts, enabling profound reinterpretations of our past experiences, increased appreciation for our present, and perhaps a new-found clarity for our future aspirations.

We expected to interact with children of another nation who would be quite similar to the American children we know, except for language differences. After all, running, jumping, throwing and kicking are actions connecting children everywhere.

Despite these similar childhood experiences, we wondered what differences we might observe. How important is family in the D.R.? Who are the role models for their children?

We expected the daily routines of people in a developing country to contrast markedly with our own. But similarities exist, right? Eating, sleeping, school, and work should be similar.

What distinct differences will surface? What are the current working conditions and career options? How do these compare with ours? Do contrasting opportunities exist, especially in education? Will observing contrasts in lifestyles and opportunities change our mindset and lifestyle?

Will contrasts lead to clarify our plans for the future? How will these contrasts influence our self-motivation? Will observing individuals with fewer life privileges increase our motivation to serve others? Will these contrasts inspire us to devote more time and energy to the AC4P Movement?

Our hope: Any contrasts observed between our lives in the U.S. and their lives in the D.R. will lead to greater clarity for our future aspirations.

Our Journey Begins

As we embarked on our journey, our entire group was united by one common belief – shared optimism. Despite countless unknowns, we were optimistic we could make a difference, despite the fact we only met a week earlier. Our shared optimism bonded our group, creating a true sense of *community*.

Furthermore, we each saw the opportunity to help others and *chose* to participate in this pioneering excursion. Each student perceived substantial *competence* in the sport they would teach the D.R. children.

Thus, we were inspired by the three C-words that fuel self-motivation (i.e., *choice*, *competence*, and *community*).[9] We hoped this journey, guided by the AC4P principles, would bring out the best in ourselves and others.

The Heart of Courage

At our first group meeting in Punta Cana, D.R., we gathered to decide collectively on a team name. We wanted to give from our heart, and demonstrate courage and compassion when teaching children. We decided to name our team "Cor" as the abbreviated version of "corazón," which is Spanish for "heart".

We shared our personal values with each member of the team. Our Cor team included the ten student-athletes, three administrators, and one teacher (the senior author). After all team members shared their values and reflections, we co-created a set of "Cor" values. Inspired by the textbook for the course, we developed a list of group values that correspond with our individual values, thereby fueling our self-motivation.[9]

We committed as a group to practice these team values. To maintain alignment between observed behaviors and team values, every team member agreed to provide each other supportive and corrective behavioral feedback throughout the trip.

Giving and receiving feedback can be awkward and uncomfortable, but we each desired to continuously improve with a shared vision and values guiding us. Our *six Cor team values were*:

1. **Appreciate the unique value of every person.** Humanistic psychology recognizes each individual as a unique human being.[11] We agreed every individual is uniquely important for optimizing our mission. We expected children and community members of diverse backgrounds and values to make their contributions to the teaching/learning process.

2. **Be a learner and a teacher.** Individuals possessing a growth mindset believe their abilities are learned and can develop continuously over time.[12] To effectively lead the sports camp, we needed to simultaneously learn and teach. To become effective AC4P teachers, we first listened to the children and assimilated into their culture.

3. **Control the controllable.** Individuals with high-internal locus of control believe most outcomes are within their personal reach.[13] Results are attributed more to individual ability and effort than chance.[14]

We flatly rejected the notion that if anything can go wrong, it will (i.e., Murphy's Law). Many factors in the D.R. were beyond our control, so we aimed to focus our energy on factors within our control and expected the best possible outcomes.

4. **Be joyful**. Optimistic people believe joy can be developed with practice.[15] We aimed to create a positive environment for the campers rather than the development of athletic skills. In our view, promoting a joyful atmosphere conducive to developing meaningful relationships trumped developing technical skills.

5. **Be authentic and courageous**. We wanted to embrace vulnerability and be authentic, showing others our openness to learn with empathy, humility, and flexibility.[16] We believed this mindset would allow us to exhibit the *moral courage*[17] necessary to effectively engage others in our teaching/learning AC4P mission.

6. **Be persistent and self-determined.** Group expectations were set by selecting group values that would be brought to life with our behavior. We realized these ideals would be a challenge to accomplish on a daily basis. Self-determination and persistence were required to consistently demonstrate actions reflecting these six *Cor* values.

Experiencing a Different Culture

For the first three days we explored the D.R. culture, seeking to understand the various situational factors we observed. An empathic and knowledgeable leader, Ben Hulefeld, taught us about the history, geography and local culture from his unique perspective as an American who had lived in the D.R. for more than two years as the Logistical Coordinator for the Punta Cana Ecological Foundation (Fundación Ecológica PUNTACANA).

This Foundation, and its parent company, Grupo Puntacana, have impacted thousands of lives in the town of Veròn. The Foundation helped establish an unprecedented partnership between the Virginia College of Osteopathic Medicine (VCOM) and the Dominican Ministry of Health (Ministerio de Salud Pública) to operate and fund the local Veròn Rural Clinic. This clinic is the only source of free health care for a population of more than 50,000 people.

In addition to improving the local healthcare facilities and networks, Grupo Puntacana and the Foundation built the Ted and Anne Kheel Polytechnic School, which offers vocational training to more than 300 high-school students a year.

We were struck with a whirlwind of emotions after seeing the extreme need for these institutions and their benefits to the D.R. residents. First sadness, then guilt for the gap between our resources and theirs. But a sense of empathic gratitude emerged for the community leaders and institutions providing support for the local health and education.

Contrasting Our American Perspective

Empathic leaders aim to understand completely the other person's intentions and perceptions.[9] Often alternative perspectives cannot be appreciated without experiencing the situational factors that determine the differential perceptions and dispositions of others. Observing the dramatic contrasts between our lives and the residents of the D.R. allowed us to be more understanding of these people and their culture.

Health. In America, our health-related concerns, such as diabetes and obesity, stem from an overabundance of unhealthy food. Many D.R. students are unable to meet basic needs for clean air and water. American patients complain when they wait minutes for quality medical care; Dominicans often wait an entire day for health care of lower quality.

Education. In America, some students do not appreciate their K-12 or college education; most Dominicans lack the financial resources to receive effective education beyond eighth grade.

With grades 1 to 8, the local school serves 900 students in classes of 30 to 70 students. School materials and supplies are out of date and worn; classrooms are crowded; and students are split into a four-hour morning and four-hour afternoon sections to accommodate overcrowding.

Many American students feel almost entitled to higher education and jobs that will sustain a comfortable existence. Most D.R. students are not graced with similar hopes. Many D.R. students do not attend school because they cannot afford the cost of transportation to get there. Many teenagers find their "careers" on the street, taking odd jobs for pocket change and no hope of a fulfilling career.

Courageous AC4P Leaders

The D.R. volunteers from our organizational partner for the sports camp epitomized AC4P leadership. They came from poor families who live in bateyes (local slum communities), yet despite enormous obstacles, they have risen to help others. We could not have imagined more formidable examples of leadership, courage, and self-motivation.

They lived the evidence-based AC4P principles daily, exemplifying *moral courage*[17] by overcoming the social norm for other individuals their age; they choose to help their local communities as opposed to focusing on themselves.

These humble leaders don't get monetary compensation for their service and receive little recognition. Yet they consistently exemplify self-motivation to teach children about basic health issues and prevention strategies.

They are not forced or required to serve others, rather they feel empowered to serve, because they can answer "Yes" to three questions from the empowerment model: 1) *Can I do It?*, 2) *Will it work?*, and 3) *Is it worth it?* (see Chapter 8).

They know *they can do it* because their competence has improved after teaching each lesson. They know *the curriculum works*, as indicated by the 30 percentage-point increase in HIV/AIDS-related knowledge from pre-test to post-intervention. Is it worth it to help others instead of helping themselves?

With numerous communities across the D.R. stricken with HIV/AIDS, they are reminded frequently *it's worth it* to reduce the suffering caused by this rampant disease. Although the consequences for prevention work are delayed and often unknown, they are rewarded daily with the smiles on the faces of engaged children after fun soccer activities and from the ongoing development of positive interpersonal relationships.

Learning and Teaching Sports

The Deportes Para la Vida (DPV) is an offspring of "Grassroot Soccer," an American non-governmental organization that uses the power of soccer to educate, inspire, and mobilize communities to stop the spread of HIV. DPV volunteers led the sports camp for the first two days with simple activities that appeared to facilitate happiness and belongingness, while educating campers on important HIV/AIDS-related issues.

The camp served 60 children ranging from 5 to 20 years of age, and represented a dichotomous socio-economic background of extreme wealth versus extreme poverty. Before beginning daily activities, it was necessary to establish clear expectations for all campers.

Commitment to Learn

DPV volunteers expected each camper to: a) show respect, b) participate, and c) lead by example. As shown in the photo, students demonstrated an active commitment to these expectations by signing the expectations poster in the presence of all 60 campers and student-athletes. As explained in Chapter 5, a personal commitment is most effective when it's: a) active, b) public, and c) involves personal choice.[18]

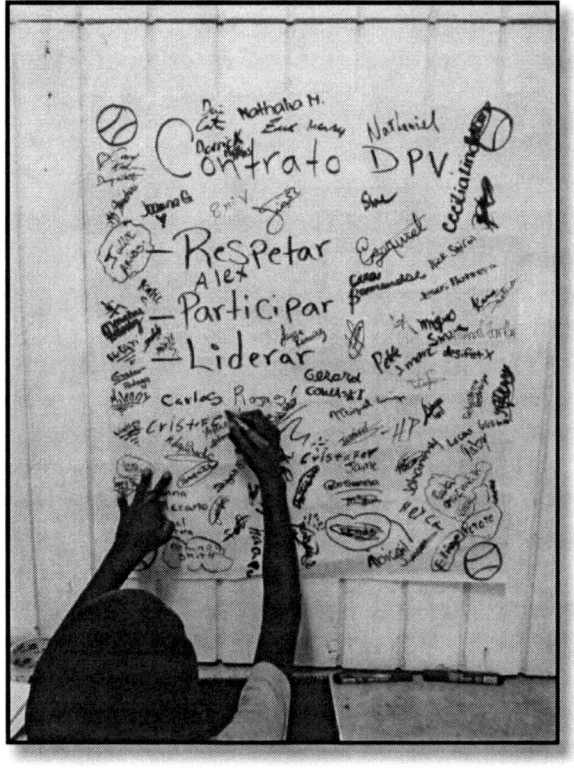

At first, campers arrived with motivation to play any sport. The DPV leaders capitalized on students' motivation for sports and applied the Premack Principle[19] to achieve their learning objectives. Specifically, in order to play further in the next engaging activity, children first listened to a lesson about HIV/AIDS.

The engaging activities taught essential lessons related to HIV/AIDS prevention. For example, we played a game called "pasa la pelota" ("pass the ball"), which began with two separate lines of campers facing each other. Each team passed the tennis ball, labeled "HIV," behind their backs to the person next to them. The opposing team guessed who held the ball behind his/her back; their guesses were rarely correct.

The activity demonstrates an important lesson: You cannot tell if a person is HIV-positive by simply looking at him or her, because the physical symptoms are unobservable.

Modeling Effective Leadership

After two days of observing successful leadership strategies of the DPV volunteers, we modeled their techniques and added our own strategies based on the AC4P principles. We benefited from observing the behavior of skilled teachers in this situation and then modeling it ourselves (i.e., observational learning).[20] In fact, we initially envisioned specific drills and activities, but we humbly changed these plans after observing the

activities on the first two camp days.

Building self-efficacy is a slow process, requiring patience from both student and teacher. We first taught simple skills and slowly increased complexity as the children's competence improved. Beyond skill development, we agreed belongingness among campers was more important than developing an athletic skill. After exploring their culture for the first two days, we integrated collegiate sports drills with activities conducive to developing positive relationships and a sense of belonging.

The language barrier was substantial, but it resulted in an advantageous consequence. We could not deliver corrective verbal feedback clearly to explain performance discrepancies. So we simply stopped, asked the camper to watch closely, and then modeled the desirable behavior.

During volleyball competition, we emphasized self-improvement and team cohesion. This fostered a win-win over a win-lose mindset within and between teams.[9] After each round, the lowest scoring team was removed from competition, but the losing teams didn't leave the field. They cheered for another team to do well. It was clear our interpersonal encouragement was developing a community spirit among everyone, even between opposing teams.

Intrinsic Reinforcement

American football is a novel game for most campers. Not surprisingly, self-efficacy was low. We recognized small successes in the drills (i.e., "small wins")[21] to enhance intrinsic motivation for campers. For example, camper Joanna dropped consecutive balls, but student-athlete Zack McCray provided encouragement. His supportive feedback about proper catching contributed to her trying harder.

Then she caught one pass, then another. She could see the natural consequences from her newly-developed skills, which increased her self-motivation to continue participating.[9]

Student-athlete Carol Kahoun reported:

Everyone exerted so much effort to improve. Seeing smiles and hearing laughs from across the field were the most rewarding feedback I could have received. I could see the natural consequences of my actions and our other coaches, which increased our self-motivation to lead.

Extrinsic Rewards

At the conclusion of camp, we recognized all campers for their achievement in the camp with a personalized VT sports camp certificate, VT t-shirt of their choice, and a VT sweatband. The campers had united into a community and the VT certificate was their common evidence. The AC4P behaviors exhibited by the children provided memorable experiences during our service-learning adventure in the D.R.

Personal Contrasts and Interpersonal AC4P Stories

Despite the lack of meeting basic needs, children in the camp were not depressed. In fact, they were some of the most caring, genuine, and joyful individuals we had ever met. The campers didn't know what they didn't have, providing no opportunity to experience a contrast. But we did. The following are examples of interpersonal AC4P stories and memorable contrasts that will forever change our future interactions and related aspirations.

Reflections from Joanne Dean Geller (Teaching Assistant)

After teaching these student-athletes, my spirit was ignited and I have renewed hope for an AC4P culture of compassion. We taught the leadership lessons to prepare the VT team for their service-learning trip abroad as if we were getting them ready for the Olympic games. Indeed, the Olympics brings together the best of the best in sports, and through this course, these students became the best of the best at teaching AC4P principles and rewarding AC4P behavior.

Our classroom lessons focused on the human dynamics of actively caring, which included empathy and patience to learn from people of a different culture. Throughout the teaching/learning process, we gained respect and admiration for the diverse talents of each individual.

I will forever cherish the time we spent together. I am very proud to have developed a positive relationship with each student-athlete who took this course; they provided me with a more optimistic outlook for the future of our world.

Reflections from Nick Smirniotopoulos (Student Athlete)

By interacting with the children, I could see the principles of leadership and self-motivation jump to life from the pages in our class textbook. For example, some Punta Cana International (PCI) students began camp as "too cool" to interact with the Veròn students. But one-on-one interactions and teamwork activities allowed them to evolve from "us versus them" (*independence*) to "we" (*interdependence*).

By the end of the week, they had more *empathy* for others.[9] For example, a PCI student told me, "This camp taught me that everyone should be treated equally – no matter where they come from and what they look like".

The intentional integration of students from extreme wealth and extreme poverty allowed for a diverse group of people to interact with each other in a collaborative and fun AC4P setting. This experience clearly reduced their unfounded prejudices about others.[22]

Julian, a Veròn student, profoundly impacted me. After watching me juggle a soccer ball in awe, he asked kindly if I would teach him how to play. He was very optimistic and interested in learning even after moments of confusion during the teaching/learning process.

I believe he had a *growth mindset*.[12] He believed his skills for soccer could improve with hard work. I was inspired by his courtesy and respect for me, as well as his intrinsic motivation to learn. So I felt compelled to recognize him with an AC4P wristband.

On the following day, he gave me his bracelet. While my wristband was intended to be given away, his was not. In fact, it was handmade and showed significant wear. I will never forget his meaningful gift of gratitude, his consistent willingness to learn, and his AC4P actions.

Reflections from Shane M. McCarty (Teaching Assistant)

In America, we often give excessive attention to independent, self-centered, and entitled individuals. As we mature, we often copy our American peers and role models for how to act and think, what to value, and who to admire. Personally, this trip brought me back to the "simple joys" of childhood.

As children, we value the present moment and interpersonal connections with others; while adults focus on the future, achieving personal notoriety and owning expensive goods. From this trip, I learned and re-learned the following lessons from children in the D.R. that I had forgotten during my transition from childhood to adulthood.

Smile. Every Dominican I observed was smiling and I found myself feeling happier and smiling back. Research shows people who smile are more trusted,[23] feel better after distressing events,[24] and can increase the smiles around them.[25]

Positive emotions, such as happiness, can spread three degrees of separation in a social network, meaning your happiness can increase the happiness of your friends', friends', friends.[26] As William James, the first renowned American psychologist taught us, "We don't smile because we are happy, we are happy because we smile".[27]

Love and Belonging. Late one night, after hearing our American perspective, the DPV leaders shared the attributes they desire in their future spouses. We specified certain appearance characteristics (e.g., height and weight), skills and abilities (e.g., athletic), and personal values (e.g., health).

Responses from the DPV leaders were simple, yet so profound. In Spanish, Kellito said, "I desire a woman who loves me for who I am, smiles all of the time, and cares". As Kenny translated his words and perspective, we felt embarrassed by ours. Our American culture has influenced our emphasis on attractiveness, status, and wealth. For Kellito, his desire is simple: to love someone and to be loved in return.

Reflections from Katie DeTuro (Student Athlete)

Upon returning home, DPV leader Kellito sent a translated Facebook message to me: "Everything is different when you are not with me. You are like a stranger I have known for years. I know I did not tell you I love you, but I hope you saw it in my eyes."

He continues, "I am so sorry I did not tell you when we were together, but I did not want you to feel bad. It was so different and you are super special to me and I will never forget." Reading these words broke my heart, but made me happy to know I impacted him.

Norman Cousins once said "If something comes to life in others because of you, then you have made an approach to immortality".[28] While I gave Kellito the strength to love again, he gave me more. He provided an experience filled with one life lesson after another. He and his teammates welcomed us with open arms, not as outsiders.

They embraced what we had to offer, and wanted to share what little they had. They displayed true empathy, not judging us for being Americans but desiring to get to know us. We still message on Facebook weekly and I plan to return to the D.R. within the year. This trip activated the start of life-long friendships between our VT students and the DPV leaders.

Life-Long Friendships

The cultivation of meaningful relationships occurred between the student-athletes and many D.R. residents, but also within the VT Cor team. Eight of ten student-athletes completed a survey on each of the five person-states at the beginning of the course and a follow-up survey on the last class day.

As shown in Figure 9.1, the students' mean score for belonging (e.g., "I feel like I really belong with students in my class") increased significantly from pre-test to post-test, while the four other person-states increased only slightly.[29] Although future research

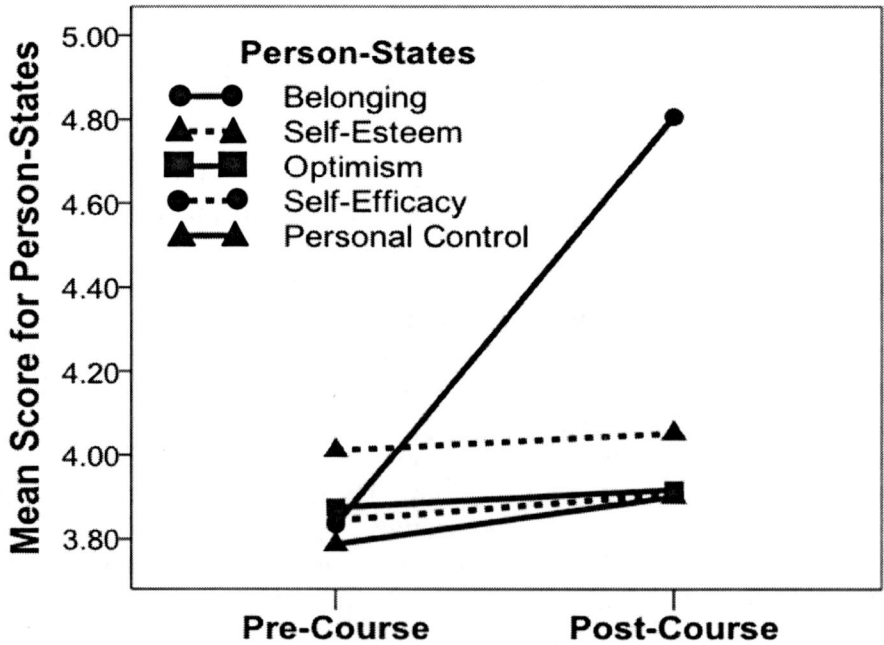

Figure 9.1. Student's person-states before vs. after their AC4P experience.

is critical, these results suggest a sense of belonging can be dramatically enhanced with an AC4P service-learning experience guided by PERMA concepts. This increase in belonging was also corroborated by students' anecdotes and personal reflections.

Different Paths but a Shared Vision

The contrast between the D.R. and the U.S. has enhanced our appreciation for our past and present. As for the future, the contrast is clear: We have so many more opportunities to enrich our future lives than do our new D.R. friends. As a result, our future plans have now changed.

We expected our future path to change as result of our experiences abroad, but we couldn't predict how much. Thanks to the transformational leadership of the DPV volunteers and our D.R. experiences, our futures now align with a shared vision to serve others and promote interpersonal compassion.

Each of us wants to create an AC4P world, but our paths, strategies, and people we impact will differ dramatically. Some of us will help families and friends while others may improve sports teams, organizations, universities, and even nations.

On the last day of our trip, we asked Peace Corps volunteer Kenny, "How often do the DPV leaders get to travel from across the Dominican Republic to Punta Cana and teach children?" Kenny said, "They will probably never experience anything like this again for the rest of their lives. This is it." The DPV leaders were trained to implement the DPV curriculum in their respective communities, but rarely travel to surrounding communities, and never to Punta Cana for a collaborative camp with Americans.

Our future plans certainly changed as a result of this trip, but the future of the DPV leaders and more than ten million D.R. residents may not. Our teaching of sports and AC4P had a positive impact on 60 children, five DPV leaders, and surrounding community members, but we wonder if the impact will be short-lived. For us, the lessons learned from our experiences in the D.R. will last forever and change our future.

We recognize our future is distinctly different from those in the D.R. and 1.7 billion others across the globe who live in poverty. Our AC4P vision is for the basic needs of every person in the world to be met and an AC4P culture to prevail.

With basic needs met, people are more likely to reach the highest level of Maslow's Hierarchy of Needs – self-transcendence. Achieving that vision will enable a world full of compassion – nations without wars, communities without violence, organizations without conflict, schools without bullying, and families without abuse.

In Conclusion

In large, public research-extensive institutions, lecture-based teaching on theory, and basic-science skills often trump student-centered pedagogies based on the discovery and development of personal values and leadership skills. Relationship building, meaningful dialogue, and contextually-rich situations rarely enter the classroom environment.

For these reasons, this course provided student leaders a unique educational journey involving theory, introspection, and real-world application. Our experience benefitted immeasurably from cooperative learning, profound interactive dialogues, engaging activities, as well as AC4P principles from psychological science.

Higher education is at a critical juncture. Opportunities are dwindling for teaching/learning experiences similar to ours. At this pivotal point, we need to reexamine the purpose of higher education.

Is the mission of higher education to provide students with functional utility or profound knowledge? The discouraging economic climate and stubbornly unacceptable unemployment rates have higher-education institutions and their students focused on efficient online courses and a "quick fix" diploma for landing a profitable job.

"In life, you can work for money or work for people," former Virginia Tech Vice President of Outreach and International Affairs, John Dooley, once said. Higher-education outcomes should not have a singular focus on high-salary employment. The opportunity presented by higher education is to use knowledge to make a difference and serve people.

Fortunately, the choice between functional utility (get a good job) and profound knowledge (translate theory, research, and technology into service) is a false dichotomy. We can do both.

Students today and tomorrow must continue to receive profound evidence-based knowledge in the classroom. But it's equally important for them to experience real-world applications of their knowledge and skills for the service of others. This is the ultimate functional utility – to actively care for the billions of people who never enter a classroom of higher education.

Notes

1. The AC4P Pedagogy was developed and implemented by E. Scott Geller (Alumni Distinguished Professor), Shane M. McCarty (Graduate Research Assistant), and Joanne Dean Geller (Former Physical Education Teacher). The service-learning component of the course was made possible by the Department of Athletics and the servant leadership of Jon Jaudon, Danny White, and Katie Cross. We are grateful for the leadership of Drs. John Dooley, Jerry Niles, and Daniel Wubah, whose forward thinking and dedication to outreach and service-learning education enabled this unique teaching/learning experience.

2. Dalai Lama. Retrieved from http://www.brainyquote.com/quotes/keywords/purpose.html

3. Seligman, M.E.P. (2011). *Flourish: A Visionary new understanding of happiness and well-being.* New York, NY: Free Press.

4. Arum, R., & Roksa, J. (2011). *Academically adrift: Limited learning on college campuses.* Chicago, IL: University of Chicago Press.

5. Luscombe, B. (2010, September 6). Do we need $75,000 a year to be happy? *Time.*

6. Hincker, L. (2012, September 30). Virginia Tech ranks fifth nationally in starting salaries of graduates from FBS schools; ACC ranked first among FBS conferences. *Virginia Tech News.* Retrieved from http://www.vtnews.vt.edu/articles/2011/09/093011-unirel-accsalaries.html

7. Confucius. *Words of wisdom.* Retrieved from http://www.trans4mind.com/quotes/quotes-parenting-education.html

8. Johnson, D.W., Johnson, R.T., & Stanne, M.B. (2000). Cooperative learning methods: A meta-analysis. Retrieved from http://www.tablelearning.com/uploads/File/EXHIBIT-B.pdf

9. Geller, E.S., & Veazie, B. (2010). *When no one's watching: Living and leading self-motivation* (Revised Edition). Newport, VA: Make A Difference, LLC.

10. Metaxas, E. (2011). *Socrates in the city: Conversations on "Life, God, and other small topics"* (p. 283). New York, NY: Penguin Group.

11. *Encyclopedia Britannica*. Humanistic psychology. Retrieved from http://www.britannica.com/EBchecked/topic/276011/humanistic-psychology

12. Dweck, C.S. (2006). *Mindset: The new psychology of success*. New York, NY: Random House.

13. Rotter, J.B. (1966). Generalized expectancies of internal versus external control of reinforcements. *Psychological Monographs, 80*(1), 1-28.

14. Weiner, B. (1974) (Ed.). *Achievement motivation and attribution theory*. New York, NY: General Learning Press.

15. Seligman, M.E.P. (1998). *Learned optimism: How to change your mind and your life*. New York, NY: Pocket Books.

16. Brown, B. (2010). The power of vulnerability. *TEDxHouston*. Retrieved from http://www.ted.com/talks/brene_brown_on_vulnerability.html

17. Geller, E.S., & Veazie, B. (2009). *The courage factor: Leading people-based culture change*. Newport, VA: Make-A-Difference, LLC.

18. Cialdini, R.B. (2001). *Influence: Science and practice* (4th Edition). Boston, MA: Allyn & Bacon.

19. Premack, D. (1965). Reinforcement theory. In D. Levine (Ed.). *Nebraska Symposium on Motivation* (pp. 128-180). Lincoln, NE: University of Nebraska Press.

20. Bandura, A. (1977). *Social learning theory*. New York, NY: General Learning Press.

21. Weick, K.E. (1984). Small wins: Redefining the scale of social problems. *American Psychologist, 39*(1), 40-49.

22. Allport, G.W. (1954). *The nature of prejudice*. Reading, MA: Addison-Wesley.

23. Scharlemann, J.P.W., Eckel, C.C., Kacelnik, A., & Wilson, R.K. (1999). The value of a smile: Game theory with a human face. *Journal of Economic Psychology, 22*(5), 617-640.

24. Ansfield, M.E. (2007). Smiling when distressed: When a smile is a frown turned upside down. *Journal of Personality and Social Psychology Bulletin, 33*(6), 763-775.

25. Hinsz, V.B., & Tomhave, J.A. (1991). Smile and (half) the world smiles with you, frown and you frown alone. *Journal of Personality and Social Psychology Bulletin, 17*(5), 586-592.

26. Fowler, J.H., & Christakis, N.A. (2008). The dynamic spread of happiness in a large social network: Longitudinal analyses over 20 years in the Framingham Heart Study. *British Medical Journal, 337*: a2338, 1-9.

27. James, W. (1890). *The principles of psychology* (Vol.1). Cambridge, MA: Harvard University Press.

28. Norman Cousins' Quotes. *BrainyQuote*. Retrieved from http://www.brainyquote.com/quotes/quotes/n/normancous111536.html

29. McCarty, S.M., Geller, E.S., & White, D. (2012). *Pedagogy for Actively Caring: Enhancing belongingness in a service-learning course*. Technical Report submitted to the Office of the Vice President and Dean for Undergraduate Education, Blacksburg, VA: Virginia Tech.

School Applications

CHAPTER 10

Sustaining Compassion after Tragic School Shootings:
Applying the AC4P principles at Virginia Tech and Chardon High School

Sophia Y. Teie, Shane M. McCarty, and Jenna McCutchen

ON MAY 15th, 2012, we traveled to Chardon High School in Chardon, Ohio with 12 additional AC4P coaches from Virginia Tech (VT). We arrived in the cafeteria and stopped at a table covered with flowers, stuffed animals, three photographs, and classmates' messages to the victims. Suddenly, we realized – this was the site of their shooting. Three months prior, a student shot and killed three others and injured three more.

We began to write a heartfelt message from our entire VT community on the cafeteria table. One by one, we passed a black sharpie and signed our names until tears streamed from our faces. We couldn't speak or hear – it was just silence – as we reflected and remembered the shootings on our campus in 2007.

This emotional experience was all too familiar because we often pass Norris Hall and West Ambler Johnston Residence Hall, the sites of the VT massacre. Reminders of our tragedy are common. Every day, we see the memorial of 32 Hokie stones on the VT Drillfield. Some of us attend brainstorming sessions about future AC4P research in Norris Hall. A few have friends living in West Ambler Johnston. All these locations remind us of our tragic past. But we are not alone.

We were standing in the cafeteria of Chardon High School – only months after their shooting. With heavy hearts and tears, we exited the cafeteria for the hallway. How could this happen again – to another community? As we stood in the hallway, only steps from the cafeteria table, a Chardon student approached us. "It's okay. Please don't cry. We are going to be okay," she said. We could feel the Chardon community's resolve to move forward, as they struggled with the aftermath of their tragedy.

The following story recounts the outpouring of sympathy from people throughout the world, the emergence of AC4P missions within communities after tragic school shootings, and a commitment to sustain compassion at Virginia Tech, Chardon High School, and other schools nationwide.

The Aftermath of the Virginia Tech Tragedy

On April 16th, 2007, a gunman took the lives of 32 Hokies and wounded 17 more on the VT campus. Within hours, a small college town in southwest Virginia became the spotlight for media outlets worldwide. In the weeks following the tragedy, media personnel cross-examined aspects of our Hokie community, searching for who and what to blame for the tragedy.[1] While this was the focus of media attention, we want to share another story – the untold story of the days, months and years that followed.

Receiving Outside Social Support

More than 90,000 condolences poured into VT from 382 college and university campuses[2] from all 50 states, and 80 countries.[3] Another 36,000 expressions of sympathy were posted online.[4] Numerous symbols of support and unity emerged, including remembrance logos, maroon and orange ribbons, and car magnets. In our darkest hours, the world reached out to VT families, survivors, and community members.

Social support is an essential ingredient for victims recovering and healing after a traumatic event.[5] But what type of social support can benefit an entire *community* stricken with grief and suffering? Sympathetic emails from distant friends? Phone calls from Mom and Dad? Condolences from strangers? Members of the VT community came to find that when a traumatic event is collectively experienced, an important source of healing is community solidarity.[6]

Experiencing Community Solidarity

Immediately following the tragedy, VT students, staff, faculty, and local community residents organized spontaneous events to aid collective grieving over the loss.[6] On April 17th, one day after the massacre, thousands attended the convocation for the victims and their Hokie family. World-renowned poet and author Dr. Nikki Giovanni closed the event by speaking about resilience and VT's future:

> *We will continue to invent the future through our blood and tears and through all our sadness. We are the Hokies. We will prevail. We will prevail. We will prevail. We are Virginia Tech.*[7]

That night, the epicenter of campus was covered with tens of thousands of candles during the candlelight vigil, reflecting our community's resolve to glow as a unified Hokie nation. For the first few days after the shootings, residents of the VT community connected interpersonally and interdependently.

Healing From Interpersonal Exchange in the Community

The weekend after the shootings, many VT students traveled home to find comfort with family and loved ones. However, VT staff and clinicians noted the unexpected volume of students who returned to attend optional classes only six days after the massacre. A campus clinician described his experiences in this way:

> *I was told again and again by students, clients, and friends alike that those who went home the weekend following the shootings could not wait to get back to Blacksburg... These students (and subsequent clients and friends) went home*

and were surrounded by those who love them the most – family. However, they all more or less stated it was not the same, no one understood and that once they got back to VT, they were surrounded by those who did understand.[8]

Distressed survivors felt a strong need to provide and seek meaningful support from those who understood the horrific event as they did, and who shared the profound emotions.[8] Sympathy from the world was appreciated and helpful, but empathy from friends sharing similar experiences was essential for healing.[9]

Community members within the town of Blacksburg became "a provider and consumer of this support system"[8] – creating a reciprocal cycle of intentional AC4P acts among neighbors, friends, and strangers. This collective effort was the manifestation of the "brother's/sister's keeper" culture envisioned in 1990 by Scott Geller.[10] The result: A model AC4P culture emerged from our 2007 tragedy.

In the aftermath, the university and local communities tried to move forward.[6] Although the events held immediately after the tragedy enhanced a Hokie community spirit, the rituals of interpersonal social support began to dissipate. A campus study revealed that solidarity had increased by 18% from a 2006 campus climate survey to a survey completed six months after the tragedy. However, solidarity among the VT community decreased from six months to nine months post tragedy.[11]

The AC4P Movement

In Fall 2008, Scott Geller and VT student leaders attempted to sustain VT's emergent culture of interpersonal compassion with a simple wristband-recognition process to reward AC4P behaviors among VT students, faculty, and staff. Then, individuals passed AC4P wristbands to recognize the AC4P behavior they observed others perform. For the next four years, they developed and evaluated interventions to enhance community and prevent bullying in elementary schools and middle schools.

Then in Spring 2012, AC4P coaches from VT shared the AC4P principles and successful applications with high-school students and various educators. Most significantly, our team led a series of AC4P workshops in Highland Hills, Ohio at the *Bullying Summit: Changing School and University Culture and Climate* (see Chapter 8).

At the summit, we met Casey Durkin, Assistant Director of Orange Schools Program, and she invited us to lead an afternoon workshop for 30 remarkable student leaders of Orange High School in Pepper Pike, Ohio. Following the AC4P workshop, those high-school students initiated "AC4P: Orange" – the first AC4P High-School Student Organization. Only weeks later, tragedy struck at a nearby high school.

Tragedy at Chardon High School

On February 27th 2012, a 17-year-old student entered the crowded school cafeteria of Chardon High School and opened fire, leaving three students fatally wounded and three others injured.[12] In Blacksburg, VT coaches were glued to TV screens and computers for news updates, feeling helpless and worlds away. Meanwhile, only 30-minutes from Chardon, leaders of the AC4P Orange club were responding to the incident by collecting notes and raising money to actively support their neighboring community.

We took comfort in the e-mail updates and text messages from our "AC4P Orange" family. They sent pictures of student-led efforts to support Chardon; one of the banners read "Orange High School believes in Chardon!" Signatures filled the banner, leaving no space, except for the final message at the bottom: "Actively Caring for People". We had met these AC4P Orange student leaders only weeks before, and they were already providing strength to Chardon survivors in the name of AC4P.

Casey Durkin had received an AC4P wristband for her AC4P leadership and now her caring extended well beyond Orange schools, helping the Chardon community in the wake of the shootings. She co-led trauma-response training for the Chardon school administrators and staff. She wrote this email update:

I asked Steve Kofol (Principal of Chardon Middle School) and Kelly Murphy (Assistant Principal) to come up to the podium and I presented them with my AC4P wristbands. Conveniently, I was wearing two that day! They started crying; I cried; and the entire place cried. The FBI joined us for an update, and I completed the training. Then, Steve came back up to close the meeting. He took his AC4P wristband off. At this moment, my heart sank, I was thinking: "Gosh, I had hoped he would have kept it for more than 20 minutes!" Then, he held it up and said, "Ever since she gave this to me, I've been trying to figure out how to cut this in 72 pieces (for each of the 72 staff members)."

Within a week of the Chardon shooting, leaders from inside and outside the Chardon community called upon us to discuss bringing the AC4P Movement to Chardon.[13]

Social Support in Chardon: A Familiar Story

Chardon received support from individuals, organizations and schools around the world. In one day, $150,000 was collected to help the families who lost their sons.[14] That same day, the local United Way established the Chardon Healing Fund to collect

additional donations in support of the families. A 20-foot banner reading "One Heartbeat" was draped in the school library, among hundreds of posters, origami cranes, and cards of condolences from concerned schools and individuals.

In the days and weeks following the shooting, the community's response provided numerous examples of AC4P behavior and interdependence. For example, community members joined a local Chardon artist to transform a school-yard tree into a living memorial. With donations from local construction and manufacturing companies, these individuals diligently wrapped the "Tribute Tree" from its roots to its branches with black and red cord (Chardon High School colors) to express sympathy for those lost and to convey hope for those who survived.

The "One Heartbeat" mantra echoed through the town, with black and red ribbons decorating trees and doors of homes for miles beyond Chardon and into surrounding communities. "After everything that has happened, I don't really want to leave," said senior Alexandra J. "I feel like we have come so close and everyone is so much more loving. It's going to be really hard to leave."[15]

Senior Kelsey C. said, "In ways, the shooting made the tight-knit senior class even closer. Classmates made it a point to check-in with each other every day. If someone was struggling or down, efforts were made to help them or cheer them up".[16]

These stories of shared sorrow echoed a powerful tale of caring – from the outpouring of condolences across the globe to the compassion that occurred among those within the victimized community. It was strikingly familiar to those of us in the VT community.

As the weeks passed, concerns about sustaining Chardon's compassion and solidarity were justified. We had seen this compassionate spirit dissipate in our own community. A Chardon student provided an example:

> *I reached out to a friend I hadn't spoken with since my elementary-school days. There were no barriers; everyone wanted to make sure others were okay... but then, we started to go back to the way things were before the shooting.*

In the aftermath of the shootings, while a more united Chardon community emerged, Chardon leaders anticipated the heightened compassion would fade. Sustainable strength and compassion was Chardon's next challenge. This became our mission: To provide AC4P principles for sustaining compassion.

Giving and Receiving Between Virginia Tech and Chardon

After seeing the success of the AC4P principles applied at VT, we were empowered to share our strategies of resilience with those in the Chardon community. We knew the great challenge facing both Chardon and VT was sustaining our AC4P cultures. How would these united communities sustain their efforts for a model AC4P community?

This model requires relationship-building *within* and *between* communities. Together, we could share and learn emergent AC4P behaviors exhibited in both communities after the respective tragedies. Together, our communities could empower one another. We could create new strategies to use in our respective schools to maintain strength within our towns. We also wanted to inspire AC4P behaviors beyond our towns.

Three months after the Chardon shooting, a contingent of VT coaches – consisting of a Blacksburg middle-school teacher, a graduate student, and 12 undergraduate students – arrived in Chardon to build our VT-Chardon community partnership.

From Shared Tragedy to Common Legacy

On the morning of May 15th, students of Chardon High School entered the school gymnasium for a school-wide assembly. VT graduate student Shane McCarty stood at the center of the gymnasium floor, looking at the aggregation of Chardon students, staff, and community members, as well as the VT coaches sitting among them. Principal Andy Fetchik introduced the AC4P leaders to his students and staff.

Shane began with stories of the origin of AC4P in safety. Then he reviewed the VT tragedy and the resolve to sustain compassion with the AC4P Movement. The students were silent, listening intently. On behalf of the VT community, Shane handed

Principal Fetchik an AC4P wristband, recognizing him for the immeasurable strength and compassion he exhibited during the past several months.

Then, the VT coaches climbed down from the bleachers to stand side-by-side with Shane at the center of the gym floor. They faced the crowd and introduced themselves, feeling overwhelmed with gratitude to share the AC4P mission with the student population. All eyes watched and waited. Shane concluded by saying:

> *We can envision a world full of compassion, because you've seen it here, and we've seen it at Virginia Tech. Although we share tragic pasts, that is not our story. Our story is one of actively caring – of people going above and beyond for others. Now, let's share the story of our actively-caring communities with the world!*

Near the rafters, two Chardon students stood and a wave emerged, as 1,150 students rose to their feet for a standing ovation. The 15 VT coaches, moved to tears, joined in the applause. We were two communities once devastated by violence, now standing together – resilient and compassionate.

At this moment, the AC4P principles transitioned beyond a safety-oriented process for industrial organizations and a bullying-prevention program for schools to a responsive, AC4P Movement for resilience-building. But our experience told us the reactive emotional responses for healing would be short-lived unless a sustained effort to promote AC4P behavior continued after the tragedy.

Sustaining Our Shared AC4P Cultures

Immediately after the assembly, 81 Chardon students attended an AC4P workshop in smaller groups led by the AC4P coaches. They walked across the gym and into the school library to meet our team. We had planned for three months for this moment to begin building relationships with students for whom we had genuine empathy.

The day-long workshop involved teaching AC4P concepts, group discussions for Chardon students to connect the principles to their daily lives, and strategy development to increase AC4P behaviors within the school and beyond.

Defining Community

The opening exercise in the workshop asked the students to share ideas on "What does an ideal community look like? Sound like? Feel like?" Students shared distinct features of this ideal community, especially aspects that enabled feelings of support after the tragedy.

We quickly picked up on one clear pattern from their responses. The ideal community for these Chardon students was their own community, within and outside their high school. They wanted to share their community spirit and the resultant interpersonal compassion they have felt since the tragedy. One of the participants, Kahrin S., reported:

AC4P gave us a new way to go out and show people that we really do appreciate what everyone has done for us, and take it a step further than sending a card, or a "Hey thanks" on the phone, but rather to really "pay it forward."[17]

In the sessions, we shared a variety of AC4P behaviors that appeared to produce greater community solidarity after a tragedy, and we brainstormed additional ways to increase the other person-states: self-esteem, self-efficacy, personal control, and optimism.

Chardon students then discussed strategies for sustaining community solidarity beyond this tragic school year. The workshop showcased the primary way to sustain an AC4P culture: Proactively demonstrate AC4P in your own community and beyond.

Paying It Forward

Following the AC4P workshop, Chardon High School students formed "AC4P Chardon" to sustain AC4P within and beyond their high school. Chardon Healing Fund member Kristin Lewis reported:

Following the initial visit from Virginia Tech in May, the Chardon High School students have embraced the AC4P program and have created an opportunity for school-wide engagement. They have been energetically working on a variety of projects over the summer months.[18]

In June 2012, another Ohio school experienced tragedy when four Brunswick High School students were killed in a car crash.[19] The AC4P Chardon students tied blue ribbons (Brunswick High School colors) around trees in the "Square" (Downtown Chardon) to show support. It reminded us of our own feelings after hearing about the shooting at Chardon back in February. We wanted to be there with Brunswick High School, but we were comforted by the ripple effect of Chardon's actions to "Pay it Forward" by helping Brunswick in their time of need.

Leaving a Legacy

At the AC4P assembly, Principal Fetchik addressed the Chardon student body:

For the graduating seniors, this is it. But never forget: You were the group that brought Actively Caring for People to Chardon High School. This will be your legacy.

On May 25th, Chardon High School held another assembly to recognize their special class of 2012. We sent two AC4P wristbands for each of the 265 seniors as a gift. Sophia Teie wrote a letter on behalf of the VT Coaches that read:

AC4P from Virginia Tech wants to wish you "good luck" with your future endeavors. Your last few months at Chardon were faced with unimaginable hardships, unique to each of you, but also shared – and you will never forget. Neither will we. One of these wristbands is from our VT family to you, as a thank you for reminding our world what it truly means to exist as One Heartbeat. If you see someone go above and beyond for someone else, pass this wristband on.

The other wristband you each have earned… as a reminder of the legacy you will each continue to create. Your Chardon community is empowered, and its ripple effect will happen through you, as you empower those beyond Chardon to actively care for people. Never forget that.

You are our heroes.

Sincerely,
Your AC4P family

Chardon Senior Eric M. expressed his gratitude for the wristbands by posting a thank-you message on the ac4p.org website, as shown below:

As the Chardon Class of 2012 graduated, AC4P gifted each senior with two wristbands for the displays of leadership, caring and community during a time of great tragedy. With these wristbands the Chardon Class of 2012 hopes to share and return the kindness and caring Chardon received when it was needed most. Thank you to everyone for your prayers, well wishes, and acts of kindness you have all shown us. One Heart Beat! Wristband #49722

On graduation day, Chardon Senior Matt L. said to a local news reporter:

We didn't want to look back in ten years and have this be the only thing we talk about, so we figured out ways to leave a positive impact on our community… We are not going to let the tragedy define our year and define us. We are going to let our actions and how we responded define us.[16]

In Conclusion

Following the April 16th, 2007 shootings at Virginia Tech, our peaceful town of Blacksburg, nestled in the mountains of Southwest Virginia, became infamous for the deadliest school shooting on a U.S. college campus.[20] Sadly, ours is not the only story of school violence.

Since our tragedy, grief and suffering caused by tragic shootings in U. S. schools have been felt by too many, including those at Delaware State University, Success Tech Academy, Louisiana Technical College, E.O. Green Junior High School, Northern Illinois University, Davidson High School, Central High School, Henry Ford High School, University of Central Arkansas, Dillard High School, Henry Ford Community

College, Wesleyan University, Canandaigua Academy, Harvard University, Larose-Cut Off Middle School, Atlanta University Center, Discovery Middle School, University of Alabama in Huntsville, Birney Elementary School, Ohio State University, Belleville Township HS East, University of Texas at Austin, Alisal High School, Mid-Atlantic Christian University, Kelly Elementary School, Marinette High School, Millard South High School, Worthing High School, San Jose State University, Pearl City Middle School, Walpole Elementary School, Chardon High School, Episcopal High School, Oikos University, Normal Community High School, Perry Hall High School, Sandy Hook Elementary School, Massachusetts Institute of Technology, University of Central Florida, Taft Union High School, and Lone Star College.[21]

The suffering caused by public shooting sprees continues to occur beyond school grounds. On July 20th, 2012, a man killed 12 people and injured 58 in an Aurora, Colorado movie theatre.[22] After this shooting, former VT Vice President of Student Affairs, Dr. Ed Spencer, wrote a letter to the community of Aurora, which included the following excerpt:

Keep in mind that one deranged person should not, cannot, and will not define your city. You will define your city. You will find that an exhilarating sense of community can and will arise from the ashes of this tragedy.[23]

In both aftermaths of the April 16th, 2007 tragedy at VT and the February 27th, 2012 tragedy at Chardon High School, our communities received an outpouring of sympathy from the world, and many members of the VT and Chardon communities went beyond the call of duty compassionately. They actively cared frequently and effectively, resulting in feelings expected within a "brother's/sister's keepers" school culture.

Tragedy led to compassion and solidarity for some survivors in the short-term. But what if this compassion and solidarity could be sustained for years? At the moment, we have yet to see a model AC4P school culture fully develop and sustain for years beyond a tragedy.

The full story of a model AC4P school culture has yet to be told, but it will. We are resilient, self-motivated, and committed to cultivating more compassionate cultures in our schools and throughout communities worldwide.[24]

Notes

1. Geller, E.S. (2008). The tragic shootings at Virginia Tech: Personal perspectives, prospects, and preventive potentials. *Traumatology, 14*(1), 8-20.
2. The higher education community lends its support. *We Remember, Virginia Tech*. Retrieved from http://www.remembrance.vt.edu/2007/higher_ed_support.html
3. April 16 memorial website. Retrieved from http://www.remembrance.vt.edu/2007/memorial/
4. Virginia Tech April 16, 2007 archives of the university libraries, 2007-2010. Retrieved from http://ead.lib.virginia.edu/vivaxtf/view?docId=vt/viblbv00656.xml
5. Haden, S.C., Scarpa, A., Jones, R.T., & Ollendick, T.H. (2007). Posttraumatic stress disorder symptoms and injury: The moderating role of perceived social support and coping for young adults. *Personality and Individual Differences, 42*, 1187-1198.

6. Hawdon, J., & Ryan, J. (2011). Social relations that generate and sustain solidarity after a mass tragedy. *Social Forces, 89*(4), 1363-1384.

7. Transcript of Nikki Giovanni's Convocation address. *Virginia Tech*. Retrieved from http://www.remembrance.vt.edu/2007/archive/giovanni_transcript.html

8. Yoder, M. (2008). Helping in the wake of disaster: A graduate student's perspective in the aftermath of the VT tragedy. *Traumatology, 14*(1), 25-31.

9. Hawdon, J., & Ryan, J. (2011). Social relations that generate and sustain solidarity after a mass tragedy. *Social Forces, 89*(4), 1363-1384.; Yoder, M. (2008). Helping in the wake of disaster: A graduate student's perspective in the aftermath of the VT tragedy. *Traumatology, 14*(1), 25-31.

10. Geller, E.S. (1991). If only more would actively care. *Journal of Applied Behavior Analysis, 24*, 607-612.

11. Hawdon, J., Ryan, J., & Agnich, L. (2010). Crime as a source of solidarity: A research note testing Durkheim's assertion. *Deviant Behavior, 31*, 679-703.

12. Achladis, T., Jovic, D., Dabrowski, J., & Taylor, L. (2012, February 28). Chardon High School shootings: Tight security in court. *Fox8.com*. Retrieved from http://fox8.com/2012/02/28/chardon-ohio-high-school-shootings/#content-start

13. We are grateful for the leadership of Joe Bergant, Kate Biddle, Joan Blackburn, Casey Durkin, Andy Fetchik, Kimm Leininger, Ellen Ondrey, April Siegel-Green, all Chardon High School students and staff, Chardon Healing Fund Board Members, and those who provided support to the Chardon Community.

14. Steer, J. (2012, March 6). $500,000 raised for Chardon Healing Fund in just a few weeks. *Newsnet5.com*. Retrieved from http://www.newsnet5.com/dpp/news/local_news/oh_geauga/500000-raised-for-chardon-healing-fund-in-just-a-few-weeks

15. Baldwin, M. (2012, June 2). The Chardon High School Class of 2012 graduated Saturday afternoon. *Newsnet5.com*. Retrieved from http://www.newsnet5.com/dpp/news/local_news/oh_geauga/chardon-class-of-2012#ixzz22cPAs3oc

16. Dissell, R. (2012, June 2). Chardon High School graduates triumph over tragedy that interrupted their senior year. *The Plain Dealer Metro News*. Retrieved from http://www.cleveland.com/metro/index.ssf/2012/06/chardon_graduates_triumph_over.html

17. Geauga Maple Leaf. (2012, May 16). Chardon High School students talk about Virginia Tech's caring. Retrieved from http://www.youtube.com/watch?v=M4EKQnN_zrI.

18. Fund sends $323,723 of healing to Chardon. (n.d.). *Chagrin Valley Times*. Retrieved from http://www.chagrinvalleytimes.com/NC/0/4484.html

19. Fourth teen dies after pre-graduation crash in Ohio. (2012, June 4). *Yahoo News*. Retrieved from http://news.yahoo.com/4th-teen-dies-pre-graduation-crash-ohio-150245089.html

20. Hauser, C., & O'Conner, A. (2007, April 16). Virginia Tech shooting leaves 33 dead. *The New York Times*. Retrieved from http://www.nytimes.com/2007/04/16/us/16cnd-shooting.html?pagewanted=all

21. Time line of worldwide school and mass shootings. (n.d.). Retrieved from http://www.infoplease.com/ipa/A0777958.html; U.S. school shootings. (2013). *Wikipedia*. Retrieved from http://en.wikipedia.org/wiki/School_shooting#United_States

22. Aurora shooting: Suspect opens fire at Colorado movie theater, killing 12. (2012, July 20). *The Huffington Post*. Retrieved from http://www.huffingtonpost.com/2012/07/20/aurora-shooting-movie-theater-batman_n_1688547.html

23. Spencer, E.F.D. (2012, July 26). A letter to Aurora from Virginia Tech: James Holmes does not define your city. *The Christian Science Monitor*. Retrieved from http://www.csmonitor.com/Commentary/Opinion/2012/0726/A-letter-to-Aurora-from-Virginia-Tech-James-Holmes-does-not-define-your-city

24. We are so proud of the 12 AC4P coaches who helped us lead workshops in Chardon High School and continue to leave an AC4P legacy: Elise Cabrisses, Jessica Cea, Mackenzie Claytor, Rohan Cobb-Ozanne, Derek Cornwell, Andrea Langston, Megan Liskey, Meredith McDaniel, Kyle Pacque, Caitlin Parker, Brittany Rivero, and Brittany Tarzia.

CHAPTER 11

AC4P after a Tragedy:
Coming together after April 16th, 2007

Victoria Jordan Stone

ON APRIL 16th, 2007 a severely troubled young man roamed the Virginia Tech (VT) campus and shot 49 people – killing 32 – before turning his gun on himself. Quiet, rural Blacksburg, Virginia is not the kind of community where a horrific massacre is ever expected.

Like those of us old enough to recall the day JFK was assassinated, everyone in this southwest Virginia town knows exactly where they were when they heard the shocking news unfolding on campus.

I was teaching a massage therapy class at Blue Ridge School of Massage & Yoga that morning from 9A.M. – 1P.M. One of my 14 students had her cell phone (despite school rules prohibiting it), and she received a text during class. During break time she told everyone a shooter was loose on the VT campus. By then we were hearing so many sirens it was clear something serious had happened.

After completing anatomy instruction, I had the students prepare for bodywork practice. Although restless, upset and agitated, the students settled down considerably with encouragement to focus on their hands, technique, and both their own and their partner's breathing.

Considerable evidence exists that the stressors rampant in our culture contribute to a condition of the Hypothalamus-Pituitary-Adrenal Cortex (HPA) Axis of the brain which promotes an exaggerated and prolonged reaction to even relatively weak stressors. An overabundance of cortisol is found in the bloodstream of susceptible individuals.[1] Eventually the hippocampus, with its focus on learning and memory, is over-ridden by fear-related learning of the over-stimulated amygdala. The hippocampus begins to atrophy in relation to the fight or flight response of the sympathetic nervous system brought on by all the adrenalin and cortisol.

Many negative consequences can result. It's believed a dysfunctional HPA Axis is related to various anxiety conditions, including PTSD. The single most effective action to both prevent and moderate this dysfunction is healthy, nurturing human contact.[2]

Students in my class may well have moderated the neuroendocrine conditions of stress in their systems during our massage exchange. Clear changes were evident in their rates of respiration, nervousness, and agitation. Students receiving massage from their classmates received nurturing, safe touching which activated a parasympathetic (rest and renewal) nervous system response, and reduced the sympathetic (flight or flight) response.

For those who may have already exaggerated HPA Axis reactivity, touch probably helped to calm their particularly extreme excitability. The same effect was apparent among those who provided massage therapy to their peers. They showed the calming effect of the massage-therapy process. One of the great qualities of massage therapy is you cannot touch another person without being touched.

AC4P Therapy Beyond the Classroom

One of my colleagues and fellow member of the Southwest Virginia Massage Therapists' Association, Tod Whitehurst, activated a telephone tree for the organization. This set up massage venues for those battered by the tragedy.

Tod works on campus in addition to being a local massage therapist, and was deeply affected and reacted, "We know what we need to do. It's an innate human quality to help in times of need."

Massage therapists from around the state, and as far away as California, responded to Tod's call for volunteers. The Virginia Chapter of the American Massage Therapy Association helped get the word out to massage therapists around the state.

Soon we were providing massages to many members of the VT community. Among the first to respond to massage therapy were police, emergency medical technicians, ministers, counselors, Red Cross volunteers, nurses, social workers, and others who worked closely with traumatized families and friends. Their respiration and pulse slowed discernibly, muscle tension melted, nervous tics and habits dropped away. Some had been awake for long periods of time, and received the benefits of some restorative sleep while on our massage tables.

The Healing of Massage Therapy

Those of us working with the early responders felt a sense of responsibility to give all we could in this time of great need. We supported each other – coordinating times to cover venues where massage therapy was being offered; sharing tables, massage cream, and overall assisting each other to provide the service we are trained to provide.

When we were tired, someone stepped in to cover our station. Providing calming and restorative massage to those dedicated responders allowed us to confront and process our own feelings of distress over what felt like a violation, a loss of innocence in nurturing, peaceful Blacksburg, Virginia.

I suspect the incidence of PTSD among the massage therapists was low because we needed to access a calm place in ourselves to facilitate the same state in those for whom we were actively caring.

The Reciprocity of Massage Therapy

The AC4P service on the part of massage therapists was reciprocal. Tara Fowlkes, one of the massage therapist volunteers said, "This is the most rewarding work I've done. Given the level of the catastrophe and the level of distress, being able to do something with our sadness and our grief helps us in the process, at least it helped me."

We were profoundly rewarded for our AC4P massage therapy. Tod reported, "The most rewarding outcome for me occurred when someone approached me and said he had finally gotten a good night's sleep".

An AC4P Community

Massage therapists were in no way the only AC4P members of the VT/Blacksburg community. Students and alumni mobilized to support Habitat for Humanity, remembrance walk/runs occurred in Blacksburg and other communities; as well as tree plantings, candlelight vigils, blood drives, and efforts to promote gun control.

It seems so right that the AC4P Movement started here. As a long-time member of the Blacksburg and VT communities, I noticed a shift occurring after April 16; once the initial shock subsided, the walls of unintentional distance between people fell. Cashiers looked into the eyes of customers, and customers looked back into the cashiers' eyes; neighbors stopped long enough to "pass the time of day" in conversation; people seemed to be more likely to stop and help others.

Overall, rather than engendering mistrust or fear among the populace, the community seems more engaged and cohesive. There seem to be fewer residents complaining about VT students' behaviors than in the past, and there's more community involvement in local projects by students. A fine, friendly, and mutually-supportive community feeling is alive and well here.

On May 11 of 2012, First Lady Michelle Obama, speaking to VT's graduating class, commented on the remarkable resilience and actively caring shown by the students at the University.

I know that as one of your commencement speakers today, I'm supposed to offer you all kinds of wisdom and advice and life lessons, but the truth is, like so many people across this country and around the world, I have been following the journey of this school. I have witnessed the strength and spirit of the Hokie Nation... And you all haven't just taught us about the power of service to lift up our families and heal our communities. You've also shown us that through service, we can heal ourselves.

From where I sit, it looks as though the Tech-Town community was empathic and proactive enough to offer a tremendous amount of support and assistance to everyone even peripherally involved in the tragedy on April 16th. We've become a more AC4P and open community by weathering the storm together. We have healed ourselves through healing each other.

Notes

1. Juhan, D. (1987). *Job's body: A handbook for bodywork.* Barrytown, N.Y.: Station Hill Press.
2. Werner, R. (2009). *A massage therapists' guide to pathology* (4th Edition). Lippincott, Williams & Wilkins; Werner, R. (2006). *"Jangled" adults - Touch and the stress response system.* Originally published in *Massage & Bodywork*. Golden, C.O.: Associated Bodywork and Massage Professionals.

CHAPTER 12

Feeling and Spreading Compassion:
From violence to an AC4P ripple effect

Rohan Cobb-Ozanne

LATE ONE NIGHT after 2:00 A.M., I'm walking on campus after collecting data on alcohol consumption for research designed and sponsored by the Virginia Tech (VT) Center for Applied Behavior Systems (CABS). I turn a corner to find an alarming scene. A very agitated young male is aggressively yelling at a tense and fearful female. He shouts, "Tell me what I want to know! Say what I want to hear!" Then he states, "I swear I could hit you right now!"

An alarm is sounding in my head as I walk toward the scene. I feel the extreme intensity of the situation, but I'm uncertain if I should intervene. I consider approaching when he calls out, "What are YOU looking at?!" as if he would not hesitate to start a fight with me. Out of concern for my own safety, I choose to continue walking.

No more than 50 yards later, I hear a noise. Immediately, I turn around to see the young woman on the ground with the man stooping over her. He hit her!

I stop the person walking behind me and tell him what occurred. I ask him to act as if we are casually talking so I can assess the situation. Another person walks over to the two and diffuses the conflict. We wait another few seconds, but the time to help proactively has passed. I missed an opportunity to prevent harm from bullying behavior.

The worst part of my failure was not my lack of *physical* courage to confront the bully by myself. Less than 100 yards behind me I had passed two police officers arresting a drunk college student. If I had been more thoughtful and observant, I could have run back to the officers for help. I could have protected the young woman and prevented an act of violence, but I did not and she suffered.

This case, however regrettable, helped shape my moral compass. Now I better understand one of the most fundamental components of the AC4P Movement. Actively caring requires more than a big heart. AC4P requires the courage to act on your caring.

I had the attentiveness to recognize a problematic situation and I felt a need to help. Unfortunately, I lacked the physical and moral courage[1] to intervene. Although I failed to prevent an act of violence, I made a personal commitment to act the next time I see a similar situation.

Connected Hearts

My next story is a discovery I made on the day I planned to tell my previous story to the 60 undergraduate research assistants in CABS. As I walked to our weekly meeting, I had a heart-warming experience. First some background information.

After the April 16th, 2007 shooting at VT, 32 stones were placed on the VT Drillfield with a name engraved for each victim. In between classes, I often placed pebbles in the shape of a heart on Austin Michelle Cloyd's stone, whose younger brother is my friend.

The act of placing the pebbles was my way of reflecting on the tragedy, our unique VT community spirit, and the value of life. Almost every week the wind and rain erased my heart of pebbles, so I created a heart anew. When I moved off campus, however, I no longer found the time to do this.

As I walk to our weekly CABS meeting on a Tuesday evening, I rehearse my story about the act of violence and my failure to prevent it. I go by the memorial and discover a pleasant heartwarming surprise: Pebbles in the shape of hearts were on *every* stone.

I am overcome with joy and feel a connection to the person or persons who modeled my behavior. I had unintentionally started something beautiful that spread to others. That moment I saw the impact people can have on each other and I felt a ripple effect – how one AC4P act can grow and help others.

AC4P as a Meme and a Movement

This experience reflects AC4P as a "meme"[2] and a Movement. A meme is an idea or element of social behavior passed on in a culture through imitation. For example, a person is recognized positively for doing an act of kindness, which results in witnesses becoming more likely to perform acts of kindness themselves (see Chapter 5). We call this the "AC4P ripple effect".

Actively caring is an idea that has become a Movement. You cannot walk on the VT campus without seeing students and faculty alike wearing AC4P wristbands. These wristbands mark us as people with a common understanding to actively care for each other. We live lives that contribute to the common welfare of others. AC4P gives you something to live up to, a vision to work towards, and a community to believe in!

An AC4P Future

AC4P forges a paradigm for the future. We cannot confront global problems – climate change, pollution, economic instability, lack of resources, over-population, nuclear weapons, and military action – while standing divided. By inviting "alien others" into our extended family, we can feel interconnected and united on compassionate terms.

Thinking, feeling, and acting for the benefit of each other – AC4P – can become a social norm.

If we can dream for a better future and love one another, then we should feel cognitive dissonance[3] when we choose not to help others in times of need. This is what I felt in my first story. We often feel regret in these situations, not because we failed, but because we did not live up to our potential to do better. This pain of regret reminds us not to make the same mistake again.

At any one moment, the sheer number of people in this world who need help is overwhelming. However, there are many more people – the silent majority – who could help others in need.

I am optimistic the AC4P Movement will spread from educational settings and work environments to activate more and more AC4P behaviors from most of us who care but do not yet act consistently on that caring. I emphasize *yet*. I am an AC4P individual on a mission to do whatever I can to help cultivate an AC4P culture of compassion.

Notes

1. Geller, E.S., & Veazie, R.A. (2009). *The courage factor: Leading people-based culture change.* Virginia Beach, VA: Coastal Training and Technologies Corporation.

2. Dawkins, R. (1989). *The selfish gene* (2nd Edition). Cambridge, England: Oxford University Press.

3. Festinger, L. (1957) *A theory of cognitive dissonance.* Stanford, CA: Stanford University Press.

CHAPTER 13

The AC4P Movement at the University of Kansas

Derek D. Reed, Jason M. Hirst, Brent A. Kaplan, and Amel Becirevic

THE DEPARTMENT OF Applied Behavioral Science (formerly, Human Development and Family Life) at the University of Kansas (KU) was one of the original hotbeds of applied behavior analysis.[1] The tradition lives on today in our undergraduate curriculum that teaches students the natural science of behavior.[2] Introduction to Applied Behavioral Science (ABSC 100) serves as the introductory course to the Applied Behavioral Science undergraduate major housed in our department.

The first author began teaching upon his hire at KU in Fall 2010. We have collaborated continually since then to enhance the impact of this course. We want to inspire our students to pursue a lifetime of human service, grounded in a strict science of behavior. Each semester we teach 200 undergraduates, most of whom are freshmen or sophomores.

ABSC 100 is a "gateway" course: Most of our students take the course as an elective to see whether this major is a good fit for them. The course is structured as a survey-level offering to expose students to the various facets of applied behavioral science. We discuss career options, seminal scientific studies, and contemporary issues facing professionals in our field.

Over time, we noticed the course was becoming overly focused on the science. It was less effective at inspiring students to recognize they each have the potential to serve as behavior-change agents and make a meaningful difference in their world. We knew we needed to add a course component more applicable to the everyday life of a student. We needed something to spark an interest in helping humanity. Something to help our students see that the ripple effect of their small acts of kindness can literally change the world. We needed E. Scott Geller's brand of humanistic behaviorism.[3]

Our Discovery of the AC4P Movement

In August 2012, we participated in the Behavior Change for a Sustainable World conference hosted by the Association for Behavior Analysis International. On the second day of this conference, Dr. Geller took to the stage to deliver his keynote address on using the science of behavior to promote envrionmental conservation. To actively care about each other and our environment was one of Dr. Geller's primary messages.

He introduced the Actively Caring for People (AC4P) Movement and discussed the good that has already come from this Movement. We vividly recall getting goosebumps as we realized this was the humanistic behaviorism we had been looking to bring into our course.

Following Dr. Geller's address the conference had programmed a 30-minute break. We spent that time excitedly discussing the potential of the AC4P Movement in our class, campus, and community. That 30-minute break turned into a two-hour discussion. We had to devise a way to work AC4P into ABSC 100.

The day we returned to the office we contacted Dr. Geller. Within a week, we had ordered 500 AC4P wristbands and began working on a new course syllabus featuring AC4P. The Movement was on at KU.

AC4P in ABSC 100

As an introductory course in applied behavioral science, ABSC 100 focuses on the scientific foundations and practical applications of behavior analysis (see Chapter 1). Before teaching procedures such as positive reinforcement, we teach skills such as observational recording and behavioral definitions.

To best integrate AC4P into the course, we break the assignment into two activities: Students select and define an instance of AC4P behavior they will target and watch for throughout the semester; and then they follow the four steps of the AC4P process (See-Act-Pass-Share).

To facilitate the experience, a major portion of our operating budget goes to purchase AC4P wristbands for every student in the class. This ensures students have the opportunity to experience fully the AC4P approach.

AC4P Assignment I. After lecturing on behavioral definitions and identifying target behaviors, we release an online discussion blog for students to post an act of caring they plan to look for throughout the semester. Students are instructed to select something of personal relevance, not just a generic "good deed" (not that there's anything wrong with that, though). Responses are publicly posted to a course blog on our Blackboard® page (see Figure 13.1).

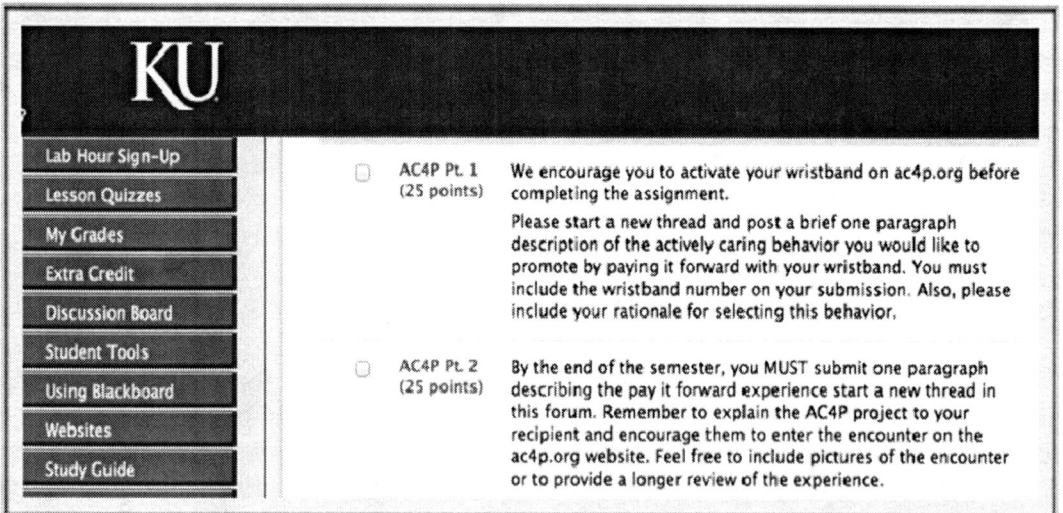

Figure 13.1 *Our Blackboard® page for the course blog.*

We personally review each entry and provide specific feedback on whether the student has selected an appropriate target behavior (i.e., something meaningful that is both observable and countable). Students who post targets such as "someone being nice to someone else" are prompted to reevaluate their response and behaviorally define "nice" such that two independent observers would agree. More appropriate definitions would be something like, "someone holding the door open for a stranger" or "someone telling a stranger s/he dropped something".

Students provide a personal rationale for their target behavior to ensure they are looking for actions they genuinely value and would like to reinforce (i.e., make more probable in the future as a function of passing on the wristband). If they do not provide a personal rationale, we prompt them to do so before assigning them the full 25 points for the assignment. Two examples of AC4P behaviors selected by our students are given in the two boxes on this page, as expressed by the students:

> My target act of caring is "communication." It may sound simple, but far too often Americans forget how to verbally communicate with each other. Maybe it's due to reliance or technology or the general hustle and bustle of modern life? It is not difficult to greet another with, "Hello, how are you?" Likewise, it shouldn't be hard to tell another person that we admire some quality they possess; e.g., "You're a great role model to your sister." From my experience, simple comments such as these could potentially lead to more happiness, success, and value to a person's daily life. If everyone took the time to simply communicate in a personal manner, everyone would feel a lot more respected!

AC4P Assignment II. Active participation in the four-step AC4P process (See-Act-Pass-Share) is the second component of our AC4P assignment. Students are instructed on each step.

First, students are told to monitor their environment for instances of their target behavior (Step 1: See). This obviously works toward the end goal of the 25 points associated with the assignment, but also serves a secondary and more meaningful purpose: Become actively engaged in seeing the goodness in humanity.

A surprising amount of charity, hospitality, and compassion occur every day, but are far too often overlooked. We aim to help students see the acts of caring that rarely make the evening news. Traditional media-reporting only reinforces the impression our communities are full of tragedy and malevolence.

In Step 2 (Act), students approach the individuals who emitted the target behavior and thank them for actively caring.

The third step (Pass)

> The actively caring behavior I would like to see happen more often around campus is picking up trash and recycling. I am disheartened when I see students throw paper scraps on the floor or toss empty water bottles on the ground... it's disrespectful to our campus and the janitors who have to pick up after them (let alone the Earth!). Imagine if every student took a few moments to identify litter or empty bottles/cans around their desk at the end of class and properly disposed of them as they left the room...campus would look so much better! The next time I see someone picking up someone else's trash, I will be sure to give them my AC4P wristband!

then includes passing the wristband to the individual and telling this person about the class assignment and the AC4P Movement. This step operates on the principle of reinforcement students learn about in our class. Specifically, students learn about behavior-specific contingent praise and are expected to apply this principle throughout this stage of the assignment.[4]

Sharing the story via ac4p.org and on the course's Blackboard® discussion blog (recall Figure 13.1) is the final step (Share).

Our students are instructed to describe the scenario of passing on the AC4P wristband, and personally reflect on their emotions and the observed reaction of the individual receiving the wristband. Student grades are privately assigned, but their stories are publicly displayed to all other students in the class. This serves two functions. First, it prompts the students to reflect on the experience and to be mindful of the emotions associated with the relevant social exchange.

Second, the public posting serves to demonstrate the collective compassion experienced and propagated within the class during the course of just one semester. Rather than a collection of nameless and faceless persons blindly sharing space in the name of education, we hope this public posting of collective compassion will portray our campus and community as environments of kindness and camaraderie.

Our vision: Students will generalize these experiences beyond the classroom. We have reason to believe they do, as exemplified by the following five student examples.

> I work in a nursing home as a CNA and every weekend I have seen many acts of kindness. One person that always stood out to me was a particular hospice nurse who comes in every Saturday. I have always admired her work because she always went above and beyond for her patients, more so than any other hospice nurse. For example, I noticed that other nurses try to hurry and get the job done, but she always took the time to talk to the patients she was caring for. She went out of her way to make each individual feel appreciated. For that reason, I decided to give my AC4P wristband to her. I thanked her for going above and beyond, for truly dedicating her time to really care for her patients by treating them as wonderful human beings. I know that she is the highlight of their day. The exchange was actually not that awkward especially since she was familiar with AC4P. She was very appreciative and thankful for the wristband.

> One day I was walking from my class to the library when I noticed a group of people on the lawn passing out pamphlets. As is typical of these scenarios, I saw that pamphlets littered the surrounding area. Almost every passerby carelessly discarded the pamphlet on the ground. However, there was a man who stopped and took the time to pick up the dropped pamphlets. He not only picked them up, but he went one step further! Instead of throwing them in a bin, he returned them back to the people handing them out. Soon I saw members of the group picking up the pamphlets from the lawn too. I told the man about my Applied Behavioral Science class and what the AC4P wristband represented. He quickly became interested! I have not seen him since that day, but I would like to think that he has passed on the AC4P wristband and message to someone actively caring.

> I gave away my wristband to somebody who demonstrated caring. It happened on my visit to my hometown when I stopped at my old high school. I was at my old high school greeting my old teachers and catching up with some friends when I overheard an argument from the back stairwell. A crowd gathered to watch a fight between two students. I decided to take action and to prevent the argument from escalating into a physical fight. After I intervened, I learned that one of the boys made fun of a gay student in the middle of class and the teacher failed to do anything. It turned out the other kid was standing up for his gay friend. The kid was a high school sophomore who was defending his friend from a senior, which takes a lot of courage. Fortunately, the fight never occurred and I was invited to attend a meeting at the end of the school day. That meeting truly surprised me and made me one of the happiest kids that day. It turned out to be a Gay Straight Alliance meeting. I came from a conservative town and when I went to high school there was never an opportunity for me to attend a Gay Straight Alliance meeting, but the two friends made it possible. I was very proud of them! If I had more AC4P wristbands I would have given everybody one, but I decided to give my wristband to the boy who defended his friend.

> I initially expected to give my AC4P wristband to someone who was helping the environment. One day, my friend and I were walking to class when I gained a whole new perspective on what it meant to actively care. On the way to class my friend and I noticed a woman was crying. My friend wanted to stop and talk to her, but I resisted since I didn't want to risk being late for class. We decided to part ways, so I ran to class. Later that day, my friend told me the woman was crying because she forgot her keys and wallet in her dorm and by the time she went back she found they were stolen. Well, her wallet was there but it was completely empty. All of her money, identification cards, and debit cards were stolen from her wallet. My friend took the time to comfort her and joined her in getting a new school ID. I gave my AC4P wristband to my friend because she was very kind to a complete stranger. That day, my friend went out of her way to help a stranger who was in need of a friend.

> As I came home from class one day, I saw a girl standing beside my car. I walked closer and saw she was attaching a small piece of paper to the windshield wiper of my car. She moved to the next car in the parking lot to place another piece of paper. The note read: "I hope you have an outstanding day!" I approached her and inquired about the note. She told me her goal was to brighten people's day and to assure everyone that somebody cares for them. This, I felt was true. Indeed, her little note has the potential of brightening somebody's day. You never know who is feeling alone or troubled, but it is comforting to know there are people who would go out of their way to spread happiness. The girl did not expect any reward for her simple, yet powerful, message. She took the effort to brighten the day of complete strangers. I presented her with my AC4P wristband and explained its purpose. In a way, the message of her inspiring note on my windshield is similar to the message of the AC4P Movement. She became very interested and eager to participate in the Movement.

Collateral Effects and Exponential Impact

At the time of this writing, we have implemented three semesters of this AC4P assignment. The effects have been amazing – well beyond the success we anticipated. Each semester we are approached by numerous students asking for additional wristbands because they find the assignment "too restrictive" – they only get to pass on a wristband once. To reinforce their active caring for the AC4P Movement we try to accommodate these requests. In one instance, a student taught a youth sports team and wanted to introduce her athletes to AC4P. In another instance, a student ran a youth Bible group and decided to implement AC4P with her pupils.

After three semesters of the AC4P assignment, we have personally distributed approximately 500 wristbands to the KU undergraduate body via ABSC 100. It has been such a pleasure to see green AC4P wristbands appearing on fans' wrists when they "Wave the Wheat" following a KU touchdown or basketball win. (Fans put both arms in the air and wave them side-to-side – a KU sports-fan tradition.) It's also inspiring to see the wristbands proudly worn by students in class, despite that not being a requisite component of the assignment.

The students' pride in the AC4P Movement has generated a buzz on campus. Other students ask about the meaning of the green wristbands they see. Faculty have approached us to ask about the AC4P wristbands. They have had students (who have not taken ABSC 100 with us) ask them where they came from and why other courses weren't distributing them.

In one case, a student who had not taken ABSC 100 with us was enrolled in one of our faculty colleague's courses. The student asked our colleague about this mysterious surge of green wristbands in the department. Our colleague directed the student to us and we forwarded her the link to ac4p.org and gave her a wristband.

After reading about the AC4P Movement, she purchased 100 wristbands to use in her role as a resident assistant in a dormitory. She informed us when we followed up that someone to whom she gave a wristband ultimately bought a dozen or more AC4P wristbands to use in her undergraduate student organization. Our vision: We will see nearly everyone (students and faculty included) walking around campus with the green AC4P wristband.

Actively Caring for the AC4P Movement on Campus

The AC4P assignment has been a major success. Given the positive feedback we've obtained from students and faculty colleagues, we plan on expanding the assignment during the coming years (including assigning this book as a required text for the course).

Still, the assignment has not been without its fair share of hiccups. We want to discuss potential pitfalls in the assignment and our recommendations and plans to circumvent these issues. In doing so, we hope to create an assignment that fully engages 100% of our ABSC 100 students.

A tendency for students to avoid giving their wristband to a stranger is the first barrier to proper engagement in the assignment. Students often identify a recipient for their wristband before ever defining the AC4P behavior in the first component of the study. This is typically flagged when we review their posts and see statements like, "I plan to give my wristband to my cousin Steve because..."

These posts are corrected and we provide feedback on making sure they identify a target behavior to look for throughout the semester. Unfortunately, we find many students who select a proper behavioral target ultimately give their wristband to a friend or relative. We are uncomfortable scoring this as "wrong" since we don't want to punish AC4P behavior.

We do worry that students rely on acquaintances to either avoid having to interact with a stranger, or to rush to complete the assignment. In either case, the student will not fully experience the benefits of seeing the good in strangers around them, or pushing their own limits in being compassionate. To help assuage this issue, we have begun requiring that students give their wristband to a stranger. This mandate does not guarantee honest reporting, but we remind our students that lying about being compassionate would be especially disappointing.

A general level of anxiety associated with being compassionate to a stranger seems to be the second barrier to engagement in the AC4P activity. This likely feeds heavily into the first barrier, as well. Students occasionally report reluctance to give praise, especially to individuals with whom they are unfamiliar. These comments are important learning opportunities, prompting us to reflect on the unfortunate reality that our culture rarely embraces interpersonal compassion. These discussions serve as a springboard for introducing the mission of the AC4P Movement.

In one semester during which the second author implemented the AC4P assignment, the discussion was kicked-off by highlighting one objective of the project: Acts of caring and empathy are perceived as strange and awkward, and this disheartening state of affairs in society needs to be corrected. Many students identified with this premise. Having students practice rewarding AC4P behavior with a wristband in class is a possible solution to the reluctance to show compassion for a stranger.

Throughout the semester, the instructor could occasionally program empathic exchanges. Instruct students to face the person to the left/right/front/back of them (direction should be varied to ensure strangers are occasionally assigned) and say one nice thing about their neighbor. The individuals comprising each dyad should then switch roles. The class can then discuss their experiences as a group, sharing their feelings during the process and offering suggestions on easy ways to compliment or thank a stranger.

Through multiple exemplars and repeated practice, we hope students become accustomed to giving spur-of-the-moment compliments and praise to persons they don't know. If successful, this practice will aid in generalization beyond the classroom.

Personal Reflections

We admit we had no idea what to expect when we began this teaching/learning adventure. In fact, we had a quite a few doubts about the assignment's success. We feared students would scoff at the assignment or find it juvenile or "uncool." We anticipated students would find loopholes in the assignment (and some probably do) and cheat their way to earning points without putting in meaningful thought or effort (that probably happens, too).

But discussing possible pitfalls and disappointments made us realize we were feeding into the very culture of pessimism and apathy the AC4P Movement aims to rectify. This pessimism in our expectations was jarring to realize and served as a stark reminder of the need for this Movement on our campus. We feel enlightened to the amazing power of the AC4P Movement as we see the macrocontingencies[5] associated with AC4P behavior unfold.

Seeing our students beam when approaching us after class to share their own AC4P stories is one of the most fulfilling experiences we've encountered in our teaching careers. Reading the scores of AC4P experiences from the AC4P assignment each semester reminds us our campus features countless instances of kindness each and every day.

Most importantly, we've learned that the sea of faces looking back at us from the seats of the auditorium are more than just tuition-paying note-takers. They are meaningful contributors of empathy and compassion to our campus culture.

For some students, AC4P behavior lies dormant until provoked. It's our job as instructors to rouse this AC4P spirit. The kindheartedness of others is often overlooked due to stereotypes of "Generation Y" or a cultural-learned hopelessness; it's our job as human beings to look for the best in people and not to assume the worst.

The AC4P Movement lives on at the University of Kansas, and we are incredibly proud to be playing a small part in its momentum.

Notes

1. Baer, D. M. (1993). A brief, selective history of the Department of Human Development and Family Life at the University of Kansas: The early years. *Journal of Applied Behavior Analysis, 26*, 569-572.

2. Catania, A. C. (2013). A natural science of behavior. *Review of General Psychology, 17*, 133-139.

3. Geller, E. S. (1995). Integrating behaviorism and humanism for environmental protection. *Journal of Social Issues, 51*, 179-195; Skinner B. F. (May/June 1971). Humanistic behaviorism. *The Humanist, 31*-35.

4. While a key aspect of the Pass Stage is to encourage the wristband recipient to pass the wristband on to another person observed performing an AC4P behavior, we did not emphasize the pass-it-on component for this assignment.

5. Glenn, S. S. (2004). Individual behavior, culture and social change. *The Behavior Analyst, 27*, 133-151.

CHAPTER 14

Is it Realistic to Expect Quality AC4P Education?

E. Scott Geller

NO, I BELIEVE IT'S unrealistic to expect quality AC4P education in contemporary U.S. schools, due to a number of barriers. These include: low teacher compensation, low teacher-to-student ratios, time constraints, public-school challenges, win/lose individualism suppressing win/win collectivism, and a national obsession on outcome scores and rankings. Plus, few if any reinforcement contingencies are in place to motivate teachers and students to improve their teaching/learning behaviors. So here's a shout out for more AC4P education in our schools.

Quality AC4P education requires interpersonal compassion, collaboration, openness to change, and contingencies that support individual and group behaviors relevant to improving both teaching and learning. From reading the AC4P principles and applications in this book, you understand this. Plus, you know what AC4P behaviors and contingencies could improve the quality of education at your school.

Now I have an assignment for you: Please share this evidence-based knowledge with teachers, school administrators, parents of school children, and the students themselves. Through your passionate participation in sharing what you've learned about humanistic behaviorism, along with examples of many small wins,[1] it may be realistic to expect quality AC4P education at your school.

Conflicting Contingencies

Let's examine the impediments that currently prevent quality AC4P education. First, grade-relevant contingencies in my classroom (and probably in many classes throughout the university system) actually support slow and redundant lecturing.
You see, the more material I present in class, the more information the students have to learn for periodic exams, and the more difficult it is to earn a high grade. And that's what university students seem focused on – grades.

Slow, redundant lecturing provides students a welcomed break from their vigorous note-taking behavior. The only thing better than a turtle-paced lecture (from the average student's perspective) would be for the class to be excused early; or better yet, for the next class to be cancelled entirely.

But why should teachers change their methods? Take my teaching behaviors early in my career, for example. My research and scholarship were more important than teaching if I wanted to keep my faculty position and obtain merit salary raises.

Moreover, my teaching evaluations – obtained from students' judgments on the last day of every class – were relatively high. In fact, those student ratings, which resulted from my basic lecturing style, helped me "win" every university-wide teaching award offered at Virginia Tech, and a teaching excellence award from the American Psychological Association in 1982.

So why change? Sure, I gave a quality lecture, according to those evaluations, but was that quality AC4P education?

Barriers to Effectiveness

To be a more effective AC4P teacher, I would need to devote an inordinate amount of time rewriting the available textbook material for my courses and planning daily classroom exercises that actively engage the students in learning and applying the principles and procedures of the course. I would also "fight" a system that requires: a) a scheduled beginning and end of a class; b) a final exam on an assigned day; and c) a normal distribution of grades.

Another challenge: Early in my career, enrollment in my undergraduate introductory psychology classes always exceeded 300, and today it exceeds 500. Given this number of students in a class, which is the norm for many introductory courses at large U.S. universities, is it realistic to expect quality AC4P education? In this situation and under these contingencies, I think not.

My opportunities for AC4P education occur when I'm guiding an undergraduate or graduate student through the various phases of a research project, from designing an empirical study to preparing a written document for professional presentation. Those AC4P teaching/learning experiences enabled my 2013 Outstanding Mentorship Award from the Association for Behavior Analysis International. Unfortunately, few undergraduate students receive this level of one-on-one customized instruction. Why?

Not only because of time constraints and low faculty-to-student ratios, but also because these opportunities require extra, self-motivated effort from students. And it seems to me the average university student (undergraduate and graduate) wants to do the least amount of work for passing course grades and an eventual diploma. Why?

It's human nature. Recall the legacy of B.F. Skinner explained in Chapter 1: *selection by self-serving consequences.* We get the behavior we reward.

Management by Numbers

Students' just-enough-to-get-by-behavior is certainly a barrier to AC4P education, but realistically, why should students change their behavior? Usually, students can obtain acceptable grades by sitting passively in their classes and taking notes sufficient to prepare for periodic exams. Or, they skip class and study the available PowerPoint slides from which the professor lectures.

Many students, working competitively for grades, limit their learning experiences to memorizing fragments of information that can be measured on objective tests. Years ago, W. Edwards Deming[2] stressed management by the numbers may get you the numbers, but the result will not necessarily be a quality product.

Quality AC4P education requires application of optimal methods and a commitment to continuous improvement – not just meeting minimum standards set by state agencies with limited expectations.

Public-School Challenges

Quality AC4P education is even more improbable in public schools, given the three-term (activator-behavior-consequence) contingencies controlling behavior. Indeed, teaching in public schools is among the most challenging professions to accomplish effectively. The working conditions and the clients (i.e., the students) in public schools indicate quite clearly that public-school teaching is much more difficult than university teaching.

University teachers do not need to be concerned with discipline management; their clients are usually willing and paying customers, selected from a pool of applicants for the privilege of higher education. This is obviously not the case for the public-school teacher, who must manage a heterogeneous (in terms of ability and personal agenda) group of young people, most of whom do not understand the value of the education they're supposed to receive.

Making lessons relevant and interesting to students raised in the alienating and isolating environment of 24/7 television entertainment, ever-more realistic and addictive computer games, and the "social network" of the internet is onerous for all teachers, but this is clearly more taxing for public-school teachers than university teachers.

University teachers are typically in charge of their customers for 50-minute blocks of time. But public-school teachers generally manage and teach the same group of pupils for much longer periods, up to several hours (and sometimes the entire day in elementary school).

Other barriers to quality AC4P teaching in public schools:

- It's no secret that teachers are not paid adequately for their arduous work, and they're not compensated according to the quality of their performance.
- Teachers in the U.S. do not receive strong cultural support for their teaching efforts, especially compared to other countries.
- U.S. high schools are publicized more for athletics than academics.
- Public expectations for the U.S. education system are seemingly narrow: higher scores on standardized achievement tests.
- Many students and their parents are narrowly focused on getting higher grades.
- With current pressures on public-school teachers to emphasize only facts and right answers over critical thinking, they avoid classroom debates and interactive discussion and tailor lessons to statewide testing programs.[3] (Many public-school teachers in my area "relax" their classroom instruction substantially after students take the SOL (standards-of-learning) exams. Often the showing of videotapes and DVD's take the place of teacher-directed learning exercises).

- Elementary and high-school teachers receive some training in colleges and universities on how to teach, but most do not receive sufficient education/training in applied behavior analysis (ABA) to accept and apply humanistic behaviorism in their classrooms.
- Privileged teachers who acknowledge the value of teaching/learning tools based on ABA are faced with insurmountable contingencies preventing their application.
- Most college/university teachers receive minimal behavior-focused training on how to be an effective AC4P teacher. As B.F. Skinner proclaimed, "College teaching is the only profession for which there is no professional training. Would-be doctors go to medical schools, would-be lawyers go to law schools, and would-be engineers go to institutes of technology, but would-be teachers just start teaching."[4]

A Memorable Day

The day that corrupted my perspective toward university teaching was Friday, November 15, 1974. This was near the beginning of my teaching career at Virginia Tech. I remember certain events as if they happened yesterday.

In my undergraduate Human Choice Behavior class, 18 of 40 students had volunteered to use an innovative student feedback device (SFD). The result was a most disappointing teaching experience, although the outcome is understandable from an ABA perspective.

I had high hopes for the SFD, an apparatus I invented and built to improve the impact of the typical classroom presentation. This prototype SFD consisted of three primary parts: a) a feedback panel with 18 indicator lights, clearly visible by only the instructor; b) 18 silent, push-button switches, each connected to a separate indicator light on the feedback panel that remained illuminated as long as the button was depressed; and c) an 18-pen recorder that documented the frequency and duration of each student's button pressing.[5]

The 18 students with feedback buttons were asked to shape an optimal lecture pace. I asked one group of nine students to keep their buttons depressed whenever the lecture pace was "too fast," and I instructed the other group of nine to hold their buttons down as long as the lecture was "too slow".

My graduate research assistant, who monitored the SFD, gave me one of two signals: "thumb up" to speed up my lecture and "thumb down" to slow me down. The plan was to maintain the signaled pace until five or more students pressed their buttons to prompt me to change.

Two other research assistants sat in the back of the classroom and independently recorded changes in the pace of my lecture. The records of these observers showed reliably I changed my lecture pace according to each signal from the research assistant. However, the students' behaviors were divergent, supporting my earlier point about classroom behavior and grade-relevant contingencies.

I had no trouble provoking simultaneous judgments of "too fast". As soon as I increased my lecture pace, five to eight lights illuminated in the "too fast" half of the feedback panel. But I could not get more than three students to indicate a judgment of "too slow" during my periods of intentionally-slow lecturing.

When switching to a slow presentation style, I attempted to activate student judgments of "too slow" and signals for me to pick up the pace. I tried these low-probability response patterns: a) returning to the same exact lecture point on as many as six occasions (as verified by the notes of the independent observers), b) standing at the lectern and paging through my lecture notes for 30 seconds, c) standing with arms folded and saying nothing for periods as long as 30 seconds, and d) pacing back and forth in front of the class for as long as 30 seconds without saying a word.

My attempts failed. Students put up with my procrastinating, rather than ask for a faster lecture pace. The button-pressing rates during each role-playing condition of this class period are published elsewhere[6] along with more details about other unsuccessful applications of the SFD.

I interpreted these disappointing findings with beliefs and self-talk like, "Students don't give a hoot about learning." Obviously that's a "cop out, blame the victim (student)" inference that lacks any AC4P direction for problem solving.

The fact is I could have developed procedures or contingencies to increase the utility of the SFD by implementing training and feedback sessions for lecture "evaluators." I could have offered rewarding consequences for appropriate or reliable judgments. But I did not.

I could have dramatically altered my teaching techniques to increase the active involvement of each student by establishing cooperative-learning groups,[7] implementing a personalized system of instruction,[8] or incorporating some precision teaching exercises.[9] But I did not. Why not?

My teaching approach was adequately rewarded. I received overall high feedback scores from students on the last day of every class, enabling me to "win" various "teaching-excellence" awards. To become a more effective AC4P teacher I would have had to dedicate more time and effort. And I did not wish to "buck the system" at that early point in my career, and perhaps jeopardize my faculty position and merit salary increases.

How Far Have We Progressed?

The impact of these barriers on the quality of teaching can be viewed on a national scale. More than two decades ago, the Secretary of Education, Lamar Alexander, set six ambitious National Education Goals to be achieved by the year 2000. Dr. Deming's words, said numerous times at his four-day seminar I attended, echoed in my ears: "What could be worse—goals without method."[2]

These National Education Goals were listed as follows in Parade Magazine by a journalist who interviewed Lamar Alexander:
1. All American children will start school each day ready to learn.
2. The high-school graduation rate will increase to at least 90%.

3. Students will leave Grades 4, 8, and 12 having demonstrated competency in challenging subject matter.
4. American students will be first in the world in science and mathematics.
5. Every adult will be literate and will possess the knowledge and skills necesary to compete in a global economy.
6. Every school will be free of drugs and violence and will offer a disciplined environment conducive to learning.[10]

Where are we today regarding the achievement of Lamar Alexander's "goals"? Does our education system deserve higher grades now than then? The disappointing answer is given in Shane McCarty's introduction to this section. But you already know the answer, right?

Here's what happened: These 1991 National Education Goals directed both teachers and students to focus on outcomes (grades), and raised U.S public expectations for higher test scores. You see, these goals gave impetus to outcome-based education (OBE).

But effective OBE is founded on three basic assumptions, verified rigorously and systematically by ABA researchers: a) all students have the potential to learn but at different rates and by different methods, b) success (or accomplishment) breeds more success, and c) the school system controls the conditions for success or accomplishment.[11]

Effective OBE applies four key principles: a) focus on significant outcomes, b) design curricula and instructional processes deductively from the ultimate desired outcomes, c) maintain high expectations for all students to succeed eventually, and d) provide expanded opportunities and support for teaching/learning accomplishment.[12]

More than two decades ago our education leaders realized OBE needs to be accomplishment oriented[13] and based on considerations of social validity[14] and notions of quality management and systems control.[2] How nice both school administrators and teachers were seemingly empowered to determine the methods for reaching OBE goals.[15] Has this ever happen on a large scale? Or even at only your school?

If quality means "superiority of kind" or "grade of excellence," as defined in my *American Heritage Dictionary*[16] and reflected in the concept of industrial quality control,[2] then quality AC4P education has not yet been achieved in the U.S. But it's surely possible.

Evidence-based technology is available today to improve substantially the quality of both teaching and learning at all levels of American education. But it's going to take more than the implementation of technology. Improved, quality education requires AC4P behavior on the part of everyone who understands and values the issues, perspectives and solutions put forth in this book.

Now you have a unique and imperative responsibility. Share your critical knowledge with others, especially educators, administrators, and parents of school children. Activate the concerned but silent majority to give a shout out for more AC4P education in your schools. Now more than ever, it's time to actively care about improving the quality of education in our United States of America!

Notes

1. Weick, K. E. (1984). Small wins: Redefining the scale of social problems. *American Psychologist, 39*, 40-49.

2. Deming, W. E. (1991, May). *Quality, productivity and competitive position.* Los Angeles: Quality Enhancement Seminars, Inc.

3. Glasser, W. (1990). *The quality school: Managing students without coercion.* New York, NY: Harper & Row.

4. Skinner, B. F. (1984). The shame of American education. *American Psychologist, 39*, 947 954.

5. Today an SFD would not require the cumbersome switches and wires I needed in 1974, but could be efficient and wireless with student feedback summarized continuously on a hand-held iPad, iPod, or smart phone.

6. Geller, E. S., Chaffee, J. L., & Farris, J. C. (1975). Research in modifying lecturer behavior with continuous student feedback. *Educational Technology, 15,* 31-35.

7. Kohn, A. (1986). *No contest: The case against competition.* Boston, MA: Houghton Mifflin; Tjosvold, D., & Chia, L. C. (1989). Conflict between managers and workers: The role of cooperation and competition. *Journal of Social Psychology, 129*, 235-247.

8. Keller, F. S., & Sherman, J. G. (1974), *PSI: The Keller Plan handbook.* Menlo Park, CA: W.A. Benjamin.

9. Lindsley, O.R. (1990). Precision teaching: By teachers for children. *Teaching Exceptional Children, 22,* 10-15; Lindsley, O.R. (1991). Precision teaching's unique legacy from B. F. Skinner. *Journal of Behavioral Education, 1,* 253-266.

10. Klein, E. (1991, August 25). We're talking about a revolution. *Parade Magazine*, pp. 4-7.

11. Spady, W. G., & Marshall, K. S. (1991). Beyond traditional outcome-based education. *Educational Leadership, 49*, 67-72.

12. Spady, W. G. (1988), Organizing for results: The basis of authentic restructuring and reform. *Educational Leadership, 46*, 4-8; Spady, W. G., & Marshall, K. S. (1991). Beyond traditional outcome-based education. *Educational Leadership, 49,* 67-72.

13. Gilbert, T. F. (1978). *Human competence: Engineering worthy performance.* New York, NY: Mc-Graw-Hill.

14. Schwartz, I. S., & Baer, D. M. (1991). Social validity assessments: Is current practice state of the art? *Journal of Applied Behavior Analysis, 24,* 231-244.

15. King, J. A., & Evans, K. M. (1991). Can we achieve outcome-based education? *Educational Leadership, 49,* 73-75; Spady, W. G., & Marshall, K. S. (1991). Beyond traditional outcome-based education. *Educational Leadership, 49,* 67-72.

16. *The American Heritage Dictionary* (1985) (2nd Collegiate Edition). Boston, MA: Houghton Mifflin.

Part III: Personal Stories of AC4P

Joanne Dean Geller

ACTIVELY CARING IS A get-well card sent to a friend or even a stranger, a cup of tea and a listening ear, returning found merchandise to its rightful owner, or shoveling a pile of snow out from an elderly person's driveway. AC4P means we appreciate people for who they are, rather than what they've achieved. When stressors and life's conflicts take the heart out of us, we need to know someone cares about our difficulties and believes in us. And we need to reciprocate, and do the same for others.

This basic level of AC4P can make a lasting difference in our lives. It's not about being judgmental, slashing people's self-esteem, and picking over faults. No, AC4P values the uniqueness of people. It recognizes human potential, and plays positively to people's strengths.

Empathy is a prerequisite. We need to perceive and care about the concerns or predicaments of others. When called to act on our caring for others, we must draw on our inner compassion and courage to act.

The following chapters include personal stories that demonstrate principles and applications of AC4P. They range from challenges of family, dealing with cancer, to the value of making time for others.

These stories will inspire you to carve out more time to actively care for family, friends, colleagues, and even strangers. Each story illustrates how AC4P helps bring out the best in both the giver and the receiver.

The testimonies cited in these chapters make an important point: AC4P behavior strengthens the compassion and caring of the person giving. Imagine the AC4P ripple effect if increasing numbers of individuals experience the rewarding, good-feeling consequences of actively caring for others.

Leaping to the self-transcendence state that sits atop Maslow's Hierarchy of Needs fulfills lower-level needs, especially our need for self-esteem and belongingness.

Self-efficacy, personal control, and optimism also are enhanced through AC4P behavior. Empowerment and self-motivation are fueled by all of these person-states, and vice versa.

Our greatest challenge is to help others feel the rewarding power of AC4P behavior. To do this, we must develop the context and implement contingencies to motivate initial occurrences of AC4P behavior. The stories in Part III provide practical suggestions for stoking the fires of self-motivation. The positive-reinforcing consequences of AC4P behavior, witnessed and experienced time and again in the personal stories that make up these chapters, support the premise that AC4P behavior is naturally rewarding and self-sustaining when nurtured within a supportive culture.

These personal stories were not due to the competence, commitment and courage of *one* heroic person. Friends, family members, teachers, co-workers, and even strangers provided direction, mentorship or supportive consequences. Performing AC4P behavior affected many authors' way of life, inspiring them to adopt an AC4P lifestyle.

Each personal story illustrates how the AC4P principles enable the development of an AC4P culture – a culture of compassion at home, at work, at school, and throughout our communities.

CHAPTER 15

My 60/60 AC4P Challenge:
When actions speak louder than words

Joanne Dean Geller

LIFE HAS BEEN a delightful ride for me. Sure, there were hard times that could have knocked me down. But the example my parents set with their style of living added appreciation and resilience to how I have lived and handled my life's challenges. I've now lived longer than my mother, who passed away when she was 57. Everyday my heart is warmed when I think of her, wishing I could hold her and tell her how much she has meant to me. She was absolutely an actively-caring person, even when suffering physical disability from a stroke and battling cancer for many years.

My mother had an optimistic aura that was contagious. She never pre-judged anyone negatively, but rather took time to understand the other person's perspective. She was a talented writer with a gift of expressing herself through poetry. She always put her family first and would sacrifice her own needs for ours.

While a mom and career person, she still found time to volunteer at church, and serve as a Councilwoman for our town. She initiated many programs to protect the environment. Indeed, our town planted trees in her memory and placed eight park benches around the fair grounds with her name on them. She made time for everyone and our house was always filled with young people who needed a place to be.

Remembering my mom inspires me to offer special support for the AC4P Movement. I'm proud to be continuing her legacy of AC4P.

I've faced potential life-destroying experiences, but the example of my mom helped me overcome these personal hardships. I had an ovarian tumor removed in high school that led to years of surgeries because of serious adhesions. My intestines had burst a number of times because of this, requiring me to be placed on a stomach pump for three months from these complications.

The doctors were sure I would need a colostomy bag for the rest of my life, but fortunately, I did not. Five years later, the adhesions attached my intestines to my diaphragm and I thought my life was over. But again, competent physicians fixed me up.

Ending a romantic relationship resulted in a person taking his life on my birthday. He left me $100,000 in his only life-insurance policy, but I chose to leave that money to his three sons. I endured the horrible process of terminating my child. Plus, I gave up a meaningful position because I would not compromise my values and tolerate sexual harassment.

I know we all deal with challenges throughout our lives, but for some reason I have been blessed with the ability to be an optimist no matter what. I am so grateful for that.

My 60/60 Commitment

I viewed turning 60 as a gift, and I wanted to share this gift with others. With new knowledge about psychological and behavioral science, as taught to me by Scott Geller,

I now have labels for my disposition to actively care, including courage, commitment, compassion, and self-motivation. Understanding the science behind each of these words provides me with insight to actively care more effectively.

My move to Blacksburg, Virginia four years ago gave me the opportunity to work with faculty and students in the Department of Psychology at Virginia Tech. Graduate and undergraduate students have told me I have been an example for the actions implied by the AC4P concept. This encouraged me to do an AC4P act of kindness for a stranger or friend each of the 60 days prior to turning 60, February 27th, 2010.

This became well-known as "Joanne's 60/60 Challenge". It was actually more of a challenge than I had expected. For me, AC4P behavior is much more than holding a door open for a friend or stranger. It involves reflectively thinking about ways to go out of my daily routine to do something special for another person. I regularly go out of my way to impact other people's lives in beneficial ways; but to give up personal time for AC4P behavior "everyday" was a different story.

My AC4P commitment began on January 1, 2010 and I was enthused. I am an outgoing person, comfortable speaking to almost anyone. But even as an extrovert, I found it challenging to come up with intentional acts of kindness everyday that were beyond the norm. I shared my daily experiences via email and phone calls with a supportive group of close friends who helped keep me accountable to achieve my 60/60 goal.

The Beginning

It's New Year's Day and I'm driving through the quiet town of Blacksburg. There's my first AC4P opportunity right in front of my eyes. Over the past two years, I had observed a young man systematically collecting litter from the sidewalk. I assumed he worked for the town. Now some might judge this "litter-control" job to be insignificant, but I've always appreciated that Blacksburg values keeping the town litter-free and has provided funds for an individual to make this happen.

So there's my "litter control" man picking up papers on New Year's Day. No one's in sight. I pull into the post-office parking lot and run into the local Starbucks to purchase a gift card for this gentleman.

Excited, I run up to him, and actually startle him. I ask for his name and proceed to tell Jason how much I appreciate his efforts to keep our town clean.

With eyes wide open and a friendly smile, Jason says, "No one has ever said anything like that to me". We shake hands and I give him the gift card. I then explain the AC4P Movement and that he's my first choice for the New Year.

What a wonderful feeling that experience gave me, and appeared to give Jason. To this day, two years later, we wave every time we see each other. One simple act of kindness and our brief conversation remind me of the power of putting AC4P words into action.

Meeting My 60/60 Challenge

I continued my daily AC4P behaviors for the next 59 days. On some days AC4P situations just happened, and some days I had to look hard and create opportunities.

My acts of kindness ranged from shoveling mounds of snow for elderly neighbors to cooking meals for families. It was a pleasure to help strangers load groceries into their cars, and to watch a smile come to the face's of cashier's after telling them I appreciate the work they do.

I took a number of days to help friends clean their homes, and I even drove my massage therapist from Blacksburg to Charlotte, North Carolina to give a massage to the wife of a special friend with ALS (see Chapter 33).

These are just a few examples of my daily AC4P experiences. Believe me, they were all well received. Some days nearly ended without finding an opportunity for AC4P behavior, and I was challenged to intentionally find someone in need of AC4P behavior.

All in all, I performed a significant AC4P action everyday for the 60 days leading up to my 60th birthday.[1] I reported each of these acts of kindness on the AC4P website for my friends and colleagues to see. Soon after my birthday, leaders of the AC4P Movement gave me a book with 60 AC4P stories, actions reflecting the achievement of my 60/60 challenge.

In Conclusion

An important lesson I learned from this two-month experience: We should appreciate all the people who donate their time on our behalf. We all want an AC4P culture of compassion. Right in front of our eyes people are already donating their personal time to help others. People who come to mind are fireman, first-aid squad members, hospital volunteers, speakers from AA programs, members of the Humane Society and many community leaders.

Growing up in the 1950s, it seemed easier to make time for such groups. In today's fast-pace life it's difficult for many people to dedicate time to others beyond their immediate family. This is why I'm thrilled to help ignite and inspire AC4P behaviors that were seemingly more common in the "good old days".

This story is about putting AC4P words into action, because our actions do speak louder than our words. The AC4P Movement is about bringing to life words of interpersonal caring, and getting on board with volunteering our time on behalf of others, including our own families.

We all have a lifetime to enjoy, and such joy is greatly enhanced when it's shared with others. There are many people out there, young and old, who can benefit greatly from a simple intentional AC4P act of kindness. And when you give some of your precious time to actively care, the enhanced boost in your own self-esteem, optimism, and sense of belonging is priceless.

Note

1. Meeting the 60-day challenge actually required me to continue my daily AC4P behaviors until March 1st, three days after my 60th birthday. But we still celebrated meeting my challenge on February 27th.

CHAPTER 16

Memorable AC4P Experiences:
Special impact of a green wristband

Justin Graves

MY DISCOVERY OF THE AC4P Movement came through an interaction in a Virginia Tech (VT) classroom. My experience as a college student and as an individual would never be the same again.

I was a freshman when I first heard about the Movement, with a purpose reflected by my University motto, *Ut Prosim* (That I May Serve).

I learned about the Movement by asking a fellow classmate – one stranger at the time – what his green wristband represented. At the time, in late 2008, there were several different silicone wristbands in circulation with a range of colors, messages, and purposes. I wanted to learn more about the AC4P wristband, and about the founder of the AC4P concept.

My quest found its destination inside Williams Hall, to Dr. Geller's office. But the timing was not right. Heavily-involved in extracurricular and leadership activities, I was unable to commit the time and energy to help the AC4P Movement. That only held true until my senior year.

My First AC4P Wristband

While I was commuting into Washington D.C. from my parent's home in Northern Virginia for a summer internship with the federal government, I was gifted a green AC4P wristband. I remember the day as if it were yesterday.

It's raining when we trek to the above-ground metro stop at L'Enfant Plaza. I ask a gentleman, "How are you doing?" He shares the story of his miserable day at work, and the prospects of an hour-long wait at the metro stop for his wife to pick him up after tending to their sick child. I listen attentively to his difficulties, and then he hands me the AC4P wristband. He had received it from a VT student while he was visiting Blacksburg.

When I got home, I turned to Google for more information about AC4P. I promptly ordered a t-shirt to support the AC4P Movement – one I still wear proudly to this day. I decided to seek out Dr. Geller again when I returned to Blacksburg. Receiving the AC4P wristband had made my day, and I wanted to join the AC4P team.

My AC4P Transformation

I sent an e-mail to Dr. Geller and Shane McCarty, asking for more information about the Center for Applied Behavior Systems, and about acquiring additional wristbands. Dr. Geller promptly e-mailed me back, and invited me to visit with him when I returned to Blacksburg. I then organized a meeting with Joanne Geller, who delivered me a box filled with 100 AC4P wristbands.

I now had my own AC4P challenge, similar to Joanne's 60/60 Challenge (see Chapter 15). My goal: Recognize at least one person with a wristband daily until the wristbands are gone. After giving someone a wristband following his or her AC4P behavior, I filled out a brief survey to document how I felt after rewarding a person's act of caring.

Before embarking on the AC4P challenge, I had set an easier goal: Meet one new person every day. Although it was sometimes awkward, and sometimes unnatural, the number of people I had met through my own AC4P challenge was remarkable. I made several new friends, many Hokies and some formerly complete strangers. I enjoyed the positive reactions I received whenever I explained the AC4P Movement.

After meeting this goal, I took a step up to the next AC4P goal. If I could meet one new person every day, then I could try and help one new person every day. I was optimistic and kept trekking through the academic year, trying to meet my commitment.

What Goes Around Comes Around

In my fourth year of volunteering at a local elementary school (Spring 2012), I met a unique first-grader – let's call him Riley. This young student had a profound impact on me throughout my weekly visits to the school. If I had gotten a haircut – Riley noticed. If I wore a different ring on my finger – Riley noticed. When I wore a new pair of shoes – Riley noticed. When I debuted my new wheelchair – Riley noticed.

One morning, just after I had received a new AC4P wristband on campus, Riley notices. "Justin," Riley asks, "What's that green wristband for?" I explain the AC4P Movement to him – the meaning of the wristband, and the pay-it-forward nature of the process. "One day, I hope to receive a green wristband of my own," Riley replies. I make note of this.

Months later, Michelle Obama, the First Lady of the U.S., was the commencement speaker for my college graduation ceremony. One week prior to the commencement, I had received a call from the White House.

The First Lady wanted to mention me in her speech. She was struck by my goal of trying to help one new person every day, having learned of this goal from a story published by the University. I was invited to meet the First Lady for a conversation prior to her speech. I saw this as a grand opportunity – an opportunity to share the AC4P message with Mrs. Obama.

The night before meeting the First Lady, I scoured my home, looking for an AC4P wristband. I rehearsed the purpose of the wristband numerous times in my head before I gave her one. Later, I saw her wearing it during interactions with University officials throughout the day. This was remarkable. Even more remarkable were her comments during her speech:

And one of today's graduates, a young man named Justin Graves, has committed himself to helping at least one person every single day. Way to go. As he put it, and these are his words – Justin said, 'Life is all about what you have done for other people.

Then, Mrs. Obama indicated that Virginia Tech could teach the rest of the world about the spirit of serving others... Wow!

Two weeks later, I'm back at the elementary school, helping out students, including Riley. The students present me with an illustrated book, each page containing students' heartfelt words of appreciation for my AC4P behavior. Then, the teacher sets

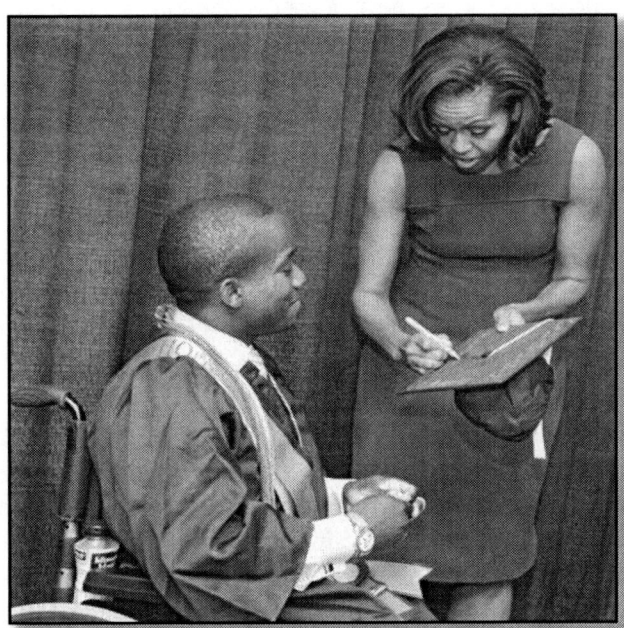

Michelle Obama discusses her 2012 commencement address with Justin Graves.

up a projector and shows a video. Low and behold, it's the video of Mrs. Obama's commencement address.

Afterwards, Riley approaches me as we walk to the lunchroom, and says, "Justin, I have something for you". I wonder what he's going to pull from his pocket. He presents me with an AC4P wristband and announces:

> *I got this bracelet at Virginia Tech some time ago. And I want you to know I really like the way you helped us in the classroom this year. Plus, you helped a lot of people too, so here's another green wristband for you to add to your collection, 'cause I bet you have a lot.*

What Goes Around *Really* Comes Around

In the summer of 2012, a close friend and I share a meal in a local Blacksburg restaurant. We start talking about the "Hokie Bucket List" – a set of items a VT student organization claims you should do before you graduate if you are a "true Hokie." Weeks earlier, the university ran a publication with an interview of me that dubbed me as "the Ultimate Hokie" and it documented reflections of my time of leadership and service at the university. I was definitely honored, but once I discover the Bucket List I realize there are some things there I would never be able to accomplish.

In November 2012, when my friend Scinju recommends we go on a local hike, I am floored. I wasn't floored because it was almost December and it had just finished snowing. I was floored because of my disability. I am a paraplegic. I ambulate with a wheelchair but always hesitate to say I am "confined" to a wheelchair because it's not a confinement. Instead, I use my disability to touch as many people as possible when they may not expect it.

After weeks of planning said hike, Scinju and I make our way to the Cascades in Giles County, Virginia with more than ten others - some are close friends, some are strangers. But by the end of the day we will have accomplished something fascinating. Scinju and friends build a make-shift cot that allows me to complete Item Number 10 on the Hokie Bucket List: Hike the Cascades Falls.

This rugged, four-mile roundtrip Hike was not only something I never imagined I'd do, but something I had admired. All of my closest friends, at some point, took the trip and took photos of the beautiful natural waterfall you meet at the two-mile point. "The Cascades" hike was an activity I had to participate in to feel I really earned that title of "the Ultimate Hokie."

Not long after I completed the hike, a video of it became viral. It wasn't all the attention it received that moved me. It was the power of AC4P that moved me. I never ever expected to be able to make this hike. I never expected to see the waterfall in person. However, thanks to some of the greatest friends on this Earth caring for me, in as active a way as possible, I was able to conquer something I thought I never could. My disability was put on the shelf when these friends stepped in to help me. And of course I had to recognize them with AC4P wristbands. I look forward to hearing how they use those wristbands to recognize others' AC4P behavior.

Unexpected AC4P Behavior

Here's how my motivation to help is enhanced. Everyone wants social approval and appreciation. This is the basic human need of belongingness (see Chapter 2). Indeed, lives can be enriched when you help someone – when you actively care for them – especially when the AC4P behavior is *unexpected*.

As a paraplegic, people often hold a door open for me. I love opportunities to make other people's day by holding a door open for them.

When a Radford student helped me put my groceries in my car at the local Wal-Mart, he didn't think I'd gift him anything, much less an AC4P wristband for him to pass on.

When I met Antwon, a homeless man on a street in Downtown Atlanta, he was just looking for money to get into the shelter on a hot summer night – not a green wristband.

When Ted Faulkner greeted me to help me meet my goal of meeting one new person every day – he didn't expect the wristband, even though he made my day.

When a prospective VT student found a Hokie ID card on the ground during his campus tour and gave it to me, he didn't expect anything in return. It's always such a pleasure to reward a person's AC4P behavior with the AC4P wristband and then share the meaning of this "small token of my appreciation".

My parents taught me to make sure people see me as an individual, before they see my wheelchair. As a disabled student at VT, I faced this challenge daily. After I became immersed in the AC4P Movement, my physical challenge became easier to handle. I looked for ways to actively care for others and for opportunities to show explicit appreciation for their AC4P behavior.

With more and more people actively caring for others, recognizing the AC4P actions of others, and sharing their stories at ac4p.org, AC4P behavior will become the norm. The result: A world we all desire to live in – a world filled with compassion.

CHAPTER 17

Living with Cancer:
The survival power of AC4P

E. Scott Geller

I REMEMBER AS IF it were yesterday. On Friday, May 3, 2002 I received unexpected, grim, and shocking news from an urologist: "You have cancer". I tell you this – not for pity or sympathy – but because of the insight I've gained from dealing with this life-threatening disease for more than a decade.

My life changed dramatically from that unforgettable news forward, from daily debilitating distress to a new appreciation of life and interpersonal relationships. I've intentionally avoided a disposition of despair and a focus on avoiding failure. With a mindset of hope, I've focused on achieving success through personal control. And, I've become more mindful of the many treasures of everyday living.

It Won't Happen to Me

I'm overwhelmed with optimism waiting for my urologist to reveal the results of the biopsy. Leading indicators gave me a 1 in 5, or 20% chance of having prostate cancer. But those statistics are based on the average 60-year old.

I consider myself much less at-risk for cancer than the average person – I don't smoke or consume much alcohol, and eat very little red meat. I exercise regularly and take antioxidant vitamins daily. I eat lots of tomatoes (which contain lycopene – a presumed protector against prostate cancer), and I spend a lot of time in the sun, providing me plenty of vitamin D (another presumed protector against this type of cancer).

I had done everything I knew to do to prevent this relatively common type of cancer. I consider my cancer an "accident," not only because it was unintentional but because it was unexpected and unpreventable with my current knowledge, tools, and methods.

Cancer of course is scary. So many of its contributing factors are unknown and/or uncontrollable (as in the genetics that likely contributed to my current plight). But through research these unknowns can be revealed, and some of the ordeals I describe in this narrative can be prevented today.

The Power of Personal Control

The immediate result of my biopsy is debilitating. I feel distressed and helpless. At the dinner table, I announce, "Well I guess it's just my time. I've lived an active 60 years, and have seen enough of this life." My 23-year-old daughter retorts, with tears streaming down her face, "But Dad, you haven't seen enough of me".

My daughter's words bring me to my senses. Why am I giving up? I can fight this thing. Famous people like Lance Armstrong, Mayor Rudy Giuliani, and General Norman Schwarzkopf have come back strong after a cancer diagnosis – I can too!

I began reading books and scouring the internet for information about prostate cancer, eventually deciding removal of the prostate was the best therapeutic approach for me. I scheduled surgery with an urologist who had performed over 350 radical retro pubic nerve-sparing prostatectomies.

I conducted substantial research to gain a perception of control over my adversity. And after this, I felt much better. Hopefulness took the place of helplessness; motivating stress overcame debilitating distress.

The Power of AC4P Support

The sense of personal control over my disease would not have occurred without AC4P behavior from family, students, friends, and colleagues. My family reassured me with words like, "We'll help you get through this". My graduate students brought me relevant books and internet material. My department chairman gave me contact information for reputable urologists.

My partners at Safety Performance Solutions, Inc. offered me optimism, including encouraging stories of their family members who have survived prostate cancer. Students in my university classes sent me e-mails to express appreciation for my teaching and to wish me success in overcoming my setback.

At the end of several classes, students approached me with words of sincere concern and comfort. Some gave me a hug, and after everyone left my introductory psychology class of 600 students, a few asked if they could pray for me. Here I am, standing in front of a mostly empty auditorium and teary-eyed, while three students take turns asking God to keep me healthy so I can keep teaching.

Research has shown over and over that interpersonal support is critical for overcoming physical illness and emotional conflict. Now I had experienced this firsthand. Through AC4P support I received the information and the inspiration to gain personal control. Indeed, without substantial actively caring I could not have maintained sufficient self-motivation and courage to endure the intense and prolonged treatment ordeal required to fight my disease – nor frankly would I want to.

I learned there's a great amount of AC4P support available when we need it, if we are willing to ask for help. As Ramakrishna said, "The winds of grace are always blowing, but you have to raise the sail".

I raised my sail in May 2002 with my announcement of being diagnosed with prostate cancer. I received a remarkable amount of genuine caring, concern, and support. All of a sudden, friends, colleagues and students expressed appreciation for my daily contributions as a teacher and researcher, along with strong sentiment and hope I will be able to continue my worthwhile work.

I soon found I would need this level of interpersonal AC4P for extended periods of time. My Senior Partners at Safety Performance Solutions, Inc. commissioned a local artist, George Wills, to draw the cartoon depicted on the next page. The message hit home for me and made me laugh out loud.

More Difficult Than Expected

I heard convalescence from prostate surgery was painful and arduous, but it was worse than I anticipated. The three-day hospital stay was a breeze compared to the following weeks of post-surgery recuperation. The only memorable problem in the hospital was lack

of sleep, largely due to intermittent interruptions by nurses who were more disruptive than necessary. It was obvious the hospital staff could have benefited greatly from some basic lessons about AC4P and applications of interpersonal observation and feedback.

I should have stayed in the hospital longer. My rush to go home and get some welcomed sleep led to extra pain and discomfort. I won't bore you with details, but the lesson is important for all kinds of recovery. Be patient and appreciate the need for incremental healing. This is a critical lesson for the doctors and hospital staff, also. They should not let unrealistic wishes and optimism of their patients overcome their empirical observations and more informed judgment.

Set Reasonable Goals

My impatience to leave the hospital was fueled by a goal to attend and participate at the 2002 Professional Development Conference of the American Society of Safety Engineers (ASSE). I was scheduled to give a day-long, pre-conference ASSE workshop just 16 days after surgery, and I had no time to lose. Yes, I gave that workshop and a keynote address two days later, and I was very glad to be able to make that trip.

Upon reflection I realize (as many had advised me) the goal I set and reached was not realistic, nor in my best interest. I'm convinced I slowed the recovery process because I tried to do too much, too fast. Bottom line: Goals are critical motivators for recovery from illness or injury, but be realistic. Trying to do more than you're physically ready for can be detrimental.

More Power from AC4P Support

My attendance at the ASSE conference was a "psychological high". While the experience may have hindered my physical recovery, it did wonders for my psychological state, including my self-esteem, self-efficacy, perception of personal control, optimism, and sense of belonging and interdependence.

I do not point out this inconsistency between mind and body healing to pit medicine against psychological science. I still believe the trip slowed my overall physical recovery and helped make the month following surgery the longest in my life. Rather, I want to demonstrate the power of AC4P support from others.

I presumed a large number of people expected and wanted me to make it to the ASSE conference, and I believed I would make some worthwhile contributions if I participated. Indeed, I signed several hundred copies of my book, *The Participation Factor: How to increase involvement in occupational safety* which was debuted at that conference.

It's noteworthy however; I could not have participated at that level without the continual assistance of my daughter, Krista. Indeed, I needed her to help me walk from one event to another. This is just more evidence for the special power of AC4P, especially from family members.

Fortunately, my interpersonal support extended far beyond my immediate family. Friends, colleagues, and total strangers called and e-mailed me with advice, well-wishes, and statements of appreciation for my prior contributions to occupational safety. Many expressed hope I would be able to get back to my research, teaching, and scholarship quickly and continue in a healthy state of mind and body.

Especially supportive were communications from others who have experienced the same illness and recovery challenges. It's so easy to feel isolated and depressed during the inactive phase of convalescence. Hearing from people who had experienced the same distress and discomfort, and who have recovered, can be extremely encouraging. These individuals can have genuine empathy, and thus can offer the most convincing advice and reassurance.

No Longer Cancer-Free

A post-surgery PSA above 0.001 indicates the presence of cancer. The patient is not cancer-free. After surgery, and for five consecutive PSA tests (i.e., 2.5 years), my score was 0.001. I was cancer-free. After three of these ideal test results, my urologist's office only scheduled me annually for a PSA test. In fact, this PSA test was self-initiated. I had not yet received a postcard to prompt a PSA check. But, I realized it had been a year since my last assessment and wanted verification of "cancer-free".

Waiting for my test results on Friday, August 17th, 2005, I'm as optimistic as I had been on that much earlier Friday, May 3rd, 2002 before learning I had prostate cancer. The doctor is friendly and cheerful as he grabs the computer printout from the holder on the door. Suddenly, his demeanor changes notably. I know something is wrong. He puts his chewing gum in a paper towel, and with a look of surprise, he delicately tells me my PSA was 0.18.

While 0.18 is close to zero, I know this is not good news. It means cancer is in my body, and can certainly grow to be debilitating and life-threatening. The urologist reviews my records and notes how unusual it is to see cancer after surgery and post-operative assessments as successful as mine. Such rhetoric does not make me feel any better.

Then he surprises me with the following: "At this time, I see no need for radiation, chemotherapy, or Lupron". (Lupron is a last-resort drug that acts like a female hormone and can have a number of undesirable side-effects, including hot flashes and complete loss of libido.) Then the doc asks me to schedule a re-assessment of my PSA in four months.

Fighting Complacency

My doc says, "Come back in four months for a reassessment. Then we'll see how fast the cancer is growing." I think: Are you kidding? The PSA test says I've gone from cancer-free to cancer-present in less than a year, and now I'm expected to wait around for another four months. Can I afford to accept this failure, and do nothing until another assessment?

Accepting my current cancer state until future PSA results indicate the need for radical treatment is the most convenient option, and is perhaps accompanied by the least amount of distress. Keep on doing what I'm doing, and I might not be worse off. In essence, this is the advice of my urologist. Keep doing what I'm doing and hope to avoid failure.

The urologist gave me no new strategy for returning me to cancer-free. He never asked me what I had done to remain cancer-free in the past, nor what I had done differently to elevate my PSA. But if he had, I couldn't have offered any meaningful answers. From my perspective, my behavior had not changed. Was the return of my cancer only a matter of bad luck? Must I accept the perspective, "Wait and watch and hope for the best?"

Must I accept the viewpoint my cancer is uncontrollable at this point? Should I keep on doing what I had been doing and merely hope my PSA does not increase dramatically? Such perceived loss of personal control does not feel right, but without evidence-based advice, that's really the only alternative. Without a credible AC4P action plan for gaining control of a personal problem, it's easy to become complacent and accept the failure you're attempting to avoid.

Raise Your Sail

Drafting this story reminds me of my most inspirational keynote address. On Wednesday, August 24th, 2005 I'm giving the closing general-session keynote at the 21st Annual Voluntary Protection Programs Participants' Association (VPPPA) Conference in Dallas, Texas. A crowded room of about 2,000 listen intently as I introduce the audience to the enviable qualities of an AC4P culture and the barriers to achieving this ideal state. They display passionate and energetic reactions to my concepts, stories, and illustrations.

Then, without pre-planning or forethought, I tell my cancer story – emphasizing how AC4P support got me through pre and post-surgery as well as the disheartening news I had heard just five days earlier.

Receiving Inspiration

This was "my most inspirational" keynote not because of anything I said, but because of how intensely the audience inspired me. I was touched by the many caring emotions displayed on the faces of the attentive listeners. And after a standing ovation, I am swamped by an onslaught of participants expressing approval, wishing me good health, and telling me I'll be in their prayers.

Many ask for my email address so they can send me information relevant for my fight with cancer, including the names of cancer specialists I could contact. Two participants wait more than 30 minutes to independently pray for me.

I left the ballroom 45 minutes after my 1.5 hour keynote feeling inspired and more ready than ever to fight again to be cancer-free. That special audience lifted my self-esteem and optimism higher than I thought possible in my current state.

In a world that seems to be experiencing more interpersonal mistrust, selfish entitlement, and debilitating fear, it was so uplifting to see so much genuine caring from so many people. Their actively caring inspired me to fight the good fight – against my cancer and for more AC4P behavior.

Living with Cancer

After 35 radiation sessions, January - February, 2006, my PSA returned to 0.004, an indication I was once again cancer free. However, the lab report I received on July 13th, 2009 burst my "health bubble" once again. My PSA had risen to 0.15; I was again no longer cancer-free. Subsequent to this distressing news, I began seeing a prostate-cancer specialist in Charlottesville, VA, who prescribed monthly PSA tests to track the growth of my prostate cancer.

My last blood test (taken August 29th, 2013) showed a PSA of 0.68, reflecting a slow but consistent germination of my prostate cancer. This doc reacted to my concern with "Wait until your PSA reaches 2.0, and then you can have a test to determine the location of the cancer. If your cancer is not systemic and found in one place, you will be a candidate for a new type of radiation therapy."

Frankly, this diagnosis and prescription is not consoling, to say the least. Again, I feel a severe loss of personal control over my disease, leading to feelings of complacency or *learned helplessness*.

I am encouraged by the informative book, *Cancer: 50 Essential Things to Do*.[1] Greg Anderson was diagnosed with metastasized lung cancer in 1984, and was told he had only 30 days to live. Refusing to accept this hopeless state, he searched for individuals who had survived cancer which doctors had labeled "terminal".

He looked for common patterns among more than 500 interviews, and from these derived his own action plan. In 1985, Mr. Anderson started the Cancer Conquerors Foundation, which later became the Cancer Recovery Foundation of America (greganderson.org).

To date, Mr. Anderson has surveyed 16,000 people who survived cancer, and he travels extensively to conduct workshops on his findings. His book on cancer survival is practical and hope-filled, and includes lessons for cancer survival, as well as overall wellness. Three of his most important strategies for surviving cancer relate directly to the AC4P principles and applications discussed in this book.

1. Take Personal Control and Expect the Best

Those who triumph over cancer do not stop with conventional treatment. They believe wellness is not a matter of luck, but requires daily commitment and effort. Active involvement is essential. They maintain a healthy outlook on life.

However, Anderson reports cancer survivors "have a refreshing sense of skepticism about 'just-think-positive' solutions". They are tough-minded realists. They don't deny the negative consequences associated with a lack of personal involvement in wellness. They maintain focus and self-motivation by imagining the most negative consequences that could occur if they don't stay actively involved. But, as we all know, many victims of cancer have done everything they know to fight this disease but still lose the battle.

2. Maintain a Sense of Purpose

Anderson reports that cancer triumphants believe they are needed – their lives have special and unique purposes. "Many are energized by an inner, even transcendent, life mission."[1] But, the author adds, "Survivors balance this profound idea of life purpose with a lighter, more playful attitude of fun for fun's sake".[2]

Furthermore, Anderson writes, "Survivors feel they are privileged to be able to help others in meaningful ways. "In helping others, they help themselves."[1] Although the author is referring to cancer survivors, this is true for the survival of most any life difficulty.

People in professions that improve the quality of life in others can take solace in the fact their daily job helps others in meaningful ways. Their professional mission statement epitomizes *self-transcendence* – the highest level of Maslow's Hierarchy of Needs[3] – which means going beyond one's self-interests to benefit others. As detailed in Chapter 2, that's AC4P behavior.

3. Nurture Supportive Relationships

From my cancer diagnosis to recovery, AC4P support from family, friends, colleagues, and students made success possible. People gave me purpose to get beyond traditional treatment and return to my pre-cancer lifestyle. While my recovery was inspired by others, I also became more aware of the value of developing profound relationships with others.

Anderson found "Cancer survivors invest more time and emotional energy in relationships that nurture them and invest less in those that are toxic".[2] In other words, survivors become "relationship sensitive," evaluating the benefits and costs of maintaining the variety of interpersonal relationships in their entire social-support system. This often leads to change that reduces negative or debilitating emotions.

Less emotional turmoil means less distress, greater reality awareness, and more opportunity for positive emotions. And positive emotions in an educational, work, or family setting lead to interdependency and AC4P behavior. Positive emotions lead to increases in self-esteem, optimism, and a sense of belonging, and these person-states increase the likelihood a person will actively care for the well-being of others.

In Conclusion

Every year since the start of my challenges with prostate cancer, I've attended the annual "Relay-for-Life" event at Virginia Tech (VT). Often I've been asked to offer a few words at the opening ceremony about the human dynamics of cancer and the value of this special fund-raising event for cancer research.

My keynote address has been different each time, except for two points. First, I point out the bold "Cancer Survivor" words displayed on my shirt and the shirt worn by over 300 other participants are wrong.

We are not cancer survivors but are *surviving* cancer. Only through continual research can treatment strategies be developed to make "Cancer Survivor" a reality. Indeed, several of the participants who wore the "Cancer Survivor" shirt at one or more of these events are no longer with us. An effective remedy had not yet been developed to save them.

The second theme I emphasize is the special value of an interdependent community of actively-caring people. This is exemplified by the impressive turnout at each of our annual "Relay-for-Life" events. In fact, for the past six years VT has led all universities nationwide in the amount of funds received at this event for cancer research. This reflects an extraordinary level of AC4P which brings to life the VT motto: *Ut Prosim* (That I May Serve).

Students, faculty, staff, family and friends walk or run around the quarter-mile track all night, each lap representing a certain amount of money donated to the American Cancer Society. Those wearing "Cancer Survivor" shirts walk the first lap. People line both sides of our entire course, cheering loudly and continuously, reaching out to shake hands or to slap high-fives with us smiling walkers.

The power of AC4P support from an interdependent community of like-minded people is exhilarating and healing. It reminds us of life's most meaningful purpose – to reach Maslow's state of self-transcendence.[3] Here we overcome our own selfish interests and issues to experience the exceptional intrinsic reinforcement that comes when we actively care for the health, safety, and general well-being of others.

Notes

1. Anderson, G. (1993). *Cancer: 50 essential things to do.* Harmondsworth, Middlesex, England: Penguin Group.

2. Anderson, G. (1993). *Cancer: 50 essential things to do.* Harmondsworth, Middlesex, England: Penguin Group, pp. 14-15.

3. Frankl, V. E. (2000). *Man's search for ultimate meaning.* New York. NY: Basic Books; Maslow, A.H. (1971). *The farther reaches of human nature.* New York, NY: Viking Publishers.

CHAPTER 18

My Starting Block and AC4P:
Developing and applying moral courage

Shane M. McCarty

AS A RESIDENT ADVISOR during my sophomore year at Virginia Tech (VT), I lived in Pritchard Hall, which at the time was one of the largest, all-male residence halls on the East Coast with 1,016 males. After hearing the words "gay" and "faggot" an average of ten times a day, I decided to act. Those unkind words made me feel uncomfortable and motivated me to actively care for beneficial change, at least among the 42 residents on my floor.

I placed a logo of the *Collegiate Times*, our school newspaper, at the top of the following words, as if they were contained in an anonymous letter to the Editor. Then, I attached this apparent letter in five bathroom stalls on my floor.

Letter to the Editor: *"Gay" is Not a Word to Use Loosely*

I am a homosexual male growing up in a heterosexual world. I feel uncomfortable almost everywhere I go. Have you ever looked down in class and seen the word faggot carved into a desk? I see it, but I also feel it. I feel that same knife cut me out – away from the group of those other Hokies around me.

The distance, the difference, between you and me, increases exponentially each time I read the word on a desk in McBryde Hall. I have seen it so many times at this point; the distance between us can no longer be measured in inches but rather in miles. I no longer feel a part of this community.

Why do you fear me? Do you fear me because I am different? I don't call you names or go out of my way to hurt you. I don't yell redneck, hick, or white trash to those of you who so proudly display your Confederate heritage. I don't judge you, the entitled upper class, for the endless privileges your parents provide – your tuition paid in full, your new car, and your designer clothes in hand with no questions asked.

If you don't want to be me, then don't discriminate against me. You throw the words faggot and gay around as if it's okay, as if nobody cares. Why do you use these words to degrade me? Is your vocabulary so limited you must attack me with the words "gay" and "faggot"? The dictionary definition of "gay" is keenly alive and exuberant.[1] Since when did that word mean *annoying* and *stupid*?

Please stop and think. Ponder your words and their impact on others. Please ask yourself the question: Who does this hurt? Because it hurts me more than you will ever know.

The Truth About That Letter

I am the last person you'd expect to author that letter, because I am a heterosexual, Caucasian, upper-middle class, Roman Catholic, male college student. Because of these identity markers, opportunities are extended to me daily. I am among the privileged class and I *realize* it. I wrote that letter to invoke reflection and potentially start a conversation among my 42 residents that could help them realize their own privileges.

If life were a race, the referee would flag me down for cheating, because my starting block was much farther along than many others. A person's starting block is mostly a product of a number of critical and sometimes invisible environmental factors (e.g., socio-economic status, ethnicity, and education level).[2]

It seems from my interactions that most people rarely consider the position of their starting block, and fewer use their privileged starting-block positions to help others. But I can't help others effectively without understanding their life experiences. Many of us consider ourselves empathic, but do we truly attempt to understand others by stepping into their shoes?

I remember my first attempt to understand the experiences of male homosexuals. Two male friends shared stories of victimization, fear of violence, and the pain caused from being different. Their college experience was markedly more stressful than mine simply due to differing sexual orientations. To reduce my own prejudices, I listened empathically to my new college friends and then attempted to capture their emotions and experiences into a letter as if I were walking in their shoes.

I wasn't born with an elevated capacity for empathy, nor did I inherit an AC4P gene. I learned how to actively care and what to care about from other people. After all, our behaviors, attitudes, and beliefs are largely determined by the various social interactions and behavioral consequences we experience throughout our lives. My family, friends, peers, and VT professors taught me the value of empathic listening, servant leadership, and the moral courage to act on my values.[3]

A Transformational Night

On a cold winter night in Blacksburg, Virginia, my understanding of passive caring versus actively caring, right versus wrong, majority versus minority, were transformed.

I'm chatting with two friends, Brandon and Joey, when I notice a group of students standing by a bus-stop shelter. The cold night causes the glass of the shelter to fog up. I see one of the group members writing a message on the glass, finishing the "t" of "faggot," I ask myself: "Why?" I've seen this scene play out too many times – the in-crowd ridiculing minority or less popular students.

I stride briskly over to the group. "Why did you write *faggot* on the window for everyone to see?" I ask the perpetrator. Silence. Nobody responds. But there is tension now where there hadn't been before.

The group looks at their friend in a way that tells me they disagree with his action. I look hard into their eyes as I erase the word "faggot" from the window. "That really offends me and I am not even gay," I say. I sense discomfort from the perpetrator's friends, but nobody says a word.

In the past, I would have reacted in a much different way. I would have expected those most affected (i.e., homosexuals) to say something – to intervene and stand up for themselves. I would have blamed the victims, thinking they must deserve it, especially if they let the ridicule occur so frequently.

But now I think: It's not exclusively the victims' responsibility to defend themselves. It's my responsibility too, and the responsibility of all bystanders, especially those with privilege and influence to exhibit moral courage[4] and speak up on behalf of others who are mistreated.

As explained in Chapter 2, intervening to help a stranger is not easy. After all, what do you say? And how do you say it? It can even be difficult to provide corrective feedback for a close friend who uses degrading or inappropriate remarks. If you have used similar language, you might assume it's not your responsibility to correct someone's verbal behavior, or you may lack the necessary skills to intervene. As discussed in Chapter 4, it takes moral courage to act contrary to the relevant social norm.[4]

From Caring to Acting

I never wrote "faggot" on a bus-shelter window, but as a high-school student only seven years ago I might as well have been that person I confronted at the bus stop. Numerous people heard "He's so gay" spew from my mouth. Fortunately, a telephone conversation with my Aunt Betsy shifted my paradigm.

When referring to a high-school teacher, I said "He's so gay" in place of "He's so stupid". She knew *punishment* was ineffective, so she provided invaluable *corrective feedback*: "You might want to think about your word choice a bit more, because using that word in such a way can really hurt people".

Sometimes people come into our lives who affect us in profound ways. It's not their beliefs that affect us; it's their AC4P behavior. My aunt displayed *moral courage* when she provided honest *corrective feedback* about my inappropriate behavior. It wasn't easy for her, but it was worth it. That single feedback conversation changed my life, and potentially the lives of many others.

Our seemingly small actions can have a far-reaching ripple effect. As I came back to my two best friends at the bus stop, I wondered how my actions affected them and the perpetrator's friends, but I never knew the direct impact of that AC4P behavior. I never mentioned that cold night at a Blacksburg bus stop again.

Two years later, I was seated at the dining room table with my family and my friend Brandon. Brandon shared that bus-shelter story when discussing courage and the challenges associated with doing the right thing. Clearly, Brandon was impacted by my act of moral courage, as were my parents after hearing that story, but what about others at the bus stop?

Did the perpetrator's verbal behavior change as a result of my corrective feedback? I believe it did. Like me, he probably never realized the negative impact caused by such hurtful words.

To this day, I wonder who I would be – my values, attitudes, and behaviors – if family, friends, colleagues, and strangers never provided me with *corrective AC4P feedback*. Numerous courageous bystanders showed genuine caring and *moral courage* when they offered me critical feedback, planting seeds for my development.

The Silent Majority

Martin Luther King, Jr. said: "In this era of social transition, the greatest tragedy is not the blaring noisiness of the so-called bad people, it's the appalling silence of the so-called good people."[5]

Those in the majority have a moral obligation to stand up for the minority. This isn't a religious obligation or a federal law, but our moral responsibility as human beings to actively care for one another.

Most human beings care about social injustice, racism, poverty, world hunger, and the many other social issues of our time, but caring alone is not enough. When we hear homophobic remarks spewing from friends' mouths, do we tell them to stop? Each day, we face choices like this one that define our character and have the potential to create a positive ripple effect we may never see.

Every time we act to benefit a stranger, we remind ourselves of a fundamental belief: Despite the differences between people, our common humanity matters most. When I graduated from high school, I had the whole world in my hands with countless opportunities, because of my advantageous starting block.

Five years later, the same world remains in my hands, but now I feel its weight. The world feels much heavier today, and it will only get lighter if I use my privilege and moral courage to improve it for others.

Notes

1. Gay. In *Merriam-Webster.com*. Retrieved from http://www.merriam-webster.com/dictionary/hacker
2. Foroohar, R. (2011, November 14). What ever happened to upward mobility. *Time*.
3. I am grateful for the countless people who have actively cared for me throughout my life. Upon reflection, I am indebted forever to those people who helped me during the most challenging and influential academic year of my life (2008-2009). Thank you Bo Hart, Brandon Carroll, Joey Zakutney, Ryan King, and Taris Mullins for inspiring me to become the person I've always wanted to be. A special thanks to each person who changed my paradigm that year, especially mentors who became close friends: Betsy Shane, Edward Spencer, John Driessnack, Leon McClinton, Lis Ellis, Ray Williams, and Steve Skripak. Finally, I am so thankful for the intentional AC4P behavior of one Hokie, because it allowed me to meet my mentor Scott "Doc" Geller, his wife Joanne Dean Geller, graduate students Ryan Smith and Chris Downing of CABS, and find my life's work: to apply behavioral and psychological science to actively care for people.
4. Geller, E.S., & Veazie, B. (2009). *The courage factor: Leading people-based culture change*. Newport, VA: Make-A-Difference, LLC.
5. King, Jr., M.L. *Martin Luther King Quotes*. Retrieved from http://www.inspirationpeak.com/cgi-bin/search.cgi?search=Dr.%20Martin%20Luther%20King&method=all

CHAPTER 19

How I Get There Matters More:
When process trumps outcome

Ryan King

MY FRIENDS AND I have an unwritten tradition on weekends in Blacksburg, Virginia. We gather at midnight at our favorite local bar, *The Cellar*, for a Guinness and pizza. The ten-minute walk from my apartment takes me past a long construction site stretching down most of Main Street.

Once a construction worker asked me, "Are you going to Taco Bell?" Reflexively I replied, "No, sorry" and hurried on to my destination. In a few minutes it hit me… He's hungry.

So I ran back to the construction worker. "Want some Taco Bell?" "Yes," and he gave me $5 to purchase his meal. I purchased a few extra tacos, put his $5 back in the bag as a surprise, and gave it all to him. "Thanks and have a good night!" he said with a broad smile.

Learning from Reflection

That AC4P story matters for two reasons: a) the AC4P moment nearly did not happen, and b) my mindset was overly-focused on my destination. Research in social psychology has demonstrated numerous situational factors influence bystander behavior.[1]

I remember Dr. Geller saying, "An event is caused by a series of contributing factors, rather than a single root cause." Here are few contributing factors that nearly prevented the occurrence of this AC4P story.

As discussed in Chapter 2, bystanders are presumed to perform a five-step sequential decision-making process to determine whether or not they will intervene in emergency situations. My story was a proactive non-emergency situation, but my decision-making followed steps similar to those given in Latané and Darley's bystander intervention model.[2]

First, I was preoccupied by my destination downtown for a beer and pizza, resulting in narrow tunnel vision and mindset (*notice a need*). Research has shown less than ten percent of people will stop to help a stranger when on route to another destination with limited time, in comparison to 63% of people who helped if they were not in a hurry.[3]

Second, the construction worker asked if I was going to Taco Bell, an indirect request to meet his underlying need for sustenance. This made it easy to reject a call for help (*interpret the situation*). Why didn't he ask me to get him dinner? I know firsthand requests for help can be awkward and uncomfortable. Sometimes pride prevents us from making a request while other times it's stubbornness and self-consciousness.

In the ideal AC4P culture, we would not feel uncomfortable asking for a favor from a stranger. We would assume the best intentions from the requester and respond honestly with, "Yes, I can help," or "No, sorry, I cannot right now".

The current social norm creates fear of rejection or criticism. But a new AC4P norm can foster appreciation over disrespect, honest and direct requests over subtle and indirect requests, and optimism (expecting the best) over pessimism (expecting something to go wrong).

Reflecting on my nearly missed opportunity to help, I am most troubled by my independent and me-first thinking. At times, we must look out for ourselves, but in this instance, there was no clear reason to be concerned with only myself (*assume personal responsibility*). I realized my two-year commitment to the AC4P philosophy and associated behaviors could not suddenly change a lifestyle I had followed for 20 years.

Assumption Amnesia

I share this story and my reflections because it made me cognizant of basic assumptions and biases I have developed throughout my life. Even in telling this story, it's apparent I've always focused on *me* getting somewhere. It was about *me* getting *my* pizza and beer. Begrudgingly I must admit when given the choice to either care about others or myself, I default to *me*.

Challenging my biases and thoughts and behaviors has been crucial to reaching the self-transcendence top of Maslow's Hierarchy of Needs.[4] My intention is to live an AC4P lifestyle. But, psychological science suggests it's harder than we think to actively care, especially when the situation involves interpersonal conversation, like in my story.

Although barriers prevent us from helping others, barriers can be overcome. We must become more aware, more courageous, and spare a few extra minutes of time each day for others.

This reminds me of something I have heard since I was a kid: Life is a journey, not a destination. The *process* of stopping to help a stranger mattered more than reaching the bar. That's the life lesson. The route we take matters more than where we end up.

Notes

1. Ross, L., & Nisbett, R.E. (2010). The person and situation. In T. Nadelhoffer, E. Nahmias, & S. Nichols (Eds.). *Moral psychology: Historical and contemporary readings* (pp. 187-196). Hong Kong, China: Graphicraft Limited.

2. Latané, B., & Darley, J.M. (1970). *The unresponsive bystander: Why doesn't he help?* New York, NY: Appleton-Century Crofts.

3. Darley, J.M., & Batson, C.D. (1973). From Jerusalem to Jericho: A study of situational and dispositional variables in helping behavior. *Journal of Personality and Social Psychology, 27*, 100-108.

4. Maslow, A.H. (1971). *The farther reaches of human nature.* New York, NY: Viking.

CHAPTER 20

Learning AC4P and Passing it On:
A domino effect

Benjamin Martin

I MET Dr. CHRIS DULA in the Fall of 2004. I was a single parent, a full-time employee, and a college student. I was also broke, frustrated and ready to quit school. Dr. Dula's AC4P behavior helped me finish my undergraduate degree.

More importantly, Dr. Dula motivated me to participate in his AC4P research and teachings. In turn, AC4P has altered my life directions, inspiring more AC4P behavior among friends and colleagues.

Being Unconsciously Incompetent

I was raised in an adverse environment where I developed poor coping styles and impaired communication skills. My misguided experiences as a teen and young adult posed a major barrier to attaining my goal of achieving a B.S. degree in psychology. I tried my best, but I had no "formula for success". I learned from my mistakes, made a conscious effort to stay out of trouble, and exhibited personal responsibility. No one seemed to notice, though. Yes, I changed internally, but external changes were needed.

You see, I was exceedingly judgmental and blunt, hurting feelings and putting people on the defensive. Countless times I worked all night and did not change clothes or shave before morning classes. My clothing was overly casual. I was an easy target for negative judgments. I did not let people feel comfortable. I anticipated negative interactions, which increased my defensiveness.

What are appropriate social behaviors and communication skills? Merriam-Webster defines ignorance as "lacking knowledge or comprehension".[1] I was unconsciously incompetent. But Dr. Dula actively engaged me in his research and seemed comfortable with me. Without his AC4P efforts, I likely would not have attained one of the "Four C's of AC4P" – Competence!

Laying an AC4P Foundation

According to Scott Geller's AC4P principles,[2] one-on-one behavioral feedback is the best way to gain competence. Serving as a research assistant in Dr. Dula's laboratory, I regularly received feedback from Dr. Dula on how I inadvertently made negative impressions on others. He challenged me to see myself through the eyes of others.

Leading by example is one of the most effective ways to teach. According to Tony Baron, "The best way to teach people…is to show them".[3] Dr. Dula always came to work clean-shaven and wearing dress clothes. He said if I adopted a higher level of professionalism, it would be more difficult for people to cast negative judgments about me.

I began shaving daily and changing after work into dress clothes I'd bought at thrift stores. This was difficult to pull off between all-night shifts and morning classes. But after making these adjustments, I was surprised to observe how quickly people's impressions of me improved.

This time of my life was one of great financial hardship. I was homeless for a short period. When Dr. Dula discovered I was sleeping in my car, he offered me his couch. His only motivation was to care for my well-being. His intentional acts of kindness helped me understand the AC4P lifestyle. I was learning empathy, but had not made a full commitment to AC4P.

Positioning the First Domino – Commitment

An AC4P lifestyle requires daily dedication to actively caring for the well-being of others. But first I needed to actively care for myself. Clean up my own backyard, so to speak. After reading relevant literature, I made critical behavior checklists[4] for professionalism and asked for feedback from people I trusted. My budding social skills led people to be more willing to give me the behavior-based feedback I needed.

I began to engage in regular AC4P behavior. People responded to me in different ways, which was encouraging and increased the frequency of my AC4P behavior. As my AC4P experiences spread I became a much more optimistic person.

Several people I'd helped cited my caring for them as an inspiration. My small but sincere AC4P acts started a ripple effect. I learned firsthand AC4P is infectious. These unanticipated results crystallized my commitment to AC4P. Still, I had yet *really* challenged myself.

Courage to "Push" Other Dominoes

As illustrated in *The Courage Factor*,[2] competence and commitment are not enough. One must have the *courage* to act when an AC4P opportunity presents itself. For months after reading AC4P scholarship by Dr. Geller, I struggled with the courage to act. I was committed to AC4P, but my acts never seemed courageous enough.

In late 2011, I attended a party at Make-A-DiffRanch, hosted by Dr. Geller. I had applied to the Ph.D. program in Industrial/Organizational Psychology in the Virginia Tech Department of Psychology, and had come to meet students and faculty members. A live band got the house rocking; people were obviously having a good time.

As the party drew to a close, cognitive dissonance[5] set in. Around me people were consuming alcohol beverages. I had decided to abstain. But I had trouble speaking up and offering rides home. What inhibited me? I had a large vehicle, a GPS, and could accommodate many people without getting lost.

Ironically, considering how brusque I used to be, social anxiety silenced me in this situation. I was rather uncomfortable in this setting; Dr. Dula and my fiancée were the only people I knew. Plus, some of those in attendance would soon be making a decision regarding my admission to the Ph.D. program.

My anxiety increased with each passing minute. Then I overheard Dr. Dula quoting from the movie *The Big Lebowski*,[6] "This is a very complicated case. You know, a lotta ins, a lotta outs, a lotta what-have-yous." I realized the situation was not complicated at all. My options were quite clear: Speak up or shut up.

Acutely anxious, I told Dr. Dula I was willing to drive others home. To my surprise, he went to the microphone and announced I was available to be a designated driver. I immediately received tremendous support from people who appreciated my willingness to help. My anxiety quickly subsided. Soon I overheard others check with friends and offer rides.

Though no one took me up on my offer, my act appeared to facilitate related AC4P behavior from others. I had found courage to challenge my inner worries and do the right thing. However, in retrospect, I believe *true* courage would be walking to the microphone myself and making the AC4P announcement. Where would such courage come from? Compassion, of course, which I had been working on.

AC4P Dominoes Fall toward Compassion

Geller and Veazie claim competence, courage, and commitment are not sufficient for consistent AC4P behavior. One must also have compassion to actively care.[2] I work daily to develop this quality.

For example, I make a conscious effort to actively listen to people in order to better understand others. I imagine what it might be like to experience the situation described by the other person. As a result, I am better able to connect with others and identify opportunities to AC4P.

My AC4P lifestyle is a work in progress. Friends and colleagues tell me they see significant improvement in my behavior across the board. I know one thing; I have become considerably less anxious. In cultivating an AC4P lifestyle, calmness now permeates all aspects of my life. And I see an AC4P ripple effect.

Regularly engaging in AC4P behavior helps us become better citizens, and our AC4P efforts nudge others to actively care. Actively caring for people begets an awesome domino effect!

Notes

1. *Merriam-Webster's Dictionary* (2003) (11th Edition). New York, NY: Wiley Publishing Company, p. 321.
2. Geller, E.S., & Veazie, B. (2009). *The courage factor: Leading people-based culture change.* Newport, VA: Make-A-Difference, LLC.
3. Baron, T. (2010). *The art of servant leadership: Designing your organization for the sake of others* (p. 9). Tucson, AZ: Wheatmark.
4. Geller, E.S. (2001). *Working safe: How to help people actively care for safety* (2nd Edition). Boca Raton, FL: CRC Press, LLC.
5. Festinger, L. (1957). *A theory of cognitive dissonance.* Evanston, IL: Row, Peterson.
6. Bevan, T., Cameron, J., & Fellner, E. (Producers), Coen, J., & Coen, E. (Directors) (1998). *The Big Lebowski* [Motion Picture].United States: PolyGram Filmed Entertainment and Gramercy Pictures.

CHAPTER 21

AC4P in My Military Career:
Mentors who had my back

Douglas R. Hole

MANY ASPECTS OF A military career truly fit the AC4P Model, especially the "I have your back" norm embedded in the military culture. My personal story transcends both my college and military experiences, and highlights several people who not only understood the AC4P philosophy but practiced it on a regular basis.

I begin with my head football coach at the College of Wooster – Phil Shipe. Phil was a good coach, but a better mentor and an AC4P person. He actively cared about all of his players as individuals. He wanted us to be the best athletes we could be. More importantly, he wanted us to grow and become outstanding contributors to society.

Promotions in the Military

As an Air Force officer, making regular promotions in an "up-or-out world" is part of the military culture. You are promoted to the next higher rank or you are deemed no longer useful. In some cases your career is cut short.

In my career, promotions came on time, up to Major. Four years after this promotion and in my 15th year, I was considered for promotion to Lt. Colonel. But I was not promoted. I feared my time in the Air Force would be cut short, and I would be separated with no retirement benefits.

Here comes my mentor, Colonel Whitey Barrows. He was the Deputy Chief of Intelligence for Tactical Air Command. He called me in and gave me a profound and thoughtful talk about continuing to do the right thing and to not be discouraged by my setback.

He advised, "Don't wear this disappointment on your sleeve. Continue to be the outstanding contributor you have been."

I followed his advice and was selected for promotion to Lt. Colonel the following year. That enabled at least a 20-year retirement.

Four years later, I faced a similar hurdle for promotion to Colonel. Again, I did not get promoted on time. But with nearly 21 years of service, I was not too concerned. As a non-flying officer, my chance of a promotion was slim at best. Brigadier General (U.S. Army) Mike Pfister, my boss at the time, put me in positions to excel with the senior leadership at U.S. Central Command. He had confidence I had "The Right Stuff" to be a Colonel in the Air Force.

The next year, 1986, I was promoted to full Colonel – a rank I could not have envisioned when I entered the Air Force in 1964. After all, only five of 100 2nd Lieutenants in the Air Force are ultimately promoted to Full Colonel.

I was immediately sent to Bahrain for a three-month stint on the USS Lasalle, the Command Ship Navy Forces in the Persian Gulf. My title was U.S. Central Command Liaison to *Commideast for* a 2-Star Admiral. It was a long title with limited responsibility. Still, I was the 3rd or 4th ranking U.S. Military Officer in the region.

A Cultural Lesson

On the day after Thanksgiving in 1986, the Intelligence Officer for the Lasalle, Marine Lt. Col. Forest Lucy and I decided to explore the Island of Bahrain where the ship was based. One of our stops was Sheik's Beach, a private beach for westerners run by the Royalty of Bahrain.

Upon arrival, we were invited by the Emir of Bahrain, Sheik Isa bin Sulman al Khalifa, to have coffee with him and his entourage. It happened to be the day the Iran-Contra Scandal broke open. As representatives of the U.S., we had to tread diplomatically on what was a troubling revelation for many in the Arab world.

Sheik Isa spoke of his wonderful trip to the U.S. and his wonderful host, then Vice President George Bush. He wanted to know why all the people who had been so nice to him wouldn't accept the Rolex watches he offered. Diplomatically we reiterated government employees are not authorized to accept gifts of this nature.

He talked about his family and said he had nine children, five girls and four boys, and he had only made five mistakes (not joking). He asked me how many children I had and I said, "None". He immediately turned his back on me; I became invisible.

I vowed to have a different answer if I received this offspring question from Arab leadership. I wrote to my sister's son, told him the story, and asked if he would mind being my son for this purpose. From then on I carried a picture of Mike Roark for conversations with Arab leadership about children.

An AC4P Mentor

Back in Wooster in the Fall of 1987, I went to see Coach Shipe. I told him of this most enlightening and embarrassing experience, since he and his wife Pem had no children either.

He sat for a moment and looked at me and asked, "Do you have a picture of you in uniform as a Colonel?" I gave him one and asked, "Why?" He replied, "The next time I'm asked if I have any kids I'm going to show him your picture and say you are my son".

This was one of the most monumental and moving experiences of my life. Coach Shipe actively cared once again. He made me feel like his most important player, though I know he felt the same about all of us. From this memorable experience, I learned the power of a few AC4P words. The AC4P phrase, "I've got your back" comes to life in many forms.

CHAPTER 22

AC4P in Australia

Martin Ralph

SINCE 2001 I'VE been privileged to serve as the CEO of the Industrial Foundation for Accident Prevention (IFAP), based in Western Australia. IFAP was founded in 1962 and is a Registered Training Organization providing national and international public and corporate safety courses. It has six training centers in Western Australia and in Queensland (the second-largest and third most populous state in Australia) located in the northeast of the country. We annually train more than 23,000 people and currently employ more than 1,800 personnel.

I regularly attend safety conferences in the U.S., and 15 years ago I met Scott Geller in New Orleans at a conference sponsored by the American Society of Safety Engineers (ASSE). I had been invited to a special book-signing event for the release of his watershed publication,*Working Safe: How to help people actively care for health and safety*. Four trips to Australia and many air miles together have seen us forge a bond that tests the many miles that separate our respective countries.

More than 600 West Australians attended Scott and Joanne's most recent trip "Down Under" as the duo presented forums to share the message of the AC4P Movement. A bit of context: Western Australia has a hard-won reputation of being an outpost community, dominated by the mining industry, with entrenched machismo attitudes, a can-do spirit and an aversion to "touchy-feely" approaches to life.

The majority of the attendees at Scott and Joanne's forums were long-term stakeholders in IFAP. I was impressed when I actively sought the opinions of many of those stakeholders, and received similar reactions: "How do we achieve an AC4P culture in our organization?" I couldn't help but wonder whether the perception of the hardened Western Australian was akin to the legend of Crocodile Dundee – nothing more than a popular myth.

So what about this AC4P Movement, and how to make it work? The prescription is so simple it's actually complex. It all comes down to the individual's willingness to go out of his or her way to help a fellow traveller in life. But this requires compassion, courage and a capacity to demonstrate personal leadership. Of these three characteristics, leadership is the most difficult to define. The academic world is only now starting to properly define what it takes to be a leader, which includes the context of both leadership and followership behavior.

Scott and Joanne have this unique ability to invigorate your soul, and to inspire you to want to go beyond the call of duty to help and/or recognize the positive actions of others. It was at a meeting in Chicago in 2011,and subsequently reinforced by Scott and Joanne in mid-2012, that my personal inspiration for the AC4P Movement began. This is the story I share here.

Contrasting Cultures

First an observation: When I was in Chicago I was privileged to witness the pride and honor on display at the Past-Presidents' reception when the then president of the ASSE,

Ms. Terrie Norris, introduced her son– a serving member of the U.S. military on leave from assignment in the Iraq conflict. The audience of esteemed contributors to the advancement of occupational safety and health in the U.S.stood to attention spontaneously and applauded the achievements of this fine young man. It was a heartwarming moment that brought a lump to the throat of this "hardened" West Aussie.

Throughout my tour of the U.S. in 2011, I saw many examples of how the serving military were given homage, from special mentions at public events to being offered first-to-board opportunities at airports. (Although I never saw a single uniformed member of the military accept this offer.) Even for a died-in-the-wool pacifist, it's difficult to mount a case against this code of honoring those who serve to protect the rights and welfare of the civilian populace.

Yet in Australia, the land of the great down-to-earth understatement, we do not venture to bring attention to those who deserve such honors. About five percent of the IFAP workforce includes ex-armed services personnel. Prior to my 2011 trip to the U.S. we did nothing particularly special to honor their contribution to our great country. We do now. And so my AC4P story begins. But first a cultural insight.

The Australian armed services have a long and proud history which semi-officially commenced in 1899 when the Boer War broke out in South Africa. Australia was made up of six colonies on the verge of becoming a federation. The war was seen as an opportunity for the emerging federation to show its commitment to Britain and to define its identity.

After the Australian Federation commenced in 1901, the new Commonwealth Government continued to support the war until its eventual conclusion in 1902. The Australian troops' reputation for bravery, toughness and cool-headedness during the Boer War became the foundation for the Australian warrior image.

Remembrance Day (also known as Poppy Day or Armistice Day) is observed on the 11th of November to recall the end of the hostilities of World War I on that date in 1918. This also serves as a memorial day to remember the members of the armed forces of the Commonwealth who had died in the line of duty. Hostilities formally ended "at the 11th hour of the 11th day of the 11th month," in accordance with the Armistice signed between the warring parties.

Australian armed services also commemorate ANZAC day on the 25th of April. This is in remembrance of the landing of the Australian and New Zealand Army Corps (ANZACs) on the shores of the Gallipoli Peninsula (Turkey)in 1915.Aiming to secure a sea route to Russia, the British and French launched a naval campaign to force a passage through the Dardanelles. After the naval operation, an amphibious landing was undertaken on the Gallipoli peninsula to capture the Ottoman capital of Constantinople (Istanbul).

The small cove on the Gallipoli Peninsula in and around which Australian and New Zealand troops landed became known as "Anzac Cove." This sector became known as "Anzac." After eight months the land campaign failed, and the invasion force was withdrawn to Egypt. The cost: 8,709 Australians killed and 19,441 wounded. New Zealand lost 2,721 soldiers, with 4,752 wounded.

The campaign is often considered to mark the birth of national consciousness in Australia and New Zealand and the date of the landing, the 25th of April, is known as

"ANZAC Day." To this day, April 25th is the date on which the sacrifice of those who had died in the Great War, and subsequent arenas of armed conflict, is remembered.

We "tough" Aussies care, but only when the country has an outpouring of nationalistic pride, which manifests itself at ANZAC day, do we *actively* demonstrate caring for our troops. I question whether this is an appropriate level of recognition. And so begins my story of AC4P.

An AC4P Paradigm Shift

In September 2011, I was fortunate to visit Istanbul, Turkey, with my wife, Michelle. I convinced Michelle to take the gruelling 20-hour round trip by road to visit Gallipoli, particularly to visit Anzac Cove, the ill-fated landing place of our armed services in 1915. Anzac Cove holds a special place in the hearts of all Australians, especially our military personnel. But as I learned, many contemporary servicemen and women never get to visit the site during their years of service.

Anzac Cove is a truly inspiring spot. It's difficult to avoid getting swept up into the mystique and unfortunate history of the place. The thought of so many young lives being cruelly cut down in a land so far from home fills one with a sense of loss that is difficult to define. It's perfectly understandable why this place is so important to our serving personnel.

While standing on the rocky beach of the Cove a thought struck me, "If IFAP's ex-servicemen and women on staff had been unable to get to this place, why not take some of this place to them?" Without much forethought I swept up a handful of the pebbles on the beach, handpicked some of the more shaped and colored ones, and stuck 13 of them in my pocket. After a thorough cleaning at the hotel, I transported them with me back to Australia.

A Special Remembrance

The closest memorial date to my return was Remembrance Day – 11th of November, 2011. Without their knowledge, I traced where each of the ex-servicemen and women on the IFAP staff would be on that day. As luck would have it, four were on duty, two at our head office, one at IFAP's southern-most site approximately 20 kilometres from our head office, and the last staff member at a remote site, 40 kilometres north of our head office.

I advised the managers of the two IFAP sites I wished them to host a formal Remembrance Day ceremony to be overseen by the ex-servicemen and women – a one-minute moment of silence at the rising of the 11th hour and flags at half-mast. The three staff at the IFAP sites were overjoyed to be honored this way. My managers willingly collaborated with my request, stopping classes and joining the ex-servicemen and women at the flag-lowering ceremony. About 70 people, staff and course participants alike, joined in at each site.

However, no flagpole was available at the remote site. Without prior knowledge of my staff member, I arranged for a television broadcast of the official flag-lowering ceremony to be broadcast from our nation's capital in Canberra to the remote site. I then opted to drive to the remote site to pay a "surprise visit" for my ex-serviceman colleague.

I arrived at the site around 10:30am, and checked out the facility, ensuring arrangements were as expected. At about 10:50am, I let myself into the room and advised my colleague of the broadcast.I asked him to officiate the "ceremony" to be held adjacent to his training room. He was astonished I would do something like that for him.

The broadcast went smoothly. We were joined by his class of about 20 course participants; and after a short coffee break, we reassembled in the training room. At this juncture I told the class of my colleague's (Rod's) service, in arenas of conflict from the Middle East, Southeast Asia and Papua New Guinea.

In typical knockabout Aussie fashion, Rod tried to dismiss his contribution as "just doing my job," but his justifiable sense of pride at being recognized was self-evident. I then presented Rod with a green AC4P wristband I had received previously from Scott when we were in Chicago. I told him it was a fitting tribute for his service. (He still wears that wristband today, despite my cajoling to "pass it forward".)

At this juncture, Rod became noticeably emotional. I then presented him with one of the pebbles I had collected from Anzac Cove, and told him of my story of how I had thought about him and my other colleagues who were ex-servicemen and women while I was taking in the Anzac Cove panorama. Rod was visibly moved.

To see this man, who had fought in some of the toughest campaigns in modern warfare, hug me and tear up was one of the most moving experiences in my life. That moving experience served to form a lasting bond between the two of us. To this day, Rod jokes with me that he will "get even," but I know he has mounted that little pebble with his war medals, and that it holds a special place of pride for him.

The same scenario (minus the flag ceremony) was repeated at the other two sites I visited during the day. My colleagues at the head office, Fiona (an ex-submariner) and Jacqui (Navy), both burst into tears upon receipt of their AC4P wristbands and pebbles. Days later they were still talking about the ceremony.

My other colleague, Dave, ex-SAS (Special Air Service), did not display such open emotion. However, he later showed me his pebble which he had mounted into a pendant he wears attached to a neck chain.

Sustaining AC4P Remembrance

This AC4P story is more than a single-yet-significant event. At IFAP we now celebrate both Anzac Day and Remembrance Day with flag-lowering ceremonies at our campuses, presided over by our ex-servicemen and women who are encouraged to wear full uniform to the functions. I have encouraged the permanent adornment of our office doorways with memorabilia of the regiments in which they served so as to mark that a proud regiment member resides within. And of course, I am in the throes of planning a major event for 2015 to mark the centenary of the fateful Anzac Day landing at Gallipoli.

Thank you Scott, Joanne and the others for inspiring me to demonstrate AC4P behavior by recognizing my ex-servicemen and women colleagues in 2011, and beyond.

CHAPTER 23

Making Time for People:
Don't delay to actively care

Joanne Dean Geller

WE HAVE ALL SAID to others or to ourselves, "I will get to that later or maybe I will have time next week." Let's be real about this and consider that waiting to do the important things we talk about can set us up for disappointment and missed opportunities. Reflect on those times you said to yourself, "Why didn't I call or visit that person when my instincts told me to do so?"

We think we have all the time in the world, but of course we don't. When it comes to AC4P we must grab opportunities to actively care as soon as we see them. This book is about inspiring you to embrace those AC4P opportunities sooner rather than later. The following experiences illustrate the meaningfulness that can come from acting on caring as soon as an opportunity presents itself.

Meeting a Distinguished Professor

For eight years now, my husband has spoken to me about an eminent professor he once worked with at the University. I've heard him say many times, "I need to visit John Cairns." Although Scott spoke so highly of this former colleague, he never acted on his words of caring. These are just those situations that call for action. If it's important, don't delay to actively care.

Formerly the Director of the University Center for Environmental and Hazardous Materials Studies at Virginia Tech (VT), Dr. John Cairns is now retired. An esteemed University Distinguished Professor Emeritus who committed his life to his family and academia is now alone. He's just the person who needs a visitor.

"So, this is it," I tell myself as I go off to find this gentleman. I had discovered Dr. Cairns lives in a Care Center in Blacksburg, Virginia. This Sunday afternoon I enter the Center and ask for his whereabouts. I find his building and am told to go to Room 207 on the second floor and knock on his door. A deep voice responds, "Just come in, I am laying in bed".

With a smile on my face, I pop my head around the corner and notice a very handsome, grey-haired gentleman. I smile and say, "I am married to Scott Geller and I just had to find you because he has spoken so highly of you." He replies, "Come sit down," and he immediately reminisces about his work with Scott, claiming, "We were both such mavericks at the University".

My next move is to call Scott, and when he answers I say, "Here's someone who wants to talk

Dr. John Cairns, Jr.

to you." I hand my cell-phone to John and John's face just lights up. I then listen and learn about the fascinating career of Dr. Cairns. Before I leave I promise to bring Scott on the next visit.

That next visit happened the following week, and listening to these two creative scholars was an opportunity I wouldn't have missed for the world.

After a few days I delivered a few of Scott's books to John. I promised to bring Scott back with three of his best students who are interested in ecological sustainability, the research domain in which John and Scott had collaborated. The research these men have accomplished will enlighten and inspire these young people.

This story exemplifies the AC4P ripple effect – how the positive impact of one kind act for one person can spread to many others.

From One Kind Act to Another

As the clock ticks, it's time to share my AC4P experience with Billy. One sunny Sunday in October of 2011 after participating in an AC4P meeting at our Make-A-DiffRanch, I drive to Christiansburg, Virginia and pass a young man walking with difficulty. I had seen this individual before on the same road and now I think to myself, "I wonder what his story is and how he had been injured".

When I arrive at the shopping mall, I sit in my car and reflect, "If I am really an AC4P person I should go back and offer him a ride." I do not ask strangers if they need a ride, but my instincts tell me to alter my paradigm this time.

I turn around and pull up next to this man and ask, "May I give you a ride?" He smiles and I tell him not to be afraid and that it would mean a lot to me if I could help. He replies, "Yes" and enters my vehicle with a smile. I ask him what had happened to him and he shares his story.

As a young man he was shot in the head because he was in the wrong place at the wrong time. He has endured years of rehabilitation and continues treatment to this day. He is lame and unable to use his right arm. He lives with his mom and walks everyday to get exercise. I ask him if he is a VT fan and he says, "Absolutely". "Do you have a VT sweatshirt?" I ask. "No I don't", Billy replies.

"Well since you are going to the mall to pay some bills how about I treat you to a VT sweatshirt?" He displays the biggest smile, and we drive to the store.

I then tell Billy about the AC4P Movement and that he's providing me the pleasure of doing something nice for someone else and I'm so grateful. I ask him if he had ever been to Panera Bread

Scott, Billy, and Joanne before a CABS meeting.

and he responds, "Never". So we have lunch at Panera.

Subsequently, I have taken Billy to some of Scott's large introductory psychology classes and to several of our weekly research meetings. Scott and I have also provided him with some work he can do with his one useful arm.

My instincts were so right on this one. If I hadn't stopped that day to offer a kind deed, I would not have met Billy and developed a special friendship to share with others. Billy is truly an inspiration to all of us, and his involvement with our group enables him to feel useful and appreciated, and to experience a sense of community.

Many of my visits to see Billy have included conversations with his mom. It's humbling to spend time with them and see the love and loyalty they have for each other. They are a very modest family, and every time I pick up Billy to attend one of our classes at VT I smile inside for this special opportunity to actively care. Indeed, AC4P behavior is rewarding and self-motivating.

The Dick Sanderson Story

My next anecdote has timeless and heartfelt meaning for me and it has touched the lives of many in special ways. This is the story of my special high-school friend, Dick Sanderson, who was stricken with ALS (Amyotrophic Lateral Sclerosis), commonly known as Lou Gehrig's disease.

Ten years ago, Dick called and asked me to reach out to our high-school friends and tell them he has ALS and soon would not be able to talk. That simple phone call provided me with opportunities that have given new meaning to my life. The photo on the next page includes my classmates from the Class of 1969 who have met each year to raise money for the Sanderson family. This challenging experience has provided us all the opportunity to actively care for Dick and his family.

Today, Dick Sanderson is totally paralyzed, requires a machine to breath, and is fed through a tube. He can hear, see and think, but is incapable of any output. He is trapped in his body with no means of communicating to others. His psychological courage to hang on under these most difficult circumstances inspires all of us to complain less about our misfortunes and to reach out to help others less fortunate.

Dick's wife Dawn and their three children work together to care for him 24/7 with daily support of in-home nurses and friends. It's both humbling and heartening to experience the interpersonal support this man has captivated. Dawn, his leading caretaker, will tell you she is blessed with opportunities to actively care for her husband with never-ending love and devotion.

All of us share this story of Dick Sanderson, which in turn motivates others to take more time to appreciate their friends and family. Each year, more than 5,000 U.S. residents are diagnosed with ALS; and following diagnosis the average ALS patient lives two to five years.[1] We have profound sympathy for those stricken with ALS, count our blessings, and embrace opportunities to actively care for individuals less fortunate than we.

My experience with John, Billy and Dick remind me each day of the power of AC4P through simple one-to-one personal communication. Make time for people and your time on earth will be enriched.

Center: Dick Sanderson. Second row: Lorna Schmitt Danckwerth, Karen Steffan Gannon, Dawn Sanderson, Dan Fagan, Wayne Meyer, Betsy Hanna Sollenberger, Sue Schwab Windt, Lynda Martenis Burns. Back row: Suzy Coutts Selby, Arnie Scalio, Michele Corona Grajewski, Ernie Blane, Steve Thomas, Rod Dorman, Brian Peters, Eddie Thomas, Joanne Dean Geller, Dan Windt, and Annie Paterson.

Note

1. Kibbs, L. (2006). ALS and Driving 4 Life. In J. Dean, & E.S. Geller (Eds.). *The power of friendship: Dick Sanderson's positive fight with ALS* (pp. 3-25). Newport, VA: Make-A-Difference, LLC.

CHAPTER 24

The Positive Addiction of AC4P:
The more you give, the more you get

John Drebinger

ACTIVELY CARING FOR People (AC4P) reminds me of the Boy Scouts. I was 11 years old when a friend asked me to join the local Boy Scout Troop. To earn the rank of Tenderfoot, I had to memorize the Boy Scout Oath. I learned early on my duty as a scout was "to help other people at all times" and the importance of the Boy Scout slogan, "Do a good turn daily".

I've spent 50 years in the Boy Scouts, a half century of being positively addicted to doing good turns, or actively caring. Back when I began to work on the Scout advancement program, I was given a brass coin with the Scout slogan. In the morning, it started in my right pocket; as soon as I had done my good turn for the day, I'd move it to my left pocket.

The Boy Scouts and AC4P

The history of the daily good turn goes back to the Fall of 1909. Chicago publisher William D. Boyce was in London looking for an office. The dense London fog had caused him to be completely lost. Boyce stopped a young man and asked for directions. The youth personally led Boyce to the location. Boyce offered the young man a tip, which he politely refused.

The young man explained he was a Boy Scout; accepting the tip would negate the good turn he had done and violate the Scout code. Boyce was so impressed he sought out the founder of Scouting, Sir Baden Powell, and brought the Boy Scouts to America.

Over the years Scouting has given me so many opportunities to personally engage in and witness AC4P, without ever calling it that. It has been a life-long education I never want to see end. For example, I learned you help others sometimes just because it's the right thing to do. You see, advancing through the ranks in the Scouts required us to log a certain number of service hours for each rank.

I cleaned up around the church where we met and coincidently, where I was a member. On occasion, cleanup involved repairing or removing acts of vandalism that had been committed: Once a swastika was painted on the sidewall of the church. I learned not every good turn will be met with an enthusiastic response.

In Scouting, selflessness is connected with helping others or AC4P behavior. At my elementary school, I signed up to raise and lower the flag every day. I had to arrive a little early and leave a little late, but I enjoyed the responsibility and it was fun.

When we worked at the church, I had a sense of pride in making the planters or the parking lot more attractive. I could proudly show and tell my parents what we had done. It was, in fact, AC4P behavior.

As Scott Geller explains in this book, AC4P builds positive feelings of self-esteem and a sense of belonging, along with other person-states. My fellow scouts and I discovered when you actively care for others, the joy and sense of satisfaction more than pay back any investment of time and effort.

Another example: Long before it became fashionable to respect the environment, I spent hours on environmental projects with other scouts. We cleaned debris and trash from a local stream and prevented soil erosion by planting trees, to name just a few of our efforts. Even though our actions benefited others, we experienced the positive personal consequences of pride, accomplishment, and fun.

At one point along my AC4P journey, I decided I wanted to pay back the organization that had given me so much. So I chose to make scouting my career. What once had been a duty became something I loved. It paid significantly less than jobs in industry, but I really wanted to give back for all I received. Scouting taught me: Every time I seek to *pay it forward* I get as much or more back than I give.

Here's proof: As a professional in scouting I studied magic to help recruit scouts. Within a few years I became a professional magician. This ultimately led to my career as a speaker in the field of safety. All this good has come from helping others. To this day, I hold AC4P as one of my highest values.

Exemplary AC4P Behavior

As a volunteer scout leader, I love to see young men embrace the value of helping others. In 2010, I saw this value displayed by one scout in my National Jamboree Troop.

Each local Boy Scout council organizes special troops for the National Boy Scout Jamboree, a gathering of more than 40,000 scouts and adult scout leaders. Scout leaders for these troops are selected from all the adults in the local council.

I've served as Scoutmaster to several Boy Scout Troops during my years in Scouting, including the privilege of serving as an Assistant Scoutmaster for the 2005 Jamboree and Scoutmaster for the 100th Anniversary Jamboree in 2010. At that time I was serving as Scoutmaster for one of the three troops going to the National Scout Jamboree from the Greater Yosemite Council. Due to my experience, I was assigned scouts who had challenging issues to deal with.

The Eager Scout

At our first troop meeting, I gave my 30-minute introductory speech to the scouts and their parents. About two minutes in, an eager scout waved his hand repeatedly. I acknowledged him and he asked a question. I answered it and two minutes later he had another question. I didn't want to squelch his enthusiasm but he was asking questions I was going to cover anyway. Another scout handled it for me by quietly telling him he should hold his questions until I was finished.

That same day I had a discussion with the eager scout's parents. They explained he was on medication for several issues. I asked about his needs and what behaviors he displayed. One that concerned me immediately was his tendency to just wander off without telling anyone. I knew in addition to the nine days at the Jamboree site, we would be on tour for ten days. I shared my concern with them. We decided to move forward and see how he did on our practice campouts.

Another challenge came to my mind. Who would I get to be a tent mate and buddy for this scout? Each scout or his parent had paid about $3,500 for the entire jamboree package and it would be reasonable for them to focus on getting the most for their money. Our eager scout was also one of the youngest in the troop; if I placed him with one of the older scouts, the older scout would be deprived of enjoying the event with boys his own age.

The AC4P Scout

During our first campout, one of our older scouts, Ross, came to me and said he wanted to be buddies with our eager scout. Ross was so attuned to AC4P, so empathic, he had observed the challenge the young scout was experiencing and volunteered even before we asked.

I saw AC4P displayed by Ross in a most exemplary way. He stuck with our eager scout and ensured he was having a great experience as well as being safe.

On our day at the Capitol Mall in Washington DC, we dropped all the scouts off at the Smithsonian and they spent the day on their own touring this amazing place. Buddy groups in this situation jumped from two to four scouts. Ross recruited two other scouts to join him to make a group of four.

What a success! At the end of each day, our young eager scout told me and the other leaders all the neat things he and Ross had done together. He always had a smile on his face. Ross joined me later and told me of their adventures and the unique experiences of our younger scout. Ross too had a smile on his face.

Despite the 100 degree heat and 95% humidity, they had a great time. The same went for Fort McHenry, Gettysburg, Mount Vernon and several other places where the scouts had time to themselves. We arrived at the Jamboree site and all went well.

The Creative AC4P Scout

One hot afternoon, I sat down at a table with Ross and his buddy and noticed our young eager scout had a one-gallon milk bottle filled with water in his hand. I asked what it was and he cheerfully replied, "It's my water bottle". I was surprised because we issued each scout a one-pint water bottle.

I took Ross aside and asked why he and our young scout were carrying such a hefty bottle. His answer was brilliant. In the extreme heat and humidity in Virginia in July, hydration was very important. We constantly reminded the scouts to drink plenty of water. Ross had the perfect solution.

If he and our young eager scout carried a one-gallon water bottle they would automatically drink more just to lighten the load. It worked great. Our young scout was never dehydrated because he began each day with that heavy bottle he and Ross would empty as the day wore on.

Ross's AC4P didn't just benefit the eager young scout; it helped everyone in our troop. My three Assistant Scoutmasters and myself could stay focused on the program for all the scouts, knowing our younger scout was safe and having a fun time.

It's a privilege to work with outstanding youth. No matter how many dollars I donate and time I volunteer, I walk away a richer person.

Just two weeks ago, I talked with Ross and heard some great news. He has been selected to be an Assistant Scoutmaster for the 2013 National Scout Jamboree at the Bechtel Summit in West Virginia.

Ross is one of the most AC4P persons I have ever had the pleasure to meet. I am proud to call him a fellow Eagle Scout and a good friend as well.

From a Process to a Lifestyle

The AC4P green wristband is just like the small brass coin I carried in my pocket as a young scout. I suppose you could start with the green wristband on one wrist in the morning and move it to your other wrist when you actively care for someone else, until you give it away to recognize another person's AC4P behavior.

The AC4P Movement will result in more and more people actively caring as the idea perpetuates itself and grows. If someone hands you a green wristband and tells you why s/he did so, s/he is giving you a unique reward for your AC4P behavior.

Then both you and that person carry the AC4P message forward. Ultimately, as others are educated, more people will actively care, which in most cases will create in them a special sense of satisfaction. I know; I've been there many times.

AC4P extends to your chosen field of work. Due to my focus on helping others, it was a natural extension to study ways people could help others work safely. All this led to my latest book I dedicated to my good friend Scott Geller, *Would You Watch Out For My Safety?*[1]

Have fun discovering all the joy in a life dedicated to helping others with AC4P behavior.

Note

1. Drebinger, J.W. (2011). *Would you watch out for my safety? Helping others avoid personal injury.* Galt, CA: Wulamoc Publishing.

CHAPTER 25

Cultivating an AC4P Family:
Bringing AC4P home

Corrine Picht

GROWING UP I LIVED on a farm with all the standard farming responsibilities. I often took risks and some might have classified me as your typical tomboy. Growing up on the farm I can honestly say thinking about my safety or anyone else's was the farthest thing from my mind. I was just lucky I was never hurt, nor any of my other family members.

After graduating from high school, I was hired at a local manufacturing facility. Ten years went by in the blink of an eye and soon I found myself just punching the time clock. One day my supervisor came to me and asked if I'd be interested in learning about people-based safety (PBS) and the AC4P Movement.

The opportunity to be a member of our PBS Team sounded interesting, so I took him up on it, although I didn't know what I was signing up for. I could never have imagined how much AC4P was going to impact my life, both in and outside the workplace.

Building an AC4P Culture among Co-Workers

As a member of the PBS Team, my challenge was to get co-workers to talk to each other about their safe and unsafe behaviors. So, we developed a formal safety coaching process where one co-worker observed another co-worker and gave AC4P behavioral feedback. Our mission was to learn from one another and share new ideas, but to also point out things that looked risky. In the beginning, this was quite a challenge because interpersonal observation and feedback is not common among co-workers.

One of my more memorable experiences involved trying to convince a co-worker to participate in AC4P coaching. He and I were chatting while walking by one of our assembly lines. During our conversation he began giving me a hard time about being so actively involved with PBS and AC4P. Our conversation went back and forth about this subject for several minutes.

Then to my surprise, he stopped talking to me and instantly stopped another man working on the assembly line. The co-worker was doing something extremely risky. Not only did he explain why the behavior was at-risk, but he also showed his co-worker the safe way to perform the task.

I just stood there in amazement, while waiting for him to finish his conversation with the co-worker. When he returned I smiled and looked him right in the eye and said, "If that wasn't actively caring then I don't know what is."

His reaction was just a simple smile. He felt good about speaking up to his co-worker and so did I. Sometimes workers just need a little encouragement to see how important AC4P is to the culture of our workplace.

Taking AC4P Home

Since I was discovering this deep passion for AC4P at work, I found myself incorporating the same concepts in my personal life. AC4P became a part of the way I interacted and communicated with people at home and in my community, as well as at work. I started to connect with people on different levels, whether they were co-workers, family, or friends. I always felt I was giving something back when I actively cared for others.

My children soon picked up on my AC4P behaviors, and very often played a large role in promoting these principles in their lives. I didn't realize the impact of AC4P on their lives until one day I was out shopping in a grocery store with my six-year old. He pointed out the way a shelf was loaded and how unstable it was. We reported it to one of the store employees. After that experience, both my boys have continued to look for different ways to actively care for the safety and welfare of others.

Several weeks later, I was out shopping again and my youngest son, who was only four years old at the time, saw an older lady drop an item on the floor. My son went right over to pick it up for her. She thanked him and commented, "What a nice little boy you are".

When he returned to me, I also thanked him for his AC4P behavior. His response, "I'm closer to the ground than she is and I didn't want to see her get hurt".

The kids began to ask themselves and others the question, "Is what I'm about to do safe or not?" As a mother, that was and still is a priceless moment for me.

From stories like these and the impact AC4P was having on my two boys, I then made up a fun game for us all to play in the car. We started with road signs and traffic lights. The boys had to explain what they meant and how they influenced the driving of other vehicles on the road.

Next, we progressed to making lane changes safely and then safety-related items we should always have in the vehicle (e.g., flashlight, first-aid kits, jumper cables). They also had no problem letting me know when I wasn't following the proper driving procedures.

The Journey Continues

As you can only imagine, we are still working on how to give effective AC4P feedback to our co-workers. The AC4P principles have changed my life in so many different ways. They have helped me develop self-confidence and enhance my capabilities to influence others. I'm sure the potential was always there, but getting involved in AC4P helped me turn good intentions to action.

Indeed, my interaction with others and my outlook on life has totally changed. I look forward to going to work where we are being more proactive rather than reactive in safety. I'm proud to say AC4P is a value I have now instilled in my children.

CHAPTER 26

Barriers to AC4P in Families:
What's the quality of AC4P on the home front?

Dave Johnson

I WAS 12 YEARS OLD when my father died suddenly, completely unexpectedly. I remember a neighbor down the street, a teacher, telling me, "Oh, you're really at a tough age for your dad to die. You were just starting to know him."

My dad came from a large family, and I recall my aunts and uncles, especially my uncles, trying to show their own form of AC4P by telling me, "Dave, we'll go to games. I'll take you to games." Maybe they included movies and watching me play sports, I don't remember.

But I know for a fact my uncles, well meaning as I think they were, never came through and took me to any games – or movies or whatever they intended as substitute dads. No AC4P behavior from them to me. I think AC4P applications in the complicated dynamics of family is damn difficult.

I didn't harbor any resentment about my uncles not coming through, at least not consciously. Instead, I was preoccupied at the time with sticking out, being different than my friends because I was the only one in seventh grade who didn't have a dad. I dreaded that first day of the school year when the teacher went around the class asking everyone what their fathers did for a living.

I don't think I even really wanted to go out with my uncles. It would be weird, not normal. During early adolescence, you want to fit in and not stick out. So the AC4P that dissipated didn't really bother me. At least I don't think it did. My uncles were raising their own kids, my cousins, and their AC4P intentions for me couldn't keep up with reality.

How do Families Actively Care?

That did leave a mark on me, however, and it relates to AC4P, though of course I never called it that. You would think the most intimate and sustained AC4P occurs within immediate families.

You might also think love and caring between parents and children, or within more extended families, is something so biologically and culturally embedded it does not qualify as AC4P. After all, if AC4P should occur naturally in any situation, it's within the family, right?

Not so. For many parents AC4P nurturing for their kids is neither instinctual nor easy. Working mothers often feel deep guilt over not doing enough, not being there, especially for their young kids.

Fathers, not as biologically connected to their offspring, nowadays join clubs and workshops on how to be better dads. Plus, fathers can feel guilt over too much business travel or long hours immersed in their work which means less "quality time" with their kids. I equate AC4P with quality time. It's a quality act.

The Quality of AC4P in Families

My future son-in-law recently told my wife and me he believes only the kids who have had easy and continual access to both parents, and years of parental support and encouragement, end up physically and mentally healthy, without resentment or outright anger directed at their parents.

So what's so difficult about giving your kid quality AC4P behavior? All they need is access, listening, questioning, observing, staying close, behavioral praise and corrective feedback, and supportive discipline? Simply put, parents need to be there for their children.

Woody Allen said life is 90% just showing up. Is it that difficult for parents to "show up" for their children? Too often the answer is "Yes".

AC4P time is problematic for many parents, especially for two-income families. Many moms and dads love their jobs, not more than their kids of course, but to the degree they will work nights and weekends. In these cases, there is simply not enough time left over to give quality AC4P to the kids.

Many moms and dads trudge through more than one job they hate in order to cover basic living expenses. The fatigue and stress, anxiety and depression, and eventual burnout, robs many parents of the ability to give quality AC4P time to their kids.

Then there are the fathers who walk out on the family. The kids are raised by their grandparents. What about parents addicted to gambling, sex, alcohol, meth, coke, and so on? So we have broken-down families and alienated children. No AC4P behavior there.

The AC4P Challenge at Home

I believe it's easier to apply AC4P principles in workplaces, schools, the military, even penal colonies than in families. Rules govern these other institutions. Behavior is easier to regulate. Peer pressure exerts itself. Families are more fluid, less structured. Unless dad is an ex-military guy running a very tight ship, which certainly happens.

Most families live in tight quarters, year after year, with so many good and bad interpersonal experiences, that all types of feelings arise among all the family members that can squeeze out opportunities for pure, unadulterated quality AC4P behavior. Call it pain, blame, scars, tension, or as the kids get older and drive and head to college, parents are just running around doing their own thing, with little occasion for sharing and caring behavior.

Finally, I think AC4P faces challenges on the home front because many moms and dads do not have the self-esteem, competence or feeling in control enough to engage in quality AC4P behavior for their kids. Maybe they had kids too young. Or they had too many kids. Or maybe they didn't get the support they needed from their own parents.

Perhaps they thought proper parenting is instinctual, and they never learned how to be an effective mom or dad. There was no sense of belonging. And so ineffective parenthood is passed down – a very undesirable example of *pay it forward*.

By the way, everything I've touched on here is relevant for spouses caring for each other. And the AC4P applications can be broadened to include extended families: grandparents, aunts and uncles, cousins.

In some cultures outside the U.S., such as Japan and other Eastern countries, and some European countries, AC4P is an unspoken multi-generational cultural bond.

The Quantity of AC4P in Families

One more thing: Missing out on my father's AC4P love, counsel, coaching, general feedback, guidance and, yes, even corrective discipline when I could have used it during my middle-school, high-school, college years and beyond, did deeply commit me to making sure I was present and accounted for to actively care for my daughter and son. Now they are both young adults, and looking back, I may have gone overboard with AC4P behavior. Is that possible? I think so.

A number of us Baby Boomers, raised by remote fathers, the norm for those "Mad Men" times, have vowed to be closer to our kids. You know, the "helicopter parents" who hover over their kids, text them daily in college, do their homework if necessary, and pace the sidelines at every youth soccer, baseball, basketball, football, ice hockey, you name the sport, since the kids were, oh, maybe five.

I believe many of us Boomers felt our parents did not actively care enough. So we more than made up for that by spoiling and codling and pumping up our kids' self-esteem to the point they demand A's from their teachers, more playing time from coaches, lucrative jobs right out of college, and often expect immediate gratification, and oh, with no adversity please.

In Conclusion

AC4P behavior is a tricky balancing act when performed in the highly emotional environment of a family and within the complexities of parenthood. This is different, and I think more challenging than AC4P applied to random strangers, or in schools and workplaces, where emotions don't run so high and organizational structure can include rules, education/training, and incentive/reward programs to prompt and motivate AC4P behavior.

I'd love to see the AC4P Movement include AC4P workshops for families. Cohesive, AC4P families sustain society. What's more important than that? The workplace? Middle schools? Prisons? No disrespect, but healthy, caring, well-balanced families come first in my book.

Part IV: Wristband Stories from ac4p.org

AUTOPILOT: Functioning in an unthinking or reflexive manner. Most of you are familiar with this term. Most people do it, function on autopilot that is. It's easier to think at System 1 and perform our daily routines, focused only on ourselves and the tasks at hand. Too often we don't think beyond ourselves and use System 2 thinking[1] to recognize those around us who might need our help.

Aly Neel was adapting to a busy schedule in a new city while interning with the Cook Political Report in Washington, D.C., but it didn't stop her from reflecting and taking time for others.

Dozens of people jam into a D.C. Metro train during rush hour – a diverse crowd of students, business people, and politicians perspiring from the heat, noses stuck in others' armpits. Conversations with riders one doesn't know is rare. On this day sly glances are made at a man catching a snooze in the corner. He's snoring obnoxiously, but no one says anything to him, no hands poke him in the arm. Strangers are not to be bothered – right?[2]

Aly Neel's Metro Story

After living in DC for some time and riding the Metro during many rush-hour mornings and nights, I have become well aware of the unwritten rule, "You just ride".

On my way home from work one day, I catch the red-line train toward Union Station per usual. A young man, wearing a suit, is sitting inches away from me. He's so close I can almost reach him. I look up and notice he seems very upset – wringing his hands, shaking his head. Unintentionally, I stare at him. I try but can't look away because he looks as if he is on the verge of tears.

I immediately think, "What can I do?" I know I have to say something, but I'm uncertain how to reach out. We finally make eye contact, and I give him a smile – the empathetic kind I would give a friend whose family member just died. I want him to know I'm sorry for whatever he is going through. Immediately after our exchange I look down, sort of embarrassed. I remember people aren't *supposed* to smile at each other on the Metro!

The Metro slows down and comes to a stop. The guy, still shaken up, stands to get off the train, but then pauses to touch me on my shoulder. He says: "You probably already forgot what you did. It didn't seem like a big deal, but this year has been the worst year of my life. What you just did a second ago, though really small, is probably the most anyone has reached out to me in this past year."

Rolling up his shirtsleeve, he tells me, "It represents a pay-it-forward notion". He hands me a green wristband, embossed with the words "Actively Caring for People".

My mouth is agape. I had heard of this AC4P Movement, but I had never received a wristband until now.

Aly N.
Washington, DC

ac4p.org Launch[3]

That wristband was one of the 2,000 AC4P wristbands distributed on the Virginia Tech (VT) campus eight months prior. After hearing this story, our AC4P team knew the AC4P wristbands could create a widespread movement far beyond VT. So, we took the green wristbands, embossed with "Actively Caring for People" that Scott Geller had been distributing at safety conferences for two decades, and added a numbering system that enabled computer tracking of the AC4P *See*, *Act*, *Pass*, and *Share* (SAPS) process.

Specifically, we asked individuals and groups to look for AC4P behavior (i.e., See) and reward such behavior with an AC4P wristband (i.e., Act). Wristband recipients are requested to look for AC4P behaviors from others and pass on the wristband (i.e., Pass). These interpersonal exchanges are documented on the AC4P website (ac4p.org) with the wristband number (i.e., Share). Tracking these positive interactions worldwide rewards and thus motivates people to follow suit and do more.

ac4p.org Stories

Stories posted on ac4p.org tell of interpersonal exchanges between people receiving and giving AC4P wristbands after specific AC4P behaviors. Wristband recognition occurs for simple gestures – such as holding the door for a stranger – and more complex acts requiring skills, financial stability, and time. These acts occur in various locations, including schools, restaurants, highways, community streets, and stores.

Many stories reflect competence, commitment, and courage. They involve people acting on behalf of family, friends, co-workers, and strangers in both reactive circumstances and in proactive situations.

Some individuals receive a wristband for AC4P in reactive situations, such as standing up for a friend after hearing a racist remark (wristband #407), rebuilding a home after tornadoes devastated Joplin, Missouri (#4766), helping after a sibling's car broke down (#2974), and saving the life of a motorcyclist after a crash (#240).

Others are recognized for proactive AC4P behavior, such as helping a friend, holding the door for extended periods of time, walking an intoxicated stranger to her home safely, taking care of a sick roommate, and giving a wallet filled with money back to the stranger who lost it.

From Random to Intentional Kindness

Every story is unique, with different people, places, and behaviors. However, one thread runs through each act of kindness: Intention. I bet you've heard of "Random Acts of Kindness".[3] This popular slogan implies that acts of kindness "just happen" without planning or forethought. Most compassionate acts of helping others are not random.

Every AC4P good-doer reminds us to be mindful and intentional (i.e., System 2 thinking[1]) regarding opportunities to actively care. Additionally, these AC4P stories suggest the helpers receive much in return: Smiles from strangers and genuine appreciation from friends. They think to themselves, "That could've been worse if I hadn't actively cared" or "I really made my friend's day".

We hope these stories inspire you to recognize others with AC4P wristbands wherever you see intentional acts of caring. Such AC4P behavior will range from small acts of kindness to heroic demonstrations of courage. Your AC4P servant leadership will help cultivate a culture of compassion worldwide.

The following AC4P stories were selected from over 2,000 stories posted on the ac4p.org website since January, 2011. The stories depict instances of individuals going "above and beyond the call of duty," intervening as a concerned and compassionate bystander on behalf of the health, safety, and/or well-being of someone else.

"Above and Beyond" Stories

From an AC4P Wristband to an AC4P Lifestyle

My freshman year I was lucky to have some crazy roommates who truly tested everything about me. At this point, I was a rough and temperamental personality trying to fit my way into the world, but struggling to adapt. However, I was given something from Benjamin Caleb George. It was a green wristband with the following words inscribed: "Actively Caring for People". At first, I wore the wristband to make Ben happy (sorry Ben but hey it's true), but the words started to etch their way into my life. I found myself trying to become better for everyone, including my friends.

It was tough and I can be a dramatic handful at times, but my life became better and I found myself smiling every day. Today, I lost that green wristband – the one that has been with me for two years, showing up in every good and bad photo. I didn't notice until I looked down and it was gone.

Its weight and words have truly sunk into my skin and I guess it has done its job. So I want to thank Ben for giving me something he might not even know would have a huge effect on my life. And for everyone who has been by my side this whole time, I know it isn't easy and you didn't have to be there, but you did. For that, I thank you. I still have more work to do to better myself, but at least I have a great start.

Nathaniel C.
Richmond, VA

A Compassionate Truck Driver

I am currently on my way back home to Virginia from New York. Long story short, my car broke down. Stuck on the side of the road we called AAA. A tow truck came, with a driver by the name of Taka (Take-a). This man is trying everything in his power to get us all the way from Middletown, Delaware to Virginia Beach, Virginia (some 215 miles) without charging us $500 dollars. He is sticking his neck out to do something for two stranded women that wouldn't benefit him at all. True human compassion! *Wristband #2974*

Jenee E.
Middletown, DE

Offering a Seat

Today, I was in Au Bon Pain and saw two girls offer a seat at their table to a blind student during the busy lunch hour. Then, they proceeded to put down their homework, and have a conversation with her as well as refill her drink when she ran out.

Without acts of kindness like these, I don't know if the student would have ever found a table during the rush hour at Au Bon Pain! I was so ecstatic to be able to give out my first wristband, especially to somebody who truly went out of her way to make somebody else's day! *Wristband #168*

Elise C.
Blacksburg, VA

Students First

I gave a wristband to Shawn Wells, Principal at Bollinger Canyon Elementary School. This is a public school that hosts five intensive special-education classrooms for students with autism and other developmental disabilities.

During the past several years, the special-education population at Bollinger Canyon has grown quite a bit, and Shawn has continued to build and support a culture that accepts, understands, and invites special education.

Just a few weeks ago, Shawn designated one of the "staff only" bathrooms to be used for an intensive toilet training program for a seven-year-old student who was not yet potty trained. This student now successfully uses the toilet on a daily basis for the first time in his life. Additionally, his parents no longer need to spend countless dollars purchasing diapers. Shawn attends and actively participates in nearly all of her student's IEP's and makes frequent visits to the special education classrooms to check in on students and ensure she is familiar with their programs.

With such a large population of special education students, this adds quite a bit of work to Shawn's already busy schedule...but she makes it happen...and she always does it smiling. In my work with Shawn, she has always put the needs of her students first. Thank you Shawn...for Actively Caring about all of your students and their families!! *Wristband #1294*

Joel V.
San Ramon, CA

Coming to the Rescue

My car has had a lot go wrong with it in the past year or so. I never take care of it. The "Check Engine" and "Maint Required" lights have been on for as long as I can remember, and it's been a joke that any day now the thing might explode (not really, I hope).

I let my boyfriend borrow my car one day, and when he returned it my brake light was fixed, the "Check Engine" and "Maint Required" lights were off, there was a brand new cap on my gas tank (I had lost it before), my oil had been checked, and fluid had been put in my windshield wiper thing.

Turns out my boyfriend had taken my car in to get a full list of what was wrong with it (a long list) and wanted to fix everything. But he doesn't know a lot about cars. Turns out Dave came to the rescue! Dave is my boyfriend's roommate. He happens to know a lot about cars and took the extra time to look over and fix the long list of things wrong with it, just because! *Wristband #22549*

Michelle L.
Blacksburg, VA

Helping a Missing Child

I was at Great Wolf lodge when the front desk called to ask if I was missing a child. I said, "No". When I woke up the next morning, I saw a lady with the missing boy.

The missing child had been in the lobby all night with the lady. She got him blankets and held him. I learned she'd been there for seven hours taking care of that boy. The boy's dad didn't even know when he woke up that his son was gone. I gave my wristband to "the lady of the night," someone actively cared! *Wristband #1425*

Logan O.
Charlotte, NC

A Compassionate Student Patrol

A student safety patrol, Eli, showed compassion to another student who boarded my bus in tears. The student proceeded to fight with her older siblings; one of them being Eli's peer.

Eli handled the situation beyond what is required of a safety patrol. She was able to immediately calm the child and find a resolution to what would have surely escalated into something very distracting for me as the bus driver. It allowed me to carry on instead of waiting for a safe place to pullover to address it myself. I gave him *wristband #8215*

Jennifer S.
Great Falls, VA

Recognition in the Worst of Times

This past February there was a shooting at my school: Chardon High School. It's been rough for everyone – some more than others. Like many teenagers, I feel as if I'm fighting the world alone, not sure if what I'm fighting for is even right. I just finished track. I'm not a star runner; I'm actually quite slow, but I do it because I enjoy it. The other faster kids are still in season and still being coached.

Anyway, after the shooting my high school received thousands of cards. They mean more to me than any of the other gifts my high school has received. Sadly we must take them down "to move on" as I keep being told. It seems as if half the kids in the school already forgot why the cards are there, anyway.

Nevertheless, I feel as if I need to read the cards just so a person's actively caring is not thrown into some box without the slightest thought. I volunteered two times to help take down the cards. Both times I read each one before sorting them into their boxes. I try not to cry but there is no shame in getting teary-eyed.

Of course some of the cards hit home, others made me smile, but in general I feel that after the clean-up I have renewed strength to deal with the confusing mess of feelings.

I can tell myself I did this clean-up for those who wrote the letters, or for the victims of the shooting, or to help the janitor who would have to deal with the thousands of cards, but I did this for me. I wanted to and that's why I did it.

The day I was taking down the cards I was extremely sad. I was thinking how I truly haven't accomplished anything since February. My grades dropped, track was not a particularly successful season. The worst part is that my relationships with friends and family are strained. I keep reading the cards, taking the strengths those individuals sent, trying to feel it.

Amazingly my track coach, Bartley comes up behind me one day and says "You're a good kid, you know that?" I needed to hear those words more than anything. He pulls off his AC4P wristband and gives it to me. I was speechless. This told me I was doing something right. I had always liked and admired him, but this was something more than I ever expected. That was my coach actively caring for me, and I look forward to paying it forward and passing on this wristband *#47735*

Megan W.
Chardon, OH

A Very Grateful Student and Fellow Hokie

I don't usually post stories but I thought this one was an awesome testament to the kind of people we have in Blacksburg. I am driving down Southgate toward Airport Drive and hit something in the middle of the road. My tire immediately bursts and I have to pull over. Of course I have no idea what to do. I get out and call my parents, as if they can help from four hours away.

With no answer I'm scared and unsure what to do. The first few cars fly by me and then finally an older gentleman offers to help. He immediately starts changing the tire and asks me to simply direct traffic. As I'm standing in the middle of the four-way intersection a student walks by. He drops his book bag and rushes over to help me.

After a few minutes of feeling like I'm going to be hit in the middle of the intersection, I call the Blacksburg Police Department to take over. In a matter of minutes two officers respond and thank me for doing the best I could. I have the spare tire in place, the student begins describing the "actively caring" campaign and he gives the older gentleman one of the green wristbands we have all seen around campus.

Until now I didn't know what "paying it forward" really meant. My crazy day turned out to be a story I'll never forget and one I will tell a million times to show people what it really means to be a Hokie. I wouldn't trade this school and town for anything in the world. UT PROSIM, and GO HOKIES. *Wristband #52517*

Kelley C.
Blacksburg, VA

Bystander Intervention Stories

AC4P Behavior Saves a Life

I witnessed a man wreck a dirt bike through a glass window. Once I heard the breaking glass, I ran to the scene and saw lacerations on his arm and several on his leg. I knew this was serious when I saw the amount of blood he lost in the 20 or so seconds it took for me to get there.

I, along with another Appalachian State University student, used t-shirts to stop the bleeding and make him comfortable until the paramedics arrived. He received more than 200 stitches for all of his wounds. We were told he would have bled out if the bleeding would not have been stopped right away. *Wristband #240*

Riley S.
Boone, NC

Corrective Feedback for a Racist Remark

I invited my friend to hang out over at our fraternity house. You might not know right away by looking at him, but he has a white mother and a black father. For most members of the fraternity, this is not an issue.

However, when we were on the porch one of the brothers, unknowing of my friend's ethnicity, begins yelling racist remarks. I immediately confronted my bro in front of guests and other brothers and told him to stop, that his bigotry was unacceptable.

After the fact, I felt guilty to belong to an organization where this kind of racism was present, and I felt incredibly troubled that my guest experienced this at my house. I didn't know the impact of me standing up for my friend until he presented me with this green wristband. The next chapter meeting we established a rule and judiciary system to handle out of line hostile or harrassing behavior. *Wristband #10805*

Scott M.
Statesboro, GA

Stopping to Help on I-95

It was the day after Christmas on a Sunday morning at 6 A.M. I'm a nurse and was driving into Baltimore for work.

I was cruising on I-95 just like every morning and saw a car that appeared stalled in the middle of the interstate about 100 feet ahead. I pulled into the right lane and slowed down. As I approached, I realized this car in the middle of the road was totaled and none of its lights were on. I immediately pulled onto the side of the road and reached into my pocket to pull out my phone to dial 911.

Before I was able to call, a woman squeezed out of the wrecked car and came running to the side of the road where I was, holding her chest. I got out of my car and asked what had happened. She told me her car was hit by another car, causing her to spin, and then a tractor trailer hit her vehicle. Both the other car and tractor trailer drove off, leaving her car smashed in the middle of the road.

I got on the phone with the police while helping to keep her calm and assessing her to make sure she was alright. As this was going on, cars were weaving around her car, which was still in the middle of the road. All of a sudden an SUV slams into her car, causing it to go flying to the side of the road about 30 feet from where we were standing. That's when I really realized: This situation is extremely dangerous.

The SUV driver got out and came running to where we were. I helped keep both of them calm, got their medical history, and assessed them for injuries – all before the police and an ambulance finally arrived. As the woman was being loaded into the ambulance, I noticed she too was wearing scrubs and was a nurse on her way to work, just like me.

I just told my brother this story today and when I did, he pulled off his wristband and gave it to me, telling me to tell my story and pass on the wristband. So that's what I will do. *Wristband #17630*

Alicia C.
Baltimore, MD

Helping a Stranger on the Side of the Road

The other day my car battery died and left me stranded. When I finally got a hold of my mom, she came and tried to jump my battery, which unfortunately fried her car's battery too, leaving us both in a rut.

While my mom started her trek to her nearest friend's house, I waited by our cars. After about 20 minutes of watching cars whiz by, a student from a neighboring district pulled over and asked if I needed any help. Not only did he stay with me as it started to get dark, but he also called his dad who happened to be an auto mechanic. His dad selflessly came and fixed both my mother's and my own car.

I gave my wristband for actively caring to the boy for being the one out of the majority who pulled over to help me – a complete stranger. *Wristband #38955*

Abi C.
Chagrin Falls, OH

Caring for Victims of a Car Crash

I showed up on the scene of a head-on car crash that happened in front of us. Myself and several friends got out to help. I went to one of the cars that had some serious damage and found a young girl inside. Both drivers' side doors were stuck shut.

When I went around to the passenger side I discovered her legs were pinned between the seat and steering wheel/dashboard. While another passerby dialed 911, I got her to give me her parents' phone number. I called them to let them know what was going on.

I stayed with her and tried to keep her calm until the paramedics arrived.

Later, after some time went by, she got my number from her parents and called me. She said she had a wristband to give me and wanted my address. A little while later I got the wristband in the mail. *Wristband #12548*

Joey B.
Chesterfield, VA

Compassionate Helping

Compassion During Times of Hardship

My sister's husband recently passed away after an extended illness. As she completed the difficult task of going through his closet, she wondered what do to with his nearly new (and even some brand new) business and casual clothes. She saw the bus driver for the faith-based school where she teaches and noticed he always wears t-shirts and jeans. She was aware this was because of financial hardship and not a fashion statement. She asked his size and he was the same size as her husband's new clothes.

She gave him all of the clothes that fit him – outfitting him with an entirely new wardrobe. He and his family are so grateful. I've sent the wristband to my sister and I know she'll not only pass it on – but continue (as she has) to actively care for people. She is an inspiration to me and all of our family. *Wristband #15260*

Theresa S.
Taylor, TX

Strengthening Friendship

I recently passed a wristband on to one of my friends at Summer Residential Governor's School. A girl I know was giving me a hard time while a bunch of our friends were spending time together. I left the room, clearly upset, to spend the rest of the night in my dorm rather than provoking the girl even more. My friend, agreeing the girl's comments were out of line, came up to spend the rest of the night in my dorm room with me. We talked mostly about other things.

I thought it was incredibly sweet of my friend to go out of her way to cheer me up. By giving her the wristband I let her know she means a lot to me as a friend and I really appreciate her. She got a little teary-eyed (in happiness of course).

My first experience giving someone an AC4P wristband was one I will truly never forget because I grew much closer with that friend as a result. :] *Wristband #12576*

Melissa D.
Radford, VA

What Goes Around Comes Around

I have always been a proponent of *pay it forward* and when I initially heard of AC4P, I felt like a younger generation now had to chance to pay it forward and understand the benefits.

My story began last winter at a restaurant. I saw a family who was told by the hostess to stand outside in the cold. I quickly finished my dinner and asked that they be seated at our table. The family was from out of town, visiting their daughter, and was truly appreciative.

Fast forward to this summer. My youngest daughter and I were at a local supermarket. I had forgotten my wallet, but had checks. However, since I did not have my license, the clerk told me to put my groceries back. Out from behind in the line, a young female said "I will pay for her". I thanked her and tried to write her a check, but she would not take it.

Then, a different young female came from the door and ran up to the girl who paid for me. She said, "You are actively caring, here's a wristband for you, pass it on." I screamed with joy and my seven-year-old child smiled.

After leaving, I realized the girl who paid for me in the grocery store was Catherine – the same young girl to whom I gave my seat at the restaurant six months earlier. Pay it forward! Actively Caring for People can become a global Movement with your help!

Donna Wertalik
Blacksburg, VA

From One AC4P Act to Another

A few weeks ago, Dr Geller came through the door, buzzing with excitement. He had just been to his bank and Dalton, one of the bank tellers, told him she had a story she needed to share.

She had been at Panera Bread, venting on her cell-phone about an unpleasant event. Frustrated, Dalton hung up, after saying, "I'm in Panera now, I'll call you later."

After she ordered, the man behind the counter smiled and told her he'd pay for her meal because she was having a bad day. Grateful and her day brightened, Dalton prepared to pass on the wristband she'd received weeks before only to realize she forgot it at home.

She explained this to him, saying she wanted to pass him the AC4P wristband. Matt proudly displayed his wrist, revealing a green AC4P wristband, "It's alright, I already have one." He had received *Wristband #5707* two weeks earlier from Joanne Dean Geller.

Eric Cunningham & Illana Elias
NSF & MAOP Students
Blacksburg, VA

Notes

1. Kahneman, D. (2011). *Thinking, fast and slow*. New York, NY: Farrar, Straus and Giroux.
2. We are grateful to Lindsey Brookbank (Writer), Kelly Wolff (General Manager), and the entire Educational Media Company at Virginia Tech for allowing us to reprint an excerpt from: Brookbank, L. (2011, January 27). Chain reaction: Actively caring seeks widespread impact. *Collegiate Times*.
3. We are grateful to the following AC4P leaders who volunteered as undergraduate students to make Part IV of this book a reality: Aly Neel (wristband recipient), John Kurlak (AC4P website developer), Harry Rosenbaum (wristband and graphic designer), Matt Wolk (AC4P website designer), and Ryan King (AC4P website manager).
4. Conari Press (1993). *Random acts of kindness*. Ermeryville, CA.

Epilogue: Where Do We Go From Here?

E. Scott Geller

I BELIEVE MOST PEOPLE want to do the right thing, and they care profoundly about the hardships of others. Unfortunately, this majority remains silent until after tragic consequences.

Consider this profound quotation from Martin Luther King, Jr., "In this era of social transition, the greatest tragedy is not the blaring noisiness of the so-called bad people; it's the appalling silence of the so-called good people."[1]

Our challenge is to speak up sooner rather than later. This call for proactive AC4P behavior is easier said than done. We don't instinctively know how to offer advice, feedback, or support to promote well-being or prevent a possible mishap. And, it's certainly easier to avoid proactive AC4P behavior and reflexively continue working for soon, certain, positive, and self-serving consequences.

But this book introduced and explained effective techniques for intervening on behalf of the welfare of others. Lack of knowledge is not an excuse. This book also shared stories of the soon, certain, and positive consequences resulting from AC4P behavior. Indeed, it *is* better (i.e., more reinforcing) to give (i.e., to actively care) than to receive. So a lack of motivation should not be an excuse.

To the silent majority, let's remain silent and inconspicuous no longer. Reflect on these issues and resolve to join the AC4P Movement to make the poeple of our world better educated, safer, healthier, and more positive. Just reading and understanding the contents of this book are not enough. You need to teach others the AC4P principles and applications shared in this book. But, teaching is not enough.

Practice AC4P Principles

If we are to make the vision of an AC4P culture of compassion real, we need you to put AC4P principles into practice. And, please make note of the worthwhile outcomes of your AC4P efforts.

When you document the methods and results of your AC4P behavior on behalf of one or more persons' well-being, your competence to teach the AC4P approach to others and convince them to get on board will be enhanced considerably.

The best teachers relate the information they're teaching to personal experiences. Interspersed throughout this book are personal stories from individuals who observed direct or indirect benefits of a particular AC4P intervention. In some cases, these authors experienced a spread of the positive intervention effects to other circumstances and settings.

Documenting your involvement with AC4P principles and practice can do more than increase your effectiveness at teaching others techniques for cultivating an AC4P culture. Your reporting of AC4P experiences can contribute to making a culture of compassion happen.

Post your AC4P stories on the ac4p.org website; email your friends and business colleagues about your positive exposures to the AC4P philosophy; write a brief newspaper report or magazine article about one or more AC4P stories; and contact your local T.V. news stations about your notable AC4P experiences.

Bottom line: An AC4P culture of compassion can only become a reality if the AC4P principles and applications are disseminated and practiced by large numbers of people. To meet this monumental challenge, we need your help to spread the word.

Our challenge is to convince ourselves and others that effective AC4P behavior is followed by soon, certain, and positive consequences. How do we do that? Through practice and feedback, of course. We need the humility to accept behavior-based feedback from others about ways to improve; and we need the courage to offer behavior-based feedback whenever it can support or improve AC4P-related behavior.

Humanistic Behaviorism

Please consider the humanistic principles of empathy, empowerment, and compassion when giving and receiving behavior-based supportive and corrective feedback. Yes, AC4P integrates the best of humanism and behaviorism – *humanistic behaviorism*. After all, *actively* means action (behavior) and *caring* is feeling (humanism).

It's noteworthy the American Humanists Association, founded in 1941 to be a clear, democratic voice for Humanism in the U.S. and to develop and advance humanist thought and action, awarded B.F. Skinner "Humanist of the Year" in 1972.[2]

B.F. Skinner has been one of my life-long inspirations. Indeed, the behavior-based safety I developed in 1979 was founded on the principles of Applied Behavior Analysis (ABA) which evolved from the Behaviorism defined and researched by Professor Skinner.[3] Skinner's legacy: We act to gain positive consequences or avoid negative consequences; and the more immediate the consequence, the greater it's behavioral impact. Furthermore, consequences for the individual usually outweigh consequences for others.

Psychologist and scholar Paul Chance purports we must prove Skinner wrong in order to solve the major problems facing humanity.[4] I agree it's a challenge to move people beyond their self-serving desires to achieve soon, certain, and positive consequences. And I can't disagree entirely with his point that these primary principles of Behaviorism give us "impulses that undermine our health; impel us toward violence; turn us into cheats, liars, and brigands, and threaten to make our world uninhabitable".[5]

However, I disagree with the implication that self-serving contingencies compel us *all* to perform undesirable behaviors, from cheating and lying to engaging in interpersonal conflict and violence. These are the individuals we hear about all too often in the news and over the internet, perhaps convincing some of us these undesirable actions reflect normative behavior.

I must also disagree with Dr. Chance's premise the ultimate challenge is to prove B.F. Skinner wrong.[4] Skinner was not wrong. We *are* motivated most by soon, certain, and positive consequences, and effective AC4P behavior *is* followed by soon, certain, and positive consequences – for others and for ourselves.

Integrating Research with Practical Applications

This book offered leading-edge strategies you can readily use to improve the health, safety, and well-being of people in various situations – from the schools to workplace and beyond.

Throughout my lengthy career as teacher, researcher, and author, I've had the good fortune to play the role of both an academic professor and an organizational consultant. While the academic researcher in applied psychology develops and evaluates interventions to improve the behavior of individuals and groups, the consultant selects and implements interventions to address problems defined by a particular client.

Consider the advantage of learning from professionals in both the academic and consulting worlds. This can assure the most effective intervention technologies are applied to current problems in ways that are acceptable, cost-effective, and employable by indigenous personnel.

Such was the mission of this book. All of the intervention tactics in Part II were developed from the results of both empirical research and practical implementation.

Only the Beginning

In his Foreword, Dave Johnson calls this book "Exhibit A" regarding the exposition of an AC4P Movement that "aspires to increase the competence, commitment, and courage needed to sustain AC4P behavior in all the nooks and crannies of daily life".

Actually, this edition is Exhibit C – a revision of our original AC4P textbook for application in schools. In addition, my students, colleagues, and I are currently expanding and developing sections of this book into a college/university textbook. Thus, Exhibit D will teach college students ways to enrich their lives with AC4P principles and applications.

Yet, we've only started to address large-scale, people-related problems that can be mitigated with AC4P interventions. Indeed, many of the AC4P methods in this book are incomplete, inconclusive, or inefficient. The potential is obvious, but more research and development are needed to demonstrate long-term beneficial impact of the proactive interventions illustrated in this book.

Please contact us with ideas and application possibilities for researching the implementation of AC4P principles. The Actively Caring for People Foundation, Inc. was established to explore and evaluate applications of AC4P principles to improve the health, safety, and well-being of people worldwide.

Continuous Learning

Tim, a participant at a recent leadership retreat at my home – Make-A-DiffRanch in Newport, Virginia – made my day with the following comment. He shook my hand and said:

What a pleasure it was to hear your latest thoughts about person-to-person actively caring to benefit individuals, organizations, and communities. I first became aware of your research and scholarship when attending your day-long workshop at the ASSE (American Society of Safety Engineers) *Convention in 2002. Since then I've read four of your books, and taught many of your principles to my colleagues at Cummins Rocky Mountain, LLC.*

I'm not sharing this comment to show off, but rather to provide context for the rest of Tim's commentary, which was most reinforcing to me.

Obviously, I was genuinely pleased to hear those kind remarks, but I had to interject, "It's so nice to learn that my teachings are reaching others through other teachers. But since you've already read several of my recent books, much of my workshop material today was redundant, right?" He replied:

For sure, I understood where you were coming from and I predicted where you were going throughout that session, and it was reassuring to hear it again. But what I really liked best was learning how your perspectives, principles, and application suggestions have evolved over the ten years I've been following your work.

That last comment was the big reinforcer for me. My teaching of practical ways to apply psychology for solving real-world problems has progressed significantly over the years, as I continuously learn from ongoing research and from my own and others' consulting experiences.

Contrary to the illustration, we're never too old to learn. For me, it's so meaningful to have an organizational leader recognize, understand, and appreciate the evolution of recommendations for managing the human dynamics of organizational and societal problems.

Why? Because it justifies continuous collaboration and mutual learning from researchers and consultants. Tim's commentary also validates the mission of this book – to connect research and practice for optimal intervention design and application relevant to cultivating cultures of compassion.

We've merely scratched the surface of societal problems that can be solved in part by applications of AC4P principles and procedures. The particular issues addressed in this book were limited to education issues, but our earlier AC4P book also addressed workplace and traffic safety, identity theft, and alcohol abuse among college students.[6]

The AC4P interventions within each of those problem domains, including interpersonal conflict and bullying in educational settings, are far from being comprehensive and optimal. We have so much more to learn from the synergistic integration of behavioral and humanistic psychology – *humanistic behaviorism*.

Share your AC4P ideas and document your AC4P stories. They could incite relevant research, suggest real-world practice, or inspire participation by others. The outcome could very well end up in a subsequent edition of this book – Exhibit E, F, or G. More importantly, your AC4P leadership is necessary to encourage others to live an AC4P lifestyle and help lead the AC4P Movement.

Notes

1. King, Jr., M.L. *Martin Luther King Quotes*. Retrieved from http://www.inspirationpeak.com/cgi-bin/search.cgi?search=Dr.%20Martin%20Luther%20King&method=all
2. *American Humanist Association*. (2008). Retrieved September 9, 2012 from http://www.americanhumanist.org/
3. Skinner, B.F. (1976). *About behaviorism*. New York, NY: Knopf.
4. Chance, P. (2007). The ultimate challenge: Prove B.F. Skinner wrong. *The Behavior Analyst, 30*(2), 153-160.
5. Chance, P. (2007). The ultimate challenge: Prove B.F. Skinner wrong. *The Behavior Analyst, 30*(2), p. 158.
6. Geller, E. S. (Ed.) (2013). *Actively caring for people: Cultivating a culture of compassion*. Newport, VA: Make-A-Difference, LLC.

Acknowledgements

For more than 30 years I've taught AC4P principles and applications in workshops and keynotes at regional and national conferences, as well as at various Fortune 500 Companies. The evidence-based AC4P lessons have always been well-received. But, periodically my evaluations have included a negative comment such as, "I appreciate the theory and principles presented by Dr. Geller, but I don't know how to apply his teachings. In other words, I like the ideas, but he didn't tell me what to do with them."

This book addressed this legitimate concern in the best way possible. How? By combining the principles with tried-and-true applications relevant to cultivating an AC4P culture in educational settings. The application chapters were written by authors who experienced the beneficial impact of AC4P applications. Plus, Parts III and IV document personal stories from individuals who experienced benefits of a particular AC4P intervention beyond an educational environment.

Thus, it's fitting to first acknowledge the 23 authors of the application chapters and personal stories exemplifying the impact of practicing one or more AC4P principles. These authors are listed in the following pages, along with their education and current position.

Thank you all for illustrating functional utility of specific AC4P principles in the real world. You have given readers specific direction for effectively teaching, implementing, and/or evaluating interventions to address the human dynamics of cultivating a culture conducive to teaching, learning, and continuous improvement.

I hope readers will be inspired to customize and apply some of the methods illustrated in Part II, and consistent with the humanistic behaviorism principles explained in Part I. I also hope the success stories from your innovations and extensions will be sent to the Actively Caring for People Foundation, Inc. for possible inclusion in a subsequent edition of this book.

Five authors contributed generously and extensively to preparing this book, beyond submitting a thoughtful chapter. In addition to authoring or co-authoring six chapters, Shane McCarty was my right-hand assistant through much of the process, from soliciting potential authors and recommending topics to helping me edit and refine chapters, including my own.

Throughout the process, Shane and I received valuable advice from Joanne Dean Geller with regard to the practicality of our ideas and concepts. With unique experiences as a high-school teacher, public relations agent, sales representative, and safety director, Joanne offered us invaluable feedback, from the relevance of particular intervention plans to the selection of words to describe principles, applications, and ramifications.

Jenna McCutchen, current coordinator of the research and scholarship in our Center for Applied Behavior Systems (CABS), not only led the preparation of Chapter 8, a practical portrayal of the preparation and delivery of AC4P workshops to prevent interpersonal bullying; she also formatted the text of each chapter, including the painstaking processing of my handwritten chapters and continuous-improvement editing of the entire book.

Sophia Teie, lead author of the inspirational Chapter 10 about helping high-school students heal and move forward after a tragic school shooting, dedicated significant time and expertise preparing the first edition of this book for final processing. This required diligent proofing of the print, photos, and illustrations to assure the document sent to the printing company was the best it could be.

It's obvious the development, preparation and refinement of the information shared in this book was an interdependent team effort. Indeed, the vision of a book to teach AC4P principles and applications could not have become a reality without the valuable assistance of the individuals listed here. But there's more exceptional support to recognize.

I'm indebted to the long-term advice, alliance, and friendship of Dave Johnson, Editor of *Industrial Safety and Hygiene News (ISHN)*. Dave and I began collaborating in 1990 when I submitted my first five articles for publication in his magazine. Every time one of my articles was published, I learned something about communicating more effectively a principle or practice from psychological science. This invaluable learning experience continued for the 19 consecutive years of my monthly *ISHN* column: *The Psychology of Safety*.

Dave was the Editor of my first safety book,[1] and two subsequent textbooks on people-based safety.[2] Plus, we co-authored a book that teaches relevant psychological science to healthcare workers.[3] In all four scholarship collaborations, including this book, Dave added his "magic" to the written expression and made it more concise, clear, and comprehensible.

Thank you, Dave Johnson, for continuing to help me make my scholarship more appreciable and appreciated by the general public. Indeed, if the contents of this book are not understood and accepted by masses of people beyond the ivory towers of university and research institutions, the applied research reported in this book has no chance of making the beneficial cultural difference it was designed to make.

Since 1990, my teaching, textbooks, and workbooks have benefitted from the artistic talents of George Wills – the creator of the instructive and entertaining illustrations interspersed throughout this book. I'm also beholden to Nancy Poes, the professional artist/illustrator who designed the cover of this book, displaying its purpose and mission so vividly and pertinently. Thanks to Nancy, you *can* judge *this* book by its cover.

I need to also acknowledge and thank a number of organizations and aggregations of individuals who believe in the mission and vision of CABS and the Actively Caring for People Foundation, Inc. They have been collaborating with us on several fronts.

Our continual partnerships with these groups will enable us to make our mutual aspirations a reality. Some of these associations of like-minded people have contributed financially to support our research Center, as well as the preparation and dissemination of this book. In particular, I'm truly grateful for the ongoing support and inspiration from:

- American Psychological Foundation (apa.org/apf)
- Angel Fund (angelfundva.org)
- Center for Peace Studies and Violence Prevention, Virginia Tech (cpsvp.vt.edu)
- Chardon Healing Fund (chardonhealingfund.com)

- Kevin R. Lawall Fellowship
- National Center for the Prevention of Community Violence (solveviolence.com)
- Safety Performance Solutions, Inc. (safetyperformance.com)
- VTV Family Outreach Foundation (vtvfamilyfoundation.org)

My 44-year teaching and research career at Virginia Tech, reflected by much of the contents of this book, has benefitted hugely from an extensive support system in both the academic and consulting worlds – professional colleagues, university students, and consumers of my books and education/training programs. All of you have offered constructive feedback to help me improve, and you've inspired me to keep on keeping on.

I thank you all very much. The synergy from your past, present, and future sustenance enables a legacy – AC4P principles and practices readers can use to enrich their lives and contribute to cultivating cultures of interpersonal compassion at work, school, home, and everywhere in between.

E. Scott Geller
October, 2013

Notes

1. Geller, E. S. (1996). *The psychology of safety: How to improve behaviors and attitudes on the job.* Radnor, PA: Chilton Book Company.
2. Geller, E. S. (2005). *People-based safety: The source.* Virginia Beach, VA: Coastal Training and Technologies Corporation.
3. Geller, E.S., & Johnson, D. (2008). *People-based patient safety: Enriching your culture to prevent medical error.* Virginia Beach, VA: Coastal Training and Technologies Corporation.

About the Authors

E. SCOTT GELLER, Alumni Distinguished Professor and Director of the Center for Applied Behavior Systems in the Department of Psychology at Virginia Tech, has authored or co-authored 37 books, 56 book chapters, 38 training manuals, 253 magazine articles, and over 350 research articles addressing the development and evaluation of behavior-change interventions to improve quality of life. His extramural grant funding, totaling more than $6 million, has involved the application of behavioral science for the benefit of corporations, institutions, government agencies, and communities.

He is a Fellow of the American Psychological Association, the Association of Behavior Analysis International, the Association for Psychological Science, and the World Academy of Productivity and Quality Sciences. He is past Editor of the *Journal of Applied Behavior Analysis* (1989-1992), current Associate Editor of *Environment and Behavior* (since 1982), and current Consulting Editor for *Behavior and Social Issues,* the *Journal of Organizational Behavior Management,* and the *Journal of Safety Research.*

Throughout his 44-year career, Dr. Geller has been honored with a number of prestigious awards, including teaching awards from the American Psychological Association, the Association for Behavior Anaylsis International, every university-wide teaching award offered at Virginia Tech, the University Alumni Award for Excellence in Research, the Alumni Outreach Award for exemplary real-world applications of behavioral science, the University Alumni Award for Graduate Student Advising, the Virginia Outstanding Faculty Award by the State Council of Higher Education, the Award for Effective Presentation of Behavior Analysis in the Mass Media by the Society for the Advancement of Behavior Analysis, and Lifetime Achievement Awards from the American Psychological Foundation and the International Organizational Behavior Management Network.

In 2010, Scott Geller was awarded an Applied Research Award from the American Psychological Association and in 2011, The College of Wooster, Dr. Geller's alma mater, awarded him the honorary degree: Doctor of Humane Letters.

Dr. Geller is a Co-Founder and Senior Partner of Safety Performance Solutions, Inc., a leading-edge organization specializing in people-based safety training and consulting since 1995 (safetyperformance.com).

Amel Becirevic, B.S. in Psychology from the University of Pittsburgh; currently pursuing a Ph.D. in the Applied Behavioral Economics Lab in the Department of Applied Behavioral Science at the University of Kansas.

Rohan Cobb-Ozanne, a Senior at Virginia Tech pursuing a B.S. in Psychology; research assistant for the Center for Applied Behavior Systems; AC4P Coach for bullying prevention.

Joanne Dean Geller, B.A. in Elementary and Secondary Physical Education from Elon University; formerly a High-School Teacher, Public Relations Agent with the New Orleans Saints and the Los Angeles Dodgers, Pharmaceutical Sales Representative for BASF, and Director of Safety for a construction company in New Jersey; currently a professional caterer and fitness instructor.

Katie DeTuro, a Senior at Virginia Tech, studying apparel, housing, and resource management: Consumer Studies Option. Member of the VT Women's Soccer Team; student-athlete study abroad trip to Punta Cana, Dominican Republic.

Cory B. Furrow, B.S. in Psychology from Virginia Tech; currently an M.S. student in Forest Resources and Environmental Conservation at Virginia Tech.

Justin Graves, B.S. in Sociology from Virginia Tech; currently pursuing an M.A.Ed. in Higher Education Administration at Virginia Tech.

Jason M. Hirst, B.S. in Psychology from Pennsylvania State University; M.A. in Applied Behavior Analysis from the University of Kansas; currently a Ph.D. student in the Department of Applied Behavioral Science at the University of Kansas.

Douglas Russell Hole, B.A. in Physical Education from the College of Wooster, Wooster, Ohio; M.A. in Political Science from Auburn University at Montgomery; 28 years in the U.S. Air Force rising to the rank of Colonel; worldwide duties in Intelligence.

Dave Johnson, B.S. in Journalism from Ohio University, Athens, Ohio; Chief Editor of the magazine *Industrial Safety & Hygiene News* (established 1967, circulation 71,400 subscribers) since 1980.

Brent A. Kaplan, B.G.S in Psychology and Applied Behavioral Science from the University of Kansas; currently pursuing a Ph.D. in the Applied Behavioral Economics Lab in the Department of Applied Behavioral Science at the University of Kansas.

Ryan King, B.S. in Finance and a B.S. in Accounting from Virginia Tech; currently working in public accounting within an advisory practice.

Andrea J. Langston, B.S. in Accounting and Information Systems and an M.A.Ed. in Curriculum and Instruction from Virginia Tech; public school teacher for middle and elementary school since 1994.

Benjamin Martin, B.S. in Psychology and an M.A. in Sociology from East Tennessee State University, Johnson City, TN.

Shane M. McCarty, B.S. in Marketing from Virginia Tech; currently a Ph.D. Student in Industrial/Organizational Psychology at Virginia Tech; research assistant in the Center for Applied Behavior Systems and the Center for Peace Studies and Violence Prevention at Virginia Tech.

Jenna McCutchen, B.S. in Psychology from Virginia Tech; currently Coordinator for the Center for Applied Behavior Systems, continuing her AC4P teaching/learning research to increase compassion and prevent bullying in educational settings.

About the Authors

Corrine Picht, Graduated from Stillwater Area High School, Withrow, Minnesota; currently an hourly employee leader for the Andersen Bayport People-Based Safety process.

Martin Ralph, B.S. in Environmental Science from Murdoch University (Western Australia) in Environmental Science and a post-graduate certificate in Organisational Human Resources and Safety, a Chartered Radiation Protection professional, and a member of the Australian Institute of Company Directors. He has been the Managing Director of the Industrial Foundation for Accident Prevention (IFAP) since 2001.

Derek D. Reed, B.S. in Psychology from Illinois State University, M.S. in Psychology and Ph.D. in School Psychology from Syracuse University; currently Assistant Professor and Director of Graduate Training, Department of Applied Behavior Science, University of Kansas, Lawrence, KS.

Nick Smirniotopoulos, Virginia Tech senior pursuing a B.S. in Psychology and B.A. in Communications; student-athlete study abroad trip to Punta Cana, Dominican Republic, University Honors, Pamplin Scholar, Features Editor for the *Collegiate Times*.

Victoria Stone, B.A. and M.A. in Political Science from Virginia Tech; Certified Massage Therapist and co-owner and instructor of Blue Ridge School of Massage & Yoga; author of *Sustainable bodywork: Wellness, self-care and injury prevention*.

Brittany Tarzia, B.S. in Psychology from Virginia Tech with a minor in Creative Writing; currently an intern at the VTV Family Outreach Foundation, Centreville, Virginia.

Sophia Y. Teie, B.S. in Psychology and Sociology from Virginia Tech; former research assistant for the Center for Applied Behavior Systems; pursuing graduate studies in Sociology at Virginia Tech.

Danny White, B.S. in Finance from the University of South Carolina; currently the Director of Student-Athlete Affairs for the Virginia Tech Athletics Department; pursuing a Ph.D. in Agricultural and Extension Education Department with an emphasis on leadership studies.

Index

A

ABA intervention 12-13, 13-14, 14-15, 17-18, 18-19, 20-21, 21, 24-25
ABA researcher 23
ABC contingency 8
ABC model 7, 114
AC4P application 121, 124, 131, 136, 141-142
AC4P at home 282-285
AC4P behavior x-xii, 28, 66, 155, 157, 160, 248, 278, 282, 285, 299
AC4P & cancer 249-256
AC4P challenge 72, 284
AC4P commitment card 72
AC4P community 214-215
AC4P culture ix, 44, 207, 281, 297
AC4P in middle school 175
AC4P lifestyle 262, 264, 282, 289, 301
AC4P mindset 289
AC4P mission 241
AC4P Movement x-xi, 148, 203, 219, 242, 245, 280, 287, 297, 301
AC4P norm 261
ac4p.org 45, 71, 111, 137, 287, 297
AC4P pedagogy 187
AC4P person-states 29, 51, 90
AC4P polite light 97
AC4P principle 239, 263, 282, 297, 301, 303
AC4P Promise Card 96
AC4P ripple effect 67, 94, 208, 218, 239, 259, 264
AC4P SAPS process 288
AC4P t-shirt 136
AC4P wristbands 45, 148, 157, 177, 180, 280, 288
Activator 7, 20, 22, 27
Actively Caring for People (AC4P) ix
Actively Caring for People Foundation, Inc. 299, 303
Actively-Caring Thank-You Card 44
Airline Lifesaver 97
Allen, Woody 284
ALS (Amyotrophic Lateral Sclerosis) 275
American Humanists Association 298
Anderson, Greg 254
Applied Behavior Analysis (ABA) 5, 19, 298
Asch, Solomon 133
Assumption amnesia 262
Atkinson, John W. 8
Attributions 26
Authority principle 137-138
  harsh factor 139
  heuristics 140
  Milgram, Stanley 138
  obedience 137
  soft factor 139
Autonomy 62

B

Baby boomers 285
Back-stabbing 83
Barrows, W. 267
Behavioral checklist 15
Behavioral commitment 21
Behavioral scientists 18
Behavior-based coaching 17
Behavior-based consequence 24
Behavior-based recognition 73
Behavior-based safety (BBS) 99
Behavior-focused AC4P 36
Behaviorism 298
Belonging 36, 49, 55, 91, 180, 184
Bem, Daryl 26
Blacksburg Middle School 176
Blue Ridge School of Massage & Yoga 213
Boyce, William D. 277
Boy scouts 277
Buckle-Up Promise Card 22
Bullying 150, 153, 157, 163
Bullying-prevention intervention 156, 182
Bullying Summit 181, 203
  high-school and college workshop 183
  middle-school workshop 182
Bystander apathy 39, 43
Bystander effect 40
Bystander intervention 261

C

Cairns, Jr. John 273
Cancer survivor 256
Candor 80
Caring 79
Carnegie, Dale 110
Center for Applied Behavior Systems (CABS) 72, 176, 217
Chance, Paul 298
Character 82
Chardon High School 136, 201, 203, 210, 291
Cho, Seung-Hui 148, 153
Cialdini, Robert 135
Classical conditioning
  Conditioned response 8
  Conditioned stimulus 8
Click it or Ticket 95
Columbine High School 153
Commitment 81, 89, 119, 264
  Active 119
  Perceived choice 119
  Public 120
Common sense 14
Communication 78
Community 66, 189, 207
Compassion 180, 265, 295
Competence 64, 189
  social competence 156
Compliance 113
Conformity 113
Consensus 81
Consistency 80
Consistency principle 67, 81, 115
  foot-in-the-door 116
  social labeling 116
Continuous learning 180
Corrective feedback 293
Counter-control 143
Courage 87, 176, 180, 189, 217,

265, 298
moral courage 90, 94, 111, 217, 258-259
physical courage 90
psychological courage 275
Courtesy driving code 97
Critical behavior checklist (CBC) 12, 16-18, 99
Culture of entitlement 148

D

Declaration of Interdependence 91
Dewey, John 110
Diffusion of responsibility 40
Direct approach 28
Direct persuasion 27
Disincentive 23
Dissemination 14, 298
DO IT process 14-18
Dooley, John 198
Driver-training score card 99
Durkin, Casey 203
Dweck, Carol
  ability vs. effort label 118-119

E

Education 20
Empathy 12, 239, 258
Empowerment 47, 150, 179, 184
  outcome-expectancy 179
  response-efficacy 179
  self-efficacy 179
Equifinality 149
Evidence-based 3-4, 61, 67, 101, 155
Experimental Behavior Analysis 11
Extrinsically motivated 24
Extrinsic motivators 61

F

Failure accepter 10
Failure avoider 9
Failure-avoiding policies 155
Family mindset 92
Feedback 24-25, 34, 65, 72
  behavior-based feedback 18-19
  continuous improvement 74
  corrective feedback 35, 52, 72, 74, 259, 284, 293
  proactive AC4P feedback 37
  supportive feedback 35, 72
    how to give 102-108
    how to receive 102-108
Fetchik, Andy 206
Flash-for-Life 94-95
Frankl, Viktor 38
Functional control 23

G

Gandhi, Mahatma 38
George, B.C. 289
Goal setting 33-35, 70-72
Group commitment 90
Growth mindset 195
Guinness, Os 188

H

Helicopter parents 285
HIV/AIDS prevention 188, 192
Human dynamics 300, 303
Humanistic behaviorism 29, 143, 298, 301
Humanistic psychology 189
Humility 298
Hypothalamus-pituitary-adrenal cortex (HPA) Axis 213

I

If-then contingency 156, 165
If-then rewards 72
Incentive 23, 165
Independence 195
Indirect approach 28
Indirect influence 27
Indirect persuasion 28
Industrial Safety and Hygiene News (ISHN) ix, 304
Institutionalize 26
Intentional acts of kindness 147
Interdependence 55, 66, 149, 180, 195
Internal justification 27
Interpersonal bullying 153
Interpersonal compassion 149
Interpersonal trust 78
Intrinsic consequences 24
Intrinsic motivation 24
Intrinsic reinforcement 193, 256

J

James, William 110, 195
Joanne's 60/60 challenge 71, 242, 245

K

King Jr., Martin Luther 259, 297
Kofol, Steve 204

L

Law of Effect 101
Learned helplessness 10, 254
Legacy 206
Liking/Ingratiation principle 122
  Compliments 123
  mere-exposure effect 124
  similarity 122

M

Maintenance challenge 26
Make-A-DiffRanch 180, 265, 274, 300
Maslow, Abraham 37
Maslow's Hierarchy of Needs 37, 255, 262
Massage therapy 213-215
Meme 218
Milgram, Stanley 138
Modeling 21, 192
Murphy, Kelly 204
Murphy's Law 189

N

National Boy Scout Jamboree 278
Neel, Aly 287
Negative reinforcement 10
Negative reinforcer 8
Negative side-effect 22

Now-that rewards 73

O

Obama, Michelle 215, 246
OBPP approach 160
Observation stage 16
Olweus Bullying Prevention Program (OBPP) 160
Operant conditioning 8
Optimism 48, 55, 183
Outcome-based incentive/reward program 25
Overstriver 9

P

Paradigm shift 65, 67
Parenthood 284-285
Pay-it-forward reciprocity 208, 293, 295
Pedagogy 187
Peer persuasion 27
Penalty 22-23
People-Based Safety (PBS) 149, 281
   coaching 281
Percent safe score 16
Perception survey 12
PERMA 187
   Achievement 187
   Engagement 187
   Meaning 187
   Positive emotion 187
   Relationships 187
Personal control 36, 48, 54, 62, 183, 249, 255
   external locus of control 48
   increase perceptions of personal control 54
   internal locus of control 48
   locus of control 48
Personality trait 10
Person-based AC4P 35
Pfister, M. 267
Positive reinforcement 10
Proactive behavior 36, 297
Prosocial behavior 150, 155, 159
Prostate cancer 250, 254
Psychological states 28
PTSD 213

Punishment 10, 22

R

Ramakrishna 250
Random acts of kindness 289
Reactive behavior 36
Reciprocity principle 109, 125
   Norm of Reciprocity 126-129
Recognition 107-110
Reinforcement 22
Relatedness 66
Relay-for-Life 256
Respondent conditioning 8
Reward 22
Rule-governed behavior 21

S

Safety Performance Solutions (SPS) 250, 307
Sanderson, Dawn 275-276
Sanderson, Dick 275-276
SAPS process 163, 288
Scarcity principle 141
   descriptive norm 142
   injunctive norm 142
   psychological reactance 142-143
Secondhand recognition 106-107
Selection by consequences 33
Self-accountability 61
self-actualization 37
Self-affirmation 33
Self-efficacy 36, 48, 179-180, 183, 193
   perception of competence 53
Self-esteem 36, 47, 52, 162, 164, 166, 183
Self-handicapping 9
Self-motivation 61, 62, 67
Self-perception 26
Self-persuasion 27
Self-serving contingencies 298
Self-talk 29, 89
Self-transcendence 38, 239, 255-256, 262
Servant leadership 289
Sherif, Muzafer 132
Shipe, Phil 267
Silent majority 259, 297

Simple reaction time 62
Skinner, B.F. x, 19, 61, 298
Small-win accomplishments 54
SMARTS Goals 70
social learning theory 48
Social-learning theory 154
Social proof principle 131
   descriptive norm 135
   injunctive norm 135
Social validity 12, 13
Spencer, Ed 210
Success seeker 9
System 1 thinking 287
System 2 thinking 287, 289
Systems thinking 66

T

Theory-driven research 19
Thorndike, Edward L. 101
Three-term contingency 7, 27

U

Unconditioned response 8
Unconditioned stimulus 8
Unconsciously incompetent 263
Ut Prosim 187, 256

V

Virginia Tech Tragedy 153, 201

W

Whitehurst, Tod 214
Wills, George 250, 304
Win-lose 81
Win-win 81

Other books by E. Scott Geller reflecting AC4P:

Actively Caring for People: Cultivating a culture of compassion (2013)

When No One's Watching: Living and leading self-motivation (2010)
(co-authored with Bob Veazie)

The Courage Factor: Leading people-based culture change (2009)
(co-authored with Bob Veazie)

Leading People-Based Safety: Enriching your culture (2008)

People-Based Patient Safety: Enriching your culture to prevent medical error (2007)
(co-authored with Dave Johnson)

People-Based Safety: The source (2005)

The Participation Factor: How to increase involvement in occupational safety (2002)

The Psychology of Safety Handbook (2001)

Intervening to Improve the Safety of Occupational Driving (2000)
(co-authored with Timothy D. Ludwig)

What Can Behavior-Based Safety Do for Me? (1999)

Understanding Behavior-Based Safety (1998)

Beyond Safety Accountability: How to increase personal responsibility (1998)

Building Successful Safety Teams: Together Everyone Achieves More (1998)

Working Safe: How to help people actively care for health and safety (1996)

The Pscyhology of Safety: Improving behaviors and attitudes on the job (1996)

Motivating Health Behavior (1994)
(co-authored by John P. Elder, Mel F. Hovell, & Joni A. Mayer)

Behavior Analysis Training for Occupational Safety (1987)
(co-authored by Galen R. Lehman & Michael R. Kalsher)

Preserving the Environment: New strategies for behavior change (1982)
(co-authored by Richard A. Winett & Peter B. Everett)